Jedrzej Georg Frynas

Oil in Nigeria

D0861219

Politics and Economics in Africa

Series Editor:

Robert Kappel and Ulf Engel

(Universität Leipzig)

volume 1

LIT

Jedrzej Georg Frynas

OIL IN NIGERIA

Conflict and Litigation between
Oil Companies and Village Communities

LIT

Cover picture: Protesting the destruction of the environment, Bori.
Ogoni, Nigeria
3. 93. 03. 10. 35   05 JAN 1993
NIGERIAN OIL
© Greenpeace / Lambon

Die Deutsche Bibliothek – CIP-Einheitsaufnahme

Frynas, Jedrzej Georg
Oil in Nigeria : Conflict and Litigation between Oil Companies and Village
Communities / Jedrzej Georg Frynas. – Hamburg : LIT, 2000
   (Politics and Economics in Africa ; 1.)
   ISBN 3-8258-3921-4

NE: GT

© LIT VERLAG Münster – Hamburg – London
   Grindelberg 15a 20144 Hamburg Tel. 040–44 64 46 Fax 040–44 14 22

Distributed in North America by:

Transaction Publishers
New Brunswick (U.S.A.) and London (U.K.)

Transaction Publishers
Rutgers University
35 Berrue Circle
Piscataway, NJ 08854

Tel.: (732) 445 – 2280
Fax: (732) 445 – 3138
for orders (U.S. only):
toll free 888-999-6778

Acknowledgements

This book, which has been developed out of a doctoral thesis at the Department of Economics, St Andrews University (UK), was assisted by academics, lawyers, oil company staff, journalists, members of non-governmental organisations and others. Unfortunately, it would be impossible to thank everyone who assisted in the writing of this study by name. I am very grateful for all the assistance I received.

I am particularly indebted to Prof. Matthias P. Beck, the supervisor of my doctoral thesis, whose skilful advice was essential in this project. I am also very grateful to my second supervisor Dr. Alison Watson.

Many thanks must go to all those who assisted in the field research in Nigeria, in particular, Nicholas Ashton-Jones, Godwin Uyi Ojo, Udeme Essien, Tunde Fagbohunlu, George Ikoli and Phillip Hall. I am also indebted to Ledum Mittee, Femi Falana, Abdul Oroh, Chief Priscilla O. Kuye, Gani Fawehinmi, Olisa Agbakoba and Oronto Douglas for their assistance in obtaining materials for this work.

Many thanks to those who gave useful comments on earlier chapter drafts: Nicholas Ashton-Jones, Uche Onyeogocha, Martin Quinlan, Sam Amadi, Daniel Omoweh and Emmanuel Ochugboju. Special thanks to Mehran Zabihollah for his kind assistance in preparing the maps and drawings. Special thanks also to Magali Perrault and Rosemarie Broadbent for comments and proof-reading at various stages.

Last but not least, I am very grateful to Prof. Mo Malek and Prof. Gavin Reid for their support and encouragement.

J.G.F.
June 1999

Contents

CHAPTER 1: Introduction and Methodology

CHAPTER 2: The Making of Nigeria's Oil Industry - Oil and the Nigerian State

CHAPTER 3: Nigerian Legal System and Oil Related Legislation

CHAPTER 4: Nigerian Legal System in Practice - Results of a Survey

CHAPTER 5: Environmental and Social Impact of Oil Operations on Village Communities

CHAPTER 6: Compensation Claims in Oil Related Litigation

CHAPTER 7: Conclusion

BIBLIOGRAPHY

APPENDICES

Major Towns and Oil Terminals in Nigeria, 1999

Nigerian States, 1999

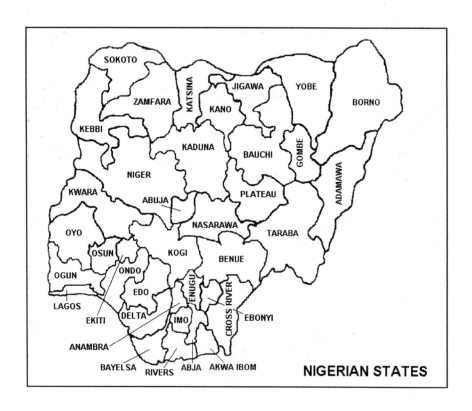

Tables

Figures

Table of Court Cases

Nigerian Cases

English Case

Table of Statutes

Nigerian Statutes

Court Reports and Legal Abbreviations

All NLR   All Nigeria Law Reports
C.J.   Chief Justice
C.J.N.   Chief Justice of Nigeria
ECSLR   Law Reports of East-Central State of Nigeria
FHC/L   Federal High Court, Lagos
F.S.C.   Federal Supreme Court
HC   High Court
H.L.   House of Lords
IMSLR   Imo State Law Reports
J.C.A.   Justice of the Court of Appeal
J.S.C.   Justice of the Supreme Court
KLR   Kings Law Reports
LFN   Laws of the Federation of Nigeria
N.L.R.   Nigeria Law Report
NWLR Nigerian Weekly Law Reports
RSLR   Rivers State Law Reports
S.C.   Supreme Court
SCNLR   Supreme Court of Nigeria Law Reports

Non-legal Abbreviations

AENR	Agip Energy & Natural Resources
CLO	Civil Liberties Organisation
CRP	Constitutional Rights Project
DPR	Department of Petroleum Resources
EIA	Environmental Impact Assessment
EMIROAF	Ethnic Minorities Rights Organisation of Africa
ERA	Environmental Rights Action
FEPA	Federal Environmental Protection Agency
HRW	Human Rights Watch
IDSL	Integrated Data Services Limited
IFESH	International Foundation for Education and Self Help
IMF	International Monetary Fund
INC	Ijaw National Congress
IYC	Ijaw Youth Council
MOSOP	Movement for the Survival of the Ogoni People
MOU	Memorandum of Understanding
MPR	Ministry of Petroleum Resources
NAOC	Nigeria Agip Oil Company
NAPIMS	National Petroleum Investment Management Services
NDDB	Niger Delta Development Board
NDES	Niger Delta Environmental Survey
NGC	Nigerian Gas Corporation
NGL	Natural Gas Liquids
NLNG	Nigeria Liquefied Natural Gas
NNOC	Nigerian National Oil Corporation
NNPC	Nigerian National Petroleum Corporation
NPDC	Nigerian Petroleum Development Company
NPRC	Nigerian Petroleum Refining Company
NYCOP	National Youth Council of Ogoni People
OEL	Oil exploration licence
OML	Oil mining lease
OMPADEC	Oil Mineral Producing Areas Development Commission
OPL	Oil prospecting licence
OPTS	Oil Producers Trade Section of the Lagos Chamber of Commerce
PRC	Provisional Ruling Council
PRO	Public Record Office in London
SAP	Structural Adjustment Programme
SEPA	State Environmental Protection Agency
SNEPCO	Shell Nigeria Exploration and Production Company
SPD	Special Project Division on the Niger Delta
SPDC	Shell Petroleum Development Company of Nigeria
WAGP	West African Gas Pipeline Project

Chapter 1: Introduction

1.1. Background

This book analyses the conflicts between oil companies and village communities in the Niger Delta.[1] These conflicts have continued for decades but, during the 1990s, they escalated further and received international media coverage. Much of that coverage focused on the anti-Shell protests of the Movement for the Survival of the Ogoni People (MOSOP) which led to Shell's withdrawal from the Ogoni area in 1993. The execution of MOSOP's leader Ken Saro-Wiwa in November 1995, combined with the suppression of the democratic opposition, galvanised the international community against the Abacha regime (1993-1998) resulting in political and economic sanctions being imposed against Nigeria. The death of General Abacha in June 1998 and the subsequent steps towards the transition to civilian rule ended Nigeria's international isolation. In February 1999, Olusegun Obasanjo was elected president. In May 1999, he took office, heading Nigeria's first civilian government since 1983.

Notwithstanding the political changes after June 1998, the conflicts between oil companies and village communities in the Niger Delta continue. While the intensity of Ogoni protests decreased from 1995, other ethnic and political groups across the Niger Delta disrupted oil activities. Seizures of oil installations and kidnappings of oil company staff have become widespread in the oil producing areas. The sources of conflicts such as the neglect of the oil producing areas and the operating practices of oil companies have not yet been adequately tackled by the government or the oil companies.

The conflicts in the Niger Delta are important beyond academic interest. Nigeria is the most populous and the largest African state. Oil is the mainstay of Nigeria's economy. Oil revenue accounts for well over 60% of the government revenue and the oil industry provides roughly 96% of Nigeria's dollar receipts (see chapter 2 for more details). By disrupting the oil production, the anti-oil protests render oil operations on the ground more difficult and may, therefore, reduce the quantity of oil and gas investment. The local conflicts, therefore, threaten the economic viability of Africa's largest state. Solving the 'Niger Delta question' is one of the key challenges facing the new civilian government.

---

[1] In this book, we often use the term 'village community'. This is because oil exploration and production activities usually affect people who live in traditional village communities in the Niger Delta. The term 'village community' is a convenient shorthand which refers to the local people affected by oil operations on the ground. But the term also signifies a common identity within a village community due to a number of factors such as common residence; a shared history and heritage; cross-cutting ties of neighbourhood, friendship and kinship; a common religious creed; and continual, intensive interaction over the entire life span with the same people in the same meeting places. Membership of a village community is defined both in terms of physical residence in a village and in terms of subscription to village social norms. This notion of a village community is derived from Todd (1978, 89-91).

1.2. Aims of the Book

This book, which has been developed out of a doctoral thesis at the University of St Andrews (UK), analyses conflicts between oil companies and village communities in Nigeria by focusing on litigation. The main advantage of using Nigerian court cases is that they provide abundant and relatively reliable evidence on these conflicts, if compared with a number of alternative methodologies.

The framework of analysis in our study is provided by the contemporary Nigerian legal system. This includes an examination of the evidence on oil-related litigation available, including exemplary cases from Nigerian courts and a survey of 154 Nigerian legal practitioners, which illustrates the conflicts between oil companies and communities and elucidates the relevant issues. By using legal materials, we place conflicts between oil companies and village communities in relation to the constraints faced by litigants, the impact of oil activities leading to conflicts and the legal principles governing disputes.

The book has three main aims. First, the study of litigation is aimed at serving as a window to an understanding of social conflicts between village communities and oil companies. Litigation typically evolves from individual and collective social conflicts. It echoes, rather than anticipates, changing situations and changing institutions. Before they can act, courts have to wait until conflicts arise and litigants file their lawsuits. In the words of Tocqueville, *'there is nothing naturally active about judicial power; to act, it must be set in motion'* (quoted in Hall 1989, 109). Writing on the development of American law, Hall has argued that issues of economic development set the judiciary 'in motion' as they bring about a dramatic rise in the demands placed on judiciaries. According to this view, the business of the courts mirrors the economic and social changes brought by economic development, while judges play a part in allocating the costs, risks and benefits of this development (Hall 1989). By implication, an analysis of litigation may, therefore, mirror the economic and social dynamic in relation to disputes between oil companies and village communities in Nigeria. In this context, such an investigation may throw some light on the social relations in Nigerian society.

Second, the book is an attempt to provide a detailed analysis of the nature of legal disputes between oil companies and village communities in Nigeria, given the dynamic processes of legal change in a developing society such as that of Nigeria. In the last one or two decades, oil-related litigation has increased in frequency. The US oil company Chevron alone was involved in over 200 pending court cases in Nigeria in 1998, while the company reportedly only had up to 50 cases in the whole of the 1980s (Frynas 1999). Shell was reportedly involved in over 500 pending court cases in Nigeria in 1998 (Frynas 1999), while only 24 compensation claims against Shell went to court in the period 1981-86 (Adewale 1989, 93). An important factor in the rise in litigation against multinational oil companies appears to have been the increased prospect of success for litigants as well as substantially higher compensation payments than before. During the 1990s, a number of high profile cases have been won by village communities, notably *Shell v. Farah*[2], in which ca. 4.6 million Naira (ca. US$

---

[2] (1995) 3 NWLR (Pt. 382) 148.

210,000 at the official exchange rate) was awarded as compensation for damage to a community.[3] The Farah case and other lawsuits appear to have been brought about by legal change. These may have benefited village communities, albeit litigants may still face problems in bringing claims. Legal disputes in the Nigerian oil industry, particularly in the light of their transformation, deserve to be the focus of an academic study.

Third, the book is aimed at making a contribution to the research and the debate on the role of multinational companies in developing countries and on the day-to-day operations of African legal systems. While numerous studies have addressed the role of multinational business, our analysis is motivated by the impression that there is a paucity of studies on the interactions between those affected by business operations and the companies in developing countries, particularly in the field of litigation. Our analysis is also motivated by a perceived lack of studies on the day-to-day operations of African legal systems. Above all, we perceive a gap in the academic writing on the Nigerian oil industry in terms of a socio-legal analysis of legal disputes between oil companies and village communities (see section 1.3. below).

1.3. Literature on Nigeria's Oil Industry

The literature on the Nigerian oil industry is extensive due to the industry's long history and its importance for the country's economy. However, it does not, on the whole, address the issue of field operations and the resultant legal conflicts.

The first serious scholarly study on the Nigerian oil industry was undertaken by Schätzl (1969) who focused on the evolution of the industry's operations in the light of the importance of oil for the country's future energy needs. A second study by Pearson (1970) concentrated on the impact of the oil industry on the Nigerian economy and investment patterns. A substantial number of other studies followed, most of which have dealt with the impact of the oil industry on Nigeria's economic development and the business side of oil operations (Emembolu 1975; Odofin 1979; Onoh 1983; Soremekun 1995a; Eromosele 1997) and the impact of the oil industry on the country's political development (Turner 1977; Ihonvbere and Shaw 1988). The most important study to-date was Sarah Ahmad Khan's pathbreaking book on the Nigerian oil industry entitled *Nigeria: The Political Economy of Oil* (1994). Khan's study focuses on business operations. It discusses the government's petroleum policy, the commercial activities of the oil companies and the nature of oil prices, among other issues.

While these studies have provided a more or less detailed analysis of business operations as well as economic and political development, they have tended to neglect the effects of oil companies on village communities and the role of the legal system as mediator and adjudicator. Some of these issues have been addressed by a small set of studies by both Nigerian and British authors. Ogbonna (1979), for instance, studied the

---

[3] In a number of other recent oil-related cases, a higher compensation award was awarded to those affected by oil operations. For instance, in *Anare v. Shell* Unreported Suit No. HCB/35/89 in Delta State HC, a number of village communities were awarded 30 million Naira (US$ 1,370,000 at the official exchange rate). However, the Farah case was an important legal precedent.

geographic consequences of the oil industry, pointing to the combined environmental consequences of oil operations in the oil producing areas. A number of recent studies by non-governmental organisations have noted the environmental and social impact of oil operations (Robinson 1996; Ashton-Jones 1998; HRW 1999a).

Two academic studies by Peter Usutu Onyige (1979) and Daniel Omoweh (1994) are particularly relevant to conflicts between oil companies and village communities. Both Onyige and Omoweh analysed the impact of oil operations on the local people, based on their own field studies in the oil producing areas.[4] The strength of their work has been in the analysis of interactions between oil companies and communities, which had largely been neglected in other studies. Onyige has been able to portray some aspects of the impact of oil operations on village communities and the attitudes of villagers towards oil companies. Omoweh meanwhile elucidated how the mechanics of the oil industry's field operations such as seismic surveys and drilling affect village communities. He described some of the resulting conflicts such as popular protests and compensation claims for damage.

However, both studies by Onyige and Omoweh have some deficiencies. Onyige's study lacks a social science basis and hence does not allow for a consistent analysis of the data. His major asset - 305 questionnaires returned by villagers – was under-utilised in the sense that the survey results were barely analysed. Omoweh's analysis is based on biased assumptions about the relationship between the state, oil companies and communities, which precludes a more balanced study of the subject. By emphasising colonialism as the root of economic underdevelopment in the oil producing areas, Omoweh's essentially Marxist outlook presupposes an adverse role for the oil companies from the outset before presenting empirical evidence. In addition, the adverse impact of oil operations may have been overemphasised by the author who claimed, for instance, that Shell was causing a land scarcity crisis in the oil producing areas without Omoweh having investigated other related factors. More importantly, neither Onyige's nor Omoweh's studies discuss the modern legal framework of community disputes in any detail.

There are a number of important studies by legal scholars on the role of law in relation to the Nigerian oil industry. Much of this literature, however, has largely failed to analyse the interaction between Nigerian petroleum legislation and the environmental and other laws related to field operations. This is due to an almost exclusive focus on either petroleum statutes or the environmental and other statutes related to field operations but not on both simultaneously. Neither of the two approaches has provided a complete picture of the legal framework in the oil industry. Major studies of Nigerian petroleum legislation by legal scholars, who have focused on the legal framework of the oil industry's commercial activities (Etikerentse 1985; Olisa 1987; Atsegbua 1993), have provided a detailed analysis of substantive law, particularly the provisions of the Petroleum Act 1969. Meanwhile, they have largely ignored either community-relevant environmental or land legislation or the legal framework in relation to oil operations in village communities. Those legal scholars who have discussed environmental law and land law in relation to the oil industry

---

[4] Onyige investigated the operations of Elf and Agip, while Omoweh concentrated on Shell's Nigerian operations.

(Omotola 1990), meanwhile, have often failed to discuss the rationales behind the commercial activities of the oil industry.

While many of these Nigerian legal studies have had strengths with regard to their analysis of the legal framework of multinational oil operations, they rarely address the socio-legal problems such as the actual enforcement of legislation or barriers to justice faced by village communities. A number of legal scholars, most notably Adewale (1989), have discussed socio-legal constraints in oil-related litigation in articles or scholarly papers. However, these studies have tended to confine their analysis to the formal legal problems involved. This is because legal scholars who engage in discussing legislation and litigation relating to village communities have often analysed law in isolation from social reality. Prototypical for this approach was an article on the relevance of the Federal Environmental Protection Agency (FEPA) Act to the oil industry by Guobadia (1993). Guobadia's article included a very brief section on the enforcement of the Act, which was limited to a discussion of the parts of the legal text that deal with the issue, but which failed to mention actual enforcement.

What emerges from the above survey of literature on the Nigerian oil industry and the legal framework of community disputes is that there is a lack of a socio-legal study on the oil industry in Nigeria, which provides a detailed analysis of the legal disputes between oil companies and village communities in relation to the institutional framework which mediates and adjudicates disputes. As indicated earlier, the objective of this book is to fill this gap within the limitations of the available material.

One of the reasons for the absence of a socio-legal study of oil-related community conflicts may be the prevailing ideas with regards to the nature of the state and with regards to social change in Africa, which rely heavily on macro-analytical frameworks. Take the example of Omoweh's study mentioned above. Based on a macro-analytical approach to the state, Omoweh ignores the dynamic processes, which have governed Nigerian legal development. This fact can be explained in part by Omoweh's view of the state as a 'monolithic block', which has led him to the impression that the judiciary, as an integral part of the state structures, lacks a dynamic of its own. In a recent study, Omoweh (1998) states: *'Since the judiciary is part of the state structure, the law court cannot be the last hope of the people in the rural oil areas in the on-going protests against the state and the oil companies over land crisis'.* This mechanistic view fails to make the distinction between political decisions at the apex of the state, on the one hand, and dynamic processes at work within the judiciary or other public bodies, on the other. This problem is perhaps characteristic of the general African Studies literature which sometimes fails to make a clear distinction between the different spheres of the state apparatus.

A further reason for a literature gap may have been the prevailing ideas about social change in Africa among scholars. As Whitaker (1991, 357) pointed out, the common feature of ideas about social change is that the essential impetus to change is assumed to be external. In particular, theories of 'development' and 'dependency' tended to concern themselves primarily with explaining the influence of Western institutions, values and power in the African context. By implication, Africans were said to merely be able to succumb, evade or obstruct the process of change, not necessarily influence it. Whitaker, on the other hand, argued that the transformation '*signifies the autonomous capacity of African social actors to generate significant change*'. The reluctance of African scholars to study this 'autonomous capacity' has led to mechanistic rather than dynamic theories of change and thus to a failure to investigate the underlying causes of the transformation of law, which can be found within the legal system and its social environment. In addition, as Whitaker (1991, 357-358) pointed out, the scholars' use of dichotomised concepts - development/underdevelopment, radical/conservative, modern/traditional - is also unhelpful to the study of change in Africa.

The formal legal approach has not been particularly useful to the study of change and the legal process in Africa because it fails to take account of socio-economic influences on legal decisions and the more dynamic aspects of the legal framework. The emphasis of African scholars on the formal legal approach may have been partly responsible for a lack of interest in the day-to-day operations of legal systems. In contrast, a socio-legal approach can provide a more holistic picture of the disputes between oil companies and village communities, which is not offered by either a purely socio-economic or a purely legal study. This approach precludes to some degree the use of the macro-analytical analysis of disputes between oil companies and village communities. A macro-analytical analysis may not be able to capture the complexity of the legal process and the dynamic processes of change which may be slow and subtle. By implication, therefore, this book is based on the assumption that a micro-analytical study is needed to investigate the nature of the legal process. A micro-analytical study could take different approaches. Our approach combines the analysis of concrete institutional arrangements with an investigation of personal experiences and perception of the legal system.

1.4. Outline of the Book

On the most basic level, our socio-legal methodology combines three main elements: an investigation of the context of oil operations, a discussion of a lawyers' survey and a detailed analysis of oil-related litigation.

We are of the view that a discussion of the context of oil operations is necessary in order to provide explanations which are both causally and meaningfully adequate in the Weberian sense. To this purpose, the book sets out by presenting the political and legal context which forms chapters 2 and 3.

Chapter 2, which discusses the making of the Nigerian oil industry and the government petroleum policy, serves as a basic background to our subsequent analysis of legal disputes. Furthermore, this chapter investigates whether the Nigerian state is biased in favour of oil companies or village communities or whether it can be considered neutral.

A discussion of the making of Nigeria's oil industry prepares the ground for a discussion of the legal system, which is at the core of the book. Chapter 3 provides an introduction to the legal framework by discussing the formal legal institutions and oil-related legislation. Issues discussed include the English Common Law, Nigerian customary law, the court system and oil-related statute law.

The contextual sections are followed by the statistical results of a survey of 154 Nigerian lawyers which form chapter 4. The survey respondents were asked about their personal knowledge of the legal proceedings and their experiences with oil companies in court. The survey allows for the use of statistical tests to investigate the quality of the Nigerian legal system by analysing answers to questions on issues such as the enforcement of court orders, extra-judicial pressures from outside institutions and problems of access to courts. Our survey analysis indicates that the judiciary and the legal process may be more biased in favour of oil companies than the opposing litigants in oil-related litigation.

The survey sets the stage for the analysis of 68 court cases involving disputes arising from oil operations on the ground. Using court judgments on topics such as oil spills and seismic surveys, chapter 5 assesses the impact of oil exploration and production on the local people. Rather than using court judgments as legal material, we utilise them as a source of factual evidence of the impact of oil operations. This enables us to identify some of the sources of conflicts between oil companies and village communities. The use of factual evidence from court cases serves as a window to an understanding of social conflicts in the Nigerian oil industry.

Chapter 6 provides a detailed discussion of the court cases in terms of substantive law. The chapter discusses the legal principles of tort law which are used as a basis for the court cases. A discussion of the legal liability under tort law and the legal defences used by oil companies exemplifies that litigation against oil companies faces severe obstacles. However, in the last decade or so, communities have been given more favourable judgments in court and some communities have been awarded relatively high compensation payments for oil company damage. This legal change, the existence of which constitutes an important finding of the book, is discussed in some detail and potential reasons are given to account for it.

Chapter 7 is the conclusion.

Chapter 2: The Making of Nigeria's Oil Industry - Oil and the Nigerian State

2.1. Introduction

This chapter, which discusses the making of the Nigerian oil industry and the government petroleum policy, serves as a basic background to our subsequent analysis of legal disputes. In order to fully understand conflicts between oil companies and village communities in Nigeria, it is instructive to examine the relationship between the foreign oil companies and the Nigerian state. Foreign oil companies and the Nigerian state depend on each other. The oil companies provide tax revenue for the state. The state provides access to the country's natural resources through the granting of oil licences as well as providing the regulatory framework such as petroleum tax and royalty, which defines the terms and conditions of operations and the financial incentives for oil companies. The state can impose minimum drilling obligations, price controls, environmental protection measures, control over the development of oil fields (including restrictions on production) and, in some cases, it can expropriate the assets of oil companies or cancel contracts. Political decisions may directly influence the day-to-day operations of the oil industry, particularly if the state has a shareholding interest in joint ventures with private oil companies as in the case of Nigeria. The state provides security protection for companies. Last but not least, the judiciary is part of the state institutions, thus legal disputes involving oil companies are regulated by the state. The nature of the state and its institutions is, therefore, relevant to the operations of oil companies and the resulting conflicts with the local people.

Our discussion of the political background of oil operations in this chapter is not exhaustive. Other scholars (e.g. Turner 1977; Ihonvbere and Shaw 1988) have provided a much more extensive account of Nigeria's political economy of oil. In this chapter, we attempt to investigate a different aspect of this discussion by exploring the link between political decision-making and community conflicts in the oil producing areas. We achieve this by examining the political context within which community conflicts in the oil producing areas have evolved. Our main concern is whether the Nigerian state is biased in favour of oil companies or village communities or whether it can be considered neutral. A number of scholars such as Terisa Turner (1976, 1977, 1978) have argued that the Nigerian state is predisposed in favour of oil interests. If it is assumed that the state is prejudiced in favour of oil companies, it has to be assumed that the state would restrict litigation against foreign investors. In order to understand the litigation between oil companies and village communities, it is thus necessary to investigate the bias of the Nigerian state in favour of foreign oil companies. This chapter examines the basic elements of Nigeria's political economy as they pertain to the relationship between the state and foreign oil companies as to the possibility of the state supporting or blocking litigation.

2.2. Colonial Origins of Nigeria's Oil

The first major oil exploratory work in Nigeria was conducted by the Nigerian Bitumen Corporation, a Nigerian subsidiary of a German company, between 1907 and 1914. In 1914, the Nigerian Bitumen Corporation was forced to withdraw from Nigeria due to the beginning of the First World War.[5] Following the end of the First World War, the company was not allowed to resume operations since the British colonial authorities gave preference to oil exploration by British companies.[6]

In 1938, a joint venture between the two major British oil companies Shell and BP was granted a licence to explore oil covering the entire territory of Nigeria.[7] This gave them a monopoly over oil exploration in the country. Shell-BP began its drilling activities in 1951.[8] In 1953, some 450 barrels of oil were discovered at the Akata-1 well. In 1956, the Shell-BP venture found oil in commercial quantities for the first time at Oloibiri. Encouraged by early successes, Shell-BP greatly expanded its drilling activities between 1958 and 1960. As a result of expanded operations, it was able to make important discoveries, of which the most promising one was the Bomu oil field in the Ogoni area in 1958. Production of crude oil began in December 1957 (Shell-BP 1960).

Initially, Nigeria's economy was not dependent on oil. Other commodities, particularly agricultural exports such as palm oil and palm kernels as well as coal and tin production, played a much greater role.[9] However, the role of crude oil in Nigeria's export portfolio increased rapidly. By 1960, crude oil exports came to provide the bulk

---

[5] It was exceptional that the British government was willing to grant a concession to a non-British oil company. This was probably because the initial exploration depended on the willingness of outsiders to come to Nigeria, since the country appeared to have no specific advantages for oil exploration, particularly as compared to alternative areas such as Russia and Persia, which provided alternative investment opportunities for British oil companies. In some other territories with British influence such as Egypt, the British government did not necessarily intervene on behalf of British companies until oil was actually found (Jones 1981, 116). Indeed, since exploration in Nigeria was considered as speculative and the capital markets were reluctant to provide financial assistance, the Nigerian Bitumen Corporation applied to the British authorities for financial support, which was duly granted (Jones 1981, 63). The Nigerian Bitumen Corporation discovered some crude oil of commercial value in 1908 but the company decided to continue exploration for crude oil of better 'lighter' quality (Njeze 1978, 165-166).

[6] Following the First World War, oil licences were granted to D'Arcy Exploration Company, a subsidiary of Anglo-Persian (later renamed Anglo-Iranian, then BP) and the Whitehall Petroleum Corporation. Both companies surrendered their respective licences by 1923 because no oil was found in commercial quantities. Petroleum Department, *Petroleum in Nigeria, Tanganyika and Kenya*, a confidential note, London, November 1936, BP Archive, the official oil company archives of BP, located at the University of Warwick, Coventry.

[7] In 1937, Shell D'Arcy (renamed Shell-BP in 1956) was formed as a joint venture between Shell and Anglo-Iranian (British Petroleum from 1954) to operate in Nigeria. As a result of the Second World War, Shell D'Arcy withdrew from Nigeria in 1941. The company returned in 1946 to resume exploration work (Shell-BP 1960, 5).

[8] According to Shell's figures, 1959 was the peak year of drilling with 53 wells drilled by Shell-BP (Shell-BP 1960, 13).

[9] In the late 1950s, the volume of coal production and oil production was similar. The difference between oil and coal production was that oil was predominantly produced for export, while coal was predominantly produced for domestic use. In 1960, 847,000 tons of crude oil were exported. In the same year, 562,000 tons of coal were produced for domestic use (Meier 1975, 457).

of the minerals exports. In 1960, 847,000 tons of crude oil were exported, compared with only 10,000 tons of tin and 2,000 tons of columbite (see Table 2.1.). Not surprisingly, by 1960, oil operations had come to play a greater role in government affairs. Petroleum matters were on the agenda of the Nigerian Council of Ministers in 6 out of 43 meetings and in 10 out of 31 meetings in 1958 and in 1959 respectively.[10]

Table 2.1. Nigeria's Exports (in thousand tons), 1919-1960

	1919-21	1929-31	1935-37	1951	1960
Palm oil	80	129	150	150	183
Palm kernels	192	255	346	347	418
Ground-nuts	45	151	242	141	333
Cocoa*	20	53	91	122	154
Crude oil	-	-	-	-	847
Tin ore	-	-	15	12	10
Columbite	-	-	1	2	2

* Cocoa exports are shown in thousand pounds sterling.
Source: Meier (1975, 457).

Table 2.2. Production of Crude Oil within the Commonwealth (in long tons)[11], 1956-1971

	Nigeria	Canada	Qatar	Trinidad	Brunei	Total Commonwealth
1956	0	22,930,855	5,783,812	4,132,681	5,547,433	40,769,100
1957	1,200	24,246,401	6,504,814	4,866,278	5,458,923	43,626,000
1958	270,000	22,066,159	8,091,813	5,336,437	5,089,492	43,803,000
1959	557,000	24,637,133	7,866,650	5,845,542	5,262,702	47,334,000
1960	867,000	25,271,229	8,083,032	6,051,047	4,473,867	47,985,000
1961	2,302,000	29,448,165	8,249,305	6,538,253	4,015,618	53,812,000
1962	3,373,000	32,548,687	8,670,919	6,982,306	3,720,253	59,887,000
1963	3,824,000	34,354,904	8,953,349	6,954,038	3,383,789	64,323,000
1964	6,027,000	36,612,711	8,802,292	7,103,495	3,488,000	73,496,000
1965	13,564,000	39,437,267	9,013,660	6,979,848	3,874,000	88,629,000
1966	20,881,000	42,856,000	8,915,387	7,943,355	4,619,000	105,909,000
1967	15,962,000	46,838,000	9,069,839	9,284,320	5,095,000	109,422,000
1968	6,900,000	50,586,170	n.a.	8,557,000	5,884,000	109,396,000
1969	25,600,000	54,798,657	n.a.	8,204,000	6,005,000	134,036,000
1970	51,970,000	61,490,674	n.a.	7,292,000	6,700,000	176,702,000
1971	74,100,000	66,729,895	n.a.	6,833,000	6,433,000	180,100,000

Source: Overseas Geological Surveys, Mineral Resources Division, *Statistical Summary of the Mineral Industry* (London, Her Majesty's Stationary Office, various years).

[10] Conclusions of Meetings of the Council of Ministers 1958 and 1959, CO1039/86, CO1039/87, CO1039/107, CO1039/108, Public Record Office (PRO), Kew, London. Despite an increase in oil-related discussions, other policy matters such as those on the Coal Corporation still took precedence over the oil industry. Petroleum policy was addressed in only 7 memos of the Council in 1958 and in 18 memos in 1959, compared with a total of almost 700 government memos in 1959 alone. The greater number of discussions on petroleum matters in 1959 stemmed primarily from the need to regulate petroleum legislation before the end of the colonial era and to issue permits for oil pipelines.

[11] 1 long ton is equal to approx. 7.45 barrels.

From an international perspective, however, Nigeria's initial oil production was not substantial. In 1960, at the time of Nigeria's independence, four oil producing countries of the British Commonwealth - Canada, Qatar, Brunei and Trinidad - produced more crude oil than Nigeria (see Table 2.2.). In percentage terms, Nigeria provided only 1.8% of the crude oil production of the Commonwealth in 1960. This had changed by 1971 when Nigeria had become the largest Commonwealth oil producing country with a production of 74,100,000 long tons, which amounted to 41.1% of the total crude oil production of the Commonwealth. By the end of the colonial era, therefore, the significance of Nigeria's oil industry did not lie so much in the actual oil production but rather in its potential for future expansion.

On the eve of Nigeria's independence in 1960, the two largest British oil companies Shell and BP were the dominant oil companies in the country and Shell (Shell-BP until 1979) has remained the dominant company in the Nigerian oil industry from the colonial era to-date.[12] However, by the early 1960s, Shell-BP had been joined by competitors. Until 1951, the venture had exclusive concessions over all Nigerian oil resources. In that year, the original exploration licence covering 357,000 sq. miles was reduced to an area of 58,000 sq. miles in Southern Nigeria. Between 1955 and 1957, Shell-BP's exploration area was further reduced to 40,000 sq. miles, mainly in the Niger Delta (Schätzl 1969, 1). The choice of exploration areas for newcomers in Nigeria was limited to areas previously abandoned by Shell-BP. Attracted by Shell-BP's successes and encouraged by the British government, other oil companies were interested in exploration work because of the suspected oil wealth. From the late 1950s, concessions were granted to a number of non-British oil companies. Socony-Vacuum (later re-named Mobil) obtained its first oil exploration licence in 1955, Tennessee (also known as Tenneco) in 1960, Gulf (later Chevron) in 1961, American Overseas (also known as Amoseas) in 1961, Agip[13] in 1962, SAFRAP[14] (later Elf) in 1962, Phillips in 1965 and Esso[15] in 1965 (Schätzl 1969, 4-5; Whiteman 1982, 340-342). As a result, nine foreign companies were engaged in oil exploration in Nigeria by 1965.

All six major foreign oil companies, which dominate the Nigerian oil industry today (Shell, Mobil, Chevron, Elf, Agip and Texaco), were already present in Nigeria by the early 1960s and were all producing by 1971. All newcomers were confined to market niches left behind by Shell-BP. The most important of these market niches were the oil resources in Nigeria's offshore area. Shell-BP had to compete with several other companies in offshore oil exploration from the start. In respect of new licences, the Nigerian Council of Ministers in 1959 agreed *'that not more than four blocks of 1,000 square miles each should be granted in the Continental Shelf area to any one*

---

[12] The Nigerian assets of BP were nationalised in 1979 (see section 2.6. below).

[13] Affiliate of the Italian government owned oil company ENI.

[14] SAFRAP (Société Anonyme Française des Recherches et d'Exploitation de Petrole) Nigeria Ltd was jointly owned by SAFRAP (50%), RAP (Regie Autonome des Petroles) (40%) and SOGERAP (Société de Gestion des Participants de la RAP) (10%). The equity share of the French government in SAFRAP and RAP was 64% and 100% respectively.

[15] Subsidiary of the US oil company Exxon.

company.'.[16] This early diversification explains in part why Shell was not able to extend its dominant position in onshore operations to those offshore.[17] In January 1964, Gulf (later Chevron) discovered the Okan oil field, the first commercial field to be found on Nigeria's continental shelf, which began to produce oil in 1965 (Whiteman 1982, 315). Gulf thus became established in offshore operations owing to its early discoveries and remained the second largest oil producing company in Nigeria into the early 1990s. Mobil made its first discovery in 1964 and began production from the offshore Idaho field in 1970 (http://www.mobil.com/world/nigeria/ mobnigeria.html, January 1998). Mobil remained the third largest oil company in Nigeria until 1992 when it overtook Chevron to become the second largest. Texaco/California Asiatic made its first offshore discovery in 1963 (Madujibeya 1975, 3). Shell's early focus on onshore areas located close to human settlements can explain why the company and its sub-contractors have been involved in significantly more local conflicts and litigation in Nigeria to-date than other oil companies operating offshore such as Mobil and Chevron.

2.3. Oil-Related Legal Arrangements under Colonial Rule

For Shell and BP to expand oil operations in Nigeria, a sympathetic system of oil licensing and a business conducive legal framework were necessary. Following Nigeria's unification in 1914, a key piece of petroleum legislation was passed in the form of the Mineral Oil Ordinance No.17 of 1914, which was amended in 1925, 1950 and 1958.[18] The Mineral Oil Ordinance was ostensibly passed *'to regulate the right to search for, win and work mineral oils'* (Ajomo 1976; Etikerentse 1985, 1).

One of the main provisions of the 1914 Ordinance was that only British oil companies were permitted to obtain oil licences in Nigeria.[19] Despite its explicit wording, this provision could be circumvented, if the colonial administration was willing to do so.[20] When Socony-Vacuum (later re-named Mobil) - a US company -

---

[16] Conclusions of the 19th Meeting of the Council of Ministers (22 July 1959), File CO1039/108, PRO.

[17] Of the 314 successful oil and gas discoveries made by 1975, 73% were in onshore areas and 27% in offshore areas. Shell-BP accounted for 77% of onshore discoveries, while three US companies - Gulf, Mobil and Texaco/California Asiatic - accounted for 76% of offshore discoveries (Madujibeya 1975, 3).

[18] Until 1914, oil companies in Nigeria operated under the Mining Regulation (Oil) Ordinance 1907 of Southern Nigeria, which was amended by Mining Regulation (Oil) Ordinances 1907 and 1909.

[19] Nigeria Mineral Oil Ordinance (Colonial Mineral Ordinance No.17) of 1914, section 6(1)(a) stipulated that:
> *No lease or licence shall be granted except to a British subject or to a British company and its principal place of business within Her Majesty's dominions; The chairman and the managing director (in any) and the majority of the other directors of which are British subjects.*

[20] A similar provision, which formally disqualified non-British companies, existed under the Mining Regulation (Oil) Ordinance 1907, section 15. However, the British authorities allowed the Nigerian Bitumen Corporation, a subsidiary of a German company and registered in Nigeria, to operate from 1907 to 1914.

was allowed to enter Nigeria in 1955, they formed a locally registered company with a British chairman and a board of directors, of whom the majority were British citizens. Since the investment of Socony-Vacuum was welcomed and even encouraged by the British government, no political objections were raised.[21] The provision of the Ordinance, which disqualified non-British companies, was eventually repealed in 1958 in order to attract US investment.[22]

The main problem of colonial petroleum legislation under the Mineral Oil Ordinance and subsidiary legislation was that it did not prescribe the terms and conditions of oil operations. These terms and conditions were fixed by oil licences issued by the colonial government. Every licence set out the specific rights and obligations of the licence holder. An oil company had to apply for each licence separately. Once a licence was granted, the company had to fulfil the conditions and obligations prescribed by the licence and had to pay the stipulated fees. There were three types of licences: the oil exploration licence (OEL), the oil prospecting licence (OPL), and the oil mining lease (OML). In addition to these three types of licences, an oil company had to apply separately for a licence to build a pipeline under the Oil Pipelines Act 1956. At first, an OEL was granted, which allowed the oil company to explore, search and drill for oil but prohibited oil production. Once the OEL for an area expired, the same oil company could either surrender the exploration area or apply for an OPL for the area in question. The OPL allowed the company to explore, search and drill for oil as well as to produce it. Once the OPL expired, the oil company could surrender the area or apply for an OML for the area in question. The OML was a long-term agreement between the company and the government to produce oil. The specific terms and fees differed between OELs, OPLs and OMLs. The most distinctive provision of an OML was the exclusive privilege to produce oil in a specific area for a period of 30 years in land areas and territorial waters and of 40 years in the Niger Delta and the Continental Shelf (see Table 2.3.).

The British authorities were prepared to amend the legal framework in Shell-BP's favour. For instance, in the early 1950s, Nigeria's colonial government, with the full authority of the British Secretary of State for the Colonies, agreed to increase the size of Shell-BP's OPLs.[23] It appears that the decision was made at the request of oil managers. An internal oil company report in 1954 read:

> As a result of representations made by Shell D'Arcy [Shell-BP venture], the Central Government have agreed that the area of these licenses shall be increased from 500 sq. miles to 2,000 sq. miles and the obligation to drill a well shall be at any time during the period of the licence.[24]

---

[21] Reported in File CO1029/255, PRO. During the mid-1950s, the British government became more sympathetic towards US private investments in Nigeria's oil industry. Before the 1950s, Socony-Vacuum (later Mobil) had already sought oil licences in African colonies such as Nigeria and the Gold Coast. The US government supported Socony-Vacuum's efforts in Nigeria throughout the Second World War, but the British government repeatedly refused to grant oil concessions to the company (Gibbs 1995).

[22] Section 2 of the Mineral Oils (Amendment) Act 1958, reported in Atsegbua (1993, 8).

[23] Letter by the Permanent Secretary, Ministry of Lands, Mines and Power in Lagos to J.M. Kisch, Colonial Office in London (June 25, 1957), File CO1029/255, PRO.

[24] K.R.H. (initials of unknown author), *Some Notes on the Administration Departments of the Shell D'Arcy Petroleum Development Company of Nigeria* (May 22, 1954), File BP 52584, BP Archive.

Table 2.3. Selected Provisions of Nigerian Oil Licences, August 1959

Type of Right	Oil Exploration Licence (OEL)	Oil Prospecting Licence (OPL)	Oil Mining Lease (OML)
Type of Right	Non exclusive (areas north of latitude 7°N)	Exclusive	Exclusive
Rental	£50 per year	2/- per square mile per year	2/6d per acre for first year rising to 10/- in sixth and subsequent years
Area	Up to 10,000 sq. miles	Up to 2,000 sq. miles onshore or 1,000 sq. miles in the Continental Shelf areas	Any size approved by government
Period Renewal (land areas, territorial waters) Period	1 year	3 years	30 years
Renewal	1 year (followed by 1 year at £50 premium)	2 years (on whole or part if work done satisfactory to C.I.M.)	30 years
Period Renewal (Niger Delta, Continental Shelf) Period	1 year	4 years	40 years
Renewal	1 year (followed by 1 year at £50 premium)	3 years	40 years
Conditions	Explore and search by geological and/or geophysical means with topographical examination and drilling may be undertaken, no production of oil allowed.	1) Explore, search and drill for oil, carry out geological, geophysical and topographical work. 2) Carry away and dispose of oil. 3) Not later than third year start training schemes for the tech. training of Nigerian staff.	1) Search, bore-for, win and work all petroleum. 2) If not already started, a training scheme for tech. training of staff must be started or contributed to.
Obligations	i) Commence geologically and/or geophysically to examine with reasonable dispatch and continue to do so. ii) Quarterly reports to D.G.S. and C.I.M. iii) Topographical and cadastral maps to Federal Surveys. iv) Samples to be given D.G.S. as required. Details any drilling to D.G.S. and C.I.M.	i) All reasonable dispatch commence and continue examination geologically and by geophysical methods. ii) Within 6 months of date of grant commence seismic investigation and be continuos until drilling operations are commenced or licence determined. iii) Before the end of third year have drill a minimum of 12,000 feet and no well shall be less than 6,000 feet in depth. This obligation will be modified if one operator is granted 2 (or more) concession areas when the single concession obligation will apply to each 2 areas in Continental Shelf. iv) Monthly drilling reports and quarterly progress reports	i) As clause 42 in Shell OML (work according to good oil-field practice) ii) Monthly drilling record to C.I.M. and D.G.S. iii) Quarterly progress report to C.I.M. and D.G.S. iv) Such other records as to production and exports as required by C.I.M.

Source: Circular Letter of A.C.F. Armstrong, Permanent Secretary in the Ministry of Lagos Affairs, Mines and Power to Shell-BP, Gulf, Pan American, Standard Oil, Mobil and California Exploration Company (4 August 1959), POWE 33/421, PRO.

Under these terms, Shell-BP had to apply for only 6 to 7 licences as against approximately 28 licences for the same area under the previous regulation. This reduced the number of wells that the company was obliged to drill to meet licence terms. With the assistance of the government, Shell-BP established its base in the oil-rich onshore areas of south-eastern Nigeria at a lower financial cost than otherwise necessary.

While the above example illustrates an instance of active support of Shell-BP by the British colonial administration, the British government largely refrained from actively assisting British oil companies in the decade before Nigerian independence in 1960. The British authorities were interested in promoting private investment by attracting new oil companies to areas abandoned by Shell-BP. British policy-making was further complicated by Nigeria's constitutional changes in the 1950s, under which petroleum policy in Nigeria increasingly became a prerogative of Nigerian politicians. The British government, moreover, was pressured by the US government into opening up Nigeria to US oil companies (Frynas and Beck 1998).

For their part, Shell-BP did not, by and large, need any active government support because the venture held the majority of oil licences at independence. In January 1960 and in January 1962, the oil prospecting licences (OPLs) granted to Shell-BP under colonial rule had expired. By the terms of the OPLs, the venture had the right to take up to 50% of the area under oil mining leases (OMLs) for a period of 30 or 40 years.[25] Shell-BP, unaffected by competitors, was able to acquire 46 oil mining leases (OMLs) covering roughly 15,000 sq. miles (38,850 sq. km) for 30 or 40 years in areas with the best geological indications for oil deposits (Schätzl 1969, 1). In comparison, the area of the Niger Delta Basin, where the bulk of Nigerian oil operations have taken place since, covers roughly 28,950 sq. miles (75,000 sq. km) onshore (Ashton-Jones 1998, 151).[26] The nature of the licensing process and the role played by Shell-BP within it enabled the company to pre-empt rivals by securing long-term leases in the most promising oil exploration areas.

By 1960, Shell-BP had established its base in the oil-rich onshore areas of south-eastern Nigeria, which has allowed Shell to retain a dominant position in Nigeria to-date. According to the *Petroleum Economist*, Shell's venture accounted for an estimated 39.6% of Nigeria's total crude oil production in May 1999, compared with Mobil's share of roughly 25.0%, Chevron's 17.5%, Agip's 6.7%, Elf's 5.0% and Texaco's 3.1% (see Table 2.4.). Shell's continuing dominance could explain why the company was involved in significantly more local conflicts and litigation in Nigeria than other oil companies operating onshore such as Agip and Elf. Shell is likely to remain the dominant player in the Nigerian oil industry, given the company's recent offshore oil discoveries, particularly the Bonga oil field (estimated future production ca. 350,000 barrels/day) in 1996 (Quinlan 1999).

---

[25] Circular Letter of A.C.F. Armstrong, Permanent Secretary in the Ministry of Lagos Affairs, Mines and Power to Shell-BP, Gulf, Pan American, Standard Oil, Mobil and California Exploration Company (4 August 1959), POWE 33/421, PRO.

[26] There exist different definitions of the Niger Delta territory. The different estimates of the Delta area range from 20,000 sq. km to 75,000 sq. km.

Table 2.4. Percentage Share of Nigeria's Crude Oil Production by Company, 1970-1999

	Shell-BP	Gulf*	Mobil	Agip	Elf	Texaco	Ashland**	Others
1970	74.47	20.05	4.68	0.45	0	0.35	0	0
1971	72.96	17.76	4.79	2.17	1.54	0.68	0	0
1972	67.50	16.86	9.17	2.87	3.04	0.56	0	0
1973	63.41	17.76	10.90	4.60	2.93	0.40	0	0
1974	59.99	16.36	13.14	6.86	3.55	0.10	0	0
1975	63.50	12.38	10.64	8.79	3.91	0.42	0.36	0
1976	59.53	14.14	11.14	8.92	3.67	1.67	0.47	0.46
1977	58.18	13.85	10.64	10.21	3.79	2.53	0.33	0.47
1978	57.20	13.80	10.52	11.08	4.08	2.27	0.46	0.59
1979	56.93	16.27	10.57	9.62	3.40	2.34	0.35	0.52
1980	56.69	16.57	10.59	8.93	4.17	2.10	0.41	0.54
1981	51.37	19.58	11.17	8.79	5.05	2.39	0.66	0.99
1982	50.82	16.37	10.57	9.96	7.21	2.91	1.26	0.90
1983	50.15	14.13	13.15	9.58	7.24	3.56	1.26	0.93
1984	50.27	13.47	12.82	9.09	7.05	4.71	1.77	0.82
1985	49.89	16.56	11.98	9.95	6.23	3.10	1.56	0.73
1986	48.30	16.85	12.30	9.12	5.87	4.45	2.44	0.67
1987	49.26	15.96	12.31	8.83	6.18	4.38	2.55	0.54
1988	n/a	n/a	n/a	n/a	n/a	n/a	n/a	n/a
1989	52.72	15.58	12.42	7.70	5.28	3.41	2.12	0.77
1990	51.18	15.29	13.16	9.50	5.30	3.24	2.11	0.22
1991	50.74	16.23	14.45	7.42	5.03	3.12	1.62	1.39
1992	49.50	16.18	16.76	7.15	4.96	2.96	1.26	1.22
1993	48.15	16.48	21.19	6.99	5.07	0	0.96	1.17
1994	48.15	16.48	21.19	6.99	5.07	0	0.96	1.17
1995	46.11	19.87	14.81	7.70	6.56	2.80	0.96	1.18
1996	46.11	19.87	14.81	7.70	6.56	2.80	0.96	1.18
1997***	42.14	18.08	20.83	6.55	5.90	3.58	1.09	1.83
1998	38.28	20.00	24.64	6.70	5.74	3.11	n/a	1.53
1999****	39.58	17.50	25.00	6.66	5.00	3.13	0.83	2.29

* now Chevron; ** Ashland lost its oil licences in 1997, Addax bought the licences in 1998; *** April figures; **** May figures.

Sources: 1970-85 data from NNPC (1986a); 1986-96 data from *OPEC Annual Statistical Bulletin* (various years), 1990 figures from Quinlan (1992, 23); 1997 data from *Weekly Petroleum Argus* (21 April 1997); 1998 estimates from *Petroleum Review* (April 1999); 1999 estimates from *Petroleum Economist* (Quinlan 1999, 3).

2.4. Evolution of Nigeria's Oil Industry after Independence

From the start of oil production by Shell-BP in December 1957, Nigerian crude oil production has steadily expanded and, more recently, billions of dollars have been invested in the development of gas production. From a level of 20,000 b/d (barrels/day) in 1960, Nigeria's oil production made a giant leap to well over 2,000,000 b/d today. During the 1960s, production was still rather insignificant but it did increase from 20,000 b/d in 1960 to 540,000 b/d in 1969.[27] From then on, production continuously

---

[27] The Civil War 1967-70 disrupted oil operations, but production then recovered and made a major leap from 540,000 b/d in 1969 to 1,530,000 b/d in 1971.

increased reaching over 2,000,000 b/d in 1973, a similar production level to the late 1990s. The expansion of Nigeria's oil production did not follow a linear trend. After a high point in 1974 and again in 1979, Nigeria's oil production declined between 1980 and 1983 in line with the decline in world market demand (see Table 2.5.). In order to stimulate oil exploration and production, the Nigerian government introduced better financial terms for oil companies, especially the Memorandum of Understanding in 1986 (this will be discussed in some detail later on). As profit margins and world-wide demand were rising, Nigerian oil production began to rise quickly from the late 1980s onwards. During the 1990s, foreign oil companies committed substantial investments to extend productive capacity in Nigeria which could account for a rise in production from 1992 onwards (Khan 1994, 55-56). Between 1992 and 1997, the number of producing oil wells in Nigeria rose from 1,701 to 2,251 (*OPEC Annual Statistical Bulletin* 1997 and 1998), while Nigerian oil production increased from 1,950 to 2,285 thousand barrels/day (see Table 2.5.).

Table 2.5. Nigerian Crude Oil Production, 1958-1997

Year	Production (000s barrels/day)	% Share of World Total	Year	Production (000s barrels/day)	% Share of World Total
1958	5	0.03	1978	1,895	3.01
1959	10	0.05	1979	2,300	3.50
1960	20	0.09	1980	2,055	3.28
1961	55	0.23	1981	1,440	2.43
1962	70	0.27	1982	1,285	2.25
1963	75	0.27	1983	1,235	2.18
1964	120	0.41	1984	1,390	2.41
1965	275	0.87	1985	1,500	2.61
1966	420	1.22	1986	1,465	2.42
1967	320	0.87	1987	1,325	2.18
1968	145	0.36	1988	1,445	2.28
1969	540	1.23	1989	1,715	2.67
1970	1,085	2.25	1990	1,810	2.75
1971	1,530	3.01	1991	1,890	2.89
1972	1,815	3.39	1992	1,950	2.97
1973	2,055	3.51	1993	1,985	3.01
1974	2,260	3.86	1994	1,990	2.97
1975	1,785	3.20	1995	2,000	2.95
1976	2,065	3.44	1996	2,150	3.09
1977	2,085	3.33	1997	2,285	3.16

Source: *BP Statistical Review of World Energy* (various years).

In percentage terms, Nigeria's share of the world crude oil production rose from 0.03% in 1958 to 0.09% in 1960 to 0.35% in 1968. From then, Nigeria's share rose enormously to 1.23% in 1969, to 2.25% in 1970, reaching 3.86% in 1974. In the 1980s, the country's share dropped to a low of 2.18% in 1983 and again in 1987, rising to 3.16% in 1997 (see Table 2.5.).

The destination of Nigeria's oil exports in terms of the world market fluctuated considerably over the years. In the first phase 1958-61, virtually the entire oil production was exported to Britain and the Netherlands, the home countries of Shell-BP. In the 1960s, new export markets were found in Western Europe, the US, Latin America, Africa and Japan. In the early 1970s, the US became the largest single buyer of Nigerian oil. In 1973, for example, over half of the Nigerian oil exports went to Western Europe, 27% to the US, 13% to the Caribbean and 5% to Japan (Madujibeya 1975, 5). The share of Nigerian oil exports to the US declined to 14.1% in 1984 as a result of the world-wide recession in the early 1980s. Nigerian oil exports to the US then recovered and peaked at 52.6% of the country's total oil exports in 1989.[28] At the same time, increased production of North Sea oil in the 1980s contributed to a relative decline of Nigerian oil exports to Western Europe (Khan 1994, 117-121), leaving the US as the main importer of Nigerian oil.[29] The main exports markets for Nigerian oil remain the US and Western Europe, with a share of 48.0% and 37.8% of the total respectively in 1997 (see Table 2.6.). Germany was the largest Western European importer of Nigerian oil, closely followed by France. Britain, Nigeria's former colonial power, accounted for only 0.2% of Nigeria's oil exports (*OPEC Annual Statistical Bulletin* 1998).[30]

Table 2.6. Nigeria's Oil Exports by Destination (per cent), 1984-1997

	'84	'85	'86	'87	'88	'89	'90	'91	'92	'93	'94	'95	'96	'97
United States	14.1	16.8	34.8	49.7	49.9	52.6	50.7	43.6	44.2	45.9	41.8	40.4	45.2	48.0
West. Europe	72.3	62.4	54.4	40.4	40.0	37.1	39.5	45.3	43.6	32.7	38.4	33.0	41.0	37.8
Latin America	8.1	16.1	4.1	1.7	1.8	1.6	1.6	2.5	2.8	4.0	4.1	5.4	3.8	4.3
Africa	3.7	3.3	4.4	6.0	6.1	4.6	4.8	5.0	5.0	5.3	4.8	8.4	2.4	4.0
Far-East Asia	n/a	n/a	n/a	n/a	n/a	n/a	0.1	n/a	0.6	7.4	6.9	9.6	5.4	4.3
Other*	1.8	1.4	2.3	2.2	2.2	4.1	3.3	3.6	3.8	4.7	4.0	3.2	2.2	1.6
Total	100	100	100	100	100	100	100	100	100	100	100	100	100	100

* mainly Canada.
Source: computed from *OPEC Annual Statistical Bulletin* (various years).

In addition to oil, gas production is becoming increasingly important to Nigeria. In an international comparison, Nigerian gas production is still relatively insignificant (see Table 2.7.). In 1997, for example, the Nigerian gas production was roughly 4.3 million tonnes oil equivalent, which was equal to roughly 30 million barrels of crude oil or, in other words, equal to approximately only two weeks of the Nigerian oil

---

[28] In the early 1980s, Nigeria's total oil exports declined from 1,960,000 b/d in 1980 to a low of 935,000 b/d in 1983. The US exports reached their lowest point at 154,000 b/d in 1984, while Western European exports reached a lowest point in 1982 with 482,000 b/d. The decline in exports to Western Europe and Latin America was, on the whole, more significant than the decline of US exports (Khan 1994, 118-119).

[29] The oil production in the North Sea played a significant role for the marketing of Nigeria's oil because the Nigerian crudes are similar in quality to North Sea crudes, their prices are related to the crude called Brent, so they compete directly with crudes in the North Sea (Khan 1994, 101).

[30] This is perhaps unsurprising since Britain is an oil producing country itself.

production at 1997 levels.[31] In percentage terms, Nigeria's share of the world gas production was only 0.21% in 1997, compared with a 3.16% share of the world crude oil production (compare Tables 2.5. and 2.7.).

Table 2.7. Nigerian Gas Production, 1971-1997

Year	Production (million tonnes oil equivalent)	% Share of World Total	Year	Production (million tonnes oil equivalent)	% Share of World Total
1971	0.2	0.02	1985	2.4	0.16
1972	0.2	0.02	1986	2.8	0.18
1973	0.3	0.03	1987	2.7	0.17
1974	0.4	0.04	1988	3.3	0.19
1975	0.4	0.04	1989	3.8	0.22
1976	0.6	0.05	1990	3.6	0.20
1977	0.5	0.04	1991	3.5	0.19
1978	0.3	0.02	1992	3.8	0.21
1979	1.2	0.09	1993	3.8	0.20
1980	1.0	0.07	1994	4.0	0.21
1981	1.6	0.12	1995	4.1	0.21
1982	1.1	0.08	1996	4.2	0.21
1983	1.3	0.10	1997	4.3	0.21
1984	2.5	0.17			

Source: *BP Statistical Review of World Energy* (various years).

Table 2.8. Nigeria's Proved Oil and Gas Reserves, 1984-1997

d	Oil			Gas		
	Reserves (billion barrels)	Reserves as % Share of World Total	Reserves/ Production Ratio (years)	Reserves (trillion cubic metres)	Reserves as % Share of World Total	Reserves/ Production Ratio (years)
1984	16.7	2.4	32.8	1.0	1.1	over 100
1985	16.6	2.3	31.0	1.3	1.4	over 100
1986	16.0	2.3	30.2	1.3	1.3	over 100
1987	16.0	1.8	34.1	2.4	2.2	over 100
1988	16.0	1.7	32.2	2.4	2.2	over 100
1989	16.0	1.6	27.5	2.5	2.2	over 100
1990	17.1	1.7	27.1	2.5	2.1	over 100
1991	17.9	1.8	26.0	3.0	2.4	over 100
1992	17.9	1.8	26.6	3.4	2.5	over 100
1993	17.9	1.8	25.8	3.4	2.4	over 100
1994	17.9	1.8	26.1	3.4	2.2	over 100
1995	20.8	2.1	30.2	3.1	2.1	over 100
1996	15.5	1.5	19.9	3.0	2.1	over 100
1997	16.8	1.6	20.2	3.3	2.2	over 100

Sources: *BP Statistical Review of World Energy* (various years).

---

[31] 1 million tonnes oil equivalent of gas is equal to 7.33 million barrels of oil.

While gas production was rather insignificant, the country's known gas reserves in 1997 amounted to 2.2% of the world total. At the 1997 levels of production, Nigerian oil production could continue for another 20 or so years. At current levels of production, Nigeria could produce gas for well over 100 years (see Table 2.8.), albeit the figures are misleading as production is still relatively insignificant.[32]

Until recently, companies were unwilling to exploit gas because there was no domestic market for gas in Nigeria, exports of gas were difficult and profit margins were low.[33] In the late 1990s, however, the Nigerian government gave the oil companies favourable fiscal incentives for gas exploitation, which can explain an upsurge in fresh investments into gas related projects.[34] Shell together with Agip and Elf engaged in the Nigeria Liquefied Natural Gas (NLNG) Project worth ca. US$ 5 billion. Chevron launched its US$ 550 million Escravos Gas Project in 1997 (further expansion planned), while Mobil launched a natural gas liquids (NGL) project worth over US$ 800 million in 1998 (*AFP*, 17 August 1998; *Oil & Gas Journal*, 22 March 1999; Quinlan 1999). Another important project is the planned West African Gas Pipeline Project (WAGP). The US$ 700 million project will export Nigerian gas to power plants in Ghana, Benin and Togo via a 990 km gas pipeline system.[35] Given the expansion of gas projects, Nigeria's gas production is bound to expand significantly but Nigeria has so far remained primarily an oil producing country rather than a gas producing country.

On the surface, the recent expansion in oil and gas projects may seem surprising, given the high political risk in Nigeria, the escalation of community conflicts and the rise in oil-related litigation. Multinational oil companies can choose between the former Soviet Union, Latin America, Southeast Asia and Africa, so it may be instructive to identify factors, which make Nigeria more attractive to them than alternative investment outlets.[36] Actual profits and profit potential in the oil

---

[32] The figures for oil and gas reserves are broad estimates.

[33] In 1965, BP discovered a large gas field in the North Sea. By then, it was clear that the European market for gas could be well served by North Sea, Libyan and Algerian gas and did not provide real opportunities for Nigerian gas exports. Difficulties with securing markets for gas and the price attached by foreign companies to gas were important obstacles to gas utilisation in Nigeria (Turner 1977, 171).

[34] Among other incentives to the gas industry, all gas development projects have been taxed under the Companies Income Tax rate of 30% rather than under the nominal Petroleum Profits Tax of 85% (as amended by the Memorandum of Understanding) with effect from 1998 (Onyenkpa 1998). The nominal profits tax rate of 85% was previously reduced to 65.75% for a maximum of five years (for new companies) under the MOU of 1991, in addition to other fiscal incentives such as reductions in the royalty rates and guaranteed minimum fiscal margins (Khan 1994, 48 and 63). Gas projects also benefit from the Oil and Gas Export Free Zone Decree No.8 of 1996. This established the Onne/Ikpokiri Export Free Zone and Regulatory Agency. The major benefits to oil companies include the provisions that remittance of profits and dividends earned by foreign investors is freely allowed and that import and export licences are not required. By the end of 1998, the NLNG plant, Mobil's Oso project, Shell's Soka gas plant and Elf's Obite gas plant, among others, were already located in the Onne zone (*PostExpressWired*, 25 November 1998).

[35] The joint developers of the WAGP are Chevron, Shell, the Nigerian Gas Corporation (NGC), Société Beninoise du Gaz, the government of Togo and the Ghana National Petroleum Corporation (Quinlan 1999).

[36] In many other oil producing countries, perception of political risk is comparable or lower than in Nigeria. For instance, Azerbaijan, Kazakhstan, Russia as well as Nigeria are rated by the Control Risks Group (1997) as medium-risk countries, while Turkmenistan and Kyrgyzstan are rated as low-

exploration and production sectors appear to be the key reason for Nigeria's importance to foreign investors.

According to a 1996 survey on the Nigerian oil industry by the consultancy firms Arthur Andersen and Andersen Consulting, Nigeria and the Middle East were ranked as the most attractive areas for oil exploration and production investments over the next five years. The high rating for Nigeria was influenced among other factors by the low cost of exploration and production, size and number of unappraised discoveries, and the preferred quality of the Nigerian oil (Arthur Andersen 1997), which we briefly examine here.

The low cost of exploration and production cannot be documented in detail because oil companies usually do not reveal the actual cost structure of their operations. Historically, production costs in Nigeria were reportedly relatively high by international comparison and they are said to have been increasing due to the use of more sophisticated technologies (Khan 1994, 85-86). Due to a shift in focus from onshore to offshore areas, investment costs per barrel in Nigeria became higher than in the Middle East. However, the costs of oil production in Nigeria can be increasingly regarded as relatively low because the Middle East no longer serves as the main comparison for oil companies. While the production costs in Nigeria are higher than in the Middle East, they are lower than in several new production areas such as the North Sea or the Gulf of Mexico. In comparison with these new production areas, Nigeria may be regarded as a low cost area.[37] According to *Petroleum Intelligence Weekly* (18 January 1999), Mobil reportedly had the lowest operating costs in Nigeria at about US$ 1.60/barrel, while the oil produced by the Shell venture cost slightly more.[38] The low cost of investment makes Nigeria particularly attractive to oil companies when oil prices are relatively low as in 1998. But technical costs cannot fully explain the profitability of oil production in Nigeria. The fiscal regime of a country largely determines the profits earned by oil companies and thus the attractiveness of a country to oil companies.

The fiscal regime of Nigeria is not unfavourable to oil companies if compared with other countries in the world (Petroconsultants 1996). While comparisons are always difficult, the 'after tax profit oil' for companies in Nigeria is higher than in several comparable countries in the world (Omalu 1996, 74).[39] The government share of 'profit oil' in Nigeria may be as low as 20%, while some other comparable countries have a share of between 60% and 90%. However, many of the arrangements gave the

---

risk countries. However, according to the Petroconsultants' rankings for political risk in 1998, Nigeria ranked as the second most risky country out of the eight major oil producing countries in West Africa, being only preceded by the war-torn Democratic Republic of Congo (Hallmark 1998).

[37] The insight into the relative merits of Nigeria's production costs in an international comparison was largely owed to personal communication with Martin Quinlan, journalist at the *Petroleum Economist*, London (September 1998). See also Quinlan (1999).

[38] In 1999, Mobil in Nigeria was planning a production of 678,000 barrels/day and operating expenditure of US$ 1.41/barrel (*Guardian*, Lagos, 22 June 1999).

[39] Profit oil is the gross revenue remaining after royalty oil, cost oil and tax oil recovery.

companies much less than 80%.[40] As Khan (1994, 93) noted, there is a marked difference between the old joint venture arrangements and the new production-sharing contracts. While the fiscal arrangements of the joint ventures were said by Khan to carry a high tax burden, the new production-sharing contracts and gas projects from the late 1980s reflected much more favourable fiscal terms. For instance, the Nigeria Liquefied Natural Gas (NLNG) contract provides for various concessions, waivers and exemptions from the provisions of Nigerian law, including a tax holiday of up to 10 years starting from the first day of production - not expected until October 1999 (Udoma and Belo-Osagie 1995). On the whole, Nigeria's fiscal regime is favourable to oil companies. According to the Petroconsultants' rankings in 1998, Nigeria ranked second in terms of fiscal incentives for oil companies out of the eight major oil producing countries in West Africa, being only preceded by Côte d'Ivoire (Hallmark 1998). There may also be hidden benefits of operating in the country owing to the companies' operational control over joint ventures (Frynas 1998; Danler and Brunner 1996, 12).[41]

In addition to low operating costs and high profit potential, Nigeria was considered attractive to oil company managers thanks to the size and number of unappraised discoveries, most of which are suspected to be in the Niger Delta and the adjacent offshore areas. Nigeria's producing oil fields are mostly concentrated in the Niger Delta Basin, which covers roughly 92,500 sq. miles (240,000 sq. km) - of which roughly 31% is onshore (Ashton-Jones 1998, 151). The Niger Delta (both onshore and offshore areas) is particularly conducive to the formation and accumulation of oil and gas for geological reasons (Hyne 1995, 90-98).

While the actual size of Nigerian oil wells is small, a key advantage of Nigeria for oil companies is the high rate of success in drilling operations, that means, the number of successful oil and gas well discoveries divided by the total number of drillings.[42] A good indicator of this success is the ratio of dry wells (i.e. drillings which do not result in any oil or gas findings) to total completed wells, which was rather insignificant in Nigeria. In 1996, this ratio was only 5.07% in Nigeria, compared with 22.01% in the US, 7.81% in Indonesia, 17.86% in Vietnam and 15.24% in Peru (see Table 2.9.). The high success rate of drilling can help to explain the rapid expansion of oil company operations in Nigeria's deep offshore areas in the 1990s. Of the 11 oil companies engaged in exploration in areas located within 200 and 2,000 metres of

---

[40] For instance, the terms of new contracts for offshore licences in 1991 gave the companies a share of only 11.7%, after allowing 30% of oil produced for cost recovery (*Petroleum Economist*, March 1991).

[41] Government officials openly suggested to the Nigerian press that oil companies bribe state officials in order to be able to deflate the operating costs in the joint ventures. Finance minister Anthony Ani suggested in 1997 that corrupt state officials benefited from the joint ventures at the expense of the government revenue (*Tell*, 24 February 1997).

[42] The actual average size of oil wells in Nigeria is relatively small due to geological conditions. Of Nigeria's 252 oil fields in 1995, 169 fields were below 100 million barrels. In 1995, there were only sixteen so-called 'giant oil fields' with over 400 million barrels (Thomas 1995), most of which were discovered before 1970. The presence of smaller oil fields, thus, renders oil exploration and production in Nigeria more expensive as more oil installations are required. It also requires continuous exploration for new fields in order to replace the existing ones and in order to increase production.

water depth, as many as 10 made a commercial discovery by May 1999 (*Guardian*, Lagos, 18 May 1999). In other words, oil and gas can be found relatively easily in Nigeria thanks to the presence of significant oil and gas reserves.

Table 2.9. Comparison of Wells Completed in Selected Countries and Regions in 1996

	Oil	Gas	Dry	Suspended	Service	Total Wells	Dry Wells as % Share of Total
Nigeria	118	2	7	10	1	138	5.07
United States	14,896	12,864	8,420	471	1,600	38,251	22.01
Indonesia	337	24	67	42	388	858	7.81
Vietnam	28	18	10	0	0	56	17.86
Peru	89	0	16	0	0	105	15.24
Africa	496	82	126	26	35	765	16.47
South America	2,538	96	244	99	83	3,060	7.97
Western Europe	328	196	139	24	69	756	18.39
Middle East	604	60	53	6	75	798	6.64

Source: *World Oil* (August 1997).

Table 2.10. Comparison of Selected Crude Oil Streams

Nigerian Crude Oil Stream	Sulphur Content (%)	°API	Foreign Crude Oil Stream	Country of Origin	Sulphur Content (%)	°API
Bonny Light	0.12	36.7	Arabian Light	Saudi Arabia	1.80	33.4
Bonny Medium	0.23	25.2	Bachequero	Venezuela	2.40	16.8
Brass River	0.09	40.9	Dubai	Dubai	1.68	32.5
Escravos	0.14	36.2	Ekofisk	Norway	0.18	35.8
Forcados	0.29	29.7	Iranian Light	Iran	1.40	33.5
Pennington	0.07	36.6	Kuwait	Kuwait	2.50	31.2
Qua Iboe	0.12	35.8	North Slope	United States	1.04	26.8

Sources: Hyne (1995, 16) and Thomas (1995).

As another important geological advantage, the quality of the Nigerian oil is generally better than elsewhere. The Nigerian light crude oil is of high °API gravity, which stands for the American Petroleum Institute standard. Nigerian crude oil streams have a low sulphur content if compared with crude oil from most other countries.[43] In 1995, Nigeria's Bonny Light (Shell) and Qua Iboe (Mobil) crude oil streams had a sulphur content of only 0.12%, compared with 1.80% in Arabian Light (Saudi Arabia), 2.40% in Bachequero (Venezuela) and 2.50% in Kuwait (see Table 2.10.). Refineries usually prefer crude oil with a low sulphur content because they must remove the

---

[43] Currently, Nigeria's biggest oil stream is Qua Iboe, produced by Mobil's joint venture.

sulphur from the oil (Hyne 1995, 14). As a result, the international price of crude oil from Nigeria is higher than that from many other countries.[44]

On the whole, Nigeria is very attractive to oil companies thanks to high profits and profit potential, the presence of significant oil and gas reserves as well as the preferred quality of the Nigerian oil. Particularly high profit potential can help to explain why oil companies have expanded their investments in Nigeria despite considerable political risks in the country and the escalation of conflicts between oil companies and village communities.

From the point of view of village communities, the intensified oil and gas exploration and production activity from the late 1980s has increased the physical presence of oil companies in the oil producing areas and contact with village communities. This in turn is likely to have increased the probability of conflicts - and thus litigation - between oil companies and the local people.

2.5. Nigeria's Political Economy of Oil

Expanding oil production as well as oil price rises stimulated by the Organisation of the Petroleum Exporting Countries (OPEC), particularly in the period 1973-74 and in 1979, rendered Nigeria almost entirely dependent on oil. Export revenues from oil rose by over 180% in 1974 and by over 70% in 1979. With this export boom, oil exports became Nigeria's major earner of foreign currency in the 1970s. In 1963, oil exports made up 10.75% of Nigeria's total exports. Ten years later, the figure had risen to 83.14%. In 1996, the share of oil exports in Nigeria's total exports was 98.2% (see Table 2.11.).

The importance of oil to the country was also reflected in the contribution of oil revenue to total government revenue, which rose from 26.3% in 1970 to 82.1% in 1974. Oil revenue has sustained the Nigerian government budgets since the 1970s. Since 1974, oil revenue has always provided more than 60% of the total government revenue (see Table 2.12.). According to Nigerian official figures, oil revenue accounted for 63.3% of the total federally collected revenue in 1997 (*Guardian*, Lagos, 19 February 1998). Even more impressively, the oil industry provided 96.0% of Nigeria's dollar receipts in 1997 (see Table 2.13.).

Forrest (1993, 133) indicated that one of the most noticeable consequences of the surge in oil revenue in the early 1970s was the neglect of non-oil tax revenues, of which some were abolished.[45] By the mid-1970s, the share of non-oil revenue in

---

[44] For instance, in December 1996, Nigerian 'Bonny Light' fetched US$ 24.53/barrel compared with US$ 23.05/barrel for 'Arabian Light' and US$ 21.82/barrel for 'Dubai' (*OPEC Annual Statistical Bulletin* 1997). In comparison with the price tag of crude oil from the Middle East, the Nigerian crude oil is also more precious because of lower transport costs. Nigeria is closer to the markets of Europe and the US than the Middle East, so an oil tanker journey from Nigeria is at least several days shorter. The buyer can therefore save money on the payment of tanker charter and insurance. This insight was largely owed to personal communication with Martin Quinlan, journalist at the *Petroleum Economist*, London (September 1998).

[45] Forrest (1993, 133-134) concluded that the expansion of state revenues was accompanied by a '*deterioration in financial discipline and accountability as the struggle to gain access to state resources intensified*'. Forrest (1993, 133-134 and 142) noted that, with rising expenditure, the government was able to afford massive tax reductions, an expansion of the public sector and

government revenue had markedly declined, in particular, the contribution of agriculture (Ohiorhenuan 1984; Ikein 1990). The contribution of the agricultural sector to Nigeria's gross domestic product fell from around 60% in 1960 to less than 10% in 1978 (Ikein 1990, 19-20). The displacement of the agricultural sector made Nigeria's economy almost exclusively dependent on a single commodity - crude oil.

Table 2.11. Growth of Nigeria's Oil Exports, 1963-1996

	Total Exports (Naira)	Crude Oil Exports (Naira)	Annual Change in Official Consumer Prices (%)	Annual Change in Total Exports (%)	Annual Change in Oil Exports (%)	Oil Exports as % of Total Exports
1963	372	40	-2.7	-	-	10.75
1964	429	64	0.9	15.32	60.00	14.92
1965	535	136	4.1	24.71	112.50	25.42
1966	568	184	9.7	6.17	35.29	32.39
1967	484	145	-3.7	-14.79	-21.2	29.96
1968	422	74	-0.5	-12.81	-48.97	17.54
1969	637	262	10.2	50.95	254.05	41.13
1970	886	510	13.8	39.09	94.66	57.56
1971	1,293	953	16.0	45.94	86.86	73.70
1972	1,434	1,176	3.5	10.90	23.40	82.01
1973	2,278	1,894	5.4	58.86	61.05	83.14
1974	5,795	5,366	12.7	154.39	183.32	92.60
1975	4,829	4,630	33.9	-16.67	-13.72	95.88
1976	6,623	6,196	24.3	37.15	33.82	93.55
1977	7,631	7,083	13.8	15.22	14.32	92.82
1978	6,328	5,654	21.7	-17.08	-20.18	89.35
1979	10,398	9,706	11.7	64.32	71.67	93.34
1980	14,199	13,632	10.0	36.56	40.45	96.01
1981	11,023	10,681	20.8	-22.37	-21.65	96.90
1982	8,206	8,003	7.7	-25.56	-25.07	97.53
1983	7,503	7,201	23.2	-8.57	-10.02	95.97
1984	9,088	8,843	39.6	21.12	22.80	97.30
1985	11,215	10,891	7.4	23.40	23.16	97.11
1986	9,044	8,368	5.7	-19.36	-23.17	92.53
1987	29,578	28,209	11.3	227.05	237.11	95.37
1988	31,193	28,436	54.5	5.46	0.80	91.16
1989	57,971	55,017	50.5	85.85	93.48	94.90
1990	109,886	106,627	7.4	89.55	93.81	97.03
1991	121,534	116,857	13.0	10.60	9.59	96.15
1992	205,613	201,384	44.6	69.18	72.33	97.94
1993	218,801	213,779	57.2	6.40	6.15	97.70
1994	206,059	200,936	57.0	-5.82	-6.01	97.51
1995	748,368	716,206	72.8	263.18	256.43	95.70
1996	1,309,616	1,286,248	29.3	75.00	79.59	98.22

Source: computed from *IMF International Financial Statistics Yearbook* (various years).

subsidies to Nigerian public enterprises. A large proportion of oil revenues was spent on consumption, particularly on imported goods, which further increased Nigeria's dependence on oil.

Table 2.12. Oil Revenue of the Nigerian Federal Government, 1970-1992

	Total Revenue (million Naira)	Oil Revenue (million Naira)	Annual Change in Official Consumer Prices (%)	Annual Change in Total Revenue (%)	Annual Change in Oil Revenue (%)	Oil Revenue as % of Total Revenue
1970	632	166	13.8	-	-	26.27
1971	1,169	510	16.0	84.97	207.23	43.63
1972	1,405	764	3.5	20.19	49.8	54.38
1973	1,695	1,016	5.4	20.64	32.98	59.94
1974	4,537	3,726	12.7	167.67	266.73	82.12
1975	5,515	4,272	33.9	21.56	14.65	77.46
1976	6,766	5,365	24.3	22.68	25.59	79.29
1977	8,081	6,081	13.8	19.44	13.35	75.25
1978	7,371	4,654	21.7	-8.79	-23.47	63.14
1979	10,913	8,881	11.7	48.05	90.83	81.38
1980	15,230	12,354	10.0	39.56	39.11	81.12
1981	12,183	8,564	20.8	-20.01	-30.68	70.29
1982	10,618	6,868	7.7	-12.85	-19.8	64.68
1983	10,509	7,253	23.2	-1.03	5.61	69.02
1984	11,193	8,210	39.6	6.51	13.19	73.35
1985	15,042	10,915	7.4	34.39	32.95	72.56
1986	12,302	8,107	5.7	-18.22	-25.73	65.90
1987	25,100	19,027	11.3	104.03	134.7	75.80
1988	27,595	19,832	54.5	9.94	4.23	71.87
1989	47,798	39,130	50.5	73.21	97.31	81.87
1990	69,788	55,215	7.4	46.01	41.11	79.12
1991	78,640	60,315	13.0	12.68	9.24	76.70
1992	138,617	115,393	44.6	76.27	91.32	83.25

* Budget estimates.
Sources: data on government revenue from the *Economic and Financial Review* and the *Annual Reports* of the Central Bank of Nigeria (various issues); consumer prices from the *IMF International Financial Statistics Yearbook* (various years).

Table 2.13. Nigeria's Foreign-exchange Revenue, 1995-97 (in million US$)

	1995	1996	1997
Oil sales, petroleum profits tax & royalties	7,898	10,891	11,994
Currency purchases by oil companies	366	551	559
Other currency purchases*	92	433	473
Other receipts	214	150	50
Total	8,570	12,025	13,076
Foreign-exchange revenue from oil as % of total	96.43	95.15	96.00

* Mainly currency purchases by banks.
Source: *Economist Intelligence Unit Country Report: Nigeria* (2nd Quarter 1998).

Dependence on oil exposed Nigeria to fluctuations in the international oil market. Unlike the low populated oil producing countries in the Middle East, the Nigerian government did not invest oil revenues in the West in order to secure a future income flow. Nor did the government set money aside in stabilisation or development funds (Forrest 1993, 142). This lack of long-term investments was not a problem as long as the oil revenues continued to increase in the 1970s. But fluctuations in the oil market could throw Nigeria's public finances into disarray. The Nigerian government budget for 1998, for example, was based on the assumption of an average oil price of US$ 17/barrel. In the same month that the budget was announced, the crude oil price fell from roughly US$ 16 to US$ 14.73/barrel, thus threatening the viability of the entire budget (*Newswatch*, 16 February 1998). In the first quarter of 1998 alone, Nigeria reportedly lost US$ 700 million as a result of the global drop in oil prices out of US$ 8 billion lost by all OPEC countries combined (*AP*, 19 April 1998). The state lacked alternative sources of financial revenue to those of oil, so the state budget was almost completely dependent on the volatile international oil markets.

The nature of Nigeria's political economy, characterised by its dependence on oil revenues, was captured in the concept of a 'rentier state'. According to this concept (Forrest 1977; Graf 1988, 218-222), the Nigerian state revenues were extracted from taxes and 'rents', largely in the form of oil revenues from foreign companies, rather than from 'productive' activity. Nigerian business was said to be restricted to 'unproductive' activities, which included (in the words of Forrest) *'commercial and service activities, small-scale capitalism and non-capitalist formations'* (Forrest 1977, 43). Forrest (1977) argued that Nigerian business had forged an alliance with foreign capital, which continued to dominate Nigeria's political economy. In other words, the Nigerian state was biased in favour of oil interests.[46]

As an extension to the concept of a rentier state, Turner (1978) has introduced the concept of a 'comprador state'. The concept of a comprador state was based on the observation that there was little indigenous industrial production of final consumer goods in Nigeria. In general, Turner (1978, 166) declared that contemporary political economies characterised by 'commercial capitalism' such as Nigeria are *'those which depend on foreign industrial production for virtually all locally-consumed manufactured goods'*. Within this system of 'commercial capitalism', indigenous business could only play a facilitating role for foreign capital within a triangular system of economic relationships, which involved foreign businessmen, Nigerian

---

[46] The concept of the rentier state in Nigeria rests implicitly on the assumption of dependency theories that Nigeria lies at the periphery of the international economic system, while the foreign companies are located within the centre of the system. Johan Galtung (1971) provided a sophisticated exposition of this theme. On the most basic level, Galtung's main idea was that the world consists of Centre and Periphery nations; and each nation, in turn, has its centre and periphery (Galtung 1971, 81). Within this Centre-Periphery structure, the Centre exploits the Periphery. Galtung (1971) argued that the centre could only extract something from the periphery nation, if there was (in Galtung's words) a 'bridgehead' between the Centre nation and the Periphery nation. According to this view, a necessary condition for imperialism was a harmony of interest between the centre in the Centre nation and the centre in the Periphery nation and a disharmony of interest within the Periphery nation. In order to continue the relationship of dominance, the centre of the Centre nation needed intermediaries in the centre of the Periphery nation (in Galtung's words a 'transmission belt' in the form of commercial firms or trading companies) who provided the 'bridgehead' for foreign capital and benefited from the economic exchange at the expense of the periphery of the Periphery nation (Galtung 1971, 84). If applied to the Nigerian rentier state, this would imply that foreign oil companies (located at the centre of the Centre nation) would need the Nigerian business elite (located at the centre of the Periphery nation) as commercial intermediaries to carry out oil exploitation.

middlemen and the collaborating 'state compradors'.[47] According to this view, a foreign business hired a local middleman as a go-between with the state. If the foreign businessman was awarded a contract, the middleman would receive a payment by the businessman, while the state comprador would receive a payment negotiated by the middleman. Turner (1978) indicated that foreign businessmen could sometimes deal directly with the state without the help of middlemen. In either case, the Nigerian state was said to serve foreign business interests to a lesser or greater extent (Turner 1978).

This view of the post-colonial state in West Africa has been challenged by a number of academics.[48] Criticism of the 'rentier state' concept rested primarily on the assumption that indigenization[49] of the economy may have enhanced the position of the post-colonial state in Africa vis-á-vis foreign business interests.[50] Indigenization measures were capable of having a serious adverse impact on the profits of foreign-owned enterprises, so they could potentially be highly damaging to oil company interests in Nigeria. Like most other African countries, Nigeria undertook many measures of indigenization of foreign enterprises, most notably the Indigenization Decrees of 1972 and 1977 (Biersteker 1987). The partial nationalization of the Nigerian subsidiaries of foreign oil companies in the 1970s was only one of those measures (this will be discussed in section 2.6. in some detail). In practice, however, effective implementation of indigenization measures was hindered by a number of factors including administrative incompetence and corruption. Indeed, Biersteker's (1987) pathbreaking study on indigenization in Nigeria suggested that the state and the indigenous business elite largely failed to wrest control over the economy from foreign capital. Confronted with Nigerian indigenization, the foreign companies in Nigeria employed 'countervailing measures' aimed at retaining effective managerial control over the joint ventures despite compliance with official indigenization decrees, which prescribed majority Nigerian ownership of business ventures. Countervailing measures included the use of managerial and technical agreements to control operations or the

---

[47] 'Comprador' is a Portuguese word for 'buyer'. According to Turner (1978), a comprador would perform the task of providing access to local markets for foreign firms. In other words, a 'state comprador' performed the role of a 'gatekeeper' for foreign firms.

[48] Collins (1983), for instance, suggested that the concept of the Nigerian state as 'rentier' or 'comprador' did not reflect reality. Instead, he argued that the role of the state *reflects a complex interplay of sectional, group and class interests'*. In practice, the state role was said to be variable. That means, the state could sometimes support nationalist interests, sometimes indigenous capitalist interests and, at other times, it might favour foreign business interests. The arguments of scholars such as Collins seemed to have been substantiated by the rise of a class of indigenous industrialists in African states which appeared to be distinct from the commercial or 'comprador' class. In his more recent studies, Forrest (1993, 9) argued that the new capitalist group in Nigeria *'is not an auxiliary comprador class. It is an active component of capital that has grown partly through collaboration with foreign capital, partly in competition with it, and partly independently'* which was a striking departure from Forrest's earlier position on the 'rentier state'.

[49] That means, measures designed to increase local (state or private) participation and control of significant business ventures.

[50] Indigenization measures in Africa were rooted in the nationalist African movements during colonial rule and after de-colonisation. Chazan *et al.* (1988, 156) argued that African political ideologies in the post-colonial period came to share a basic concern to overcome poverty and underdevelopment, which resulted in some sort of economic nationalism across Africa. In general, the intellectual climate in Africa's post-colonial states appeared to favour economic nationalism which usually implied the assertion of broadly defined national economic interests as opposed to the interests of foreigners.

training of indigenous managers to become 'company people' loyal to the oil company.[51] In general, Biersteker (1987, 299) concluded that *'indigenization has certainly not contributed significantly to Nigerians' control of their economy'* despite its limited success. If judged by Biersteker's analysis, indigenization did not result in the demise of the 'rentier state'.

The concept of the 'rentier state' indirectly implies that the state would not support litigation against foreign oil companies in Nigeria. The concept assumes that the state lacks autonomy vis-á-vis foreign investors. By implication, since foreign oil companies are said to have unrestricted access to state officials, they could use their influence with these officials to increase their prospects of success in court cases filed against them. The key question in the subsequent sections is, therefore, to what extent is the Nigerian post-colonial state biased in favour of foreign oil companies, given the indigenization measures undertaken in the oil industry. The government petroleum policy and the role of the state in community conflicts are key factors in this discussion.

2.6. Nigerian Petroleum Policy in the 1960s and 1970s

Nigeria's petroleum policy has never been entirely coherent due to factors such as the frequent change of petroleum officials and differences within the ruling elite (Frynas 1998), so any generalizations must be treated with caution. [52] In terms of state involvement in the Nigerian oil industry, Obi and Soremekun (1995) distinguished three distinct historical phases. According to this typology, the first phase extended from the colonial period until the end of the 1960s and involved little state participation in the oil industry. The second phase, as a response to political changes during the Civil War 1967-1970, was said to have been marked by an increase in state participation in the 1970s. Obi and Soremekun (1995) argued that Nigeria moved from the collection of oil rents to direct intervention in the running of the oil industry. The third phase, as a response to the economic crisis of the 1980s and the introduction of the Structural Adjustment Programme (SAP) in 1986, was said to be marked by a limitation of some of the earlier policies of state intervention. Greater fiscal incentives for the oil industry were said to be the key element of the third phase. All three phases are briefly outlined below with a view to investigating a link between petroleum policy and state bias in favour of oil companies.

---

[51] On 'countervailing measures' used by foreign companies in Nigeria, see Biersteker (1987, 112-131 and 218-242).

[52] For instance, during the rule of General Abacha 1993-1998, the Minister of Finance Anthony Ani repeatedly clashed with the Minister of Petroleum Resources Dan Etete over petroleum policy. Ani proposed in 1996 to sell all government shares in the oil joint ventures by the year 2000. He also intended to transfer joint venture agreements into production sharing agreements. However, Etete, who succeeded Don Etiebet as oil minister in March 1995, opposed the plan. In late 1996, Ani suggested that the government was committed to a total privatization of the oil industry. In early 1997, Etete announced that the government would make sure that the *'sector remains in the hands of Nigerians'*. Etete prevailed and privatization plans were shelved in 1997 (*Tell*, February 24, 1997). Both Ani and Etete lost their government positions in August 1998.

During the first phase of state involvement in the Nigerian oil industry until the end of the 1960s, the role of the Nigerian government in the oil industry was largely limited to the collection of tax and rent or royalty from foreign oil companies. The most notable change in petroleum policy in the 1960s was the increase in the amount of oil rents paid to the federal government.[53] The government was assigned an increasingly higher share of oil revenues at the expense of oil companies. But it did not attempt to intervene directly in the running of the oil exploration and production sectors in Nigeria. In 1962, Agip gave the Nigerian government an option to take a 33.33% stake in the Nigeria Agip Oil Company (NAOC) in the form of a clause in its concession agreement, but the government did not take up the offer until April 1971 (Obi and Soremekun 1995, 12). Agip was a subsidiary of the Italian state-owned company ENI. Under the leadership of Enrico Mattei, ENI embarked on aggressive world-wide expansion by offering better financial deals for governments of oil producing countries, which shocked competitors (Sampson 1975, 147-151). A confidential circular of the British Foreign Office in 1961 noted with anxiety that ENI *'has actively encouraged the development of state oil organisations (...) by political means'.*[54] The Nigerian government declined Agip's offer and, by and large, limited petroleum policy to fiscal changes throughout the 1960s. The only notable exception to the rule was the government participation in the construction of an oil refinery in Port Harcourt initiated by Shell-BP.[55] From the point of view of village communities, virtually nothing had changed since the government largely abstained from directly intervening in the running of the oil exploration and production work on the ground.

Obi and Soremekun (1995) suggested that the second phase of state involvement in the Nigerian oil industry started during the Civil War 1967-70 (also known as the Biafran War), which changed the perception of the oil industry in government circles.[56] Pearson (1970, 139) suggested that the Civil War made the government realise the strategic importance of oil for Western countries because foreign intervention had drawn Nigeria into the international politics of oil. Furthermore, the war required stricter government control of the oil industry and the

---

[53] In 1967, Nigeria's government proclaimed the Petroleum Profits Tax (Amendment) Decree 1967, which adopted new terms for tax assessment and allowed for higher government revenue. Pearson (1970, 24-29) estimated that the new arrangements were capable of increasing the government share of profits from 50% to as much as 66%, although any comparison of actual profits was difficult as profits depended on changing oil prices. In the 1970s, the petroleum profits tax was further increased from 50% to 55% in 1973, to 67.75% in 1974 and to 85% in 1975, while royalty rates were increased from 12.5% to 16.67% in 1974 and to 20% in 1975 (Khan 1994, 16-18).

[54] Confidential Circular No.029 of the British Foreign Office, prepared by the Ministry of Power (30 March 1961) DO177/33, PRO.

[55] Initially, the government agreed to take up only a 40% stake in the refinery and the oil companies seemed satisfied. Letter from J.S. Sadler, the UK Trade Commissioner in Lagos, to J.A. Davidson, Commonwealth Relations Office (18 September 1961), DO 177/33, PRO. Later the government share was increased to 50%. A joint venture was formed between the government (50%), BP (25%) and Shell (25%) as a separate company called the Nigerian Petroleum Refining Company (NPRC). The NPRC refinery was commissioned in 1965 near Port Harcourt in Rivers State under the management of BP (Pearson 1970, 92).

[56] In May 1967, the Governor of Nigeria's Eastern Region Colonel Ojukwu declared the independence of Biafra. In July 1967, a full-scale war was declared between Biafra's regime and Nigeria's federal regime based in Lagos. Biafra surrendered in January 1970. On the Civil War, see e.g. Forsyth (1969).

state came to rely on oil revenue to promote economic development (Pearson 1970, 139).

Following the Civil War, Nigeria joined the OPEC in 1971. The most important effect of OPEC membership on Nigeria's oil policy was in regards to indigenization which was encouraged by the OPEC.[57]

At this stage, it must be pointed out that some indigenization measures were not inherently contrary to the interests of foreign companies. In line with the government's indigenization policy, for instance, foreign oil companies have increasingly replaced expatriate managers with Nigerians. Yet this process was already under way before the promulgation of the Petroleum Decree in 1969 since it probably made good business sense to employ indigenous managers. In fact, Shell-BP was committed to greater 'nigerianization' from the 1950s, but the oil companies in Nigeria experienced the problem of finding educated recruits.[58] Nigerian institutions also had problems filling positions with qualified Nigerians, particularly during the shortage of trained staff in the early 1970s (Turner 1977, 68). Indigenization was hindered by practical concerns.

Indigenization measures in the Nigerian oil industry were greatly expanded in the 1970s. From 1971, the government gradually set up joint ventures with oil exploration and production companies in Nigeria and acquired shareholdings in these ventures (Turner 1980, 107-109). By July 1979, the government had acquired a 60% ownership in all the major foreign oil companies except for the production-sharing agreement with Ashland and the Tenneco-Mobil-Sunray venture (Khan 1994, 70) (see Table 2.14.).[59]

---

[57] A resolution at the OPEC Conference in 1968 advised member countries to acquire *'participation in the ownership of the concession-holding companies'* (OPEC 1992, 21). Indigenization measures in the Nigerian oil industry had already been launched before the country joined the OPEC. As early as 1968, the Companies' Act forced all companies to become incorporated in Nigeria. This provided the government with a greater access to company accounts, a move resented by the US oil companies in Nigeria (Turner 1977, 48-49). In 1969, the Petroleum Act forced oil companies to recruit and train a greater number of Nigerians. According to the Petroleum Act, at least 75% of the total number of employees in senior and supervisory positions should be Nigerians within ten years from the grant of an oil mining lease. Companies were further obliged to restrict all employment opportunities for skilled, semi-skilled and unskilled work to Nigerians (Petroleum Act No.51 of 1969, section 37). The Petroleum Act also proclaimed that only companies incorporated in Nigeria could be granted oil licenses (Petroleum Act No.51 of 1969, section 2(2).

[58] E.J. Pearce, the British Trade Commissioner at Enugu, wrote as early as 1959 that Shell-BP were committed to greater Nigerianisation and were *'indeed anxious to fulfil their promise'*. Pearce also noted that it is *'extremely difficult to secure and train the right type of Nigerian'* (Report of a visit of Mr. E. J. Pearce, the United Kingdom Trade Commissioner at Enugu, to the Shell-BP Exploration Company's installations at Owerri, Port Harcourt and in the field, 31 August - 3 September 1959, POWE 33/421, PRO). The proportion of Nigerians in senior and supervisory positions at Shell-BP increased from 7% to 45% between 1957 and 1970 despite the fact that no legal provision forced them to employ Nigerians (Madujibeya 1976, 300). Since Shell-BP was voluntarily prepared to employ Nigerians, it has to be assumed that the company had commercial reasons for doing so.

[59] As a result of nationalization in the 1970s, the share of foreign capital in Nigeria's mining industry declined from 100% in 1971 to 40.8% in 1977, to 21.8% in 1989 (*Economic and Financial Review of the Central Bank of Nigeria*, various issues).

Table 2.14. Evolution of Government Participation in Major Oil Companies in Nigeria, 1971-1999

	Government Participation (%)	Date of Acquisition
Shell-BP	35	April 1973
	55	April 1974
	60	July 1979
Shell*	80	August 1979
	60	June 1989
	55	August 1993
Mobil	55	April 1974
	60	July 1979
Gulf (Chevron)	55	April 1974
	60	July 1979
Agip/Phillips	33.33	September 1971
	55	April 1974
	60	July 1979
Safrap (Elf)	35	April 1971
	55	April 1974
	60	July 1979
Texaco	55	May 1975
	60	July 1979
Pan Ocean	55	January 1978
	60	July 1979

* Shell-BP until August 1979.
Sources: Turner (1977, 1980); Khan (1994); Whiteman (1982); *Petroleum Economist* (October 1993).

The nationalization of BP in 1979 showed that the Nigerian government was able to fully nationalise a foreign oil company, if it was determined to do so (Khan 1994, 70-71). The nationalization of BP, however, was conducted out of foreign policy considerations, not for economic reasons.[60] For the Nigerian oil industry, the nationalization of BP changed little. In the exploration and production sector, Shell continued to operate the joint venture on behalf of the government, which was previously jointly operated by Shell and BP (Khan 1994, 70).

From the perspective of village communities, the nationalization of BP and indigenization of the oil industry changed virtually nothing since the foreign oil companies retained managerial control of the joint ventures. Despite the fact that foreign companies operate the joint ventures with a minority shareholding, two out of

---

[60] The Nigerian government aimed at influencing British policies on Rhodesia (which later became Zimbabwe), which was then ruled by a white supremacist regime. The government under General Obasanjo was committed to the cause of black majority rule in Rhodesia. The government wanted to exert political influence on the British foreign policy towards Rhodesia. The British government looked set to lift sanctions against Rhodesia, which finally prompted the Nigerian decision to nationalise BP. The nationalization of BP was undertaken shortly before the Commonwealth Conference in Lusaka where Britain was expected to take a softer approach to sanctions against Rhodesia. An official excuse for nationalization was coincidentally provided by an arrangement between BP and the US company Conoco. According to this arrangement, BP was to sell North Sea oil to Conoco in return for Conoco's supply of non-OPEC oil to South Africa (Aluko 1990). In other words, BP was participating in supplying oil to South Africa, which was opposed by the Obasanjo government.

three of the multinational oil companies interviewed by Biersteker claimed that they had retained effective control over venture operations (Biersteker 1987, 241). In general, Terisa Turner (1977, 152) argued that *as long as they* [oil companies in Nigeria] *remained operators, participation had little more than financial implications for them'*. While the government formally commands the joint ventures with its ownership equity, the foreign oil companies control the day-to-day operations of the joint ventures.[61] Despite the creation of joint ventures, the same oil companies thus continued their production activities in village communities.

Indigenization measures were accompanied by a re-structuring of the state oil administration. In April 1971, the Nigerian National Oil Corporation (NNOC) was created to acquire any liabilities and interests in existing oil companies on behalf of the government.[62] The creation of the state oil corporation had a significant impact on village communities as far as oil exploration was concerned. Until the 1970s, only foreign oil companies and their business partners carried out oil exploration. After 1971, the state oil corporation, its subsidiaries or sub-contractors also became involved in oil exploration on the ground in village communities.

In 1977, Nigeria's oil corporation was re-organised. In that year, the NNOC was merged with the Ministry of Petroleum Resources (MPR) to form the Nigerian National Petroleum Corporation (NNPC).[63] Until 1986 when the MPR was re-established, the NNPC combined the functions of an oil company with the extended regulatory powers of a ministry.[64] This peculiar role allowed the NNPC, for instance, to issue licences to its so-called competitors. The NNPC's ambitious goal was to eventually control the entire oil industry in Nigeria including oil exploration and production (NNPC 1986b, 27).[65]

The NNPC never carried out its threat to fully nationalise the oil industry. In the same year the NNPC was established, the government paradoxically introduced new financial incentives for foreign oil companies in order to stimulate new exploration. Alli (1997) observed that a decline in oil exploration by foreign companies in the 1970s had forced the government into a more accommodating tone towards the foreign oil companies. Between 1977 and 1983, the fiscal incentives for foreign oil companies were improved four times, although the new fiscal terms failed to significantly increase foreign investment in oil exploration (Alli 1997). According to Aluko (1990, 386), when NNPC officials were summoned by General Obasanjo in 1979 to opine on the

---

[61] Nominally, the government owned roughly 58% of Nigeria's total oil production in April 1997. But the foreign oil operators - including Shell, Chevron, Mobil, Agip, Elf, Texaco - produced roughly 98% of Nigeria's total daily oil output in April 1997 (*Weekly Petroleum Argus*, 21 April 1997).

[62] NNOC Act No.18 of 1971.

[63] NNPC Act No.33 of 1977.

[64] The MPR was once again formally abolished in 1998.

[65] The NNPC was intended to become *'a commercial, integrated, international oil company, engaged in exploration, production, processing, transportation and marketing of crude oil, gas, by-products and derivatives'* (NNPC 1986b, 27). In negotiations between companies and the government, the ultimate threat of the complete nationalization of the oil industry was less effective because of the inability of the NNOC to operate successfully. Among other advantages, the creation of an effective state oil corporation could allow the government to do more than just bluff in negotiations (Turner 1977, 209).

potential impact of BP's nationalization, they reportedly showed little enthusiasm for nationalization of the oil industry. They were said to have argued that the nationalization of BP would slow down oil production, which would in turn result in a fall in Nigeria's oil revenue in the short-term (Aluko 1990, 386). This cautious attitude towards nationalization exemplified a marked shift from the earlier calls for full nationalization of the oil industry among NNOC officials only a few years earlier. It has to be assumed that government officials recognised in the late 1970s that they could not dispense with foreign investment. Contrary to the assertion of Obi and Soremekun (1995), it thus appears that the third phase in Nigeria's petroleum policy started in the late 1970s rather than in the mid 1980s.

2.7. Nigerian Petroleum Policy in the 1980s and 1990s

During the 1980s, faced with the immediate problems of falling oil revenue and political crises, the government further improved the fiscal terms for oil company operators in order to woo foreign investors (Alli 1997). Most importantly, the so-called Memorandum of Understanding (MOU) was introduced in 1986 as a comprehensive improved financial agreement between the government and the oil companies. Amongst other fiscal incentives, the MOU of 1986 ensured a guaranteed so-called minimum fiscal margin of US$ 2.00/barrel of oil (after royalty and tax payments), which was an increase from US$ 1.60/barrel in 1982 (see Table 2.15.).[66] Changes in fiscal arrangements from the 1970s onwards signified the state's greater reliance on revenues from foreign oil companies. It is likely that this reliance rendered the state more receptive to the needs of oil companies rather than village communities in the oil producing areas.

Table 2.15. Changes in Selected Financial Incentives in the Nigerian Oil Industry

	1977	1982	1986	1991
Guaranteed Fiscal Margin (US$/barrel)	0.80	1.60	2.00	2.30
Guaranteed Technical Cost (US$/barrel)	1.00	1.60	2.00	2.50

Source: Alli (1997).

---

[66] The margin of US$ 2.00/barrel applied as long as the actual technical cost of oil companies did not exceed US$ 2.00/barrel and the oil price remained between US$ 12.50 and US$ 23.00/barrel. Under the MOU, the calculation of tax was changed from the so-called Official Selling Price (OSP) to a market based price, which allowed higher profits for the oil companies. Other incentives included the reduction of the petroleum profits tax, security of tenure and investments, generous tax holidays, guaranteed export earnings including permission to operate offshore escrow accounts and reserves addition bonuses. In 1991, the MOU was reviewed and the financial incentives were slightly increased (Adepetun 1996). In 1993, the government introduced further incentives for exploration in deepwater offshore areas, including lower royalty rates and higher cost recovery allowances (Barrows 1995). In April 1999, the Deep Offshore and Inland Basin Production Sharing Contracts Decree was passed for the development of deepwater offshore areas which included fiscal terms favourable to the industry. Among other incentives, the nominal Petroleum Profits Tax of 85% (as amended by the Memorandum of Understanding) was cut to 50% for oil production under production sharing contracts (PSCs) in deepwater offshore areas (section 3 of the Decree).

During the third phase of petroleum policy in the oil industry, the government continued to pursue diversification and indigenization measures. As the key element in diversification strategies, the Nigerian government was prepared to grant oil licences to newcomers. Attracted by favourable fiscal arrangements after 1986, many new companies - including the Statoil-BP Alliance, Exxon and Du Pont (an affiliate of Conoco) - started exploring for oil and gas in Nigeria (Khan 1994, 90-91). Several newcomers made a number of important oil and gas discoveries such as Conoco's discovery of the giant 'Chota' field in 1998 and Statoil's successful drilling of the 'Nnwa-1' well in 1999 (*NewReport Journal*, 10 July 1998; Quinlan 1999).

As a result of diversification measures, the number of oil companies operating in Nigeria has greatly expanded. In 1966 and in 1986, eight and twelve oil companies respectively had oil prospecting licences or oil mining leases in Nigeria. By 1998, their number had risen to over 50 (see Appendix B). A large proportion of the oil licences was held by the NNPC and its subsidiaries as well as by joint ventures with an NNPC share. The total concession area (excluding exploration licences) had grown from 118,156 sq. km in 1966 to 225,444 sq. km in 1998 (see Table 2.16.).[67] The concession area has further grown since 1998. In March 1999, at least 11 oil prospecting licences (OPLs) were allocated to indigenous oil companies (*Guardian*, Lagos, 18 May 1999.

As a result of indigenization measures, private indigenous oil companies came to own a significant number of oil licences in the 1990s.[68] In March 1999, there were 46 indigenous companies holding 55 oil licences in Nigeria (*Hart's Africa Oil and Gas*, 31 March 1999). The majority of these companies obtained their oil licences between 1990 and 1993 (see Appendix C). The rise of private indigenous oil companies is important because it could mean that the Nigerian state is no longer dependent on oil rents from foreign firms. It is thus instructive to explore whether the rise of indigenous oil companies resulted in less state bias in favour of foreign oil companies.

From the early 1990s, indigenous oil companies have expanded their exploration and production operations.[69] Wealthy Nigerian businessmen such as Yinka Folawiyo and Moshood Abiola came to invest substantial funds in the oil exploration

---

[67] Many of the companies, which obtained exploration licences or prospecting licences, withdrew from Nigeria at a later date. By 1975, 19 oil companies had concessions in Nigeria (Madujibeya 1975, 2). As shown in Table 2.16., only 12 companies had either a prospecting licence or an oil mining lease by 1986.

[68] Until the late 1980s, there were virtually no serious indigenous oil companies in Nigeria, except for Henry Stevens in the 1970s and Nigus Petroleum in the 1980s, of which neither survived (Avuru 1997, 292). The first successful indigenous private oil company was Henry Stevens Petroleum in the early 1970s under Henry Fajemirokun, president of the Lagos Chamber of Commerce. Henry Stevens operated in partnership with the US company Westates Petroleum, which was granted an offshore oil exploration licence in 1970 (*Africa Confidential*, December 17, 1971). From the late 1980s, many new indigenous oil companies were founded starting with Dubri Oil which bought an oil licence from the foreign oil company Phillips Oil in 1987. By the end of 1993, the government had allocated oil licences to almost 40 indigenous oil companies (see Appendix C).

[69] Their total production rose from 5,000 b/d in 1993 (Avuru 1997, 300) to 55,500 b/d at the end of 1996 and it is still rising (*PostExpressWired*, 19 March 1998). According to Avuru (1997, 301), indigenous oil companies and their business partners invested over US$ 800 million in the Nigerian oil industry in the period 1991-1996.

and production business.[70] Yet only a handful of indigenous oil companies have actually set up properly equipped operating companies. There were only few exceptions such as Moshood Abiola's Summit Oil which was able to self-finance its operations (*Vanguard*, 10 July 1998). Most other indigenous oil companies lacked the technical know-how and the financial resources to develop their oil licences. Therefore, they generally sought experienced Western partners and formed joint ventures, in which the foreign company usually had a 40% equity share (see Appendix C). Of the nine 'active' companies in 1996, seven were operating with a foreign technical partner (Avuru 1997, 293).[71]

Table 2.16. Oil Companies with Oil Prospecting Licences (OPLs) and Oil Mining Leases (OMLs) in 1966, 1986 and 1998

Company	1966 Concession Area (sq. km)	Company	1986 Concession Area (sq. km)	Company	1998 Concession Area (sq. km)
Shell-BP*	48,946	Shell	31,309	Shell	43,052
SAFRAP**	23,600	Elf	8,256	Elf	21,542
Gulf***	17,754	Gulf	14,138	Chevron	23,726
Tennessee	8,721	Mobil/Tennessee	2,259		
Agip	5,260	Agip/Phillips	5,259	Agip/Phillips	5,259
Mobil	5,245	Mobil	2,562	Mobil	5,619
Amoseas	5,001				
Phillips	3,629	Phillips	232		
		Texaco	2,570	Texaco	2,570
		Pan Ocean	1,005	Pan Ocean	503
		Nigus	1,025		
		Agip Energy	360	Agip Energy	5,060
				Statoil-BP	6,059
		NNPC	40,440	NNPC	690
				NPDC****	2,625
				NAPIMS****	24,000
				over 40 others	84,739
Total Concessions	118,156	Total Concessions	109,415	Total Concessions	225,444

* Shell from 1979; ** later Elf; *** later Chevron; **** NNPC subsidiaries.
Sources: 1966 data computed from Schätzl (1969, 8); 1986 data from Khan (1994, 21); 1998 data from Petroconsultants (1998).

---

[70] Folawiyo provides an example of a Nigerian businessman who was able to shift from commercial to industrial activities. From the late 1950s to the 1970s, Yinka Folawiyo's business interests centred around the importation of foodstuffs, cement and other goods into Nigeria. In the 1970s, Folawiyo established a cement manufacturing company and large-scale farming plantations. In July 1991, Folawiyo moved into oil exploration and production through Yinka Folawiyo Petroleum. By the late 1990s, Yinka Folawiyo Petroleum became Folawiyo's largest investment (*PostExpressWired*, 6 July 1998). Moshood Abiola founded Summit Oil in 1990, which was managed by his eldest son Kola Abiola (*Vanguard*, 10 July 1998). In 1994, the Abacha government withdrew Summit Oil's OPL for political reasons (*Constitutional Rights Journal*, October-December 1994). The licence was later returned.

[71] Of the 38 indigenous oil companies in 1996, Avuru (1997, 293) considered 20 as entirely inactive. Avuru (1997, 293) only considered 9 companies as active in the sense that they have been '*engaged in a sustained effort at exploration and production*'.

Indeed, the rise of indigenous oil companies has increased the penetration of Nigeria's oil exploration and production sectors by foreign oil companies. Technical partnerships with Nigerian companies have proved an effective strategy for smaller foreign oil companies such as the Canada-based Abacan to set foot in oil exploration and production in Nigeria.[72] While it is too early to make a prediction on the success of the indigenous oil companies, their combined share of oil production is likely to remain insignificant for some time. In April 1997, the two largest indigenous producers Amni International and Consolidated Oil accounted for only 0.7% of Nigeria's total oil production each. The six established companies - Shell, Mobil, Chevron, Elf, Agip and Texaco - accounted for over 97% of Nigeria's oil production (*Weekly Petroleum Argus*, 21 April 1997). In other words, the diversification and indigenization measures did not threaten the dominance of the six established oil companies. The impact of the indigenous oil producers was too small to significantly alter the position of the Nigerian state vis-á-vis foreign oil companies.

The position of the Nigerian state vis-á-vis foreign capital appears to have been strengthened under the oil minister Dan Etete in the period 1995-1998. Etete introduced a number of policy measures, which ran counter to the interests of the foreign oil companies.[73] Above all, he inflicted a blow to foreign oil companies with the Petroleum (Amendment) Decree No.23 of 1996 (also known as the Marginal Fields Decree), which empowered the government to recover all undeveloped marginal oil fields from foreign oil companies and re-allocate the same to indigenous oil companies (Adepetun 1996; Atsegbua 1997). The Decree is an important test of the bias of the Nigerian state in favour of foreign capital because it violated the interests of foreign oil companies. Most foreign oil companies considered this compulsory acquisition of parts of existing concessions as a breach of existing agreements (Adepetun 1996; Atsegbua 1997). Foreign oil companies previously claimed that the development of marginal fields was unprofitable. Yet a large number of oil companies, mostly foreign, have reportedly indicated an interest in exploiting these oilfields following the Decree No.23 (*Vanguard*, Lagos, 13 August 1998). According to Avuru (1997, 301), marginal fields can often be more economically exploited by smaller oil companies with lower overhead costs than by large multinational companies. The government's decision to develop the marginal oil fields thus potentially benefited the Nigerian state, which would receive greater oil revenues, and small indigenous oil companies, which would be able to start oil production from marginal fields without the financial burden of oil

---

[72] In early 1998, for example, Abacan had a 40% equity share in five joint ventures with Nigerian companies, which covered six oil prospecting licences (OPLs): Yinka Folawiyo (OPL 309), Optimum Petroleum (OPL 310), Petroleum Products (OPL 233), Alfred James Petroleum (OPL 302) and Amni International (OPL 237 and 469).[72] Abacan and its Nigerian partners made a number of oil discoveries such as Amni's Ima offshore field (Petroconsultants 1998).

[73] There was a delay over the re-negotiation of the MOU from 1996 because the foreign oil companies could not agree with the government on new fiscal provisions. In 1997, Etete launched two new committees to monitor the oil industry: the Joint Venture Cash Calls Monitoring Committee and the LNG Project Monitoring Committee. Several months earlier, Etete accused the foreign oil companies of tax evasion, spurious contracts, lack of accountability and other transgressions. The new committees were charged with greater scrutiny of operating budgets of oil companies and greater physical monitoring of projects, among other things (*The Guardian*, Lagos, 24 January 1997).

exploration. At the same time, the Decree would constitute a substantial loss of capital assets for the established foreign oil companies.[74]

The Marginal Fields Decree, however, had a number of legal loopholes and had not been enforced by 1999, which left the profit potential of the foreign oil companies unaffected.[75] The lack of enforcement of the Marginal Fields Decree underlines the *ad hoc* nature of policy making in Nigeria. The one-page decree was hastily drafted and even failed to define the word 'marginal field', so the oil companies could, legally speaking, claim that they do not have any marginal fields. Shell indeed claimed that it did not have any marginal fields and refused to declare any of its fields as marginal (*PostExpressWired*, 19 March 1998). More importantly, the reluctance of the government to enforce the Decree suggests that the government is well aware of the adverse consequences of alienating the foreign oil companies, which could result in diminishing the foreign investment upon which Nigeria is dependent. In any case, it must be remembered that marginal fields only constitute a peripheral asset of the foreign oil companies. One could thus consider the use of marginal fields by indigenous producers as merely a profitable niche within the foreign-dominated oil sector. The Marginal Fields Decree does not put into question the concept of the rentier state in Nigeria, which explicitly allows for those indigenous business opportunities within the foreign dominated sector of the economy.

In general, the government largely continued to offer attractive financial incentives to foreign oil companies in order to ensure the flow of foreign investment. The 1999 budget of the federal government, for example, provided for new fiscal incentives for gas development projects, including an increase in the so-called 'investment capital allowance' from 15% to 35% (Adepetun and Segun 1999). It is not yet clear in what way petroleum policy will be altered under the new Obasanjo regime. Since the death of General Abacha in 1998, the Ministry of Petroleum Resources - the government's monitoring agency for the oil industry - was formally abolished and was replaced with a Special Adviser on Petroleum Resources to the president.[76] In March 1999, the NNPC subsidiary NAPIMS was transformed into an independent limited liability company and was vested with the government's exploration and production assets.[77] The long-term impact of these decisions on petroleum policy cannot be fully predicted at this stage. But the Abubakar regime (June 1998 - May 1999) could be said

---

[74] According to Avuru (1997, 303), there were 183 marginal fields in Nigeria with estimated proven reserves of 2.3 billion barrels of oil. Based on the oil price of US$ 14/barrel, the marginal fields could yield US$ 32.2 billion in gross oil revenues.

[75] A number of marginal fields have been surrendered by the established oil companies on a voluntary basis. For instance, Chevron agreed to surrender three marginal fields to African Petroleum in a commercial deal (*PostExpressWired*, 22 February 1999).

[76] Garry Aret Adams, NNPC's former managing director, was appointed the President's Special Adviser on Petroleum Resources in 1998 (*PostExpressWired*, 31 August 1998 and 8 October 1998). In June 1999, he was replaced by Alhaji Rilwanu Lukman, former Secretary-General of the OPEC (1994-1999) and Nigeria's former Minister of Petroleum Resources (1986-1989) (*Guardian*, Lagos, 2 June 1999).

[77] Deep Offshore and Inland Basin Production Sharing Contracts Decree No.9 of 1999, sections 16(1) and (2). However, by June 1999, the provisions of the decree related to NAPIMS only existed on paper, as NAPIMS continued to operate as a division of the NNPC.

to have been more sympathetic to foreign oil investors than the previous regime.[78] Amongst other policy measures, Abubakar backed the partial privatization of the country's four refineries and part of the government shareholdings in the oil exploration and production ventures (*Vanguard*, 24 September 1998; *Energy Compass*, 26 February 1999). Privatization of the government's oil assets also received support from key members of the new Obasanjo administration.[79]

Greater fiscal incentives to oil companies from the late 1970s and plans for partial privatization of the oil industry underline a continuing contradiction in Nigeria's petroleum policy. On the one hand, the government pursued the goal of transferring control over the oil industry to Nigerians. The indigenization measures of the 1970s were not reversed. The foreign oil companies in Nigeria continue to operate joint ventures, which are majority government-owned. On the other hand, the government and the emerging indigenous oil companies continued to require the foreign companies' technical expertise and investment. Therefore, the plans for the complete nationalization of the oil industry were never carried out and the government has consistently attempted to avoid alienating the foreign oil companies. The third phase of petroleum policy making thus suggests that state bias in favour of oil companies was ensured by the continuing reliance of the state and the business elite on foreign oil and gas investment. It is likely that this bias rendered the state less receptive to the needs of village communities.

Even if the Nigerian state were not biased in favour of oil companies, an adequate policy on the oil producing areas would be hindered by corruption among government officials who benefit from private deals with oil companies. Indeed, it appears that a significant part of Nigeria's public resources has been used for private gain by private middlemen and state officials (or in the words of Turner 'state compradors'). According to Soremekun (1995b), during the civilian rule 1979-1983, the Nigerian state lost 12.5 billion Naira in oil revenue as a result of fraudulent practices, largely as a result of private middlemanship. In comparison, Nigeria's total government revenue from oil was 8.9 billion Naira in 1979 (Central Bank of Nigeria, *Economic and Financial Review*, June 1982). The respectable periodical *Africa Confidential* revealed that some US$ 3-4 billion were reportedly siphoned off in oil deals by the ruling elite and its business partners in less than four years from November 1993, when General Abacha came to power (*Africa Confidential*, 24

---

[78] A number of foreign oil companies arguably benefited from petroleum policy under General Abacha (1993-1998), most notably the French oil company Total. During General Abacha's rule, the French government regularly flouted visa restrictions imposed by the European Union on Nigerian government officials and argued for those sanctions to be lifted (HRW 1999a, 32). Total benefited from the improved French-Nigerian relations. In October 1997, Total was awarded a contract worth over US$ 200 million to conduct a so-called turn-around-maintenance of the Kaduna refinery and to operate the plant for a three-year period (*Inter-Press Service*, September 16, 1997). In 1998, the much-sought after OPL 246 was allocated to South Atlantic, a new indigenous oil company owned by Lieutenant-General Theophilus Danjuma, which had business links with Total (*Guardian*, Lagos, 24 March 1999).

[79] Vice-President-Elect Alhaji Abubakar Atiku said in May 1999 that the privatization of the NNPC assets in the oil company joint ventures was *'inevitable'* (*Guardian*, Lagos, 10 May 1999).

October 1997). In comparison, Nigeria's total government revenue from oil was US$ 12 billion in 1997 (*Guardian*, Lagos, 19 February 1998).[80]

Until recently, corruption in the oil industry has persisted and middlemen as well as state officials have continued to provide access for foreign companies.[81] Under General Abacha's rule 1993-1998, foreign trading companies such as Glencore, Addax (both Swiss-based) and Arcadia (British-based) reportedly paid commissions of about 10-15% to government officials for the allocation of term-contracts (*Africa Confidential*, 24 October 1997).[82] The term-contracts exemplified the role of Nigeria's private middlemen such as the businessman Mike Adenuga, owner of the indigenous oil firm Consolidated Oil. Adenuga acquired term-contracts in the names of Tradoil and Crownway Enterprises from the Nigerian state. The fuel cargoes were in turn handled by the British-based firm Arcadia (*Africa Confidential*, 21 June 1996). Under General Abubakar's rule (1998-1999), oil licences and crude oil lifting contracts were reportedly allocated to oil companies owned by serving and retired senior military officers or their associates. Above all, the government allocated at least 11 oil prospecting licences (OPLs) to indigenous oil companies in March 1999 without opening a public competitive tender. For instance, OPL 243 was awarded to Ozoko Energy Resources, reportedly owned by Okhai Akhigbe, Chief of General Staff (*The News*, 3 May 1999). Of the 11 oil companies which obtained OPLs, only Amni International had any previous experience in oil production.[83] Following the handover of power in May 1999, President Obasanjo announced that the allocation of the 11 OPLs would be reviewed (*Guardian*, Lagos, 1 June 1999). While it is too early to make a prediction on the significance of this decision, past experience would suggest that anti-corruption measures may be difficult to implement in Nigeria.

Evidence of the prevalent corruption in Nigeria seems to confirm one of the key elements of Turner's model of the 'comprador state', in which a foreign business partner may seek a contract from the government through bribes. What is obvious is that revenue made in these operations by Nigerian officials and middlemen ultimately depends on the production capacity of the foreign oil companies. Any serious infringement of the operations of these companies would be counter-productive to the interests of those involved in these dealings.

---

[80] Among other financial arrangements, more than US$ 2 billion allocated to the NNPC for refinery repairs in the period 1993-95 had gone missing. From general Abacha's rise to power in 1993, financial transfers involving the oil industry had to go through the presidential office, which suggests that the government was fully informed of the extent of corruption and financial deals in the oil industry (*Africa Confidential*, 24 October 1997).

[81] Conversely, the failure to pay bribes could endanger a company's survival. In 1997, the oil ministry demanded a 'signature bonus' on top of the required fee, before awarding the oil mining leases (OMLs). The indigenous firms Amni International and Yinka Folawiyo, which complained about paying those bribes, had problems obtaining their respective OMLs (*Africa Confidential*, 24 October 1997).

[82] In 1997, those three foreign companies were said to control roughly 80% of Nigeria's term-contracts between them, exporting 1.1 million b/d of crude oil from Nigeria (*Africa Confidential*, 24 October 1997). In comparison, Nigeria's total oil production was 2.3 million b/d of crude oil in April 1997 (*Weekly Petroleum Argus*, 21 April 1997).

[83] According to *The News* (3 May 1999), the son of Colonel Sanni Bello, the chairman of Amni International, was married to General Abubakar's eldest daughter. Bello is believed to have protected General Abubakar's interest in the company.

Even if corruption did not provide an obstacle to an adequate policy on the oil producing areas, the government's ability to carry out effective reforms may be limited by other factors characteristic of the current Nigerian political economy. In 1981, the Nigerian state attempted to curb some of the worst excesses of corruption and mismanagement in an effort to re-organise the Nigerian National Petroleum Corporation (NNPC, the successor of the NNOC). This followed evidence from an US accountancy firm that some 2.8 billion Naira (roughly US$ 4 billion) had not been accounted for by the bank records of the NNPC. The Irikife Tribunal, which investigated the matter, even failed to summon Generals Buhari and Obasanjo, who were responsible for supervising the NNPC and controlled oil sales during the period in question. This suggests that the scope of the inquiry was limited (Turner and Badru 1984). Khan's (1994, 24-27) account of the restructuring of the NNPC following the Irikife Tribunal's report describes how the organisation of the NNPC was split up into nine subsidiaries. These were intended to be independent. An 'independent' regulatory agency called the Petroleum Inspectorate was also created.[84] As most of the reforms failed to improve efficiency, the NNPC was again re-structured as a 'commercial and autonomous' entity in January 1992, which was intended to be run more like a private corporation.[85] In practice, however, the government retained the main position of influence within the NNPC, which in turn continued to run joint ventures on behalf of the government (Khan 1994, 24-27). Despite the commercialisation of the state oil corporation, Khan (1994, 26) described the NNPC as an *'essentially weak organisation'* with *'excessive red tape and bureaucratic delays'*. These reform attempts exemplified the great difficulties involved in the creation of an effective regulatory authority within the Nigerian oil industry. Ultimately, these difficulties in running an effective production and regulation entity have benefited the foreign oil companies, which have been able to continue business as usual in the absence of effective challenges by the state.

From the perspective of village communities, the question arises whether the Nigerian government would have pursued more beneficial policies for the people in the oil producing areas, if the state were less biased in favour of oil companies and government officials had less to benefit from commercial deals with foreign oil companies. While this question is largely hypothetical, the persisting government dependence on oil, corruption and inefficiency appear to restrict the range of choices available to policy-makers in Nigeria. In the face of those constraints, the Nigerian state is likely to be more receptive to the needs of oil companies rather than village communities in the oil producing areas.

---

[84] The Petroleum Inspectorate was later merged with the newly re-established Ministry of Petroleum in 1986 (Khan 1994, 25).

[85] The NNPC essentially had three subsidiaries engaged in the oil and gas exploration and production sector: the Nigerian Petroleum Development Company (NPDC), the Nigerian Gas Corporation (NGC) and Integrated Data Services Limited (IDSL) (Khan 1994, 26). However, the National Petroleum Investment Management Services (NAPIMS) was vested with the government's exploration and production assets in March 1999. See Deep Offshore and Inland Basin Production Sharing Contracts Decree No. 9 of 1999, sections 16(1) and (2). Until 1999, NAPIMS was an NNPC subsidiary which oversaw the financial aspects of oil operations (see also footnote 77).

2.8. Ethnic Factionalism and Allocation of Resources

The bias of the Nigerian state in favour of oil companies has an ethnic dimension. Crude oil has been almost exclusively located in rural areas on the land of ethnic minority groups in the south-east of the country.[86] Due to their small numbers, these groups - the Ijaw, the Ikwerre, the Edo, the Itsekiri, the Urhobo, the Isoko, the Ndoni, the Andoni, the Ibibio, the Etche, the Ogoni and other smaller groups - wielded little political power (HRW 1999a, 91-92; Danler and Brunner 1996, 12).[87] The available Nigerian census data is not particularly reliable, so it is not entirely clear how many people live in the oil producing areas. The Ijaws clearly constitute the largest ethnic group in the Niger Delta and the fourth largest ethnic group in Nigeria. According to Ijaw leaders, there are twelve million Ijaws, but they are divided into ethnic sub-groups which speak mutually unintelligible dialects of the Ijaw language (Nanakumo 1999).

At the time of Nigeria's independence in 1960, political power was distributed between the three major ethnic groups - the Hausa-Fulani, the Ibos and the Yorubas, who dominated the Northern, the Eastern and the Western Regions, representing roughly 66% of Nigeria's population. In each of the regions, the dominant ethnic group lived alongside many smaller groups.[88]

While the oil producing areas have been mainly located in the Christian-Animist South, the mainly Muslim North has wielded greater political power throughout Nigeria's history to-date.[89] Out of eleven Nigerian heads of state since independence in 1960, eight came from Northern groups (including three from the so-called Middle Belt of Nigeria)[90], two were Yorubas (Obasanjo ruled twice), one was Ibo. Heads of state from the North also tended to rule much longer than their Southern counter-parts (see Table 2.17.).[91]

From 1966 until today, control of the armed forces has largely remained in the hands of officers from the North. The change of government in Nigeria was often determined by the conflicts within this Northern-dominated military rather than by ethnic conflicts. That means, different factions of the military battled over the

---

[86] Based on the 1991 census, roughly 70% of the population in the three oil producing states - Delta, Rivers and Bayelsa - lives in rural delta communities (World Bank 1995, volume I, 2).

[87] However, ethnic loyalty has limits. Government participation of ethnic minority leaders does not necessarily result in a better treatment for those minorities. Dan Etete (oil minister 1995-98), for example, was an Ijaw from an oil producing area (*Africa Confidential*, 9 May 1997). But Etete concentrated on arranging lucrative business deals in the oil industry for himself rather than assisting the Ijaws (*Africa Confidential*, 24 October 1997).

[88] Olowu (1990, 200-201) estimated the number of ethnic groups in Nigeria at between 250 and 400.

[89] Nmoma (1995, 314) argued that the religious divide between the northern-Muslim and the southern predominantly Christian cultures was probably greater than the purely ethnic divide. Nigeria's population has diverse religious backgrounds comprising of Islam, Christianity and Animism unevenly spread in the regions. According to Ibrahim (1991, 115), Muslims, Christians and 'pagans' made up 47%, 34.6% and 18.2% of the population in 1963 respectively, though the true extent of Animism may have been much greater.

[90] The Middle Belt are largely non-Muslim areas populated by northern ethnic minorities. Some of the conflicts within Nigeria's ruling elite were instigated by Middle Belt officers (Othman 1989).

[91] The rule of Ironsi, an Ibo from the Southern region, in 1966 and Shonekan, a Yoruba from Western Nigeria, in 1993, whose power was very weak, only lasted for a few months each.

distribution of government posts (Othman 1989). But ethnic causes of political instability have continued to play an important role in Nigeria's history. President Babangida's cancellation of the democratic election in 1993, for example, was said to have been designed to prevent the South from taking control. Moshood Abiola, the election victor, was a Yoruba from Western Nigeria who had not received the approval of the traditional rulers in the North (Nmoma 1995, 340).[92] The long-term significance of the 1999 presidential elections, in which the two principal candidates were Yoruba, cannot be predicted at this stage.

Table 2.17. Nigerian Governments, 1960-1999

Period of Rule	Head of State	Type of Government	Ethnic Origin	How the Rule Ended
1960-1966	Balewa	Civilian	Hausa	Attempted Coup/ Assassination
1966	Ironsi	Military	Ibo	Coup/ Assassination
1966-1975	Gowon	Military	Angas/Middle Belt	Coup
1975-1976	Mohammad	Military	Hausa	Attempted Coup/ Assassination
1976-1979	Obasanjo	Military	Yoruba	Elections
1979-1983	Shagari	Civilian	Fulani	Coup
1984-85	Buhari	Military	Fulani	Coup
1985-1993	Babangida	Military	Minority Group in the Niger State	Elections results nullified in June 1993, stepped down in August 1993
1993	Shonekan	Civilian	Yoruba	Head of Interim Government, Coup
1993-1998	Abacha	Military	Kanuri*	Presumed heart attack
1998-1999	Abubakar	Military	Middle Belt Group	Elections
1999-	Obasanjo	Civilian	Yoruba	

* Abacha grew up in Kano, Central Hausaland.
Source: Khan (1994, 13), various newspapers and periodicals.

With Nigeria being dominated by the Northern elite, resource allocation was biased against the interests of the people in the oil producing areas. As federal budgets were becoming increasingly dependent on oil revenues, the Nigerian regions and later states were allocated a smaller proportion of the locally collected revenue. Following Nigeria's independence in 1960, each region was allowed to retain 50% of the tax revenues derived from that area. The allocation on the basis of derivation was reduced to 45% in 1970 and to 20% in 1975 (Suberu 1996, 29-31). The oil producing states benefited from this revenue allocation, particularly before 1975. Under the derivation

---

[92] Abiola was imprisoned in June 1994 and died in detention in July 1998, shortly before his expected release.

principle between 1970 and 1975, an oil producing state would receive 45% of the oil rents and royalties derived from onshore oil production. However, the derivation principle was subsequently abolished in favour of a special account for the oil producing areas. In 1982, 1.5% of the government revenue was thus earmarked for the development of the oil producing areas, in addition to the revenue allocated by the federal government to the states and the local government councils (Forrest 1993, 53 and 83).[93] The abolition of the derivation principle was to the detriment of the people in the oil producing areas because a higher share of the oil revenues generated in their local areas was allocated to states that were non-oil producing. Of the central government's net payments to the federal states in 1997, the three oil producing states - Delta, Rivers and Bayelsa - received a share of only 3.36%, 2.85% and 2.38% respectively (*Guardian*, Lagos, 19 February 1998) despite the fact that these states provide the bulk of Nigeria's government revenue. In comparison, in the fiscal year 1974/75, the oil producing states - Bendel and Rivers - received a share of 23.7% and 17.1% respectively (Forrest 1993, 53).

A comparison of revenue allocation from 1960 to-date is not entirely conclusive since only a small fraction of locally raised revenues ever reached village communities in the oil producing areas.[94] Williams (1992, 106 and 117) noted that the current principle of resource allocation in Nigeria is flawed because allocation takes place on the basis of the states rather than on the basis of ethnic minorities, yet state boundaries do not correspond to ethnic boundaries. Members of the dominant ethnic group in an area usually control the spending by a state or a local government council. They might, therefore, put other minorities in that area at a disadvantage in terms of allocation. Within that system, ethnic minorities in the oil producing areas are marginalised because they tend to have little control over spending decisions. Due to the current system of revenue allocation, as Osaghae (1998, 11) argued, the creation of separate states and local government areas '*has been highly positive for minorities*' because it provided '*a pedestal for direct access to and participation in the federation's politics and governance*' for the larger ethnic groups. Under pressure from various ethnic and interest groups, Nigeria went from being divided into four regions until 1967 to 36 states by 1996 (see Table 2.18.). The number of local government areas rose from 301 in 1976 to 776 in 1996 (Osaghae 1998, 11; HRW 1999a, 47-48). This allowed the larger ethnic groups such as the Ijaws to participate more actively in the allocation of resources.

Ethnic or other interest groups in the oil producing areas often lobbied for a new state or a local government area to be created within their respective area with the aim

---

[93] In 1997, the federal funds were officially allocated as follows: 48.5% for the federal government, 24% for the federal states and 20% for the local government councils, while the rest went to 'special funds', which included 3% for the oil producing areas (*Guardian*, Lagos, 19 February 1998).

[94] Between 1960 and 1963, for example, the government of the Eastern Region was entitled to 50% of the oil revenues. But the Eastern Region, of which oil producing areas formed a small fraction, was ruled by members of the Ibo ethnic group from non-oil producing areas. It is thus likely that only a small fraction of the oil revenues reached the oil producing areas.

of being able to allocate financial resources themselves.[95] The Ogoni leaders, for example, have long advocated a federal state of their own, although they have failed so far (Osaghae 1995). The Ijaw leaders also demanded a state of their own. In October 1996, their demands were met with the creation of Bayelsa State which was carved out of the riverine areas of Rivers State (HRW 1999a, 94). But the creation of Bayelsa State and new local government areas did not satisfy the demands of the community leaders in the oil producing areas for more financial resources. Indeed, ethnic competition over resource allocation in the oil producing areas persisted, or even intensified, as a result of the creation of new states and local government areas. For instance, the re-location of a local government headquarters led to ethnic clashes between Ijaws and Itsekiris in Warri in Delta State in the period 1997-1999, which forced Shell and Chevron to close several oil flowstations on a number of occasions.[96] One Ijaw group recently called for the creation of three separate federal states for the Izon (a sub-group of the Ijaw nation) alone.[97]

Table 2.18. Creation of Nigerian Regions and States, 1954-1999

1954	1963	1967	1976	1987	1991	1996
3 regions	4 regions	12 states	19 states	21 states	30 states	36 states

Sources: Forrest (1993, 50); *The Guardian* (Lagos, 19 February 1998).

While ethnic conflicts in the Niger Delta have existed for a long time, it appears that the government has helped to aggravate existing ethnic disputes and used ethnic factionalism as an excuse for repressive measures by security forces on at least a number of occasions. For instance, the government blamed some of the violence in the Ogoni area in the early 1990s on 'ethnic clashes'. It was claimed that over 1,000 Ogonis were killed in ethnic clashes with the Andoni and Okrika ethnic groups in 1993 (Osaghae 1995). However, Human Rights Watch (HRW 1995, 11) has provided evidence that the government played an active role in *'fomenting such ethnic antagonism'* and that *'some attacks attributed to rural minority communities were in fact carried out by army troops in plainclothes'*. Osaghae (1995, 337) argued that such views were *'plausible because Andoni leaders interviewed denied having any problems with the Ogoni neighbours'*. In general, conflicts on the micro-level may have been exploited by the authorities in the past.

On the macro-level, the dominance of the three major ethnic groups from the non-oil producing areas seems to have prejudiced resource allocation in Nigeria against the interests of the oil producing areas. Osaghae (1995, 342) indeed argued that

---

[95] The three principal oil producing states are Bayelsa (created in 1996 out of parts of Rivers State), Delta State (created in 1991 out of parts of Bendel State) and Rivers State (created in 1967 out of parts of the Eastern Region) (Forrest 1993, 50; *The Guardian*, Lagos, 19 February 1998).

[96] Dozens, if not hundreds, of local people died in the conflict (*AFP*, 31 March 1997; *Africa Confidential*, 9 May 1997; *Newswatch*, 9 and 16 November 1998; *Phone News International*, 12 May 1999).

[97] The Bayelsa Indigenes Association, headed by R.J.A. Hobobo, supplied a list of demands including a call for the withdrawal of troops from the Niger Delta and a development plan for the area (*Guardian*, Lagos, 18 January 1999).

the 'Ogoni uprising' of the early 1990s illustrated that *'the state exists to further the interests of the majority groups against those of the minorities and that it colludes with the multinational oil companies'*. In other words, the Ogoni uprising suggested that the Nigerian state was biased in favour of the dominant ethnic groups and, arguably, their foreign business partners. This could be seen as an important factor in the escalation of conflicts between oil companies and village communities.

2.9. Community Protests against Oil Companies

The most wide-spread demand of the local people in the oil-producing areas, as Suberu (1996, 29-31) pointed out, is that a significant proportion of Nigeria's oil revenues should be returned to their areas on the basis of derivation. This would result in fewer funds for non-oil producing areas which, until recently, appeared to be unacceptable to those who rule Nigeria, particularly the Northern elite. The failure of the Nigerian state to channel a significant amount of financial resources to the oil producing areas has resulted in protests against the state and oil companies.

Throughout Nigeria's history, protests against the government and oil companies were usually peaceful and limited to a single community. An exception was the rebellion of Isaac Adaka Boro, Sam Owonaro and Nottingham Dick, who proclaimed a short-lived independent Niger Delta Republic in 1967 over oil-related grievances (Osaghae 1995). However, in the last decade or so, ethnic groups in the oil producing areas have become more militant in their demands as more and more people came to realise that they received little investment in their areas, while Nigeria's economy was thriving on oil revenues extracted from their land. Since the late 1980s, these groups such as the Ogoni, Ijaw, Urhobo, Isoko and other groups have intensified their demands for increased investment and stepped up their protests against oil companies and the government. As a result of the rising militancy of protesters, the number of community disruptions to oil operations in Nigeria rose during the 1990s. Shell was mostly affected because of the company's large onshore concessions.[98]

Organisations advocating the rights of the people in the oil producing areas have grown in numbers and appear to have become more influential in the last decade or so. The main political threat to oil company operations in the 1990s came from the formation of the Movement for the Survival of the Ogoni People (MOSOP) under the leadership of Ken Saro-Wiwa, whose protests targeted Shell. Like many other ethnic groups in the Niger Delta, the Ogonis - a minority group of 500,000 people - felt that they should receive greater benefits from oil operations in their communal areas. Although the crude oil was produced in their areas by Shell's joint venture, the communities received little economic benefit and were marginalised politically in Nigeria. Another reason for anti-Shell protests was that environmental damage had left many communities more impoverished than before due to the destruction of crops, fish and community lands (Fabig 1998; Mittler 1996). In October 1990, the leaders of

---

[98] In 1997, Shell reportedly lost 67 working days to community disturbances out of 117 lost in the Nigerian oil industry. Shell was followed by the indigenous company Consolidated Oil with a reported loss of 34 working days (*Guardian*, Lagos, 24 February 1998).

MOSOP and traditional Ogoni rulers presented the 'Ogoni Bill of Rights' to the federal military government, in which they demanded political autonomy for the Ogonis. In December 1992, MOSOP asked Shell, Chevron and the NNPC for billions of US dollars in compensation for damage from oil operations and the Ogoni protests became more militant (Osaghae 1995). The protests received international support from Western non-governmental organisations such as Amnesty International and Greenpeace which put further pressure on the Nigerian government and the oil companies, particularly Shell (Mittler 1996).

Until 1993 when Shell officially withdrew from the Ogoni area, oil operations were disturbed either in spontaneous protests or under the direction of MOSOP or the more radical National Youth Council of Ogoni People (NYCOP) and the Ethnic Minorities Rights Organisation of Africa (EMIROAF). For instance, villagers at Bomu in Ogoni protested against pipeline construction by Shell, which prompted the withdrawal of the sub-contractor firm Willbros.[99] When Willbros returned to the area in April 1993, a crowd successfully prevented the company's work.

The 'Ogoni uprising' helped to spark off anti-oil protests elsewhere in Nigeria. Many new local associations were formed with the aim of advocating the rights of the people in the oil producing areas such as the Ijaw National Congress (INC), the Ogba Solidarity, the Urhobo Progressive Union, the Niger Delta Environmental Forum, among others (Ogbnigwe 1996). Not all of these groups were organised along ethnic lines. For instance, in August 1997, the Chikoko movement was launched as an alliance of different ethnic groups and staged mass protests against oil companies (*Delta Magazine*, October 1997). In addition, a number of Nigerian non-governmental organisations such as Environmental Rights Action/ Friends of the Earth Nigeria campaigned for the rights of the people in the oil producing areas.

The 'Ogoni Bill of Rights' of 1990 helped to popularise the demand for the control of Nigeria's oil resources by the local people. In December 1998, a conference attended by over 5,000 Ijaw youths from over 500 communities adopted the so-called 'Kaiama Declaration of the Ijaw Ethnic Nationality'. The 'Kaiama Declaration' stated that *'all land and natural resources (including mineral resources) within the Ijaw territory belong to Ijaw communities and are the basis of our survival'*. Furthermore, it demanded self government and control of resources for the Ijaw people within *'a federation of ethnic minorities'* (HRW 1999a, 130). Since its pronouncement, the 'Kaiama Declaration' has received the support of many non-governmental organisations and interest groups in Nigeria (*Phone News International*, 25 January 1999).[100]

Conflicts between oil companies and village communities have continued until today. In January 1999, for example, Isoko youths shut down five of Shell's

---

[99] This was described in a report for Shell in Nigeria, prepared by Shell's sub-contractor Willbros. "Review of Events Leading to the Withdrawal of Workforce from the Bomu Area," Willbros West Africa Inc. for Shell Petroleum Development Company of Nigeria, 3 May 1993.

[100] Other ethnic groups such as the Ogbia, the Urhobo and the Ogba produced similar documents (*Guardian*, Lagos, 28 April 1999). For instance, the Ogbia people produced the 'Charter of Demands of the Ogbia People' in 1992. The Charter demanded, amongst others, 50% of the oil revenues from the Ogbia area to be paid to the local people and the payment of £ 226.5 billion as rents and royalties arising from oil operations between 1956 and 1992 (HRW 1999a, 129-130).

flowstations in Delta State (*Guardian*, Lagos, 19 January 1999). However, privately industry officials admit that the threat from the millions of Ijaws, behind the bulk of the recent incidents, is greater than that from the 500,000 strong Ogonis or from other ethnic groups. Ijaw protests and ethnic clashes have caused severe disruptions to oil company activities since 1997. In March 1997, for instance, over 100 Shell workers were taken hostage by Ijaws armed with automatic rifles and oil installations were occupied by groups of Ijaws. Eleven of Shell's oil pumping stations, accounting for 210,000 b/d, were shut down during the hostage-crisis (*Phone News International*, 25 March and 7 April 1997). On 1 January 1999, the Ijaw Youth Council (IYC) formed at Kaiama launched the so-called 'Operation Climate Change', a programme of protests against the oil companies in the Niger Delta (HRW 1999a, 130-131). The Ijaw protests are unlikely to end in the foreseeable future.

The economic cost of the anti-oil protests to Nigeria has been substantial. Consider the example of the Ogoni area. Shell withdrew from the Ogoni area in 1993, the company was hence unable to produce any crude oil. According to Shell, the oil wells in the Ogoni area are capable of producing 28,000 barrels a day (SPDC 1995b). If we take the relatively low oil price of US$ 13/barrel, Nigeria lost US$ 133 million per year in oil revenues from the Ogoni area.[101] According to this conservative estimate, Nigeria lost almost US$ 800 million in oil revenues from the area between May 1993 and May 1999. All of these calculations are, of course, hypothetical but they can, nevertheless, tentatively indicate the extent of economic loss resulting from anti-oil protests.

On the most basic level, one can distinguish at least two ways in which the Nigerian government and the oil companies have responded to anti-oil protests: by granting concessions to the oil producing areas in the form of greater social expenditure and by relying on repressive security measures. These two responses are briefly described in the two following sections.

2.10. Government and Oil Company Concessions to Protesters

As a reaction to anti-oil protests and under pressure of public opinion, the Nigerian government and the foreign oil companies were prepared to invest more in the oil producing areas.

As a gesture of goodwill towards the oil producing areas, the Niger Delta Development Board (NDDB) was established in 1961.[102] Amongst other goals, the NDDB was responsible for agricultural development projects in the Niger Delta. Britain provided technical assistance to the NDDB but government officials considered the Board an ineffective institution. A.R. Melville, an agricultural adviser at the British Ministry of Overseas Development, noted in a confidential report in 1965 that

---

[101] The price of Bonny Light, Shell's main crude oil stream in Nigeria, averaged US$ 12.77/barrel in 1998. However, our estimate is rather conservative since the oil price was significantly higher than US$ 13 in previous years. In 1996 and 1997, the price of Bonny Light averaged US$ 21.17/barrel and US$ 19.40/barrel respectively (Quinlan 1999).

[102] Niger Delta Development Act 1961.

The impression gained was that the Board had no clear idea of its objectives or how they should set about the task of sorting out desirable projects into priority order. At the same time there was a desire [among Nigerian politicians] *to have something spectacular to show for political motives and this is one of the reasons for the misguided effort being put into rice development.*[103]

In other words, the NDDB was regarded as little more than a public relations exercise. A focus on public relations is likely to have limited the Board's effectiveness in executing development projects in the Niger Delta.

The 1990s saw the most wide-ranging concessions to the oil producing areas. As a result of protests against oil companies, the federal government launched several committees and commissions to inquire into the socio-economic and environmental problems in the oil producing areas. These included the Justice Alfa Belgore Commission of Inquiry in 1992, the Ministerial Fact-Finding Team in 1994 under the oil minister Don Etiebet and the Niger Delta Development Panel headed by Major-General Oladayo Popoola in 1999 (*Guardian*, Lagos, 28 April 1999; *Newswatch*, 25 May 1999). The detailed recommendations of these bodies have not always been followed. Nonetheless, the government's financial contributions to the oil producing areas were significantly increased in 1992 and again in 1999.

In 1992, the Babangida government increased the amount of financial contributions to the oil producing areas from 1.5% to 3%. The Oil Mineral Producing Areas Development Commission (OMPADEC) was established as a sort of development agency to distribute the 3% allocation to the oil producing areas. Yet the OMPADEC, like many previous government development efforts, failed to satisfy the demands of the local people in the oil producing areas.

The example of the OMPADEC is instructive for an understanding of some of the conflicts arising from the allocation of oil revenues in Nigeria. Osaghae (1998) observed that conflicts have arisen between different ethnic and common interest groups over the composition of the OMPADEC board and over the formula for distributing the OMPADEC budget.[104] Projects were supposed to be distributed in proportion to a community's share of the current oil production. This formula was considered unjust by some communities such as Oloibiri, on whose land oil companies had produced a significant fraction of the oil in the past, but were no longer producing. In addition, the data used by the OMPADEC was said to be unreliable (Osaghae 1998).

While a number of communities in the oil producing areas were able to benefit from OMPADEC projects such as gaining electricity and water provisions, a significant proportion of the funds allocated to the OMPADEC was mismanaged. OMPADEC's chairman Albert K. Horsfall was to report directly to the head of state, but there was no supervisory authority over the agency. Okonta and Douglas (1998) observed that Horsfall and the other commissioners were empowered to undertake any projects they liked anywhere they liked, including setting up banks and manufacturing

---

[103] Confidential Report of an advisory visit to the Federation of Nigeria by A.R. Melville, agricultural advisor, Ministry of Overseas Development in London (22 March - 22 May 1965), OD30/43, PRO.

[104] In 1996, ten of the twelve members of the OMPADEC board were from the oil producing areas (Osaghae 1998, 23).

companies and awarding substantial public contracts. With the absence of any performance guidelines or controls, the OMPADEC proved inefficient and corrupt.[105] In the face of inefficiency and under public pressure, the Nigerian government launched an investigation into the running of the OMPADEC in 1996 and Albert K. Horsfall was sacked in December 1996 (Okonta and Douglas 1998). The appointment of Eric Opia as OMPADEC's sole administrator in 1996 did not appear to have improved efficiency as the structures of the agency did not, by and large, change. In 1998, Opia was removed from the OMPADEC after he failed to account for 6.7 billion Naira (almost US$ 80 million) he received on behalf of the OMPADEC (*PostExpressWired*, 19 July 1998). The OMPADEC was subsequently re-structured under the new chairman Vice Admiral Preston Omatsola (*PostExpressWired*, 2 October 1998, 12 and 13 November 1998).[106]

Even if the OMPADEC had been successful in effectively distributing funds to the people in the oil producing areas, a 3% share of government revenue was regarded as too low by many community leaders.[107] One of the major demands of the minorities' leaders in the oil producing areas at Nigeria's constitutional conference of 1994-95, as Osaghae (1998, 12) noted, was that communities from those areas should be part-owners of the oil, jointly with the federal government, and should receive a part of the oil revenues. Indeed, the 1995 draft constitution proposed that 13% of the federal revenue should be distributed to the states on the basis of derivation. This new revenue allocation formula was eventually introduced into law under the 1999 Constitution (*Guardian*, Lagos, 6 and 7 May 1999). In other words, 13% of the oil revenue will be allocated to the states from which it is derived. Furthermore, the Abubakar government announced a US$ 170 million development plan for the Niger Delta as recommended by the Niger Delta Development Panel in early 1999 (*Inter-Press Service*, 15 April 1999). In the meantime, the demands of the people in the oil producing areas have increased. One pressure group in the Niger Delta recently demanded that the allocation of government funds to the oil producing areas be increased from 13% to 60% (*PostExpressWired, 27 January 1999*). Imo Itsueli, the managing director of Dubri Oil, recently called on the Nigerian government to increase the allocation from 13% to 25% (*Newswatch*, 9 and 16 November 1998).[108]

The mere establishment of the OMPADEC and the recent allocation of 13% to the oil producing areas suggests that political pressures on the micro-level can influence government policy on the oil industry, even though the state may remain biased in favour of oil companies. The failure of the OMPADEC to channel resources

---

[105] In a single project, for example, the OMPADEC reportedly financed the construction of the Eleme Gas Turbine in Port Harcourt at a cost of US$ 20.7 million in 1993. At the end of 1995, the project was still uncompleted and it transpired that more funds were needed to conclude the project (Okonta and Douglas 1998).

[106] Omatsola, an Itsekiri indigene, was the former Chief of Naval Staff and a former member of the Provisional Ruling Council (PRC).

[107] The Ogoni leader Ken Saro-Wiwa considered the OMPADEC an 'insult' and decried that the agency was designed to *'bait us and destroy our will to resist injustice'* (quoted in Suberu 1996, 38).

[108] Itsueli was a former chairman of NNPC's board of directors and a former vice-chairman of the Oil Producers Trade Section (OPTS) of the Lagos Chamber of Commerce.

to the oil producing areas illustrates the use of public oil revenues for the private benefit of specific individuals at the expense of village communities affected by oil operations on the ground.

Since the Nigerian government was unable to channel adequate financial resources to the oil producing areas, the local people demanded the creation of development projects by oil companies such as hospitals or schools. Oil companies engaged in development projects in the Niger Delta from at least as early as the mid-1960s. In 1965, Shell-BP commissioned research from agricultural experts on possible community development projects in rural areas (Odogwu 1991). Shell sought the support of the British Ministry of Overseas Development, which already had some experience in assisting rural development projects in Nigeria. The company approached A.R. Melville, an agricultural adviser at the British Ministry of Overseas Development. Said A.R. Melville in a report in 1965:

> In the course of my discussion with Mr. Max Davies of the Shell/BP Petroleum Development Co. of Nigeria Ltd. the view was strongly put that when it became apparent that oil developments were bringing prosperity to the relatively few in urban areas there might well be considerable resentment in agricultural areas especially where oil operations were involved. What was needed was some sort of public relations effort.[109]

Judging by the above report, Shell sought community development projects primarily for public relations purposes, an approach which perhaps limited the effectiveness of the early development projects.

Until the early 1990s, the scope of oil company development projects in Nigeria remained relatively insignificant. As a reaction to anti-oil protests and under pressure of public opinion, oil companies greatly expanded their development projects in the 1990s. In 1996 alone, Shell claimed to have spent over US$ 36 million on community development in Nigeria (SPDC 1997). Based on figures for the 1980s, this would constitute a substantial increase. In comparison, according to Shell's figures, the company had spent 13.7 million Naira (roughly US$ 1.4 million at the 1991 official rate) between 1980 and 1991 on various development projects in Nigeria (Odogwu 1991).

Other companies also claim to have spent substantial amounts of money on community development projects in the 1990s. Mobil claims to have spent on average approximately US$ 8 million per year on community development projects between 1994 and 1997, while Chevron claims to have spent approximately US$ 28 million on those projects between 1990 and 1997 (HRW 1999a, 104).

The substantial increase in the scope of development projects suggests that the anti-oil protests and the international pressures on oil companies were successful to some extent. But the oil company figures appear to have been artificially inflated. For instance, SPDC's 1996 community budget included US$ 7.4 million spent on roads.

---

[109] Confidential Report of an advisory visit to the Federation of Nigeria by A.R. Melville, agricultural advisor, Ministry of Overseas Development in London (22 March - 22 May 1965), OD30/43, PRO. A.R. Melville advised the Ministry that 'we should be prepared to help them [Shell-BP] in ensuring that effective projects are initiated'.

However, the company's advertising brochures failed to mention that oil companies require roads for access to oil fields as part of their business operations. Most of these roads lead to oil installations, by-passing the local villages (Danler and Brunner 1996, 23-24). Furthermore, US$ 1.1 million of SPDC's community budget was reportedly spent on compensation for damage in the process of land acquisition, which companies are legally obliged to pay anyway (SPDC 1997). As Danler and Brunner (1996, 23) pointed out, the cost of development projects can be offset against tax, so the oil companies have an economic incentive to inflate the figures for social expenditure. Oil company figures may, therefore, conceal expenditure which is part of the company's standard commercial operations.

More importantly, there are some indications that a significant proportion of the oil companies' community budget was misappropriated by oil company staff, local contractors or chiefs.[110] Of the money actually spent on community projects, a significant proportion appears to have been misspent. Some of the projects are inappropriately planned and others never become functional. For instance, Human Rights Watch reported that Shell built a fish processing plant in Iko, Akwa Ibom State which stands empty. The plant was constructed a long distance from trade markets, it lacked electricity for cold storage and suitably qualified personnel to run the plant (HRW 1999a, 105). As another example, Shell promised to construct a sandfill project at the Ojobo village in Delta State in 1991. The initial work involved site clearing, but the project was later abandoned (*Guardian*, Lagos, 18 January 1998; *Tell*, 27 January 1997). In general, a recent Human Rights Watch report concluded: '*virtually every community in the delta has a non-functioning water or electricity scheme or other project sponsored by one or other of the oil companies or by OMPADEC and since abandoned*' (HRW 1999a, 105). While this claim is likely to be an exaggeration, the available evidence would suggest that a significant number of development projects in the oil producing areas have failed to satisfy the demands of the local people.

There are indications that a number of oil companies have recently attempted to explore new avenues of appeasing village communities. In November 1998, three companies - SPDC, Mobil and NLNG - signed a Memorandum of Understanding (MOU) with representatives of the Bonny Kingdom, the first agreement of that nature ever signed between oil companies and a community. According to the MOU, the three companies agreed to construct a 2.7 km road on Bonny Island and to provide pipe-borne water and electricity within two years (*Newswatch*, 9 and 16 November 1998). If successful, such agreements could perhaps produce fewer conflicts than previous ones because an oil company would enter land with the express consent of a whole community rather than with the mere consent of the state governor. Furthermore, there have been attempts to introduce self-help projects based on the premise of sustainable development. Perhaps the most notable example is Statoil-BP's Akassa project which was executed by ProNatura International and the Niger Delta Wetlands Centre, two non-governmental organizations, rather than by the oil company itself. If successful, self-help projects could perhaps satisfy the demands of communities better than previous development projects because the local people would have a much greater say

---

[110] See, for instance, reports by Human Rights Watch (HRW 1999a, 105 and 165), Brot Für Die Welt (Danler and Brunner 1996, 18-24) and Environmental Rights Action (ERA 1997).

in the execution of the project.[111] While it is too early to predict the relative success of these projects, the new initiatives could mark a new beginning in the relationship between oil companies and village communities. Nonetheless, the scope of the MOU and the self-help projects is still rather insignificant, if compared with the OMPADEC projects and the other oil company development projects.

Obviously, any discussion of the previous failures of government and oil company development efforts must remain speculative. One of the most likely explanations is the influence of the prevalent corruption and inefficiency in Nigeria on the conduct of government officials, oil company staff and local contractors. Corruption is a severe impediment to business operations in Nigeria. Indeed, the Control Risks Group describes Nigeria as *'one of the most difficult places in which to do business'* (1997, 71). According to a KPMG survey, threequarters of British firms would not do business in Nigeria because of its reputation for fraud (*Guardian*, London, April 16, 1996). It could be expected that corruption has also affected the implementation of development projects.

Another explanation for the failures of development efforts may be the government's and oil companies' focus on public relations (PR) strategies in the execution of development projects rather than the need to address the real life problems of village communities in the oil producing areas. Some of the oil companies' community development projects in Nigeria have been used in advertising materials despite the fact that they had been abandoned and were not functional. For instance, in the case of the Ojobo sandfill project mentioned earlier, Shell used the abandoned project for PR purposes. In the company's 1996 calendar, Shell in Nigeria printed a photograph of an aerial view with the caption *'An SPDC sandfilled scheme at Ojobo in the trans Ramos Area of Delta State'*. Shell's project in Ojobo had not yet been built by then and the photograph was of a different village (*Guardian*, Lagos, 18 January 1998; *Tell*, 27 January 1997). As another example, Shell claimed in an advertising brochure in August 1996 that the Kolo Creek flowstation provides associated gas for a rural electrification scheme (SPDC 1996). When the author of this book visited the flowstation in early 1997, gas was still being flared there. Examples like these would suggest that the oil companies' PR claims may be at variance with reality. This reliance on PR successes as opposed to real improvements in the government's and the oil companies' performance may in turn fuel anger amongst the inhabitants of the Niger Delta (see e.g. ERA 1997).

While the scale and the causes of failed development projects cannot be fully ascertained at this point, it has to be assumed that broken promises of the government and oil companies further fuel conflicts between oil companies and the local people.

---

[111] Personal interviews with Nick Ashton-Jones, Environmental Rights Action (London, January 1998), and Philip Hall, ProNatura International (Lagos, February 1998). See also 'Delta People – Akassa Community Development Project', video produced by Take 3 Video & Film Production (London 1998). Another self-help project was the US$ 5 million Western Niger Delta Development Programme, launched by Chevron in partnership with the International Foundation for Education and Self Help (IFESH) in May 1999 (*Phone News International*, 21 May 1999).

2.11. Repression of Protests and Security Arrangements

While oil companies and the Nigerian government were prepared to grant some concessions to the protesters in the oil producing areas, a frequent response to anti-oil protests was the use of repressive security measures. Anti-Shell protests by the Ogonis, as documented by Human Rights Watch (HRW 1995), were met with violence by the state, which involved extrajudicial killings, rapes, arrests and floggings of protesters. In November 1995, Ken Saro-Wiwa and eight other Ogoni leaders were executed, an act which was seen as linked to anti-Shell protests (e.g. *Observer*, 19 November 1995).[112] More recent protests have also been met by state violence. In the wake of the 'Kaiama Declaration', dozens of anti-oil protesters - most of them non-violent - were killed and their houses burnt by the Nigerian security forces in December 1998 and January 1999 (*Reuters*, 31 December 1998; *Phone News International*, 25 January 1999; *AP*, 1 February 1999; HRW 1999b). Activists from human rights and environmental organisations which advocate the rights of the oil producing areas faced regular harassment from the authorities. This included arbitrary arrests, intimidation and beatings (HRW 1999a, 131-133). In dealing with anti-oil protests, the authorities used regulary units of the police and the army as well as the navy. The Nigerian authorities also created special units of the security forces, consisting of the police and the military, to deal with anti-oil protests such as the Rivers State Internal Security Task Force in 1994 (HRW 1995, 14).[113]

There are indications that the oil companies supported the repression of anti-oil protests. For instance, Chevron equipment such as helicopters and boats was reportedly used in attacks on anti-oil protesters in 1998 and 1999 (*Hart's Africa Oil and Gas*, 3 February 1999; HRW 1999b and 1999a, 151). Several years earlier, a secret memo revealed that oil companies provided the infamous Rivers State Internal Security Task Force with financial assistance. In an internal memo in May 1994, Major Okuntimo called for '*pressure on oil companies for prompt regular inputs as discussed*'.[114] The money was probably used for internal repression since the Task Force was mainly used in the Ogoni area to deal with anti-Shell protests. In the same internal memo, Major Okuntimo wrote: '*Shell operations (are) still impossible unless ruthless military operations are undertaken for smooth economic activities to commence*'.

In addition to assistance by state security services, oil companies maintain their own security forces. These security forces are drawn from the Nigerian police and perform duties at oil installations. Paid by the oil companies, they are known as Shell Police or Mobil Police. The best evidence on security co-operation comes from the court case *XM Federal Limited v. Shell*[115], in which an arms supplier sued Shell over

---

[112] The *Observer* (19 November 1995) indeed reported that Shell had refused to help Saro-Wiwa unless anti-Shell protests were called off. Following the 1995 execution of Ken Saro-Wiwa, Ledum Mittee became the leader of MOSOP in exile. Mittee returned to the Ogoni area in October 1998.

[113] In 1997, 'Operation Salvage' was formed in Bayelsa State with the aim of protecting oil installations. A similar unit called 'Operation Flush' was established in Rivers State (HRW 1999a, 121-122).

[114] Memo written by the then Chairman of the Rivers State Internal Security, Major Paul Okuntimo, to the then Military Administrator of Rivers State, Lt.Col.Dauda Komo, 12 May 1994.

[115] Unreported Suit No. FHC/L/CS/849/95.

breach of contract in the Federal High Court of Nigeria.[116] Among others, the court case revealed that the Nigerian government provides policemen to guard oil installations. In a letter dated 1 December 1993, Shell's Managing Director Philip B. Watts[117] applied for an increase in 'supernumerary police guards' (also known as 'spy police') from 1,200 in 1993 to 1,400 in 1995 for the company. Of these policemen, 200 men were to be stationed in Shell's headquarters in Lagos, 400 men were to be stationed in Warri (Shell's Western Division) and 600 men were to be stationed in Port Harcourt (Shell's Eastern Division). Furthermore, oil companies employ private security staff. According to Human Rights Watch, Shell employed roughly 2,300 people (or roughly 20% of the total workforce including contractors) on security duty in Nigeria in 1998 (HRW 1999a, 116).

Evidence from the court case *XM Federal Limited v. Shell*[118] also revealed that Shell was negotiating to import weapons into Nigeria in breach of an arms embargo between 1993 and 1995. According to court evidence, Shell sought tenders from Nigerian arms suppliers to procure weapons worth over US$ 500,000. These included 130 Beretta 9mm calibre sub-machine guns, 200,000 rounds of bullets and 500 smoke hand grenades. Nigeria's Inspector General of Police approved the arms purchase under pressure from Shell managers. Following revelations in the British press on Shell's arms dealings in 1996, a Shell International spokesman later admitted that one of three bids for arms purchases had been 'selected' by Shell in March 1995, although the arms deal had not gone ahead (*Observer*, 11 February 1996).

Oil companies, of course, have a legitimate right to protect themselves against violent attacks, particularly in an unstable region such as the Niger Delta. But it must be noted that, until recently, most protests in Nigeria were peaceful. It is likely that overreliance on security forces can lead to unnecessary bloodshed. An example of how the oil companies' overreliance on security forces can lead to violence was provided by an official inquiry into the Umuechem massacre (Rivers State of Nigeria 1991). On 30 and 31 October 1990, local youths at Umuechem demonstrated against Shell. Shell had been operating in the area from the late 1950s, resulting in the pollution of a stream, destruction of farm crops and other losses to property. The community had received little or no compensation, while villagers called for social amenities such as the provision of electricity. Shell did not respond to the dissatisfied community members, but decided to rely upon security protection. On 29 October, J.R. Udofia, Shell's

---

[116] The first plaintiff was XM Federal, an international arms dealer. The second plaintiff was Humanitex Nigeria Limited, a Nigerian arms dealer approved by the government. Humanitex was employed by XM Federal as security adviser and its Nigerian agent. Shell ordered arms from Humanitex but later withdrew its order, most likely because the arms were considered too expensive by Shell. Brian Anderson, Shell's managing director, wrote in a letter in September 1994: '*We consider this quotation to be excessive, based upon our own investigations from other sources of supply*' (Letter from Brian Anderson, Shell's Chairman and Managing Director, to Alhaji Coomassie, Inspector-General of Police, 12 September 1994). The arms supplier subsequently filed a lawsuit.

[117] In 1994, Philip B. Watts left Nigeria to take up the post of Shell's Group Regional Co-ordinator for Europe. He was succeeded as managing director of Shell in Nigeria by the Nigerian born Brian Anderson. Anderson was in turn replaced in July 1997 by Ron van den Berg, former chief executive of Shell in Brunei.

[118] Unreported Suit No. FHC/L/CS/849/95.

Eastern Division manager wrote a letter to the Commissioner of Police in Rivers State informing him of an *'impending attack'* on oil facilities allegedly planned for the next day. Udofia did not merely appeal for security protection but explicitly requested the assistance of a unit of the Mobile Police, which was well-known for its brutality. Udofia requested the Commissioner to *'urgently provide us with security protection (preferably Mobile Police Force) at this location'* (Rivers State of Nigeria 1991, Appendix G). In the course of the next few days, the Mobile Police moved in with teargas and gunfire, killing around 80 people and destroying almost 500 houses. In the wake of the incident, a judicial commission of inquiry was set up by Colonel Godwin Osagie Abbe, the Rivers State Military Governor. The inquiry found that there was no imminent threat of attack and that the demonstrators were neither violent nor armed (Rivers State of Nigeria 1991).

The incident at Umuechem exemplifies oil company overreliance on security co-operation in dealing with conflicts in village communities. Rather than engaging in negotiations with the Umuechem people, Shell decided at an early stage in a peaceful protest to call on the security forces for assistance. In general, the judicial report of the official inquiry into the Umuechem massacre concluded:

> It is the view of the Commission that there had been lack of meaningful contact and consultation between the Oil Company/Companies and the Communities in which the Oil Companies operate and therefore lack of understanding between both parties. Where there is such lack of understanding there is always confusion, disorder and all that make for disturbances [sic] (Rivers State of Nigeria 1991, 14).

Any explanation of the oil companies' overreliance on security protection must remain speculative. One of the most likely explanations is the close relationship between the government and the oil companies. Foreign oil companies form joint ventures with the NNPC, a state-controlled company, and have many formal and informal agreements with state agencies that range from questions of land acquisition to the purchase of arms for the police. As shown earlier, oil companies and the Nigerian state maintain close ties of co-operation in terms of security arrangements. Furthermore, oil company managers often become Nigerian bureaucrats, and vice versa. It is perhaps no coincidence that a former SPDC director, Ernest Shonekan was to become Nigeria's head of state in 1993, if only for less than a year. Former SPDC staff, Edmund Daukoru, while still working for Shell, was in 1992 appointed Group Managing director of NNPC and subsequently retired from his SPDC post. Others have also held government positions. Rufus Ada George, the former Governor of Rivers State, and O.C.J. Okocha, the former Attorney General of Rivers State, worked for Shell at some point (Frynas 1998). The available evidence would suggest that oil companies have much closer ties with the Nigerian administration than with village communities. By implication, it has perhaps been much more convenient for a manager to summon the police or the military than to engage in negotiations with the local people.

The government's suppression of the anti-oil protests and the companies' overreliance on security protection exemplified that the ruling Northern elite was unwilling to yield to the demands of community leaders in the oil producing areas.

Following the death of General Abacha in June 1998, there have been signs of a policy shift. In particular, as indicated earlier, there has been an increase in the government's financial contributions to the oil producing areas. In June 1999, the Obasanjo administration decided to create a new government body for the Niger Delta to produce a comprehensive masterplan for the social development of the region (*Guardian*, Lagos, 8 June 1999). However, the new civilian government is likely to face at least two obstacles in terms of distributing money to the Niger Delta. First, the 'Kaiama Declaration' has indicated that the local people seek control over oil resources, not merely the creation of development projects in their areas. Second, if judged by past experience, a significant part of the funds for the Niger Delta may be lost to corruption and ineffective development projects, thereby causing further frustration among the local people. At this stage, it cannot be predicted whether the new Obasanjo government is either willing or capable of offering concessions acceptable to the radical local leaders in the oil producing areas. Until now, the oil companies and the government appeared to rely on repressive security measures which have fuelled conflicts between companies and the village communities.

2.12. Conclusion

This chapter served as a basic background to our subsequent analysis of local conflicts by examining the making of the Nigerian oil industry and Nigeria's government petroleum policy. We have seen that despite partial nationalization and nominal control of the Nigerian government, oil companies have largely retained effective managerial control over joint venture operations. Operational control implies the legal liability of foreign oil companies as operators (both in joint ventures and production-sharing contracts) for any damage caused in the course of oil operations. Within the framework of the book, it can thus be argued that government policy plays only a limited direct role in the village community as far as day-to-day oil operations are concerned. If oil operations cause damage, those affected have to deal with the foreign oil companies rather than with the government. This is important for the study of litigation between village communities and the oil industry, not least because companies, not the government, are usually named as defendants in court cases involving damage from oil operations.

In addition to providing the historical background to the subsequent analysis of legal disputes, we have investigated the basic elements of Nigeria's political economy with a view to exploring the question of whether the Nigerian state is biased in favour of oil companies. On the surface, evidence on the bias of the state in favour of foreign capital puts into question the concept of the rentier state. Some policies such as the Marginal Fields Decree indeed ran counter to the interests of the foreign companies. The notion of a rentier state can be supported, however, to the extent that foreign oil companies have largely continued to dominate the economic development of the Nigerian oil industry and government revenue. In the 1970s, the Nigerian federal finances came to rely primarily on oil rents and the state was forced to continually attract foreign investment in the oil sector in order to ensure a continuation of oil exploration and production. While foreign oil companies could not dictate petroleum policy, it has to be assumed that the state largely avoided imposing policy measures, which would alienate foreign investors. The Marginal Fields Decree, for instance, was promulgated in the best interests of the state and the indigenous business interests, but it was never implemented as it contravened the interests of the foreign oil companies and their allies in the state administration and the state was too weak to attack those vested interests. Judging by the evidence discussed in this chapter, there are indications that the Nigerian state is predisposed in favour of oil companies at the expense of those affected by oil operations.

This speculative finding on the bias of the state finds support in the government's inadequate budgetary contributions to the oil producing areas. The failure to satisfy the monetary demands of the community leaders in those areas could, in turn, be assumed to trigger anti-oil protests. By implication, the rise in social unrest and litigation may be partly attributed to the unequal allocation of social costs and benefits arising from oil operations within Nigerian society, a fact which cannot be directly derived from our later discussion of court cases. The government's and the oil companies' monetary concessions and repressive security measures have not, until today, been able to contain anti-oil protests in the oil producing areas.

With the executive arm of the government being biased in favour of oil interests, it could be expected that the state would restrict litigation against oil companies. However, the discussion in this chapter cannot answer the question of whether there also exist biases within Nigeria's formal legal system and the judiciary. These questions will be explored in the two subsequent chapters.

Chapter 3: Nigeria's Formal Legal System and Oil-Related Statute Law

3.1. Introduction

Conflicts and litigation between village communities and oil companies are constrained by the structural character of the legal system and oil-related statute law which are discussed in this chapter.[119] The structural character of the legal system determines the venues in which legal disputes between companies and communities are located. Statute law determines the legal rights and obligations of village communities and oil companies when dealing with each other. The constraints and opportunities provided by the legal system partly determine the responses of village communities and oil companies to socio-economic conflicts. In other words, the structural character of the legal system and statute law determine what is feasible in litigation between village communities and oil companies.

In addition to providing a legal background to the subsequent discussion of court cases, we investigate whether the Nigerian legal system is biased in favour of oil companies. If the Nigerian state is indeed prejudiced in favour of oil companies as the previous chapter suggested, it has to be assumed that it would restrict the legal rights of those adversely affected by oil operations. In this context, this chapter examines those factors within Nigeria's formal legal system and statute law which may have given rise to an advantageous legal position for oil companies vis-à-vis village communities.

The Nigerian legal system has much in common with other legal systems in Africa, particularly those in former British colonies, in which English Common Law was introduced under colonial rule. However, despite the influence of the English legal tradition, the Nigerian legal system has at least three distinct features which have also had an effect on the relationship between oil companies and village communities. First, the Nigerian legal system is very complex and rich. Its main characteristic (similar to other countries in Sub-Saharan Africa) is the 'plurality' of legal systems. In general, as Allott (1965, 220-221) noted, the British colonial governments in Africa introduced the legal system of the mother country, while, at the same time, permitting the regulated continuation of traditional African law and judicial institutions unless the latter were deemed contrary to the interests or morals of the colonisers. This plurality (in Allott's words, duality) of legal systems was often accompanied by the existence of different court systems. African customary law usually consisted of unwritten indigenous customs and traditions and was tribal in origin. It commonly applied to Africans only with some exceptions in the so-called 'native courts'. English law was commonly applied to non-Africans as well as to transactions between non-Africans and Africans

---

[119] For an introduction to the Nigerian legal system, see Obilade (1979), Akande (1982) and Okonkwo (1980). For an introduction to Nigerian petroleum law, see Etikerentse (1985), Olisa (1987) and Atsegbua (1993).

in the territorial or British courts (Allott 1965, 220-222).[120] For the oil industry, the existence of this plurality meant that companies were able to operate in a village setting according to Western colonial laws and contracts, while the local population was able to continue living according to customary legal systems. In other words, the oil companies and the village communities came to live according to different legal systems during colonial rule.

Second, the Nigerian legal system is not stable but dynamic, particularly owing to the nature of customary law.[121] It is accepted among scholars that African customary law is far from being 'immutable' but rather is subject to constant change. Thus the content of legal rules in Africa may be highly flexible (Allott *et al.* 1969, 9-15). As Park (1963, 67) noted, customary law in Nigeria develops from time to time and modifies itself in order to keep pace with changes in social conditions. Not unlike US or English law, Allott *et al.* (1969, 10) maintained that African judges as well as researchers have to select from a variety of principles and rules in a particular case, which marks any *'living, adaptable, functional system of law'*. In their view, the crucial problem is that of a time factor. Given the flexible nature of law, law may undergo changes at different levels - principles, norms or rules - at any time, so it may be difficult to reconstruct the contents of traditional law at a particular period (Allott *et al.* 1969, 9-15). By implication, oil companies may sometimes be unaware of the changing customary law in their areas of operations.

Third, the significance of African customary law to Africa's socio-economic development may be greater than some observers think. Standard Western sociological studies recognise that society is governed by rules and norms, although many of them are not called 'laws'. Anthony Giddens (1989, 117), for example, stated that the world *'would collapse into chaos if we did not stick to rules which define some kinds of behaviour as appropriate in given contexts, and others as inappropriate'*. In the African context, Gluckman (1965, 2-3) argued that societies which have no formal legal system, nonetheless, abide by well-established and widely accepted customary rules.[122] Since customary rules in Nigeria do not resemble written Western law, it is possible that oil company staff may sometimes underestimate the significance of those rules and norms when dealing with village communities.

The three features of Nigeria's legal system mentioned above may have had wide repercussions for conflicts between village communities and oil companies.

---

[120] African customary law could also be applied to non-Africans in West Africa and Northern Rhodesia in cases where a non-African contracted with an African and a court found that to rely strictly on English law would result in substantial injustice to either party (Allott 1965, 222).

[121] Scholarly research on the introduction and development of legal systems in Africa, particularly in former British colonies in West Africa, has a rich tradition going back to the early 1960s (Allott 1960; Elias 1962; Daniels 1964) but there has been surprisingly little emphasis on the dynamic change of legal systems. Scholars have researched some administrative and judicial innovations introduced in colonial as well as post-colonial states in Africa, yet there has been little research on the changing nature of the Common Law applied in Nigeria.

[122] Writing on African customary law, Gluckman (1965, 2-3) stated that societies without any formal institutions of government such as courts and powers to legislate may have such *'well-established and well-known codes of morals and law, of convention and ritual, that even though they have no written histories, we may reasonably assume that they have persisted for many generations'*, so they are far from living in a state of lawlessness.

Conflicts between the companies and communities may arise if one party does not recognise the validity of the other party's laws. As shown below in greater detail with the example of land legislation (see sections 3.5. and 3.6. below), village communities have continued to recognise customary land rights despite the introduction of the Land Use Act 1978, which re-defined the legal position on land ownership in Nigeria. A company's ignorance regarding land titles may render it difficult to identify the correct receiver of compensation payments for land acquisition. This may lead to conflicts with the local people over land for oil operations (this will be explained in greater detail in chapter 5). In general terms, the existence of competing legal systems may thus lead to conflicts. By implication, in order to reduce the quantity of community conflicts, oil companies must address the presence of customary law when dealing with village communities.

To sum up, Nigeria's legal system has a distinct identity which is relevant to our discussion of conflict and litigation. In order to understand the evolution of the contemporary legal system in Nigeria, we use the three-fold typology of the pre-colonial, colonial and post-colonial law, as suggested in Allott's (1965, 220) analysis of African legal history.

3.2. Pre-colonial Law

Before the British government took possession of the African colonies, Nigeria (or rather the area of what later became Nigeria) was ruled by traditional customary law. The development of the plurality of legal systems mentioned earlier ensured that customary law has continued to play a role in the Nigerian legal system until today.[123]

In theory, customary law is derived from ancient customs. In practice, as Allott (1965, 220) pointed out, customary rules in Africa have sometimes been modified by the pronouncements of state, local and traditional authorities as well as by formulations of adjudicators and arbitrators.[124] Customary law in Nigeria is not a single uniform set

---

[123] While the main characteristics of the formal-legal institutions of colonial and post-colonial states have been largely undisputed among academic scholars of law in Africa, African customary law has become the main focus of study and a source of academic debate. Research on customary African laws has been undertaken by both legal scholars (Sarbah 1968 - first published 1897, Danquah 1928, Allot 1960) and anthropologists (Schapera 1935, Gluckman 1965, Roberts 1972).

[124] Writing on the content of customary law in the actual enforcement process, several scholars (Chanock 1985, Snyder 1981) have argued that the so-called customary law implemented in 'native courts' was not necessarily a relic of a traditional society but rather a historical construct of the colonial rule, influenced by a struggle between the colonisers and those colonised. In Senegal, for example, Francis Snyder (1981) found that modernising elites often took a leading role in defining 'indigenous law'. In this context, the nature of law changed as it was reshaped from an adaptable traditional, mostly unwritten, system into fixed, formal and written rules enforced by native courts. Martin Chanock (1985), for example, traced the development of customary law in Zambia and Malawi from the late 19th century to independence in the 1960s. His research demonstrated that customary law was reconstructed from a fluid, shifting set of principles and procedures to a fixed, written sets of codes. These written (or 'invented') codes, nevertheless, claimed continuity with an African past and were used as the basis for the formation of a new national legal system of the post-colonial state (Chanock 1985, 55). Far from being a set of pre-colonial African social rules, customary law became a historical product created by colonial administrators and the emerging African elites who shaped the law to meet their own, often changing, political and economic interests (Chanock 1985, 145). While this type of research may have yielded important insights on

of Nigerian customs, but operates only within an ethnic group or a community living in the same area. As Park (1963, 65) noted, there may also be local variations between communities of the same ethnic group. Unwritten customary law on a particular matter in one part of the Ibo land, for example, is usually, but not always, the same as that in another part of the Ibo land. Written Islamic Law is also referred to as customary law, although it originates from outside Nigeria, so it is not, strictly speaking, customary to Nigeria at all. In Northern Nigeria, Islamic Law has largely supplanted ancient local customs (Park 1963, 65-68). The oil producing areas in south-eastern Nigeria, however, are almost exclusively non-Islamic, so Islamic Law is not relevant to our discussion. Traditional customary law is important to an understanding of oil-related litigation because village communities in oil producing areas still tend to observe customary rules. From the perspective of oil companies in Nigeria, it may have been better if the oil reserves had been located in Muslim areas since Islamic Law is codified as well as being more static and more predictable. The dynamic and unpredictable nature of traditional customary law may lead to misunderstandings and thus conflicts between oil companies and village communities.

Today, points of customary law are decided in the so-called customary courts, which are headed by an indigene from the area who has special knowledge of the local customs and traditions of the local people. With some exceptions, these courts only involve indigenes from the same community or the same ethnic group. Customary courts are thus never directly involved in litigation against oil companies. Those cases are always adjudicated by higher Nigerian courts, which make a different use of customary law. As Adaramola (1992, 73) observed, contemporary customary courts accept customary law as given law, while higher courts accept Nigerian law and English Common Law as given law. As a result, customary law is merely treated as fact or evidence in a court case in a higher court, not as law (Adaramola 1992, 73). Since all court cases involving oil companies are located in a higher court, the significance of customary law is limited as far as oil-related litigation is concerned. In other words, the venue of oil-related court cases limits the exercise of customary law in oil-related cases.

Customary law, however, continues to be used in oil-related litigation when facts are disputed, for example, when the ownership of a piece of land is disputed. As Adaramola (1992, 73) noted, in order to establish customary law in a higher court, witnesses must prove the existence of customary rules by oral evidence, alternatively books or manuscripts must be presented, which are recognised as established authority in the specific locality. Customary law can also be established by judicial notice (Adaramola 1992, 73), in which case the judge simply assumes that a customary rule exists without asking for evidential proof.[125] A customary rule is established within the legal context of a particular case. For instance, a particular law of inheritance among

---

the nature of the formal-legal institutions in Africa, it may have overstated the actual influence of colonial rule and its manipulation of local customary laws, particularly in Britain's West African colonies where virtually no European colonists settled.

[125] As Park (1963, 92) argued, certain customary rules and institutions become so well known to the judges that they no longer need to be proved. When these rules and institutions are established in a court case by judicial notice, they effectively cease to be questions of fact and are converted into matters of law.

the Ogoni may help a judge to establish the ownership of a specific house, which is disputed in a court case, but only after the customary rule is either accepted by the judge outright or is proved through oral or written evidence.

Courts may allow different types of factual evidence depending on the particulars of the case or the available evidence. In reference to land property, for example, Fatayi-Williams, J.S.C., in the case *Idundun v. Okumagba*[126], defined five ways in which ownership of land may be proved in Nigeria.[127] First, ownership of land may be proved by traditional evidence. Second, it may be proved by production of written documents of title. Third, acts of the person (or persons) claiming the land such as selling, leasing or renting out a part of the land or farming on it, are also evidence of ownership, provided that the acts extend over a sufficient length of time and are numerous enough. Fourth, acts of long possession and enjoyment of the land may also be *prima facie* evidence of ownership. Fifth, proof of possession of connected or adjacent land may also be used to prove ownership. To sum up, evidence presented in court cases involving oil companies may combine elements of customary law and formal Nigerian law.

Not all customary rules are admitted by courts, however. In order to be recognised by Nigerian courts, customary law must, above all, fulfil a number of conditions. A customary rule is subject to four legal 'tests' of validity called the criterion of repugnancy, the criterion of incompatibility, the criterion of public policy and the criterion of applicability. First, a customary rule is only valid, if it is not *'repugnant to natural justice, equity and good conscience'*. These terms are difficult to define, as Obilade argued (quoted in Adaramola 1992, 74), but generally the purpose of the rule under colonial administration was to invalidate 'uncivilised' customs. The problem with the rule is that Nigerian judges can use the rule of repugnancy in an *ad hoc* manner, particularly if they perceive a particular rule as 'uncivilised' or unjust. In one case, for instance, the Supreme Court invalidated a rule of Maliki Law that prevented persons accused of highway robbery from defending themselves.[128] Second, a customary rule is only valid, if it is not incompatible with any Nigerian legislation or regulation. As indicated earlier, certain customary rules may be abolished by legislation. For instance, Nigeria's Eastern regional government eradicated the so-called Osu customary law. Under the Osu law, certain persons, known as 'Osu' (outcasts) were subject to legal and social disabilities. This practice was abolished by legislation in 1956 (Park 1963, 47). In addition to the explicit legislative abolition of customary rules, a rule may be invalid, if it is considered to be inconsistent with the intention of legislation, even though the piece of legislation did not expressly abolish the specific customary rule. For instance, in the case *Agbai v. Okogbue*[129], Nigeria's Supreme Court ruled that a certain customary law was incompatible with Nigeria's

---

[126] (1976) 9 & 10 S.C. 227.

[127] As Aluko (1998, 14) pointed out, however, the precedent in *Idundun v. Okumagba* does not apply where the boundaries of the land between communities have previously been demarcated. In this case, the court will resolve the issue of ownership by referring to the boundaries demarcated, for instance, by a previous customary court ruling.

[128] *Guri v. Hadejia Native Authority* (1959) 4 F.S.C. 44, cited by Park (1963, 71).

[129] (1991) 7 NWLR (Pt. 204) 391.

Constitution.[130] Third, a customary rule is invalid, if it is contrary to public policy, although this criterion is rarely used in Nigeria. On one occasion, it was held that the Yoruba law of legitimisation was contrary to public policy because it would encourage promiscuity (Adaramola 1992, 76). As Adaramola (1992, 74-78) argued, the fourth criterion of applicability derives from the three above criterions. In order to be applicable, a customary rule must be shown to be in existence at a particular time and must be recognised and adhered to by the community. It is not enough for a custom to have been in use in the past, it must still exist and still be accepted. Any customary rule must fulfil all the above four conditions in order to be admitted by a judge of a higher court. However, even if a judge refuses to adopt a particular customary rule in a court case, the rule still remains law within the given community as it continues to be accepted as law within that community (Adaramola 1992, 74-78).

Nigerian judges may find it particularly difficult to adjudicate oil-related cases involving disputes over questions of customary law.[131] It is not always clear to what extent specific litigants still abide by specific rules of customary law. It is likely that customary law is less prevalent in bigger towns where members of different ethnic groups live side by side and have adapted to modern urban lifestyles. It is likely that customary law is still prevalent in rural areas, particularly where communities are less exposed to modern lifestyles. But the use of specific customary rules may vary from community to community and is likely to change over time. The use of customary rules also varies according to the subject matter of the dispute. A survey by Uwazie (1994) among rural and urban members of the Ibo ethnic group indicated that community members preferred to resolve disputes according to customary rules and alternative channels of dispute-resolution, rather than through the country's formal legal system. According to the survey, potential litigants tended to use formal legal institutions,

---

[130] In that case, Samuel Okogbue from Abia State was invited to become a member of a so-called age grade in his community. In his community, it was a custom to group community members into age grades for the purpose of community development. The Amankalu age grade, to which Okogbue was assigned, decided to construct a community hospital and impose a compulsory levy on its members in order to pay for the construction. Okogbue refused to join the grade and to pay the levy on the ground that he was a Jehovah's Witness. Upon his refusal to join the age grade and to pay the levy, members of the age grade entered Okogbue's premises and seized his sewing machine, claiming that they acted on the authority of the custom of the people. In the first instance, the magistrates' court ruled that a custom, which made it compulsory for a person to belong 'willy nilly' to an association, violated the 1963 Constitution. In addition, the court ruled that, since the plaintiff refused to join the age grade on religious grounds, a compulsory membership further violated his constitutional right to freedom of religion. On appeal, the High Court reversed the judgment of the magistrates' court. The Supreme Court, to which the matter went from the Court of Appeal, agreed with the magistrates' court that the above mentioned custom violated the Constitution. Said Nwokedi, J.S.C.:

Much as one would welcome development projects in the Community, there must be caution to ensure that the fundamental rights of citizens are not trampled upon by popular enthusiasm. These rights have been enshrined in the Constitution which enjoys superiority over local custom.

[131] Section 252 of the 1979 Constitution provided that certain judges of the Supreme Court and the Court of Appeal must be learned in Islamic personal law and customary law. But the judges of the Supreme Court and the Court of Appeal, like those of any other higher court, are not likely to be knowledgeable in all areas of customary law. Since there are many systems of customary law in Nigeria, no Nigerian judge can be an expert on all areas of customary law. By implication, any courts except the local customary courts may find it difficult to adjudicate court cases involving the knowledge of customary law.

police and customary or higher courts, to handle cases of murder, injurious assault, grand theft, rape and divorce. However, they were least likely to resolve land disputes in courts. About 98% of the respondents said that they would solve land disputes in indigenous institutions, including village and family tribunals, while only 2% would seek redress from the courts or police.[132] These results suggest that alternative modes of dispute resolution and customary law have survived in Nigeria, even though their use varies according to subject matter (Uwazie 1994).[133] The significance of customary law in disputes over land ownership is particularly important to oil companies since the acquisition of land rights in rural areas plays a key role in oil operations.

To sum up, customary law is likely to continue to play a limited role in oil-related litigation as far as factual evidence is concerned. But the use of customary law is severely constrained in court cases involving damage from oil operations. Oil-related cases are located in higher courts, in which legal rules are derived from colonial and post-colonial law, so litigants from village communities cannot rely on the legal principles of customary laws with which they are familiar. Local customary laws designed to protect the village communities such as customary environmental laws are not effective in court cases filed against oil companies.[134] In this sense, the legal system is biased against village community litigants.

---

[132] **Table:** Survey among Ibos on the Question 'To whom would you complain about the following cases?'

Type of Case	Complaint to Police or Court (%)	Informal dispute resolution* (%)	Total Number of Respondents
Land	2	98	212
Murder	76	24	208
Injurious assault	66	34	207
Grand theft	71	29	207
Petty theft	32	68	199
Minor assault	22	78	178
Adultery	15	85	179
Spousal abuse	4	96	178
Rape	71	29	147
Divorce	60	40	159

* Includes village/family tribunals and other indigenous institutions. Source: Uwazie (1994).

[133] Uwazie (1994) concluded in general that *'despite the rise of national legal systems in Africa, indigenous modes of justice persist'*. In the context of Nigeria, Uwazie concluded that the future of indigenous justice seems assured despite the impact of economic development, missionary activity and Western education.

[134] As Douglas (1997) revealed, Niger Delta communities recognise a multitude of environmental customary laws aimed at protecting their environment. These include laws for the protection of forests, the soil and the aqueous environment. If enforced, environmental customary laws would be likely to outlaw certain oil company practices which lead to environmental damage. Non-enforcement of those laws is therefore advantageous to oil companies.

3.3. Colonial Law

The imposition of colonial rule in Nigeria resulted in the introduction of English law. The Nigerian post-colonial state inherited the general formal-legal structure of the colonial period which has formally continued to form the basis of the Nigerian legal system until today.

English law introduced in Nigeria comprises English Common Law, the so-called doctrines of equity and various British statutes. Some of the British statutes have ceased to be in force. Some of them have been specifically repealed and replaced by Nigerian legislation. English statutes only apply in Nigeria in so far as local circumstances and the Nigerian legislation permit. These are mainly very old statutes which were operating in England before 1900. In theory, English Common Law and the doctrines of equity formally apply in Nigeria as they exist in England today. Until 1963, the Judicial Committee of the Privy Council in Britain acted as the highest court for Nigeria. As Obilade (1979, 123) noted, court decisions of the Privy Council given before the abolition of appeals to the Council are still binding on Nigerian courts, which means that a Nigerian court must follow them. Park (1963, 62-63) argued that contemporary decisions of the British House of Lords are also binding on Nigerian courts as they *'present the conclusive expositions of English law and that being so it will not be open to the Nigerian courts to depart from them'*. This view has been put into question by Obilade (1979, 134).[135] While it is not entirely clear to what extent the Nigerian legal system is still embedded into the English Common Law, the legal system is firmly based on the legal principles of the English Common Law.

In practice, however, it is unclear how far the Nigerian legal system has deviated from the English Common Law doctrine. Allott (1960, 24-25) argued that practically all African legal systems allow for some modification of English law. In addition to the inherent possibility of judges modifying legal rules, colonial and post-colonial statute law in Africa contained express provisions, which allowed for substantial changes in the law applied.[136] The Nigerian Constitution 1979, for instance, was interpreted by courts as having abolished the distinction between the right to sue under so-called 'public' and 'private nuisance' in Nigeria, a distinction which persists in England.[137] More important than statute law, as Allott (1960, 24-27) showed,

---

[135] Obilade (1979, 134) argued that *'no English court forms part of any Nigerian court hierarchy. Therefore, no Nigerian court is bound by a decision of any English Court under the doctrine'*. Obilade (1979, 134-135) concluded that decisions of English courts can only have a persuasive authority on Nigerian courts, that means, a Nigerian court can decide whether to follow an English precedent or not. In any case, the Nigerian legal profession and the judiciary continue, to a large extent, to accept English court precedents as guiding principles in their work. Nigerian legal textbooks also continue to rely on many English rather than Nigerian court cases. The use of English court precedents depends on the area of law. In some areas of law, English court precedents are used almost exclusively. For instance, a textbook on tort law by Kodilinye (1982, 190-194) cited English court cases on the issue of trespass to chattels 21 times, while it cited Nigerian court cases only twice.

[136] Article 17 of the Tanganyika Order in Council, for example, referred to by Allott (1960, 22), stated that *'the said common law, doctrines of equity and statutes of general application shall be in force in the territory... subject to such qualifications as local circumstances may render necessary'*.

[137] Karibi-Whyte, J.S.C. pronounced: *'The restriction imposed at common law on the right of action in public nuisance is inconsistent with the provisions of section 6(6)(b) of the Constitution, 1979 and to that extent is void.'*. Per Karibi-Whyte, J.S.C. in *Adediran v. Interland Transport* (1991) 9

African judges had a great scope to modify English law in the African context. Therefore, we do not know to what extent Nigerian law can still be called English Common Law.

While Nigerian judges observe English court judgments made in the past, they also rely heavily on Nigerian judicial precedents. To a large extent, the application of English Common Law and the doctrines of equity in Nigeria ties judicial decisions to the pattern of legal development in England. Nevertheless, as in most other post-colonial states in Africa, Nigerian judges may reject an objectionable rule of English law outright or adapt or modify the objectionable rule, which can lead to considerable modification of English precedents (Allott 1960, 24). Nigerian judges often cite Nigerian precedents rather than English ones even if the same legal rule applies. In the case *Shell v. Farah*[138], for instance, the judge of the Court of Appeal cited 36 Nigerian court cases and only 12 foreign cases. A number of procedural practices also differ. For instance, Nigerian judges have on some occasions physically visited the site of a disputed subject matter in a civil court case, a practice uncommon in England. Most important of all, Nigerian precedents sometimes apply somewhat different legal rules from English ones. The greatest difference between Nigerian judicial precedents and the English Common Law is that Nigerian courts make limited use of Nigerian customary law, which stems from the need to adapt English law to the actual reality of Nigerian society. In referring to Africa in general, Allott (1960, 25) argued that it would indeed be impossible to leave English law unadapted in the face of different social norms and customs in Africa.[139] Like property law in several other West African countries, Nigerian property law, for example, is quite different from English law as far as land ownership is concerned, which finds an expression in Nigerian court precedents. As Daniels (1964, 377-378) pointed out, transactions in land may be governed either by the received English law or by the appropriate customary law.[140] As shown in the sections on land law below (sections 3.5. and 3.6.), Nigerian court precedents continue to recognise the existence of communal and family land ownership, which exists under Nigerian customary law, but not under the English Common Law.

NWLR (Pt. 214) 155 at page 180. Karibi-Whyte, J.S.C. further stated: *'Having held that in the institution of actions, the distinction between public and private nuisance in this country has been abolished by the Constitution 1979, the exercise of the right of action for nuisance is no longer based on or determined by the distinction.* Per Karibi-Whyte, J.S.C. at page 182. In other words, the 1979 Constitution clearly abolished the common law distinction between public and private nuisance as far as the right to institute actions in nuisance before Nigerian courts is concerned.

[138] (1995) 3 NWLR (Pt. 382) 148.

[139] Writing on the local modification of colonial law in Africa, Allott (1960, 25) concluded:

'The most important single factor requiring the adaptation of English law is the existence of local African populations, to whom the English law is to be applied. The African populations are living under their own forms of society, having their own customs, own religion, beliefs, social organisation, patterns of marriage and divorce, land law, etc. How can English law be applied to them unadapted?'.

[140] English law is usually applied *'where English conveyancing forms have been used to transfer land'* (Daniels 1964, 377). On the other hand, land originally held under customary law is not necessarily converted to land held under English law as a result of subsequent transactions. In a number of West African court cases under colonial rule, it was held that customary law applied to a transaction, although a mortgage was executed in accordance with English law (Daniels 1964, 377-378).

Irrespective of the degree to which the Nigerian legal system has deviated from the traditional English Common Law, the introduction of the Common Law in Africa has often been regarded by scholars and administrators as inherently conducive to a country's economic development.[141] Nigerian legal scholars have often supported the retention of British colonial law (as opposed to a re-enaction of African customary law) after the country's independence from Britain partly because of its perceived benefits to business. T.O. Elias (1989, 5), Nigeria's most eminent legal scholar to-date and former Chief Justice of Nigeria, argued that the main function of jurisprudence in a developing society was indeed *'to promote economic growth and social well-being'*. From the perspective of oil companies and other private enterprises, the legal continuity ensured through English Common Law, particularly English commercial law, was considered the best method of promoting economic growth as African customary law was considered incapable of providing a coherent framework for commercial transactions. Said A.A. Schiller: *It is generally recognised that the indigenous systems of law in Africa are deficient in the areas of commerce, finance and social welfare. Further, the indigenous law is considered inadequate in the field of obligations and property* (quoted in Seidman 1968, 31). English common law, supplemented by statute law such as petroleum legislation, has therefore continued to guide the economic decisions of oil companies. From the perspective of oil companies, the introduction of English law into Nigeria was beneficial as companies require a stable legal framework in order to make investments with some degree of security. Furthermore, in legal disputes with village communities, oil companies are able to use the legal principles of Common Law with which company lawyers are familiar rather than customary laws. The introduction of English law into Nigeria has therefore ultimately been to the advantage of oil companies.

---

[141] This position is generally supported by law & economics theorists such as Richard Posner. In general terms, Posner (1986) argued that the Common Law is economically efficient. Posner (1986, 229-230) stated that the Common Law doctrines *'form a system for inducing people to behave efficiently, not only in explicit markets but across the whole range of social interactions'*. This 'efficiency theory of the Common Law' does not imply that every Common Law rule is inherently efficient. Posner (1986, 21), for instance, merely suggests that the *'Common Law is best (not perfectly) explained as a system for maximising the wealth of society'*. According to Posner (1986, 230), one example of an efficient Common Law rule is the doctrine of the 'eminent domain', which allows private companies to compulsorily obtain private property for the sake of economic development. While the doctrine limits private property rights, Posner (1986, 230) argued that it allows a value-maximising exchange.

In the African context, both radical and liberal scholars have agreed that the introduction of the Common Law was conducive to capitalist development. The role of law in Africa's socio-economic change has been directly addressed by several scholarly studies (Seidman 1968; Ghai *et al.* 1987). According to radical scholars such as those in the edited work of Ghai *et al.* (1987), received colonial law was indeed seen as a precondition for capitalist development in Africa as it served to integrate peripheral areas into the world economy. According to more moderate scholars such as Allott *et al.* (1969, 11), *'legal development does not keep exactly in step with socio-economic development; and that more general development itself is not precisely phased in all its parts'*. However, judge-made law as well as statute law is likely to keep law in some accord with socio-economic developments. The problem Allott *et al.* faced was that of a time factor: when does the judicial or popular disregard of a traditional rule mean that the rule is abrogated and loses the force of law? Individual Kipsingis in Kenya, for example, began to enclose and appropriate community grazing lands, which raises the question at what point in time does what was originally a flagrant disregard of established rights become an approved method of acquiring property? Allott *et al.* (1969, 11-12) concluded that there is generally a time-lag between social and legal evolution.

3.4. Post-colonial Law

The basic framework of colonial law has largely remained in place in African post-colonial states, as Jacques Vanderlinden (1983, 95) argued. According to Vanderlinden (1983, 95), most legal modifications have been undertaken in the area of public law. Most importantly, as Vanderlinden (1983, 97) noted, the formal legal structures became in theory accessible to all citizens, while hitherto they had merely been accessible to non-Africans and a small group of 'Westernised' Africans. In practice, however, the formal legal system has only been opened to the 'Westernised' parts of the population, mostly in urban areas, while the rural majority continued to rely more on customary law and its institutions (Vanderlinden 1983, 97). The main consequence for the oil industry was that members of village communities in oil producing areas were given the opportunity to use the courts, if only in theory, to freely sue the oil companies.

In the former British colonies in Africa, as Allott (1965, 222) argued, the most striking changes to the legal system occurred with regards to the unification of the court systems, which involved four main changes. First, the appellate court structure was integrated by permitting appeals from lower, formerly 'native', courts to the superior courts. Second, the practice and procedure of the formerly 'native' courts was anglicised and standardised, by applying the procedure of the general, formerly British, law courts. Third, the laws administered by the courts were harmonised by applying statutory law in the local courts and customary law in the general law courts. Fourth, the jurisdiction of local courts was extended to non-Africans in some places (Allott 1965, 222).

While the Common Law has remained the basis of the formal-legal structure in Nigeria, the post-colonial Nigerian state introduced a multitude of statutes. Nigerian statute law comprises statutes and subsidiary legislation, both at the federal and the state level. From the beginning of military rule in 1966, the legislative powers of the federal government were gradually expanded at the expense of state governments. Most of the important matters of government are within the Exclusive Legislative List established by the 1979 Constitution. States may only legislate on matters not on the Exclusive List. Any state laws may be declared inconsistent with the Nigerian Constitution. The Exclusive Legislative List includes *'mines and minerals, including oil fields, oil mining, geological surveys and natural gas'*.[142] This means that the federal government has the exclusive right to legislate on any issues related to the oil industry. The federal government and state governments sometimes delegate power to government officials, departments or other public authority to make subsidiary laws. These are regulations and orders to supplement the so-called primary legislation or statutes. For instance, the federal government established the Petroleum Act 1969 which can be considered to be primary legislation, while the minister responsible for petroleum affairs established the Petroleum (Drilling and Production) Regulations 1969 which can be considered to be subsidiary legislation. The Petroleum Act

---

[142] Constitution of the Federal Republic of Nigeria 1979, schedule 2, part I, Exclusive Legislative List, item 37.

established a general legal framework for oil companies, while the Regulations established specific legal provisions for oil operations.

In general, if judged on evidence from secondary sources, the evolution of Nigeria's post-colonial law, both statute law and judicial precedents, does not appear to support the view that the Common Law is inherently beneficial to economic development.[143] First, the existence of the rentier state meant that the formulation of legal rules did not follow a completely nationalist agenda. By implication, it could be expected that legal rules were on occasion beneficial to the ruling elite and the oil companies at the expense of economic development in Nigerian society as a whole (see chapter 2). Second, the Common Law was generally biased in favour of corporate interests.[144] Most important of all, the introduction of Common Law in Nigeria put commercial interests expressed in Common Law doctrines above the rules of Nigeria's customary law. This bias meant, for instance, that the government expropriated the land of village communities for the benefit of foreign oil companies at an inadequately low cost (as will be shown in greater detail in sections 3.5. and 3.6. on land law below). This expropriation benefited the oil companies at the expense of village communities.[145]

The example of environmental law and the Federal Environmental Protection Agency (FEPA) is indicative of the inherent contradictions in the making of post-colonial law (as shown in greater detail in the section on environmental law below). Before the establishment of the FEPA, the Common Law doctrines proved largely insufficient to curb environmental pollution by oil companies. This was despite the fact that village communities in the oil producing areas were adversely affected by oil operations without receiving adequate compensation from oil companies. The formation and the continuing existence of the FEPA were the result of a nationalist agenda in policy-making and of popular pressures at the micro-level. However, the non-enforcement of FEPA rules in the oil industry could be seen partly as a result of an

---

[143] By implication, the evolution of post-colonial law in Nigeria puts into question Posner's view that the Common Law is economically efficient (compare footnote 141).

[144] In general terms, some scholars in the field of the sociology of law would argue that law usually serves as a vehicle of domination by the ruling classes. As a prototypical exponent of this view, Alan Hunt (1993, 21) argued that *'law plays an important part in sustaining the domination of the ruling class'*. Hunt distinguished between coercive and ideological domination. Coercive domination refers to the organised power of the state (including courts, the prison system and the police) which may be used to coerce individuals or groups to behave in a certain manner. According to Hunt, the main application of coercion is to protect the 'general conditions' of the capitalist order, above all, to protect and reinforce capitalist property relations. Ideological domination refers to activities and processes whereby (in Hunt's words) *'the assent of the existing social order is produced and mobilised'* (Hunt 1993, 25). Law is said to transmit ideological attitudes and values prevalent in society. These attitudes and values in turn reinforce and legitimise the existing social order. Coercive and ideological domination are closely related. For instance, the coercion of an offender reinforces the general values and attitudes associated with the existence of private property in society as a whole. As shown in this chapter, evidence on both substantive law and the structural character of the legal system provides substantial support for the view that Nigerian law is a vehicle of domination for the ruling elite. The elite's economic well-being is in turn dependent on the corporate interests of foreign oil companies. It could be argued that the elite is thus inevitably compelled to protect those corporate interests by using law or other means available.

[145] By implication, in Nigeria, the doctrine of the 'eminent domain', mentioned by Richard Posner as an efficiency maximising device, benefited the ruling elite and the oil companies at the expense of Nigerian society as a whole (compare footnotes 141 and 143).

alliance between the Nigerian elite and the foreign oil companies. This may help to explain why environmental rules were usually not properly enforced, although Nigeria as a whole was losing billions of dollars in revenues due to financial losses from gas flaring and oil spills. The case of Nigerian environmental law and the FEPA, therefore, questions the view that the Common Law is inherently conducive to economic development.

While the economic advantages of the Common Law are questionable in the Nigerian context, the post-colonial legal system confirmed the applicability of Common Law to Nigeria as opposed to the re-introduction of customary law. As previously argued, the displacement of customary rules in higher courts and the introduction of English law ultimately prejudiced the legal system in favour of oil companies and against the community litigants.

Until today, the legal rules of both colonial and post-colonial law have continued to determine what is possible in court cases between oil companies and village communities. In the context of oil operations, the most relevant substantive rules are statutory. They include statutes on land, petroleum matters and the environment, which we examine in some detail below. Of those three types of statutes, Nigerian land legislation is the oldest.

3.5. Customary Land Rights and Land Acquisition Before 1978

Land acquisition is a precondition for oil operations since crude oil is located under the earth's surface. While land legislation determines the legal principles of land acquisition for economic activities, land allocation in village communities continues to be regulated by customary land rights. Oil companies are legally bound to pay monetary compensation for land acquisition, so they are forced to deal with customary landowners and/or their tenants in the course of acquiring land.

From the point of view of oil companies, proof of land ownership can be difficult in Nigeria's rural areas as land is usually held according to local unwritten customary laws. These customary laws differ from ethnic group to ethnic group and from village to village, although customary land rights in Nigeria share a number of common principles. Above all, the Western concept of 'ownership' is in itself foreign to Nigerian customary law and was introduced into Nigeria under British rule.[146] Customary law distinguishes, nevertheless, between some sort of permanent land ownership and mere possession of land. In the case *Shell-BP v. Abedi*[147] in 1974, the plaintiffs sued Shell-BP for having damaged a piece of land previously cultivated by themselves. The Abadiama people claimed that they were the land owners. The trial judge established that the plaintiffs were *'in actual occupation of the land'* but were not *'de jure owners of the land'*.[148] In other words, they were merely customary tenants, while the people of Gbekebor were the owners. The plaintiffs would have won

---

[146] On problems of terminology, see, e.g., James (1973, chapter 2).

[147] (1974) 1 All NLR 1.

[148] Quoted per Fatayi-Williams, J.S.C. at page 11.

compensation, if they had pleaded possession of the land rather than ownership and if they had successfully provided proof of a tenancy agreement. They lost the case on appeal because the basis of their claim was as owners of the land so they could not claim compensation as customary tenants. The appeal judge said that '*A de facto possession of land gives right to retain the possession and to undisturbed possession of it as against all wrong doers. It is not, however, sufficient against the lawful owner*'.[149] Although one must remember that customary rights may sometimes be ambiguous, the Abedi case indicates that customary law distinguishes between ownership and mere possession of land and that land can be leased to a tenant.

The nature of ownership under customary law is different from Western concepts of ownership. In the West, ownership relates to a named individual or a group of individuals, who can administer, rent out or sell a particular plot of land. In Nigeria, on the most basic level, the land is traditionally held by village communities or families, not by individuals. A useful starting point is the court judgment in *Tijani v. Secretary of Southern Nigeria*[150] of the early 1920s, in which Viscount Haldane said:

> The next fact which it is important to bear in mind in order to understand the native land law is that the notion of individual ownership is quite foreign to native ideas. Land belongs to the community, the village or the family, never to the individual. All the members of the community, the village or family have an equal right to the land, but in every case the Chief or Headman of the community or village, or head of the family, has charge of the land, and in the loose mode of speech is sometimes called the owner. He is to some extent in the position of a trustee, and as such holds the land for the use of the community or family. He has control of it, and any member who wants a piece of it to cultivate or build upon, goes to him for it. But the land still remains the property of the community or family. He cannot make any important disposition of the land without consulting the elders of the community or family, and their consent must in all cases be given before a grant can be made to a stranger (quoted in Elias 1971, 72).

In line with the above judgment, this study makes the distinction between communal, family and individual land.[151] Communal land belongs to all the members of the village community. By customary law, each member of the community is entitled to acquire a portion of land, which is usually used for agricultural purposes. Members who seek grants of communal land must approach the chief who decides on their applications. The Chief or Headman is not an owner of communal land but merely a quasi trustee. The most important prerogative of the chief is distribution of land, in particular virgin land. Grants of land are usually made subject to conditions which may vary according to ethnic group or village and relate to the length and form of grant. For instance, in Ebiama, an Ijaw village, parcels of land were held indefinitely

---

[149] Per Fatayi-Williams, J.S.C. at page 17.

[150] (1923), 4 N.L.R. 18.

[151] Haldane's statement that land never belongs to the individual under customary law has been criticised by scholars. Tobi (1992, 46) and James (1973, 22) pointed out that individual ownership of land was known to customary law even before the arrival of the British in Nigeria.

as long as they were farmed, while in some other Ijaw communities land was usually re-distributed among its members every year. In the same manner, the laws of succession vary according to ethnic group and village.[152] Land may have to be returned to the community after a period of time depending on local customary law such as after one farming season or after the death of the occupiers. When land is returned to the community, it may be re-allocated once again. The chief has the right to revoke a grant of land and to evict the occupier under certain circumstances, in which case the land is returned to the community.[153] In any land conflicts involving communal land, the chief legally represents the community to the outside world.[154] However, a chief's powers as a trustee are limited. He cannot sell communal land without the consent of the community members. Any money collected by the chief on behalf of communal land must be shared within the community.

Real world forms of ownership, as opposed to the world of legal categories, may be even more complex. Leis (1972, 16) described an Ijaw village in the Niger Delta where most of the farm land and fishing sites are owned by sections and sub-sections of the village rather than by the village as a whole. But in those cases one can also speak of communal land.

Family property in Nigeria is distinct from communal property and requires an understanding of the distinction between a family and a community. On the most basic level, a family is understood here to be a kinship group of people who trace descent from the same ancestor, who usually live together and share the economic benefits of the same area of land.[155] The smallest family can be composed of only a man, his wife or wives and their children, but a family can have many more members related through marriage, kinship or adoption. The composition of a family and the rights to family land are determined by local custom and can vary considerably according to ethnic group and community, but a family is always a kinship group. In contrast, a village community is a settlement inhabited by families linked by common economic, cultural and historic relationships, not necessarily close kinship.[156] A chief or a headman is a leader within a community, while a family head exercises family rights within the family.

Communal land can become family land through allotment by the chief. This means that the communal land is partitioned and allotted to a family. It is henceforth controlled by the family. An allotment is different from the mere allocation of communal land to a family for cultivation because it means permanent transfer of

---

[152] On general laws of succession in Nigeria, see, e.g. Okoro (1966).

[153] On the right of revocation and eviction, see Elias (1971, 87-96).

[154] On the chief's representative status, see Elias (1971, 84-86).

[155] In everyday speech, the word 'family' usually refers to a group of people linked together by kinship, irrespective of whether or not they live together. Since one could go a long way back in tracing descent, the common sense meaning of the word 'family' cannot form the basis of any sociological inquiry. In this study, the word 'family' only refers to persons who are linked by close kinship bonds, live together and typically engage in common economic activities. On the basic concepts of rural sociology in general, see Galeski (1972).

[156] The oral history of Nigerian villages sometimes traces the community's distant origins from a common ancestor, but its value is largely symbolic.

ownership.[157] In the case of allocation, land is allocated to a family for a period of time after which it is returned to the community for re-allocation. However, family heads sometimes claim allocated plots as family land after a few generations, especially when no one in the community can remember the original land allocation (James 1973, 56). In effect, as James (1973, 46) argued, with increased population pressures and allotment of communal land to families, there has been a gradual shift from communal to family land holdings in Nigeria.

The family head, usually the oldest male member of the family, is in charge of distributing family land. He allocates plots to family members and others for cultivation, collects the rents and represents the land in disputes with outsiders. The rights of a family head over family land are much the same as that of a chief in charge of communal land (Elias 1971, 107). However, if the entire family dies out or if the family land is abandoned, the land holdings are returned to the community and may be re-allocated once again.

While communal and family ownership has survived in Nigeria, there has been an increase in individual land holdings. Individual land ownership has become common in urban areas, particularly in Lagos (James 1973, 22).[158] The shift towards individual land holdings is attributed to a number of factors including the commercial exploitation of land property, the influence of English legal concepts of individual ownership and the shortage of land due to population growth (e.g. Meek 1957, 131-136; Mbakwe 1987). Collective land rights have, nevertheless, continued to co-exist with individual land rights until today, particularly in rural areas.

The colonial administrators recognised the existence of collective land ownership in Nigeria, even though they generally held that a change towards Western-style individual land rights was both inevitable and beneficial to Nigerians.[159] Since no white British settlers in Nigeria ran large-scale plantations, in contrast to Eastern Africa, the British colonialists largely refrained from expropriating the land of the Niger Delta communities. However, colonial mining legislation vested the ownership of natural resources such as oil in the colonial state. The Minerals Ordinance 1916 provided that *'The entire property and control of all minerals, and mineral oils in, under or upon any lands in Nigeria, and of all rivers, streams and watercourses throughout Nigeria, is and shall be vested in the Crown'*.[160] Following Nigeria's independence, oil rights remained vested in the state under section 1 of the Petroleum Act 1969.

---

[157] Elias (1971, 84) used the term 'partition of land' rather than allotment. However, the use of different definitions should not obscure the issues. Whether one speaks of partition, allotment or gift, the meaning signifies permanent rather than temporary transfer of ownership.

[158] As early as 1948, it was estimated that roughly half of the Ikeja area (part of Lagos today) belonged to individual owners (Meek 1957, 136).

[159] Frederick Lugard, Nigeria's first Governor in the period 1914-1919, stated that *'conceptions as to the tenure of land are subject to a steady evolution, side by side with the evolution of social progress, from the most primitive stages to the organisation of the modern state'*. He continued: *'These processes of natural evolution, leading up to individual ownership, may, I believe, be traced in every civilisation known to history'* (Lugard 1965, 280-281).

[160] Section 3(1).

Oil rights, however, were distinct from land ownership. Oil companies could only get access to oil resources by applying to the government, not the local land owner, for a licence (see chapter 2). In return, the oil company paid rents and royalties to the government. Once an oil company obtained an oil licence from the government, it had to separately negotiate with the village community or families over the sale or the lease of specific pieces of land. The government therefore reserved for itself the sole right to dispose of oil resources, while the land itself was left in the hands of the local people, a distinction which largely survived until 1978.

Oil companies encountered problems in dealing with collective land rights because the chiefs as protectors of the tribal heritage were sometimes unwilling to sell or allocate communal land to outsiders. Europeans had already encountered the problem in the pre-colonial era when collective land holding hindered European penetration of the African interior. The Castle of Sao Jorge di Msia, the most important Portuguese base in pre-colonial West Africa, was accordingly built not on purchased but on leased land because the local ruler opposed the sale of land (Dike 1956). Since land owners were often reluctant to sell or allocate land to outsiders, including land for oil operations and may have taken an uncompromising stance in negotiations with oil companies over compensation, the government in Nigeria gradually introduced specific legislation in order to compulsorily acquire land for economic development.

Nonetheless, until the promulgation of the Land Use Act 1978, the government was not legally empowered to expropriate land for the private needs of oil companies. It was only empowered to expropriate land for public purposes by the Public Lands Ordinance 1876, later re-enacted as Public Lands Acquisition Act 1917, and other similar statutes. In cases of land acquisition, compensation was to be paid to the owners (Olawoye 1982, 15-16). Despite the legal limitations, the government had often compulsorily acquired land for oil companies before 1978 under the so-called power of 'eminent domain', which gave it the power to seize private property for public use. Oil operations were generally considered by the government to serve the 'public interest'. Both the Oil Pipelines Act 1956 and the Petroleum Act 1969 specifically provided for powers of 'eminent domain' as long as compensation was paid to the land owners.[161]

In the court case *Nzekwu v. Attorney-General East-Central State*[162], for example, the Ogbo family sued the government for compulsory acquisition of their land. According to the government representatives, the land acquisition was intended for the 'economic development' of the area. The Ogbo family had previously leased parcels of land to oil companies. Hence, it must be assumed that oil companies would have been amongst the beneficiaries of the government's land acquisition. From the perspective of the oil companies, one of the advantages of compulsory land acquisition is that oil operations can proceed notwithstanding the conflicting claims of different land owners. The Nzekwu case exemplifies this point. At the time of public acquisition, ownership of the land was disputed between the people of Onitsha and the people of Obosi. Christian Onyedike, chartered surveyor and government witness at the trial, said that '*it was a big risk for an investor to invest his money on it* [the land]

---

[161] Oil Pipelines Act 1956, sections 19(4) and (5); Petroleum Regulations, section 17(1)(c).

[162] (1972) All NLR 543.

for fear that if his vendor lost his claim he would lose his money'. The compulsory land acquisition hence lowered the risk for private investors. Interestingly, in the Nzekwu case, the plaintiffs did not refuse to deal with the oil companies or the government but demanded higher compensation than they were actually offered. They did not attempt to hinder economic development but tried merely to benefit from it.

The above case and similar ones exemplify that land owners did not necessarily challenge compulsory land acquisition for oil operations, but were often more concerned with the quantum of compensation owed to them.[163] Until 1978, however, the land owners were able to challenge compulsory acquisition by suing the government, even though it is unclear whether many owners took this course of action. An important case was *Ereku v. the Military Governor of Mid-Western State*[164], in which the Itsekiri Communal Land Trustees and other community representatives sued the government for expropriation of land on behalf of McDermott Overseas, an oil company sub-contractor. In that case, McDermott attempted to acquire approximately 50 acres of land near Igbudu in the then Warri Division of the Delta province in the Mid-Western State of Nigeria for the company's operations. In April 1966, the government published an acquisition notice declaring that the land had been acquired for public purposes under the Public Lands Acquisition Law of Western Nigeria 1959. Subsequently, the government granted a lease for 99 years to McDermott. The plaintiffs sued the government seeking a declaration that the notice of acquisition was invalid and seeking an order setting aside the compulsory acquisition. They lost in the first instance, but won the case on appeal to the Supreme Court. The lawyers representing the government had argued that the oil company benefited the public not least because it *'employs a large number of Nigerians'*. The court was unmoved by those arguments and declared that the government was not empowered to acquire land for McDermott even though the court found that the company had the same objectives as the government and served the Nigerian public. It held that the acquisition was on behalf of a private company and not the government. T.O. Elias, Chief Justice of Nigeria, accordingly allowed the appeal and declared the notice of acquisition *'unconstitutional, ultra vires and void'*.[165]

The Supreme Court went even further declaring that the Public Lands Acquisition Law (Amendment) Edict 1972, of Mid-Western State, was invalid. The Edict was specifically introduced by the government of the Mid-Western State in order to allow expropriation of land on behalf of private companies. The Edict allowed compulsory land acquisition *'required by any company or industrialist for industrial purposes'*, which broadened the meaning of *'public purpose'*. The Supreme Court declared that the Edict was *'unconstitutional, ultra vires and void'*.[166]

---

[163] In the case *Aghenghen v. Waghoreghor* (1974) All NLR 74, two communities were engaged in a dispute concerning a compensation payment for land compulsorily acquired for Shell-BP's oil operations. Another example is the case *Okwuosa v. Adizua* (1977) 1 IMSLR 217, which involved a dispute over the compensation payment for land compulsorily acquired for Agip's oil operations.

[164] (1974) 10 S.C. 59.

[165] Per Elias, C.J.N. at page 74.

[166] Per Elias, C.J.N. at pages 74-75.

The above case reveals some of the potential legal difficulties that oil companies could encounter in acquiring land for economic development before 1978. The situation changed dramatically with the promulgation of the Land Use Act 1978.

3.6. Land Use Act

The Land Use Act 1978 vested the ownership of all land within a state in the state governor. The most important provision of the Act read:

> Subject to the provisions of this Decree, all land comprised in the territory of each State in the Federation are hereby vested in the Military Governor of that State and such land shall be held in trust and administered for the use and common benefit of all Nigerians in accordance with the provisions of this Decree.[167]

The Act makes explicit references to the oil industry. In particular, section 28 stipulates that the military governor can revoke a right of occupancy for 'overriding public interests', which include the 'requirement of the land for mining purposes or oil pipelines or for any purpose connected therewith'.[168] These provisions empowered the governor to use any land holdings in Nigeria for oil operations. In theory, a governor could legally acquire the entire state territory and then assign it to a single company. In practice, the procedure for acquiring land for oil operations did not change significantly. Before and after 1978, an oil company had to acquire an oil licence for a given area. Subsequently, the company approached the State Ministry of Lands in order to work out the conditions for entry into the land in question and the compensation to be paid to communities (Ajomo 1982, 339). In this respect, little changed for the oil companies.

However, there have been major changes concerning village communities following the Land Use Act 1978. First, a community no longer has the right to question the entry of an oil company onto its communal land. The governor can acquire any land on behalf of private or public oil companies. The precedent established in *Ereku v. the Military Governor of Mid-Western State*[169] no longer applies. Second, compensation for land must be paid to the governor and not to the community as before. A distinction is made between compensation for land and compensation for improvements to land. Until 1978, oil companies either paid annual rent to the land owners for the use of their land or purchased a plot of land. In addition, they were legally bound to make compensation payments for any improvements to the land such as destroyed buildings and crops. Since 1978, oil companies have only paid compensation for improvements to the said land (Omotola 1980, 38-39). In practice, a community only receives a single payment, if any, from the oil company when something has been destroyed. Third, according to the Land Use Act, no court has the jurisdiction to inquire into any question concerning the adequacy of compensation paid to land owners (Ekemike 1978, 16).

---

[167] Section 1.

[168] Sections 28(1), (2c) and (3b).

[169] (1974) 10 S.C. 59.

From the perspective of the oil companies, the Land Use Act brought advantages and disadvantages. Perhaps the main advantage is that community conflicts or prolonged negotiations over land can no longer delay land acquisition for oil operations. Previously, conflicts over land could delay oil operations. For instance, in the case *Ereku v. the Military Governor of Mid-Western State*[170] described earlier, McDermott's operations were delayed by a local dispute with the Itsekiri Communal Land Trustees. Compulsory land acquisition by the government renders the process of acquiring land quicker and more efficient for the oil companies. A key disadvantage of the Land Use Act for oil companies is the payment of rent to the governor rather than to the actual land owners. Since the land owners receive inadequate compensation, they may become more aggrieved by oil operations. It could be more beneficial for an oil company to pay compensation to the actual land owners rather than to the governor in order to prevent any potential dissatisfaction with oil operations within the community (chapter 5 discusses the link between such dissatisfaction and community protests against oil companies, which can disrupt oil operations).

On the whole, the advantages to oil companies may have outweighed the disadvantages. The Land Use Act has allowed the government and oil companies to obtain land for economic development, which was one of the key objectives of the Act. Brigadier Musa Ya'Ardua said at the inauguration of the Land Use Panel in 1977 that *'Both the Anti-Inflationary Task Force and the Rent Panel Reports identified land as one of the major bottlenecks to development efforts in the country'* (quoted in Olawoye 1982, 14). By implication, the 1978 Act eliminated this bottleneck.[171]

In terms of customary law, the Act has changed little. Admittedly, there has been confusion among lawyers as to the true meaning of the Act.[172] In particular, according to the Act, a community, family or individual no longer owns the land but only has a mere right of occupancy. Despite the promulgation of the Land Use Act and despite growing pressures on land, there is strong evidence that land owners' attitudes to land have not markedly changed and collective land rights persist in Nigeria's rural areas.[173]

---

[170] (1974) 10 S.C. 59.

[171] Even though the Act is beneficial to oil company interests, there are no indications that oil companies lobbied for a change in Nigeria's land use legislation. Said Olisa Agbakoba, a prominent Nigerian lawyer:

> *Clearly, the reason behind the Land Use Act was to acquire land for what the government considered the economic development of Nigeria. Because of customary rights, land was not readily available for oil exploration or other activity. So, clearly, the Act benefits the oil companies, but one cannot say that there is a link between oil company activities and the Act* (Personal interview with Olisa Agbakoba, Lagos, February 1997).

[172] Among other things, there has been a long standing argument between lawyers over whether the Land Use Act amounts to the nationalisation of land in Nigeria by the state. See, e.g. Umezulike (1986).

[173] For instance, Oshio (1990, 91) argued that *'the institution of family property with its incidents under customary law largely survive the Land Use Act, 1978'* despite several court judgments to the contrary. On the impact of the Act on customary systems of tenure, see e.g. Omotola (1980, chapter 2). According to Omotola (1982, 40), *'the land struggle continues as if the Act had not come into effect'*.

Interesting evidence on land ownership is provided by a survey conducted by Winston Bell-Gam (1990) in the Bonny local government area.[174] The survey is of interest to the present study because Bonny Island has served as the site of Shell's crude oil export terminal for several decades (SPDC 1995a). According to the survey, in the Bonny area, 53.8% of the land used for house construction was virgin land allocated by the local chief and 26.7% was land inherited by the present owner. Only 6.9% of the land was purchased by the owner (Bell-Gam 1990, 62). In some places, no land purchases took place whatsoever such as in the village of Finima. These results are significant since the area around Bonny experienced a steady growth in population and was heavily affected by oil company operations, so one could expect a dynamic market for land property to have developed. More importantly, the results are significant since collective land rights have survived not only in remote villages but also in towns such as in Bonny Town where land for house construction could be expected to be more scarce than in villages.[175]

In general, the survey of Bonny Island indicates that individuals as well as families in Nigeria continue to acquire land through allocation by the chief, inheritance or purchase, not through a grant by the state governor. By implication, the land owner

---

[174] Bell-Gam was not interested in ownership rights as such, but the findings on ownership were incidental to the survey. The survey investigated the nature of land use with regards to land obtained for house construction, not on land in general. Nonetheless, since Bonny Island is largely made up of non-farming communities and is not industrialised, land is mainly required for house construction. Bell-Gam's evidence on house construction can hence provide a fair indication of the form of ownership rights. In the course of the survey, Bell-Gam asked the question 'how was land obtained for this house?'. The respondents' replies included land allocation by the chief, inheritance and purchase. It is assumed here that land allocated by the chief indicates communal ownership. Inherited land may be both family and individually owned, so it is a less reliable indicator of ownership structures.

[175] **Table:** Results of a Survey in Bonny on the Question 'How was land obtained for this house?'

Place (estimated population)	Bonny (18,075)	Opobo (23,580)	Okrika (26,425)	Finima (2,760)	Queenstown (2,379)	Oloma/ Ayaminima (946)
1. Virgin land allocated by local chief	77.88%	28.90%	37.75%	54.72%	51.52%	56.41%
2. Site of former house inherited by present owner	5.76%	50.78%	34.69%	45.28%	36.36%	43.59%
3. Site of former house obtained by arrangement with former owners	3.84%	12.50%	3.06%	-	6.06%	-
4. Virgin land purchased by present owner	11.54%	0.78%	7.14%	-	3.03%	-
5. Site of former house purchased by present owner	-	1.56%	1.02%	-	3.03%	-
6. Any other (specify)	-	-	-	-	-	-
7. Don't know	1.04%	6.25%	2.04%	-	-	-
8. No response	-	-	14.28%	-	-	-

Source: Bell-Gam (1990, 96, 146, 171, 183, 189, 199 and 205).

can still expect to enjoy his or her land rights until the government or an oil company becomes interested in a particular piece of land. In that case, land can be compulsorily acquired while the owners receive no compensation for the land.

The Land Use Act remains the most significant piece of legislation on land issues in Nigeria to-date. The provisions of the Land Use Act were valid from 1978 onwards and did not apply to events before 1978. In spite of this, oil company lawyers unsuccessfully attempted to use the Act in order to discharge of their obligations to village communities for operations before 1978. In the case *Adomba v. Odiesi*[176], two families were involved in a dispute over who should receive a compensation payment from Agip. Agip had entered communal land near Oloibiri in Rivers State in 1977, a year before the Land Use Act was promulgated. In court, Agip as the second defendant claimed that '*the plaintiffs had no right to institute the claim because of the Land Use Decree*' as they allegedly failed to fulfil certain requirements of the Act. The judge rightly considered Agip's statement to be irrelevant. Even though the court judgment was made in 1980, Agip had to pay compensation for the land because the company entered the land before 1978. The Adomba case suggests that the year 1978 was a clear-cut dividing line in terms of compensation for oil company land acquisition in Nigeria. From 1978 onwards, village communities enjoyed fewer land rights in relation to oil companies.

To sum up, the Land Use Act allowed oil companies to gain easier access to the land and to the oil resources through the government. Companies were no longer obliged to negotiate over the sale or allocation of land with the customary land owners, albeit they were still required to pay compensation for destroyed crops and other improvements to land. As a consequence, companies had a lesser economic incentive to investigate the local patterns of land ownership, which can partly explain the carelessness with which oil companies deal with village communities (this will be explained in some detail in chapter 5). At the same time, the Land Use Act failed to safeguard the rights of customary land owners, despite the recommendations made to the government by the Land Use Panel in 1977.[177] In this sense, the Nigerian land legislation after 1978 was biased in favour of oil companies at the expense of village communities.

3.7. Petroleum Legislation and Operating Arrangements

Once oil companies acquired land in village communities, they still required the backing of a business conducive legal framework to expand their operations. In order to fully understand the nature of legal disputes between oil companies and village

---

[176] (1980) 1 RSLR 139.

[177] In preparation for the Land Use Act 1978, the Nigerian government convened the Land Use Panel between May and November 1977, under Justice Chukwunwelke Idigbe as chairman. Referring specifically to the oil industry, the Panel recommended that the '*Federal government should take a serious look at the effects of oil exploration and exploitation*' with a view to '*improving the quantum of compensation payable to land owners*' and to compelling oil companies into '*complete reclamation*' of all leased land (Land Use Panel 1977). But these recommendations have never been followed.

communities, it is instructive to broadly outline the general legislative framework for the functioning of the oil industry in Nigeria.

The main oil-related statute in Nigeria is the Petroleum Act 1969. The promulgation of the Act repealed the colonial Mineral Oils Ordinance, the main piece of petroleum legislation until 1969. While the Act was a creation of the post-colonial state, it largely confirmed provisions of the colonial oil legislation. As Atsegbua (1993, 35) observed, provisions related to the assignment and revocation of oil licences as well as the rights and powers of licence holders remained much the same as under colonial rule (see chapter 2). The greatest changes concerned oil mining leases (OMLs). Until 1969, OMLs were granted for a period of 30 or 40 years. After 1969, OMLs were merely granted for 20 years. In addition, the oil company was obliged to relinquish one-half of the area of the lease ten years after the grant of an OML. This new provision encouraged a faster rate of exploration because oil company managers were aware that they would have to relinquish part of the area and were likely to speed up exploration (Atsegbua 1993, 35-37).

While the nature of oil licences remained largely unchanged, the nature of the arrangements between oil companies and the government changed significantly. From 1971, the foreign oil companies were not merely granted oil licences by the government, but had to operate joint ventures with the government (see chapter 2). Perhaps surprisingly, for many years to come, no formal operating agreements were signed between the joint venture partners. Operating agreements spell out the legal relationship between the partners and also lay out the rules and procedures for specific areas of responsibility as well as the meaning of joint property. In the joint venture between Shell and the Nigerian government, which has been operating since April 1973, no formal operating agreement was signed until July 1991.[178] The agreement in 1991 was the first formal legal agreement to formalise the working relationship between Shell - the joint venture operator - and the other joint venture partners - NNPC, Elf and Agip (Atsegbua 1993, 43).

More recently, production-sharing contracts, first introduced in an agreement with Ashland in 1973, have become more popular than joint venture arrangements, particularly in offshore operations. The same company may indeed have different arrangements with the government.[179] For instance, Shell operates a joint venture on behalf of the government under the name Shell Petroleum Development Company

---

[178] The participation arrangements with foreign oil companies were divided into two parts: the financial agreement and the operating agreement. The financial agreement with Shell-BP, for example, was signed in 1973. A draft operating agreement was drawn up in 1973 but it was not acceptable to the management of the NNOC. In their view, the agreement gave the NNOC little direct control over oil operations. While NNOC staff would be represented as directors in the joint ventures, no powers were provided for the day-to-day running of the oil operations. In addition, the government was to abide by the terms of the oil mining leases and concession agreements. The Ministry of Mines and Power refused to present an alternative draft, so the issue remained unresolved. The joint ventures were forced to operate according to informal and formal procedures agreed with government officials. The draft agreements provided a basis for interim operational procedures (Turner 1977, 146-148).

[179] Apart from joint ventures and production-sharing contracts, Nigeria introduced the so-called risk-service contract in 1979. A contract between Agip Energy & Natural Resources (AENR) and the NNPC, first signed in 1979, is the only active risk-service contract remaining (on risk-service contracts, see Khan 1994, 79).

(SPDC) of Nigeria. In addition, Shell Nigeria Exploration and Production Company (SNEPCO) has been operating since 1993 in deep-water acreage offshore and in so-called frontier areas onshore under a production-sharing arrangement with the government.[180] Both SPDC and SNEPCO are wholly-Shell owned, but they operate under different legal arrangements which, above all, affect the financing of oil activities.

In a production-sharing contract such as Shell's SNEPCO offshore venture, the contractor advances all funds towards running costs. In a joint venture such as SPDC, the operator and the other joint venture partners share the operating costs. Since Shell owns a 30% share in the SPDC-NNPC venture, the company pays 30% of the running costs. A similar Operating Agreement with Topcon Company (Texaco Overseas) of 1988 read:

> *All costs and expenses incurred by the Operator shall be borne by the Parties in proportion to their respective Participating Interest.*
> *Operator shall initially advance and pay all expenditures of whatever nature and kind incurred in Joint Operations. Operator may at its election, require each Non-Operator to advance its share of Joint Operation net cash requirements ('Cash Call'). Operator shall have a first and prior lien on all rights and interests of each Party in the Leases, Joint Property, and in production to secure payment* (Barrows Company 1995, 772-779).

Thus, on the most basic level, in a production-sharing contract, the government does not have to invest anything, while in a joint venture, it must advance substantial funds at regular intervals. While the old joint venture arrangements continue to exist, new arrangements made in the 1990s have tended to be production-sharing contracts. During the 1990s, many of the large foreign oil companies in Nigeria (including Shell, Mobil, Elf, Exxon and BP-Statoil Alliance) signed production-sharing contracts (Khan 1994, 74). Both under joint venture and production-sharing contracts, the foreign oil company has retained effective operating control over day-to-day operations in village communities. The company rather than the government has continued to be legally liable for any breach of law or for any damage arising from oil operations in village communities. From the perspective of village communities, the post-colonial petroleum statutes hence changed little.

With regard to the day-to-day operations of oil companies, the Petroleum Act 1969 and other pieces of legislation (see below) contain various legal provisions designed to discourage village communities from hindering oil activities. The Oil Pipelines Act imposed a penalty of fifty Naira or imprisonment for three months for obstructing any activities related to the possession of any oil pipelines or any ancillary installations of oil pipelines.[181] The Petroleum Act[182] extended these sanctions to other types of oil operations by providing that:

---

[180] As another wholly-owned Shell subsidiary, Shell Nigeria Gas (SNG) was launched in 1998 to market natural gas (*Vanguard*, 20 July 1998). SNG is not directly involved in oil exploration and production.

[181] Section 25.

[182] Section 12(1).

Any person who interferes with or obstructs the holder of a licence or lease granted under section 2 of this Decree (or his servants or agents) in the exercise of any rights, power or liberty conferred by the licence or lease shall be guilty of an offence and on conviction shall be liable to a fine not exceeding £100 or to imprisonment for a period not exceeding six months, or both.

Punishment for interference and sabotage became stiffer over the following two decades. The Petroleum Production and Distribution Anti-Sabotage Decree No.35 of 1975 created the offences of sabotage in respect of wilful acts calculated to prevent, disrupt or interfere with the production or distribution of petroleum products. Under the Decree, offenders are to be tried by military tribunals and, if found guilty, are liable to death sentence or to imprisonment for up to twenty-one years. As if the threat of the death penalty were not enough, the Special Tribunal (Miscellaneous Offences) Decree No.20 of 1984 prescribed that those who unlawfully and wilfully break, damage, disconnect or otherwise tamper with any pipe for the transportation of crude oil or refined oil or gas shall be tried by the Miscellaneous Offences Tribunal. Those found guilty are liable to death by firing squad (Olisa 1987, 155-156). The death sentence was changed to a term of life imprisonment by the Special Tribunal (Miscellaneous Offences) Amendment Decree 1986 (Adewale 1989).

The common feature in all the above anti-sabotage statutes was trial by military tribunals. As Nwabueze (1992, chapter 3) showed, the legal rights of those tried by military tribunals are severely constrained. By implication, the anti-sabotage statutes were designed to offer security protection to oil companies without offering adequate legal safeguards to those suspected of tampering with oil installations. This would suggest that the anti-sabotage statutes are biased in favour of oil interests. This does not, however, imply that petroleum legislation as a whole or the administration of justice is biased against village communities in the oil producing areas. Above all, anti-sabotage legislation has rarely been applied in practice.[183] Furthermore, a number of petroleum statutes, which specifically deal with oil company field operations, contain legal provisions for the protection and compensation of those adversely affected by oil operations (provisions for compensation will be discussed in section 3.10. below). More importantly, a number of environmental statutes contain provisions which are capable of limiting the adverse effects of oil operations on village communities and offering legal recourse to those affected. An analysis of those statutes is instructive in discussing the question of whether the legal system is biased in favour of oil interests.

---

[183] In one case, five men were accused of attempting to break a pipeline belonging to the NNPC in Ogun State and were tried by a military tribunal in accordance with the provisions of the Special Tribunal (Miscellaneous Offences) Decree 1984 (*ThisDay*, 23 January 1997). Cases such as this are rather infrequent, however. It appears that oil companies have exaggerated the extent of sabotage in order to avoid compensation payments to communities, although one cannot deny the existence of sabotage (this will be shown in chapter 6).

3.8. Oil-Related Environmental Legislation

While Nigerian petroleum statutes may or may not be biased in favour of oil companies, environmental law is likely to be capable of acting as a constraint on oil operations in village communities. The most important piece of environmental legislation in Nigeria is the Federal Environmental Protection Agency (FEPA) Act 1988, as amended by Act No.59 of 1992. The Act created the FEPA, a public body with the responsibility of protecting, developing and managing the Nigerian environment. It was also meant to advise the government on national environmental policies and priorities and on activities affecting the environment.[184] Until 1988, Nigeria had no national institution and no comprehensive detailed legislation to deal with environmental issues.

In addition to the general provisions of 1988 and 1992, the FEPA established detailed guidelines and standards for environmental control (FEPA 1991). The Agency co-operates with other governmental bodies. It is headed by a governing council with members drawn from various federal ministries. In addition, since 1992, the Agency has had a technical committee, also mostly drawn from federal ministries, to advise the governing council on technical issues.[185] In addition to the creation of FEPA, the 1988 Act encouraged the federal states and the local government councils to set up their own environmental protection bodies to deal with environmental issues in their respective areas.[186] Since 1988, many federal states have created State Environmental Protection Agencies (SEPAs).

The creation of the FEPA illustrates the growing interest in environmental issues in Nigeria which dates back to the 1970s at least. In 1979, the Nigerian National Petroleum Corporation (NNPC) held the first conference on environmental issues in the oil industry. The 1979 Conference called for the enactment of an environmental law similar to the Environmental Protection Agency (EPA) in the US. Since 1979, the NNPC has regularly organised environmental conferences. Calls for environmental legislation became louder (Odogwu 1991).[187] The final creation of the Agency in 1988 was in direct response to the so-called Koko incident when toxic waste from Europe was brought to Nigeria, which was followed by an outcry in the Nigerian press (Ilegbune 1994, 93). In other words, FEPA's creation was directly sparked off by public pressure at the micro-level.

The FEPA was given broad legal powers to enforce environmental controls in the oil industry and, thus, to intervene in the running of the industry. The FEPA Act and guidelines regulate areas such as water quality, effluent limitation and air quality. Section 20 of the Act prohibits the discharge *'of any hazardous substances into the air or upon the land and the waters of Nigeria'*. Pollution of Nigeria's natural environment is also made a crime and monetary penalties are imposed upon polluters. Under section

---

[184] Section 4.

[185] Section 2.

[186] Section 24.

[187] During the civilian rule in Nigeria 1979-1983, an Environmental Protection Agency Act was actually passed. However, the Act had not been signed into law before the Shagari government was overthrown in 1983 (Areola 1987, 284).

20, a company may be fined up to 500,000 Naira for non-compliance with the Act and an additional 1,000 for every day that the offence continues. Section 21 of the Act makes specific reference to spiller's liability. If the text of section 21 were followed, in the case of an oil spill, the company would be liable for a penalty, the cost of removal including any governmental expenditures and the cost of third parties in the form of reparation, restoration, restitution or compensation.

However, the limitations on FEPA's *de facto* environmental control in the oil industry are substantial. The FEPA Act provided for representatives of the Ministry of Petroleum Resources to sit on both the governing council and the technical committee. Petroleum officials could thus potentially influence FEPA's policy initiatives in favour of oil companies. Most importantly, the oil industry was explicitly mentioned in the FEPA Act. Section 23 of the Act reads:

> *The Agency shall co-operate with the Ministry of Petroleum Resources (Petroleum Resources Department) for the removal of oil-related pollutants discharged into the Nigerian environment and play such supportive role as the Ministry of Petroleum Resources (Petroleum Resources Department) may from time to time request from the Agency.*

Section 23 is sufficiently vague to leave doubt about the relationship between FEPA and the Ministry of Petroleum Resources. The words 'co-operate' and 'request' indicate that FEPA may be restrained from acting on matters relating to oil pollution without the consent of the oil ministry. As Adewale (1992, 64) argued, section 23 makes the Department of Petroleum Resources independent of FEPA, a status which can be attributed to the strategic importance of oil to Nigeria. In theory, the administrative competencies of the Ministry of Petroleum Resources and FEPA largely overlap in the area of environmental protection (see Table 3.1.). It appears that section 23 of the FEPA Act may have taken the oil industry out of the purview of the Agency. It is still unclear to what extent the abolition of the oil ministry in 1998 has influenced the relationship between petroleum officials and the FEPA.

Table 3.1. Administrative Competencies in Environmental Matters in the Oil Industry

Ministry of Petroleum Resources	*Federal Environmental Protection Agency*
• Environmental permitting authority for oil operations	• Environmental permitting authority for all industries in Nigeria, including the oil industry
• Licensing authority with regard to oil operations	• Regulation of industrial effluent discharges
• Review and approval of Environmental Impacts Assessments (EIAs) for oil operations	• Review and approval of Environmental Impacts Assessments (EIAs) submitted in support of the authorisation process

Source: Petroconsultants (1997, 12).

Several sections of the FEPA Act create loop holes which enable the offending oil company to escape legal responsibility for pollution. Among other exemptions, the Act permits the discharge of hazardous substances into the environment where such discharge is authorised by a law in force in Nigeria.[188] An example is the Oil in Navigable Waters Act which permits the discharge of hazardous substances or petroleum in certain circumstances.[189] For instance, a vessel may discharge oil into Nigerian waters if the escape of oil was due to leakage and the leakage was not due to any want of reasonable care and all reasonable steps were taken to stop or reduce the discharge. Therefore, as Adewale (1992, 58) argued, section 4 of the Oil in Navigable Waters Act destroys the stringent deterrent which might have been provided by the FEPA Act. Considering the above discussion, the text of the FEPA Act bears many limitations.

Perhaps more importantly, the enforcement of the FEPA Act has, until recently, been largely ineffective.[190] Scientific regulations established by FEPA in 1991, by and large, failed to restrict the adverse impact of oil operations on the ground. For instance, the *'emission limit for particulates from stationary sources'* was 50-250 mg/m^3 for oil burning (FEPA 1991). Shell's own figure for emissions from gas flaring in Rivers and Delta States of Nigeria was 240 mg/m^3 (World Bank 1995, volume II, annex I). A more comprehensive analysis of FEPA standards was carried out by Environmental Rights Action (ERA), a Nigerian environmental group. Samples taken in Shell's production area in Akwa Ibom State were compared with FEPA standards. Most of the actual values measured by ERA were lower than FEPA standards, except for temperature and sulphur. Yet, at the same time, oil operations had an adverse environmental impact on the area, for instance, through the destruction of the mangrove vegetation (ERA 1995, 15 and 19). It therefore appears that FEPA's environmental standards may have been tailored in such a way that the oil industry can comply with them without taking any additional measures. This fact is not surprising since most of FEPA's oil industry standards were directly taken from the Department of Petroleum Resources (DPR), which is primarily concerned with oil production. This once again underlines the significance of section 23 of the FEPA Act. Even if the DPR strived to minimise the environmental impact of oil activities, it lacked the monitoring and basic office equipment to do so. Referring to environmental control, the World Bank concluded that the DPR is *'currently not able to perform its duties and is limited to obtaining oil company spill reports'* (World Bank 1995, volume II, annex J).

Like the DPR, FEPA lacks basic equipment and skills to enforce environmental controls. According to the World Bank, the FEPA office in Rivers State had 25 staff in 1995, including 10 environmental professionals of which only 3 dealt with oil pollution, and only few activities were being implemented. The World Bank concluded that FEPA's funding and environmental expertise had to be substantially increased in order for it to be able to have a significant impact on environmental control. FEPA's main deficiencies in Rivers State were limited funding, weak monitoring and enforcement capacity, and few appropriately trained staff. In 1995, while at least

---

[188] Section 20.

[189] Oil in Navigable Waters Act, section 4.

[190] As yet Adewale and other Nigerian scholars have largely failed to analyse the enforcement of the FEPA guidelines and standards. For instance, a study by Guobadia (1993, 413-414) was limited to a recitation of sections of the legal text that deal with enforcement but failed to discuss actual enforcement.

represented in Rivers State, FEPA had not even been active in Delta State, Nigeria's other major oil producing area at the time (World Bank 1995, volume II, annex J). The operations of the FEPA also appeared to have been hindered by corruption. In October 1996, the chief executive of the FEPA, Dr. Evans Aina was arrested for fraud involving 1,115 million Naira (*Guardian*, Lagos, 27 January 1997). Yet, even if the FEPA were effective and an oil company had to pay a fine, the FEPA Act stipulates a fine not exceeding 500,000 Naira and an additional fine of 1,000 Naira for every day the offence subsists. Based on the 1995 average official exchange rate, this amounts to a little less than US$ 23,000 per incident, which appears to be a rather insignificant amount for any foreign oil company.

The State Environmental Protection Agencies (SEPAs), created by different states from 1988 onwards, also appear to lack effectiveness. The World Bank investigated the ineffectiveness of the SEPA in Rivers State. In 1995, the SEPA only had one vehicle and not a single boat, although much of the oil production takes place in riverine areas which requires movement by boat. Lacking a laboratory, the Agency was unable to monitor water or air quality standards. The Agency commissioned a study on the environmental effects of gas flaring, but ran out of funds to complete it. Much of the SEPA's work on the oil industry was limited to visiting the sites of oil spills and certifying that clean ups were completed. The World Bank concluded that the Agency's ability to assess and manage oil pollution was very limited (World Bank 1995, volume II, annex J). This evidence indicates severe limitations in the FEPA Act, the key environmental piece of legislation in Nigeria.

The lack of enforcement of the FEPA Act illustrates the inadequacy of environmental controls in Nigeria in general. The Associated Gas Re-injection Act 1979 and the Associated Gas Re-injection (Amendment) Act 1985 are the most significant environmental laws dealing specifically with the oil industry, promulgated in order to reduce gas flaring.[191] The 1979 Act required oil companies to re-inject the gas into the earth's crust or, alternatively, to provide detailed programmes for the utilisation of associated gas. The Act also set out the objective of prohibiting gas flaring by January 1984. The 1985 Act amended some of the provisions of the earlier Act and added new ones including a penalty for gas flaring. These gas related laws have no direct impact on litigation brought by village communities but they can illustrate the problems of enforcing environmental legislation in Nigeria.

Despite the imposition of fines for non-compliance, the gas legislation has hardly been implemented in practice as the government failed to initiate an appropriate policy for gas utilisation.[192] Non-enforcement was to some extent due to the fact that

---

[191] As Turner (1977, 174) pointed out, the Petroleum Act 1969 already provided for gas utilisation. The Petroleum (Drilling and Production) Regulations stated: '*Not later than five years after the commencement of production from the relevant area the licensee or leasee shall submit to the Commissioner any feasibility study, programme or proposal that he may have for the utilisation of any natural gas, whether associated with oil or not, which has been discovered in the relevant area*' (quoted in Turner 1977, 174). The Petroleum (Amendment) Decree No.16 of 1973 was further passed to '*enable the Federal Military Government to take natural gas produced along with crude oil (and presently flared) on terms agreed upon between the Government and the producer*' (quoted in Turner 1977, 176).

[192] As early as 1969, the 'Report of the Fact-Finding Mission' of the Nigerian government alluded to the problems of gas related legislation in the following words:

the Nigerian National Petroleum Corporation (NNPC) was not willing to contribute towards the costs of gas development. For instance, Shell's Associated Gas Gathering Project was cancelled in 1994 because of financial problems. The project was aimed at reducing gas flaring in SPDC's Eastern Division by 25% by selling the excess gas to industrial plants nearby (van Dessel 1995, 23). Furthermore, gas projects such as the Nigeria Liquefied Natural Gas (NLNG) project were delayed as a result of political decisions (Frynas 1998).

Gas related legislation in Nigeria has had little effect on the day-to-day operations of oil companies for two main reasons. First, the government was willing to grant exemptions to companies for non-compliance with legislation. Most oil wells were indeed exempted from compliance with the gas related statutes.[193] As many as 55 out of Shell's 84 oil wells in 1985 were exempted from the provisions of the gas legislation and over half of the wells belonging to the other companies (see Table 3.2.).

Second, the fines for gas flaring were insignificant. It was often cheaper for oil companies to continue gas flaring than to invest in gas projects. In 1985, the fine for gas flaring was set at 2 Kobo per one thousand cubic feet (28.317 standard cubic metres) of flared gas to be paid according to the same procedure as for royalty payments, that is, in foreign currency into a designated foreign account (Olisa 1987, 51). For instance, Mobil paid 142,172,123 Naira in gas flaring fines in 1994, which is insignificant if compared with the 3,035,262,789 Naira paid in petroleum royalty in the same year. Payments by the other oil companies were similarly insignificant (see Table 3.3.). At the end of the 1980s, Chevron (formerly Gulf) noted that switching from water injection to gas injection would cost the company US$ 56 million (quoted in Akpan 1997, 267). In effect, compliance with the Gas Re-injection Decree would cost the company US$ 56 million, compared with a mere US$ 1 million/year which the company had to pay in gas flaring fines. It was therefore cheaper for the company to continue gas flaring.

Table 3.2. Gas Flaring Exemptions and Fines in the Nigerian Oil Industry in 1985

	Shell	Mobil	Gulf*	Texaco	Elf	Ashland	Tenneco	Pan Ocean
Wells fined	29	5	10	2	2	2	0	0
Wells exempted	55	10	7	3	4	1	1	1
Total wells	84	15	17	5	6	3	1	1

* today Chevron.
Source: Synge (1986, 37).

> '...the nation's interests are not identical with [those of] the companies. This is clearly demonstrated in Nigeria by the fact that the companies have as yet not considered it necessary to take any action to commercialise the gas which is necessarily produced with the oil and which right now is flared. [Elsewhere] at least equal importance is given to the question of commercialisation and conservation of gas as is given to oil. While a nation can legislate about these [matters] or regulate them, it is only the positive initiative which it gives which actually means anything or gives rise to concrete results' (quoted in Turner 1977, 172).

[193] Exemptions were made on the basis of technical and economic factors rather than environmental ones, for instance, in cases where re-injection would not increase production.

Table 3.3. Gas Flaring Fines and Royalty Payments of the Major Oil Companies in Nigeria (in thousand Naira) in 1994

	Mobil	Shell	Agip	Chevron	Texaco	Elf
Flaring fine	142,172	45,812	19,121	41,127	4,886	5,631
Royalty	3,035,262	7,867,852	1,780,944	3,436,626	714,578	3,178,406
Fine as % of royalty	4.68%	0.58%	1.07%	1.20%	0.68%	0.18%

Source: Nigeria's Oil and Gas Publications (1996, 52).

The percentage of flared associated gas fell from around 95% in the 1970s to 74% in 1985, but the oil companies have so far failed to comply with the gas legislation of 1979 and 1985 (Akpan 1997). The World Bank (1995, volume II, annex J) argued that the gas flaring fines *"proved to be too small an incentive to induce companies to reduce flaring"*. The Bank further commented on the impact of gas related legislation:

> *Although gas utilisation will increase, in the near term it will be based on economical non-associated gas supplies and not reduce gas flaring. The largest outlet for Nigeria's gas, the Bonny LNG plant, will liquefy primarily non-associated gas.* (World Bank 1995, volume II, annex J).

The gas flaring fines were recently substantially increased. In 1996, the fine was increased from 2 Kobo to 50 Kobo per thousand standard cubic feet (*Daily Times*, 20 July 1996) and was further increased to 10 Naira in 1998 (*Oil & Gas Update*, January 1998). The increase in 1996 did little more than to offset inflation.[194] The increase in 1998 was significant. In the meantime, the financial incentives for gas projects were substantially enhanced in the late 1990s (see chapter 2). As a result, gas exploitation became more important. Indeed, Shell aims to eliminate gas flaring in Nigeria by the year 2008, while Mobil aims to achieve the same by the year 2001 (*Weekly Petroleum Argus*, 19 May 1997). In the long-term, gas flaring is therefore likely to end within the next one or two decades. But it would appear that this is not the result of gas related legislation but the result of improved fiscal incentives for oil companies. In the short-term, there is little commercial incentive for oil companies to stop gas flaring and to comply with the gas related legislation.

Like the FEPA Act and the gas related legislation, the other environmental legislation in Nigeria also failed to significantly curb the adverse environmental impact of oil operations. A confidential study commissioned for the Shell-initiated Niger Delta Environmental Survey (NDES) of 1996 concluded: *"From our investigation all the legislation in the Niger Delta as regards environmental pollution control are more in the interest of industry than the community"* (Ogbnigwe 1996, 16). The study provided a brief summary of the different areas of legislation, which clearly indicated that environmental legislation was generally unenforced, favoured the government and the companies or entailed implementation problems (see Table 3.4.). The NDES-commissioned report, although too generalised and partially inaccurate, argued that

---

[194] In the decade 1985-1994, Nigerian consumer prices rose by over 1,100%, that means, 50 Kobo in 1994 were worth an equivalent of just over 4 Kobo in 1985.

current legislation had so far failed to protect village communities from the adverse impact of oil company operations.

According to the World Bank, there are three major constraints to the regulation of the energy and minerals sector in Nigeria. The first constraint is the absence of requirements for community participation in the planning and development of oil activities. The second is corruption and inadequate compensation for damage to property. The third is lack of enforcement of environmental regulations. In addition, unlike other oil producing countries, Nigeria does not have a separate statute for the conservation of oil (World Bank, volume II, annex J).

Some of these problems can be illustrated with the help of factual evidence from the case *Douglas v. Shell*[195], in which Oronto Douglas[196] - an environmental rights activist - sued Shell, the state oil corporation NNPC, the Nigeria Liquefied Natural Gas (NLNG) project, Mobil and the Attorney-General for non-compliance with the Environmental Impact Assessment (EIA) Decree No.86 of 1992.[197] The EIA Decree required companies and public bodies to undertake a so-called environmental impact assessment (EIA) survey prior to embarking on any project or activity where *'the extent, nature or location of a proposed project or activity is such that is likely to significantly affect the environment'*.[198] Douglas' lawyers contended that the EIA was not strictly applied in the execution of the NLNG project and Mobil's Natural Gas Liquids (NGL) recovery project, having violated section 7 of the Decree which intended to give members of the public and interested groups the right to make comments on EIA surveys. Douglas maintained that no adequate opportunity was provided for public comments on the gas-related surveys in question.

The Douglas case revealed the questionable role of the FEPA, which was legally bound to certify EIA surveys. It appears that the FEPA did not take notice of the public criticism of the EIA surveys for the gas projects. However, after the commencement of the Douglas case on 26 June 1996, the FEPA then altered its position and placed a Public Notice in the Daily Times (1 July 1996), a Nigerian daily newspaper, requesting information and comments on the EIA survey on Mobil's NGL project, which it had failed to do until then. One could conclude that the publication of the advertisement was in direct response to the lawsuit. Furthermore, the court case revealed that construction work on Mobil's gas project had already been allowed to start before the EIA survey was submitted to the FEPA. The Douglas case reflected two of the problems raised by the World Bank study mentioned earlier in relation to environmental protection: lack of community participation in planning and development as well as lack of legal enforcement.

---

[195] Unreported Suit No. FHC/L/CS/573/96 in the Federal High Court, Lagos.

[196] Oronto Douglas, an environmental lawyer, is one of the leaders of the Ijaw Youth Council (IYC), a spokesman of the Chikoko movement and one of the directors of Environmental Rights Action (ERA).

[197] The Douglas case was dismissed in the first instance. In December 1998, the Court of Appeal ruled that the Federal High Court was in breach of a number of procedural rules when deciding the Douglas case and the case was remitted back to the Federal High Court to be re-tried before a different judge.

[198] Section 2(2).

Table 3.4. Legislation to Protect Communities, Compiled for the NDES-commissioned Report in 1996

Legislation Area	Laws/Regulations	Degrees of Community Protection
Noise	- Workmen Compensation Acts 1990 - State Environmental Sanitation Edicts - Factories Act - FEPA and SEPA Decrees & Edict	Not in force [sic] at all and inadequate laws
Wildlife Conservation	- Endangered Species Act Cap 108 LFN* 1990 - Natural Resources Conservation Council Act Cap 286 LFN 1990 - Forestry Law	Not properly enforced and inadequate laws
Pest Control	- Public Health Laws - FEPA Act Cap 131 LFN 1990	Laws are antiquated in terms of penalties, implementation and application and have been dropped in the present laws of the federation
Fishery	- See Fisheries Act Cap 404 LFN 1990	Lack of enforcement and poor co-ordination and inadequate laws
Water	- Mineral Oil (Safety) Act Cap 350 LFN 1990 - Mineral Resources Act Cap 226 LFN 1990 - Oil in Navigable Waters Act Cap 339 LFN 1990 - Petroleum Act Cap 350 LFN 1990 - River Basins Development Authorities (RBDA) Act Cap 396 LFN 1990 - FEPA Act Cap 131 LFN 1990	- Inadequate, antiquated and finally omitted in the Federal Laws but still effective in the Delta States - Colonial and not in use [sic] - Not adequately in force [sic] and do not favour the communities
Land	- Land Use Act Cap 202 LFN 1990 - Handful Wastes Act Cap 16 SLFN 1990 - Natural Resources Conservation Council Act Cap 131 LFN 1990 - FEPA Act Cap 131 LFN 1990	- Favour and protect interest of government and not communities - All these laws favour and protect government not the communities - Not properly enforced
Industry	- FEPA Act Cap 131 LFN 1990 - Harmful Wastes Act Cap 165 LFN 1990 - Environmental Impact Assessment (EIA) Decree 1992, No.86 - SEPA Edicts	- Not properly enforced - FEPA not equipped to enforce the regulation - Provisions to witch hunt communities and rob them of right to compensation i.e. sabotage
Oil and Hazardous Substance	- Petroleum Act Cap 350 LFN 1990 - Petroleum (Drilling and Production) Regulations 1969 - Associated Gas Re-Injection Act Cap 20 LFN 1990	- Did not adopt environmental consideration and so cannot protect communities interest - Not effective
Sanitation	- Public Health Law - Environmental Sanitation Edicts - FEPA Act Cap 131 LFN 1990	- Antiquated - Not properly in force [sic] - Not properly in force [sic]; waste dispersal and not waste disposal
Air	- FEPA Decree No.56 of 1988	

* LFN stands for the Laws of the Federation of Nigeria.
Source: Ogbnigwe (1996, 16-17).

On the whole, it appears that the implementation of Nigeria's environmental statutes has so far offered little protection to village communities, especially since the government has shown little interest in enforcing environmental legislation. The companies meanwhile have little financial incentive to comply with environmental laws. In this context, government policy and corporate interests have resulted in inadequate enforcement of statute law. Environmental legislation or rather its loopholes and lack of enforcement have prejudiced the administration of justice in favour of oil company interests at the expense of village communities.

3.9. Nigerian Court System

In addition to statute law, conflicts between village communities and oil companies are also constrained by the structure of the court system. The court system in Nigeria has two layers: the federal courts and the state courts.

The courts established for the federation are the Supreme Court, the Court of Appeal, the Federal High Court, and the courts of the capital territory of Abuja. The Supreme Court, first established in 1914, is the highest court in Nigeria, headed by the Chief Justice of the federation. It exercises exclusive appellate jurisdiction over the decisions of the Court of Appeal and various disputes concerning presidential elections and between states and the federal government. The Court of Appeal, first established in 1976, can entertain appeals from state courts[199] and has exclusive appellate jurisdiction over various issues. The Federal High Court, first established in 1973 as the Federal Revenue Court, has exclusive jurisdiction over certain matters but no appellate jurisdiction (Nwankwo et al. 1993, 8-14).[200] The Court of Appeal and the Federal High Court have divisions in different towns across Nigeria in order to facilitate the courts' workings.

The courts established for the states of the federation include the State High Courts, magistrates' or district courts, area or customary and Sharia (Islamic) courts, Customary Courts of Appeal, and Sharia Courts of Appeal.[201] District, Area and Sharia Courts mostly exist in Northern Nigeria. Customary courts exist mainly in Southern Nigeria. A State High Court exists in each state with jurisdiction for the whole of the state but has divisions in different towns across each state. Customary and Sharia Courts of Appeal only exist in some states. At the beginning of the 1990s, only 19 out of 30 states had a Customary Court of Appeal. A Customary Court of Appeal has the

---

[199] Appeals can be entertained from the State High Courts, the Sharia and Customary Courts of Appeal and the Code of Conduct Bureau. Until 1976, there was no intervening appellate court between the State High Courts and the Supreme Court.

[200] As Oyakhirome (1995) pointed out, the Federal Revenue Court was originally constituted as a specialised court for cases dealing with federal revenue matters such as the taxation of companies, banking and government fiscal policies. The court was re-named the Federal High Court under the provisions of the 1979 Constitution but its original purpose as a specialised court of revenue matters largely persisted until 1993. The Constitution (Suspension and Modification) Decree No.107 of 1993 extended the original jurisdiction of the court to a wide range of matters including oil-related litigation, drugs and aviation.

[201] Other courts may include Rent Tribunals or Sanitation Courts.

jurisdiction to entertain appeals on matters concerning customary law. A Sharia Court of Appeal has the jurisdiction to entertain appeals on matters concerning Islamic law. Magistrates' courts exist all over Nigeria. In many northern states, the magistrates' courts only entertain civil cases, while district courts entertain criminal cases. Area or customary courts are at the bottom of the court system. Area courts mostly deal with Islamic law, while customary courts mostly deal with customary law (Nwankwo *et al.* 1993, 8-14).

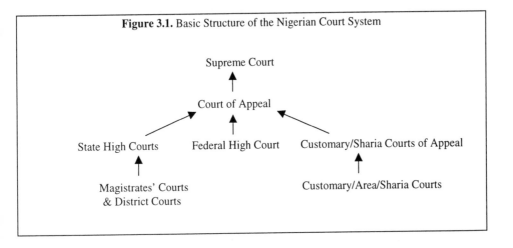

Figure 3.1. Basic Structure of the Nigerian Court System

In terms of oil-related litigation, the State High Courts were the courts of first instance until 1993. As a result, a potential litigant was able to file a suit against an oil company in any of the divisions of a State High Court. This situation radically changed in 1993 when the government introduced the Constitution (Suspension and Modification) Decree No.107 of 1993, which extended the original jurisdiction of the Federal High Court to oil-related matters. The Decree vested the Federal High Court with the exclusive right to decide on matters related to oil mining, seismic studies and related matters.[202] Pending oil-related cases are still tried in the State High Courts and other relevant courts. All new oil-related lawsuits, which started after 1993, must be brought to the Federal High Court, although the Court of Appeal has disagreed with such an interpretation of the 1993 Decree. In *Shell v. Isaiah*[203], the Court of Appeal stated that the 1993 Decree did not affect oil spillage matters.[204] Notwithstanding the

---

[202] The original jurisdiction of the Federal High Court over oil-related matters was pronounced in the Federal High Court (Amendment) Decree No.60 of 1991. But the 1991 Decree was suspended by Decree No. 16 of 1992. The Constitution (Suspension and Modification) Decree No.107 of 1993 re-enacted the provision that any lawsuits involving mining operations must be directed to the Federal High Court.

[203] (1997) 6 NWLR (Pt. 508) 236.

[204] Katsina-Alu, J.C.A. stated that the Decree No.107 of 1993 *'does not affect the jurisdiction of the State High Court to adjudicate this matter. The Decree is inapplicable because the subject matter of the claim in this case did not arise from "mines and minerals, oil fields, geological surveys or natural gas". The subject matter arose from oil spillage from the defendant's oil pipelines onto the plaintiffs' swampland and farmlands'* (per Katsina-Alu, J.C.A. at page 247). This view appears to

impact of the Isaiah case, from the perspective of litigants in oil-related cases, an important feature of the structural character of the legal system changed as a result of the 1993 Decree.

3.10. Nigerian Legislation and Compensation for Damage

While the venues for court cases between oil companies and village communities have changed in recent years, statute law relating to compensation also underwent some changes following Nigeria's independence in 1960.

A variety of Nigerian laws, including petroleum legislation, describe the numerous circumstances under which compensation may be paid to those adversely affected by oil operations. The right to compensation was first entrenched in the Oil Pipelines Act 1956 which obliges a holder of a pipeline licence to pay compensation to any person who suffer damage caused by oil operations.[205] The Oil Pipelines Act states:

> (...) the court shall award such compensation as it considers just in respect of any damage done to any buildings, lion crops or profitable trees by the holder of the permit in the exercise of his rights thereunder and in addition may award such sum in respect of disturbance (if any) as it may consider just [sic].[206]

The 1956 Act specifically deals with pipelines and related damage, particularly oil spills. However, it was not until the promulgation of the Petroleum Act 1969 that more comprehensive provisions were made in respect of 'fair and adequate compensation' for damage from oil operations. In particular, the Petroleum Act provides that:

> The holder of an oil exploration licence, oil prospecting licence or oil mining lease shall, in addition to any liability for compensation to which he may be subject under any other provision of the Decree, be liable to pay fair and adequate compensation for the disturbance of surface or other rights to any person who owns or is in lawful occupation of the licensed or leased lands.[207]

---

be a very narrow judicial interpretation of the Decree as it could be expected that the original legislators probably intended to include the issue of 'oil spills' within the ambit of 'mines and minerals' or 'oil fields'. In addition to Decree No.107 of 1993, the federal government enacted the Admiralty Jurisdiction Decree No.59 of 1991, which placed all court cases arising from oil pollution within the exclusive jurisdiction of the Federal High Court. It appears that the scope of the Decree was merely confined to maritime areas, however. Katsina-Alu, J.C.A. stated: '*The phrase "any claim for liability incurred for oil pollution damage" contained in section 1(1)(e) of the [Admiralty Jurisdiction] Decree cannot be read in isolation but within the context of Admiralty jurisdiction meaning any claim for liability incurred or oil pollution damage by ships, oil tankers and related property. I am in agreement with the learned counsel for the plaintiffs that the decree cannot apply to claims for oil spillage from pipelines onto swampland and farmlands like in the instant case* [sic]' (per Katsina-Alu, J.C.A. at page 246).

[205] Sections 19-23.

[206] Section 20(1).

[207] Paragraph 36 of schedule 1.

The Petroleum Act 1969 and the related Petroleum (Drilling and Production) Regulations 1969 list the items for assessment of compensation, including economic trees, structures affixed to the land, fishing rights, shrines and venerable objects. In addition, those affected by oil operations are entitled to compensation for the so-called disturbance and injurious affection. Disturbance means a depreciation in land value or an interest in land due to damage, which could include any consequences of eviction from the land, legal costs of the purchase of comparable property, increased rental or other expenses and loss of profits. Injurious affection refers to some anticipated depreciation in the value of the land (Omotola 1990).

The right to adequate compensation for compulsory acquisition of property (not for environmental damage) was further entrenched by the Nigerian Constitution 1979.[208] Section 40 provided that any compulsory acquisition of property

> 'requires the prompt payment of compensation thereof; and gives the person claiming such compensation a right of access for the determination of his interest in the property and the amount of compensation to a court of law or tribunal or body having jurisdiction in that part of Nigeria'.[209]

In essence, the text of the 1979 Constitution did not simply insist upon the payment of compensation but stipulated that the compensation paid must be adequate. The payment of adequate compensation for the compulsory acquisition of property became a constitutional right, which was important since the Constitution ranked above the provisions of the Petroleum Act 1969.

While the 1979 Constitution secured the right to adequate compensation for the compulsory acquisition of property, the African Charter on Human and People's Rights, which was ratified and made enforceable in Nigeria in 1983, secured the right to adequate compensation for environmental damage.[210] In the case *Fawehinmi v. Abacha*[211], the Charter was placed above every other Nigerian legislation, which even rendered it superior to constitutional decrees. Article 24 of the Charter provides that *'all peoples shall have the right to a general satisfactory environment favourable to their development'*. Article 21 provides for the right to *'freely dispose of their [all peoples'] wealth and natural resources'*. In addition, it provides that *'in case of spoliation the disposed people shall have the right to the lawful recovery of its property as well as to an adequate compensation'*.

While 'adequate compensation' for damage has become an entrenched right, Nigeria has no comprehensive legislation dealing with the issue of compensation. Furthermore, some types of damage such as psychological damage are not explicitly provided for by statutes. Most importantly, the quantum of damages has not been

---

[208] The 1979 Constitution included a number of provisions, which appear to be aimed at environmental protection. For instance, section 17(2)(d) required the state to prevent the *'exploitation of human or natural resources in any form whatsoever for reasons other than the good of the community'*. Nonetheless, as Ajai (1996, 242) pointed out, the 1979 Constitution did not recognise environmental rights as such. The Constitution did not, moreover, contain a provision which explicitly guaranteed the right to compensation for environmental damage.

[209] Section 40(1).

[210] African Charter on Human and People's Rights (Ratification and Enforcement) Act 1983.

[211] (1996) 9 NWLR (Pt. 475) 710.

explicitly defined. The term 'adequate compensation' can be subjective and vague, thus compensation appears to be a matter for the claimants to negotiate or for the judge to resolve. Since no comprehensive legislation relating to compensation for damage exists, the open market value of the subject matter for assessment has been considered the *'yardstick for compensation'* (Omotola 1990, 289).

Subject matters of assessment which have an open market value include the land, buildings, installations and crops. In addition, there are official government guidelines for compensation payments for crops, trees and land (see Table 3.5.). However, official rates for crops and trees tend to be considerably lower than the actual market value. For instance, the World Bank (1995, volume II, annex M) noted that the fruit from a mango tree was worth 200-300 Naira per year, while the official compensation rate for a mango tree was a mere 25 Naira in 1995. Since the compensation rates are so insignificant, oil companies are even prepared to pay higher rates of compensation than prescribed by the government. A sub-committee of the Oil Producers Trade Section (OPTS) of the Lagos Chamber of Commerce, an association of oil producing companies, periodically releases a comprehensive list of compensation rates. These rates are merely recommended to oil companies and are not binding, but companies reportedly use them (Frynas 1999, chapter 3). A simple comparison between the official rates and the OPTS rates reveals how insignificant the official rates are. In 1997, for instance, the OPTS rate for rice was 15,860 Naira per hectare, while the 1995 official rate was a mere 1,375 Naira. Even if adjusted for inflation in 1996 and in 1997, the official rate would amount to only 1,924 Naira, which would amount to roughly one-eighth of the OPTS rate (see Table 3.5.).

Table 3.5. Comparison of Official and OPTS Rates of Compensation for Damage from Oil Operations

Type of crop/ tree	1995 Official Rate per Hectare/ Tree (in Naira)	1995 Official Rate Adjusted for 1996-97 Inflation (in Naira)*	1997 OPTS Rate per Hectare/ Tree (in Naira)	1995 Official Rate per Hectare/ Tree (in US$)**	1997 OPTS Rate per Hectare/ Tree (in US$)***
Rice	1,375	1,924	15,860	62.80	724.66
Beans	290	406	10,660	13.25	487.07
Yams	835	1,168	48,000	38.14	2,193.18
Cocoyams	625	874	16,000	28.55	731.06
Most vegetables	625	874	5,850-16,000	28.55	267.29-731.06
Mango tree	25	35	500	1.14	22.85
Banana tree	2.50	3.50	160	0.11	7.31
Plantain tree	2.50	3.50	160	0.11	7.31
Agbono tree	18.75	26.23	340	0.86	15.54
Timber hardwoods	50	69.95	600	2.28	27.42

* Inflation was 29.3% in 1996 and 8.2% in 1997; ** at 1995 average exchange rate; *** at 1997 exchange rate.
Sources: World Bank (1995, volume II, annex M, 76), Compensation Rates Recommended by OPTS Sub-Committee on Land Acquisition (April 1997 Edition).

The compensation rates paid by oil companies, however, cannot be considered adequate from either a social or a legal point of view. In 1995, the World Bank calculated compensation rates for damaging forest land. Based on an annual rent of 5,000 Naira, the Bank concluded that the quantum of compensation should at least be 50,000 Naira per hectare. In reality, oil companies in Delta State only paid 1,000 Naira per hectare (World Bank 1995, volume II, annex M, 75). The rates paid by oil companies are thus considerably lower than those recommended by the World Bank. A further problem with the rates paid by oil companies is that they are not based on lost profits or some anticipated depreciation in the value of the land. The OPTS rates are called 'farm gate rates', which means that they are merely comprised of the market value of buying a crop or a tree plus the transport and other incidental costs of carrying them to the village. It was argued that the current method of compensation payments for crops and trees used by oil companies does not lead to the adequate compensation prescribed by law (Uduehi 1987, 104). As shown earlier, the Petroleum Act 1969 includes provisions for payments for disturbance and injurious affection, but these are not being observed by either the oil companies or the government.

In order to better understand the issue of compensation, consider the example of a coconut tree with the OPTS rate of 600 Naira. A mature coconut tree is potentially capable of yielding 30-80 coconuts, worth roughly 50 Naira each. If we assume an average of 50 coconuts per harvest, we arrive at a figure of 2,500 Naira as gross income for a single harvest. Less expenditure (costs of labour, maintenance etc.), the net income may be half, say, 1,250 Naira.[212] This means that the net income from one harvest of one coconut tree would already be considerably higher than the 600 Naira supposedly paid by an oil company. In order to properly calculate the loss of profits, the average net income from one harvest would need to be capitalised over a given estimated life span for the tree. The life span of a coconut tree could be 25 years or more. Assuming a period of only 10 years, one would arrive at a figure of 12,500 Naira. According to this conservative estimate, a coconut tree would be worth 12,500 Naira to a Nigerian farmer, which is roughly 20 times more than the current OPTS rate of 600 Naira. All of these calculations are, of course, hypothetical and do not take into account the so-called discount rate, which is common in calculating capital value. They can, nevertheless, tentatively indicate the gap between the rates paid by companies and the considerably higher economic value of the trees and crops to the farmer.

Similar calculations can be made for other economic trees, crops or fishing rights. Considering the above discussion, it appears that the current method of compensation payments is inherently flawed and fails to reflect both the social reality and the letter of the Petroleum Act 1969. In addition to the above problems, there are no compensation rates for subject matters which have no open market value such as loss of expectation of life, deteriorating health or psychological damage. In essence, there is no adequate statutory provision for the quantum of compensation in Nigeria.

Legislative gaps are not necessarily a crucial problem since legislative provision cannot be entirely explicit as technology changes, inflation rises and human needs

---

[212] These insights are owed to a personal interview with Nick Ashton-Jones, Environmental Rights Action (London, February 1998). See also Uduehi (1987) for alternative methods of assessment of compensation. The approximate market prices used in the example were for early 1998.

change. Therefore, statutes need to be flexible to a certain extent. However, the lack of legislative provision and inadequate government policy in Nigeria have had highly adverse effects on village communities. Amounts of compensation arrived at during negotiations with village communities are still being paid according to the OPTS and government rates, which have been shown to be inadequate.

Existing gaps in legislative guidelines require judicial discretion, although Nigerian legislation provides for various circumstances under which compensation for damage from oil operations can be awarded. Since the phrase 'adequate compensation' can have different meanings, it is essential to analyse the way in which judicial interpretation has evolved on the issue (this will be shown in greater detail in chapter 6).

3.11. Conclusion

The formal-institutional structure of the Nigerian legal system is highly sophisticated, based on an elaborate fusion of English Common Law and typically Nigerian features, particularly customary law. Nigerian statute law, especially the FEPA Act, offer some scope for the protection and compensation of those adversely affected by oil operations but it contains major loopholes. It is not yet clear in what way oil-related regulations will be altered under the new Obasanjo government. Since the death of General Abacha in 1998, the Department of Petroleum Resources - the government's monitoring agency for the oil industry – has been abolished and there have been tentative indications that the Nigerian government may impose stricter environmental standards on the oil industry.[213] Until now, the guidelines for the operation of the oil industry and their actual enforcement have offered little protection to village communities.

In contrast to the enforcement problems experienced with environmental laws, Nigerian land law appears to be biased *per se* against village communities and their customary rights. With the advent of the Land Use Act 1978, land owners have been deprived of their land rights to the benefit of oil companies, which can compulsorily acquire any piece of land they desire with the permission of the state governor. In addition, land owners no longer receive any rents from oil companies for land acquired for oil operations, which underlines the fact that the government has favoured the interests of private companies in Nigeria before those of village communities.

In general, our discussion of land legislation and environmental law has indicated that statute law is either inadequate or unenforced which renders it incapable of restricting the adverse impact of oil operations on the ground. While statutory law has offered little protection to village communities, it promised monetary

---

[213] In November 1998, for instance, a new regulation was announced which stipulated that the volume of oil in drilling mud waste must not exceed 1%, which meant a change from 10% to 1%. If this environmental regulation is enforced, the cost of drilling is likely to rise for the oil companies (*PostExpressWired*, 30 November 1998). More importantly, in June 1999, the Obasanjo administration created an Environment Ministry (*Guardian*, Lagos, 21 June 1999). It is not yet clear whether recent changes precipitate a fundamental shift in Nigeria's oil-related legislation. However, it is likely that FEPA will continue operating as a department of the new ministry.

compensation for those adversely affected by oil operations. However, statutory provisions for the payment of compensation contain gaps and the actual quantum of compensation prescribed by the state appears to be inadequate in relation to the damage caused by oil companies. Considering the inadequate nature of legislation and its enforcement, one can understand why village communities tend to feel aggrieved by the inadequate compensation payments offered by oil companies. A farmer is not likely to understand legal or economic concepts such as capital value, but he or she is likely to notice that the farm income fell as a result of oil operations, while this loss was not matched by the oil company's compensation payment.

On the whole, this chapter has indicated that Nigeria's legal system tends to be biased in favour of the state and the oil companies at the expense of village communities. In this context, an alliance of the political elite and private interests in Nigeria (see chapter 2) obstructs the development of legal remedies for environmental and land related problems experienced by village communities. In other words, the rentier nature of the Nigerian state continues to prevent the formulation and enforcement of legislation which would benefit the interests of society as a whole, as opposed to the interests of the ruling elite and the oil companies. The inadequate legislative provisions and legal enforcement may result in social unrest in the oil producing areas by groups dissatisfied with the prevailing economic, social and legal order. This social unrest may result in litigation against oil companies. The litigants' only hope is that the judiciary is sufficiently independent of state structures as well as positively disposed towards them in order to give a wider scope to legal remedies. This calls for an analysis of the actual-practical operations of the legal system presented in the following chapter.

Chapter 4: Nigerian Legal System in Practice - Results of a Survey

4.1. Introduction

This chapter discusses the actual-practical operations of the legal system by using the results of a survey of Nigerian legal practitioners carried out by the author (the questionnaire is reproduced in Appendix A). The survey serves as a window to an understanding of conflict and litigation between oil companies and village communities in Nigeria, the main focus of the book.

The survey was aimed at evaluating the opportunities and constraints faced by potential and actual litigants in oil-related litigation. Inevitably, the survey does not address all correlates of legal disputes such as socio-economic and political factors including the marginalisation of ethnic minorities in the oil producing areas (see chapter 2). Rather than developing a comprehensive model of conflict and litigation in Nigeria's society, the main goal of our survey was to illustrate the incentives and disincentives of the legal process, which can either encourage or discourage litigants from engaging in litigation.

In this context, the survey results can verify or falsify two hypotheses as to whether the legal system is biased against oil companies or village communities. One of these hypotheses is that the formal-legal system is biased against village communities. Previous discussion in this book has suggested that there are indications of a bias in Nigeria's statute law in favour of oil companies (see chapter 3). The fact that statute law may be predisposed in favour of oil companies, however, does not automatically imply that the legal system as a whole is biased. Our previous discussion did not raise the issues of bias within the cumulation of judicial precedents, the court process or the day-to-day behaviour of the judiciary. If the legal system as a whole were found to be prejudiced in favour of oil companies, it could be reasonably assumed that a number of potential litigants had been discouraged from instituting lawsuits against oil companies. This would mean that the current level of litigation against oil companies is merely a small fraction of the potential court cases, which could arise as a result of valid legal claims to compensation for damage from oil operations. A further hypothesis would be that the legal system *per se* has no inherent biases but rather that the existing distribution of resources favours the claims of oil companies.

This chapter examines those factors within Nigeria's legal practice which may have given rise to an advantageous position for oil companies vis-à-vis village communities. It should be noted at this stage that possible explanations are not necessarily mutually exclusive. The day-to-day operations of the legal system may embody factors which operate against the interests of village communities to a varying degree, while some factors may operate against the interests of oil companies.

Of central importance to our discussion in this chapter is the question of access to courts (sections 4.3. and 4.4.). The extent of the barriers to justice can indicate the motivations of the potential plaintiffs who decide not to pursue a valid legal claim in court. Constraints to the institution of lawsuits also influence the perceived image of the formal legal system among potential litigants. These constraints could lead to a feeling among potential litigants that law is on the side of the opposing litigants. This feeling, combined with economic inequality and lack of political representation, could in turn increase the likelihood of extra legal forms of protest. An examination of the day-to-day operations of the legal system in relation to village community claims can hence serve as a window to an understanding of why village communities abandon litigation in favour of extra legal forms of protest such as seizure of oil industry equipment.

We start with a brief discussion of survey methodology. Readers who are not interested in methodology are advised to proceed directly to section 4.3.

4.2. Methodology, Survey Analysis and Profile of Respondents

As previously stated, the purpose of this chapter is to identify factors which can either encourage or discourage individual and community litigants from engaging in oil-related litigation. We investigate this topic on the basis of a survey of 154 Nigerian legal practitioners. This approach has to be weighted against alternative methodologies. One of those alternative methodologies would be to survey potential and actual litigants from village communities in the oil producing areas. Such a survey could investigate extra-legal forms of dispute resolution such as informal negotiations and settlements, which cannot be analysed through a survey of legal practitioners. A survey of village community members, moreover, would be likely to highlight barriers to justice as perceived by community members. It is likely that many potential litigants with a valid legal claim have never approached a lawyer in the first instance. A survey of legal practitioners does not account for those potential litigants. Lawyers can only report on actual experiences with potential litigants whom they have met. But the vast majority of legal practitioners in our survey have had at least some experience with obstacles in terms of access to courts. This indicates a high level of awareness amongst the respondents with regard to the problems encountered by potential litigants.

More importantly, a survey of legal practitioners is likely to yield superior returns to a survey of potential litigants in village communities. While all legal practitioners speak English, a high proportion of the members of village communities does not speak English but a local language and/or pidgin English. Survey questions would need to be translated into a number of local languages. The members of village communities, moreover, may be illiterate which is likely to render the use of standardised multiple-choice questions very difficult. By implication, a survey of village communities would pose severe problems of consistency. A survey by Onyige (1979) in the oil producing areas exemplified some of the language and communications problems. For instance, with regards to the question on the impact of oil operations, respondents in Onyige's survey named oil pollution and oil spills as major problems of oil operations, without noticing that oil spills are part of oil pollution. Onyige's survey encountered a number of problems, which cannot be solely ascribed to the inadequacies of survey design. His study exemplified that a survey of village communities may produce misleading and statistically inconsistent results.

An important strength of a survey of legal practitioners as opposed to a survey of potential litigants is that lawyers can be attributed some ability to answer questions accurately; an ability which perhaps exceeds that of the average member of society. All Nigerian lawyers have a university degree and have been trained to use language in a precise way. This is likely to ensure an adequate standard of the respondents' replies.

The main strength of a survey of lawyers as opposed to a survey of potential litigants is that it can assist an analysis of broader questions regarding the legal system, as compared to the individualistic view of litigants. A survey of legal practitioners has thus allowed for an assessment of key characteristics of the legal system such as the quality of the judicial services provided by courts of different types.

For practical reasons, survey distribution in Nigeria can be a difficult undertaking. Given Nigeria's problems with communications services, it would have been very difficult, if not impossible, for a researcher to distribute questionnaires to a random population of lawyers in different locations. Problems included delayed distribution or loss of mail. The reliable alternative taken in our survey was to distribute questionnaires in person. However, survey distribution in person does not always lead to a high response rate. In Nigeria, even well known and established organisations encounter problems in conducting standardised questionnaires distributed in person. For instance, the Constitutional Rights Project (CRP), a well-known Nigerian non-governmental organisation, conducted a survey among judges and legal practitioners in 1993. Despite repeated efforts by the CRP staff to retrieve the questionnaires in person from the judges and lawyers, the response rate was relatively low. Out of 1,000 questionnaires, only 511 were returned, which represented a response rate of 51.1% (Nwankwo *et al.* 1993, 6-7). We assumed that Nigerian legal practitioners would be even less likely to respond to a researcher based at a British university, whom they had never met before and who has no affiliation to an established organisation in Nigeria. Therefore, our efforts concentrated on finding a way of ensuring an effective distribution and collection of questionnaires.

In this context, it was assumed that the distribution and collection of questionnaires would be helped by an affiliation with an established Nigerian organisation. The author sought the support of Abdul Oroh, executive director of the Civil Liberties Organisation (CLO), a Nigerian non-governmental organisation, and Chief Priscilla O. Kuye, former head of the Nigerian Bar Association. Both Mr. Oroh and Ms. Kuye offered to assist in the distribution of the survey by providing lists of names of law firms which were said to have had previous contacts with the oil industry. Additional names of law firms were provided by several legal practitioners known to the author. The main rationale behind the choice of respondents was to find lawyers who had professional experience in dealing with oil-related cases. It was assumed that, unless our respondents included a significant number of experienced lawyers, the analysis of the respondents' views would provide little information on oil-related litigation. We are confident that the names of law firms obtained for our survey probably reflect the best possible sample of lawyers, which an outsider would be likely to get in Nigeria. A limitation of the survey to those locations where personal contacts with legal practitioners could be established has yielded an adequate response rate.

Of the names obtained, the vast majority of law firms were located in Lagos, Port Harcourt and Warri. Lagos is Nigeria's commercial centre where the greatest number of lawyers reside and where the major oil companies tend to have their headquarters. A large proportion of lawyers dealing with the oil industry are employed in law firms in Lagos, several of which have a subsidiary in Port Harcourt or in Warri. Port Harcourt is the main centre of the Nigerian oil industry being located in Rivers State, the oldest oil producing area in Nigeria, which hosts, for instance, the operational headquarters of Shell's Eastern division. Warri is the second most important city in the oil producing areas, which hosts, for instance, the operational headquarters of Shell's Western division. Many law firms dealing with oil-related litigation are based in Port Harcourt and Warri. Port Harcourt rather than Warri was chosen for the location of the survey because the number of law firms with oil industry work is greater in Port Harcourt than in Warri. Given the concentration of oil activities in the Port Harcourt area, we felt justified in limiting the location of the survey to Lagos and Port Harcourt.

In the course of several weeks in February and March 1998, 240 questionnaires were distributed among Nigerian lawyers in Lagos and Port Harcourt. In Lagos, 180 questionnaires were distributed in person to the law chambers and were also collected in person by the author or by the chief legal adviser of the CLO, Udeme Essien, with whom the author collaborated. Visits to the law firms took place between 9:00 A.M. and 7 P.M. At each address the author introduced himself as an academic researcher and presented a letter from the Department of Economics, St Andrews, which indicated that the survey was supported by the Department and by the CLO. The chief legal adviser of the CLO did not need an introductory letter because he could gain access to a law firm owing to his affiliation with the CLO. This approach proved effective in terms of securing an entry into the law firms.

At each address the author or Mr. Essien asked to speak to a senior partner in the law firm. If necessary, an appointment was made to call again later. If no contact was established after two visits, the address was given up. In each firm, between 1 and 5 questionnaires were left with the senior partner to distribute randomly among the lawyers. The number of questionnaires left in a law firm depended on the willingness of the partner to support the survey. It was felt that it would have been better to distribute only one questionnaire in each law firm to ensure greater representativeness. But we had feared that, unless several questionnaires were distributed in each firm willing to support the survey, the number of respondents could turn out to be too small to represent a significantly high sample of respondents. In order to ensure consistency in the lawyers' responses, all respondents were asked to provide their personal assessment of the legal system, as opposed to the views held by their employers or colleagues. This was important in order to avoid the possibility of the lawyers reflecting the perceived views of their employers or colleagues on the legal system rather than their own views. All respondents were advised that their responses were anonymous and would be treated with confidentiality. It was hoped that this approach would encourage respondents to provide a more candid assessment of the legal system.

In Port Harcourt, 60 questionnaires were distributed in person by a volunteer member of the CLO, in a similar manner to the one described above for Lagos.

This approach allowed for an effective distribution and collection of questionnaires. Out of 240 questionnaires, 154 were returned, representing a response rate of 64.2%. This was significantly higher than the response rate of 51.1% in the CRP survey mentioned earlier. By the end of the author's stay in Nigeria, only 19 questionnaires were retrieved from Port Harcourt, compared with 135 in Lagos, representing response rates of 31.7% and 75.0% respectively. The low response rate in Port Harcourt can be explained by the fact that a number of lawyers failed to return their questionnaires on the date of collection. The high response rate in Lagos can be explained by the fact that a significant number of lawyers were visited more than once to collect the questionnaires.

Since we are mostly interested in describing the legal system in relation to the oil industry operations and oil-related litigation, our survey analysis attempts to assess the views of lawyers with experience in dealing with oil-related cases. We attempted to strengthen this analysis through a series of oil-related questions in the survey. As it turned out, a number of the law firms surveyed had no or virtually no dealings with oil-related litigation. In a significant proportion of firms, oil-related litigation constituted only a small fraction of the firm's total work. The survey, nevertheless, reflects a significant pool of expert knowledge on oil operations since as many as 128 respondents (83.1%) state that they have previously had some professional contact with the oil industry, of which 85 (55.2%) have previously acted as legal counsel for an oil company, its subsidiary or a sub-contractor and 97 (63.0%) have previously acted as counsel in a lawsuit against an oil company.

The analysis of the survey relies on frequency distributions, percentage tables and statistical tests.[214] Among other questions, we investigated whether specific sub-groups of respondents (e.g. lawyers specialised in environmental law or lawyers who previously worked for the oil industry) hold different views from those respondents who do not fit into the sub-group.[215] The views of lawyers who previously worked for the oil industry or those who had previous contacts with the oil industry are likely to reflect their professional experiences in dealing with oil-related cases. A comparison of those lawyers with the other lawyers highlights the differences between oil-related litigation and other types of litigation. In this context, the presence in our sample of a significant proportion of lawyers with no previous oil industry contacts is useful as it provides a comparative reference.

When using the term 'oil-related litigation', one needs to remember that there are different types of oil-related cases. These include employment-related litigation, environmental cases and commercial disputes. We are, of course, mostly interested in

---

[214] In the following analysis of the survey, all results are depicted in percentage terms. The figures may not always add up to 100.0% but range from 99.8% to 100.1% as the figures were rounded off.

[215] We approached this question by conducting non-parametric chi-square (χ^2) tests for independence. A similar method was applied in a study by Adigun and Stephenson (1992), which utilised chi-square tests in an analysis of job satisfaction in the UK and Nigeria. In our analysis, the alpha value was set at 10% ($\alpha = 0.10$). If one or more cells had expected frequencies of less than 5, they were combined with others until new cells were formed with expected frequencies of at least 5. For each chi-square test quoted in this book, the corresponding χ^2 and p-value are provided in a footnote.

court cases between village communities and oil companies. These cases involve mainly environmental claims. We have thus utilised the distinct category of environmental lawyers vis-à-vis the other lawyers in order to distinguish between views on oil-related litigation involving village communities and other types of oil-related claims.

Before going into the depth of survey analysis, we will briefly describe the profile of respondents in our survey. Of the 154 respondents, 124 lawyers (80.5%) are male and 28 lawyers (18.2%) are female, while 2 lawyers give no response. This broadly reflects the dominance of men within Nigeria's legal profession. The average age of respondents is 40 years. Respondents are relatively young, roughly 50% of them are under 36 years of age.[216] Lawyers have been, on average, members of the Nigerian Bar Association for 11 years.[217] A large proportion of respondents - 40.9% - have between 6 and 10 years of professional experience. The relatively young age and the short experience of the respondents can be attributed to the recent expansion in legal education in Nigeria.[218]

The size of law firms, in which respondents have been employed, varies widely. The largest law firm has approximately 55 employees while the smallest has only 2 employees. The average firm size is approximately 12 employees.[219] The largest firm has approximately 40 support staff while the smallest has no support staff at all. The average number of support staff is roughly 5.5.[220] The majority of law firms - some 61% - has between 1 and 5 support staff. In general, one could say that the size of Nigerian law firms is relatively small. Respondents, many of whom had dealings with the oil industry, can be expected to work for more flourishing firms with a larger number of staff because legal advice for the oil industry can be very profitable. Therefore, the average size of the law firms in our survey is likely to be greater than the size of Nigeria's law firms in general.

Of the 154 lawyers, 30 (19.5%) state that they specialise in criminal law, 93 (60.4%) in civil law, 47 (30.5%) in environmental law and 102 (66.2%) in commercial law. The large number of lawyers with specialisation in commercial law can be explained by the fact that many respondents work for the oil industry, which requires specialised knowledge of commercial law. A number of lawyers indicates that they specialise in all types of law since they are employed by a general law practice. In Nigeria, there is no professional distinction between barrister and solicitor so a general practitioner is theoretically expected to be familiar with all aspects of the legal

---

[216] Birth year MEAN = 1957.97.

[217] Year of admission to the Bar MEAN = 1986.91.

[218] Enrolment in the Nigerian Law School, which has recently been relocated from Lagos to Abuja, has increased significantly in the last two decades. According to Oko (1994), the Law School had 225 students in 1973. The number of Law School students increased to 796 in 1983, to over 2,000 in 1988 and to 2,611 in 1992. By 1999, the number had reportedly increased to roughly 3,000 (Guardian, Lagos, 20 May 1999). The number of Law School students is a good indicator of the expansion of Nigeria's legal profession because all prospective lawyers must attend the school before they can be called to the Bar. As a result of the recent expansion in Nigeria's legal education, it is not surprising to encounter so many relatively young lawyers in the country.

[219] Size of law firm MEAN = 12.09.

[220] Number of support staff MEAN = 5.49.

practice. However, lawyers who declare to be specialists in all areas of law are considered 'unclassifiable' for the purpose of the survey precisely because they do not indicate a particular specialisation. The replies of lawyers who provide no information on their specialisation are classified as 'no response'. This system of classification can explain the relatively high percentage of 'unclassifiable' and 'no responses'.[221]

To sum up, respondents are predominantly male, under 40 years old and have 10 or less years of professional experience. They tend to work in small law firms, with 1 to 5 support staff, and they are predominantly specialised in civil law. The profile of respondents appears to reflect the fact that the Nigerian legal profession is relatively new in composition, dynamic and dominated by small, under-funded law chambers.

4.3. Problems of Access to Courts

The degree of access to courts determines as to whether potential litigants can file a lawsuit or not, so it constitutes a key test of the quality of a legal system. Unfortunately, there has been relatively little academic research on the access to courts in Africa. Writing on Francophone Africa, Degni-Segui (1995) has identified five basic problems of access to courts in Africa: geographical distance to courts, delay in the disposal of cases, lack of funds, African political systems and ignorance of legal rights. In this section, we analyse whether our survey results support or do not support the findings of Degui's study on access to courts.

Respondents have been asked whether they have encountered instances in which potential litigants have been discouraged from seeking legal recourse although they have had a valid claim to compensation, an injunction or another form of legal recourse. Excluding 'no responses' and 'don't knows', as many as 78.5% of the respondents state that they have had some experiences with potential litigants who were discouraged from seeking redress in court. Some 71.6% note that they have had those experiences at least sometimes, if not often (see columns 3 and 4, Table 4.1.). These figures indicate that the problems of access to justice in Nigeria are very significant indeed.

Lawyers have been asked to rank reasons which would prevent potential litigants from seeking legal recourse. The responses suggest that the main constraints of access to courts are financial problems and ignorance of potential litigants. Out of 154 lawyers, the lack of funds is regarded as a very important reason by 75.3% of the lawyers and by 13.6% as an important reason. The second and third most important reasons are the lack of general education and ignorance of legal rights. These two problems are considered very important reasons by 57.1% and 51.3% respectively, and are considered important reasons by 24.7% and 37.7% respectively. These answers suggest that victims of crimes and civil wrongs in Nigeria are frequently ignorant of their legal rights. The other important problems of access to courts are: delay in the disposal of cases, intimidation by public bodies, intimidation by tort-feasors and

---

[221] In the following analysis of the survey results, all unclassifiable responses are counted as 'no response'.

uncertainty about the potential success of a suit. Other problems such as ethnic origin and the geographical distance to courts are considered less important (see Table 4.2.).

Table 4.1. Answers to Question 11a 'Have you encountered instances in which potential litigants have been discouraged from legal action although they had a valid claim to compensation, an injunction or another form of legal recourse?'

	1	*2*	*3*	*4*
	Percentage of Respondents	*Cumulative Percentage*	*Percentage of Respondents (excl. 'no responses' & 'don't knows')*	*Cumulative Percentage (excl. 'no responses' & 'don't knows')*
Very often	7.1	7.1	9.5	9.5
Often	17.5	24.6	23.3	32.8
Sometimes	29.2	53.8	38.8	71.6
Rarely	5.2	59.0	6.9	78.5
Never	16.2	75.2	21.6	100.1
Don't know	20.8	96.0	-	-
No response	3.9	99.9	-	-
Total	99.9	99.9	100.1	100.1

Table 4.2. Answers to Question 11b 'Amongst the following rank reasons which you think would prevent potential litigants from seeking legal recourse?' (per cent)

	Very important reason	*Important reason*	*Less important reason*	*No response*
Lack of funds	75.3	13.6	4.5	6.5
Lack of general education	57.1	24.7	9.1	9.1
Ignorance of legal rights	51.3	37.7	3.9	7.1
Delay in the disposal of cases by courts	48.7	39.0	7.1	5.2
Intimidation by public bodies	35.1	35.1	16.9	13.0
Intimidation by tort-feasors	24.0	43.5	19.5	13.0
Uncertainty about the potential success of a suit	21.4	55.2	13.6	9.7
Ethnic origin	15.6	27.3	42.2	14.9
Geographical distance to courts	10.4	33.8	40.9	14.9
Living in a rural area	10.4	33.1	42.9	13.6
Organisational structure of villages	5.8	20.1	57.1	16.9
Being a woman	4.5	20.8	59.7	14.9
Young age	3.2	20.8	59.1	16.9

A significant proportion of respondents maintain that the problems of access to courts are greater in litigation involving oil companies. Excluding 'no responses' and 'don't knows', some 48.9% state that the problems of access to courts are more severe in oil-related litigation than in other types of litigation, while 40.3% state that the problems are equal (see columns 3 and 4, Table 4.3.). The high percentage of respondents who note that the problems are equal in oil-related litigation and in other types of litigation suggests that a significant proportion of the potential litigants in oil-related cases are not particularly disadvantaged if compared with other types of litigation. But the responses suggest that, by and large, the problems in oil-related litigation are greater.

One commercial lawyer from Lagos states that the problems are more severe in oil-related litigation because *'claims against oil companies often occur in rural areas in which educational levels are low, there is general ignorance and lack of funds'*.[222] It could be argued that the main reason why problems are greater in oil-related litigation is the financial imbalance between the affluent oil companies on the one hand and the poor village communities on the other hand. Oil companies have clearly more financial resources than community litigants, which they can spend on the country's leading lawyers and expert witnesses. The village communities in oil producing areas belong to some of the poorest income groups in Nigeria. Bayelsa State, one of the main oil producing areas, is one of the poorest regions in Nigeria.

Table 4.3. Answers to Question 11c 'Are the problems [of access to courts] particularly severe in oil-related litigation?'

	1	2	3	4
	Percentage of Respondents	*Cumulative Percentage*	*Percentage of Respondents (excl. 'no responses' & 'don't knows')*	*Cumulative Percentage (excl. 'no responses' & 'don't knows')*
Much more severe	11.7	11.7	14.0	14.0
More severe	29.2	40.9	34.9	48.9
The same	33.8	74.7	40.3	89.2
Less severe	6.5	81.2	7.8	97.0
Much less severe	2.6	83.8	3.1	100.1
Don't know	9.7	93.5	-	-
No response	6.5	100.0	-	-
Total	100.0	100.0	100.1	100.1

There appear to be two important reasons why the financial imbalance between oil companies and village communities has become less significant in recent years. First, those affected by oil operations usually sue oil companies as a group rather than as individual plaintiffs so they may share some of the financial costs between themselves. Village communities and families have had greater problems in litigating successfully in the past (this will be shown in greater detail in chapter 6). In the 1970s, it was not uncommon for a judge to dismiss a suit or to limit its scope because he or

---

[222] Lawyer no.83, 1998 survey of Nigerian lawyers.

she found that the plaintiffs had not proven their authority to sue as a group.[223] Successful cases, in which oil companies have been sued by plaintiffs representing a village community or a family as a whole, have become more widespread.[224] Second, many lawyers in the oil producing areas appear to increasingly view court cases against oil companies as a financial investment, as pointed out by a number of respondents. Therefore, they no longer demand a standard fee from the litigants but instead demand a contingency fee.[225] In practice, this means that lawyers work for free for their client during the legal proceedings but in turn demand a high share of the compensation payment in return, if the suit succeeds. In other words, the lawyer rather than the litigant increasingly carries the financial risk of losing a case. The attraction of lawyers to oil-related litigation may be high because the financial rewards are potentially higher than in other types of litigation. In *Shell v. Farah*[226], for example, in which the plaintiffs were awarded 4,621,000 Naira by the court in 1994, the lawyers did not receive a standard fee but instead received roughly 2,500,000 Naira or 54% of the total compensation payment.[227] In comparison, according to Nwankwo *et al.* (1993, 28), the Chief Justice of Nigeria, the highest paid judicial officer in the country, received 77,400 Naira per annum in 1993 (excluding housing and other additional benefits). Since the potential earnings in oil-related litigation are substantial, several lawyers in the oil producing areas such as Lucius Nwosu in Port Harcourt have specialised in litigation of village communities against oil companies.[228] In some cases, the lawyer may even be willing to pay for expert evidence if he or she can expect a high share of the potential compensation payment.[229] In effect, lawyers such as Nwosu help potential litigants to gain greater access to courts in oil-related litigation. The two reasons discussed above - group based claims and the nature of lawyers' fees - may explain

---

[223] For instance, in *Chinda v. Shell-BP* (1974) 2 RSLR 1, the plaintiffs' claim was dismissed as the judge held that they *'have not proved their authority to sue in a representative capacity, and are therefore deemed to be suing only in respect of themselves individually'*.

[224] Several recent high-profile cases by communities against oil companies from the 1990s can be cited: *Geosource v. Biragbara* (1997) 5 NWLR (Pt. 506) 607, *Shell v. Tiebo VII* (1996) 4 NWLR (Pt. 445) 657, *Shell v. Farah* (1995) 3 NWLR (Pt. 382) 148. In all of these cases, plaintiffs sued an oil company in representative capacity, not as individuals.

[225] Lawyers employed by oil companies usually receive a standard fee rather than a contingency fee, so they earn a fee independently of the success of a suit. For instance, Shell in Nigeria reportedly pays roughly US$ 2,500 on average in lawyer's fees for a single case, including the standard fee, court fees, tax and other bills, no matter whether a suit succeeds or not (Frynas 1999). A standard fee may be less profitable for a lawyer than a contingency fee but it carries little financial risk for the lawyer. A standard fee may still be very profitable for legal practitioners, in particular, those working for the oil industry. According to Ibidapo-Obe (1995, 186), some Nigerian lawyers charge a standard fee of between 250,000 and 1,000,000 Naira for a single brief. The vast majority of potential litigants in village communities would not be able to afford those sums. In contrast, a contingency fee may enable potential litigants to file a lawsuit.

[226] (1995) 3 NWLR (Pt. 382) 148.

[227] Personal interview with Ledum Mittee, one of the lawyers in the Farah case (London, February 1998).

[228] In the Farah case alone, Lucius Nwosu reportedly received roughly 2,000,000 Naira. Personal interview with Ledum Mittee, one of the lawyers in the Farah case (London, February 1998).

[229] In the Farah case, for example, Lucius Nwosu reportedly covered the costs of the scientific report presented in court. Personal interview with Ledum Mittee, one of the lawyers in the Farah case (London, February 1998).

why the problems of access to courts in some oil-related litigation have become less severe in recent years. This can, in turn, help to explain the rise in litigation against oil companies.

While the financial burden of litigants in oil-related cases appears to have decreased, the lack of funds remains the most important problem of access to courts in Nigeria, whether in oil-related litigation or other types of litigation. The limited Nigerian legal aid scheme, introduced in 1976, initially only provided financial assistance in criminal proceedings (Collett 1980). In 1986, the Nigerian legal aid scheme was extended to cover civil claims in respect of accidents (Ibidapo-Obe 1995, 188). But the vast majority of oil-related litigation does not qualify for any legal aid. Village communities have to hire a lawyer and expert witnesses themselves, which is expensive and burdensome. Several respondents emphasise that plaintiffs in oil-related cases often lack funds to pay for expert evidence. This favours oil companies which can afford to hire some of the country's best scientific experts. According to a 1994 field survey of Okoosi and Oyelaran-Oyeyinka (1995), undertaken in 14 oil producing communities in Delta State, the average daily income ranged from 7 Naira (US$ 0.30 at 1994 official rate) in Uzere to 50 Naira (US$ 2,27) in Agbasho. In comparison, in the case *Shell v. Farah*[230], the two expert referees appointed by the court tendered a bill for 515,800 Naira, which included 415,800 Naira for their fees and 100,000 Naira for a soil test. Considering the relatively low incomes of the local people, potential litigants can rarely afford to engage lawyers and expert witnesses.[231] Hiring a lawyer on a contingency fee could solve the financial problems of potential litigants. But it could be expected that access to contingency fees may be limited due to the significant cost of expert witnesses and the financial risk faced by legal practitioners.

Even if a lawyer is prepared to forego his standard fee and is also prepared to pay himself for expert evidence, there may be other costs related to negotiations with oil companies and litigation, in particular costs of travel and court fees. Litigants may need to travel to visit their legal counsel, to negotiate with oil company staff and to attend court proceedings. The geographical distance is a problem, since those affected by oil operations live mostly in the Niger Delta where it may take many hours or even days to find a regular means of transport. Transportation in the Niger Delta is relatively expensive for the local population. The chief of Okoroba, a Niger Delta village, explained that a single trip to Shell's Western headquarters in Port Harcourt would cost him as much as the income from several months fishing.[232] According to the World Bank (1995, 79), a return trip between many riverine communities in the Niger Delta and Port Harcourt costs as much as the monthly salary of a government employee. Court fees may also be a burden. If a court case is lost, they may amount to a total of over 10,000 Naira.[233] If the case is lost on appeal, the general costs may be higher,

---

[230] (1995) 3 NWLR (Pt. 382) 148.

[231] In general, a World Bank (1996, 25) report stated that 34.7 million Nigerians out of a population of some 102 million lived below the poverty line in 1992. According to the World Bank (1996, 38), the average per capita expenditure of rural households was 780 Naira per annum (at 1985 prices). In Southern Nigeria, the figure was 937 Naira per annum. Considering those low incomes, it is understandable that the lack of funds is the key problem for any potential litigants in Nigeria.

[232] Personal interview (Okoroba, February 1998).

[233] Personal interview with Mr. Vera-Cruz, partner at Victor & Charles (Lagos, February 1998).

especially if the litigants have to travel to the Supreme Court in Abuja, which is located in Northern Nigeria.

While the lack of funds is the main obstacle faced by potential litigants, the second and third most important problems of access to courts are related to ignorance. Communities in the oil producing areas are often ignorant of their legal rights, as exemplified by the village Okoroba in Bayelsa State visited by the author of this book. Prof. Bruce Powell, biologist at the University of Port Harcourt, estimated that the number of fish in the vicinity of Okoroba fell by approximately 80% as a result of canal dredging by a Shell sub-contractor. The oil operations clearly damaged the local economy dependent on fishing.[234] However, the villagers were unaware that they could sue Shell for the loss of income from fishing, although they were aware that they could sue oil companies for destroyed crops and trees.[235] According to a number of lawyers, villagers are usually aware that they are entitled to compensation for damage from an oil spill while they tend to be ignorant that they are entitled to claim compensation for damage from other oil company activities. This may partly explain why a substantial quantity of court cases against oil companies are initiated in respect of oil spills.[236] Ignorance of formal legal rights can be partly explained by the existence of customary laws, which govern Nigeria's village communities. Community members usually prefer to resolve disputes according to customary law, rather than through the country's legal system (see chapter 3). Potential litigants from village communities are likely to be highly familiar with their own customary law rights, but in oil-related disputes they must seek redress in the formal legal system whose rules are usually alien to them. To sum up, the problems of access to courts appear to be greater in oil-related litigation, which involves village communities.

4.4. Views on Access to Courts by Different Sub-Groups

The views on access to courts vary across different groups of respondents.[237] The environmental lawyers have particularly strong views on barriers to justice. In 5 out of 6 questions, in which the views of the environmental lawyers differ from the other lawyers, the environmental lawyers consider problems of access to courts more severe than others (see Table 4.4.).[238] Perhaps not surprisingly, they regard the lack of general

---

[234] Personal interview with Prof. Bruce Powell, Port Harcourt (February 1997).

[235] Personal interviews with villagers at Okoroba, Bayelsa State, Nigeria (February 1997).

[236] Another reason for the substantial quantity of litigation involving damage from oil spills may be that the case law is relatively well settled and makes it relatively easy to claim damages (see chapter 6). In 1998, 70% of all Shell's pending court cases in Nigeria involved damage from oil spills (Frynas 1999, chapter 6).

[237] Of all chi-square tests for independence conducted on the issue of access to courts, the most significant deviations occur in respect of the lawyers' professional background. Environmental lawyers and commercial lawyers hold diverging views from the other lawyers in 6 and 5 out of 15 questions respectively. Views also vary according to years of professional experience (in 4 questions out of 15), according to size of law firm (in 4 questions), according to age (in 3 questions) and according to gender (in 3 questions).

[238] In cross-tabulations, in which the responses of environmental lawyers vary from the rest, the p-value varies from p = 0.065 to p = 0.0002, that means, all results are highly significant at $\alpha = 0.10$.

education as the main problem. Of the environmental lawyers, 73.3% consider the lack of general education a very important obstacle. This is not necessarily surprising since an understanding of environmental damage can be expected to require more technical knowledge than other types of legal disputes. Interestingly, environmental lawyers consider intimidation by public bodies and tort-feasors a particularly important problem of access to courts. Of the environmental lawyers, 60.5% and 44.2% regard the intimidation by public bodies and tort-feasors as very important problems respectively, compared with 28.2% and 20.0% of the other lawyers respectively. These results suggest that the government and some private bodies may attempt to frustrate environmental litigation.[239] By implication, the views of the environmental lawyers appear to indicate that potential litigants seeking compensation for environmental damage in oil-related litigation may be more likely to encounter problems of access to courts than litigants in other types of litigation. Furthermore, these views imply that lack of general education and intimidation are more important problems of access to courts in oil-related cases involving environmental damage than in other types of cases. These are important facts since lawsuits between village communities and oil companies usually involve claims for environmental damage.

Perhaps somewhat surprisingly, the views of lawyers who had previous contact with the oil industry diverge from the other lawyers in respect of only one question, namely on the question how often lawyers have met potential litigants discouraged from legal action despite a valid legal claim.[240] Of the lawyers with previous oil industry contact, 10.9% pronounce that they have met potential litigants who have been discouraged from legal redress very often, compared with none of the other lawyers. Of the lawyers with previous oil industry contact, 73.3% state that they have met potential litigants who have been discouraged from legal redress at least sometimes if not often, compared with only 35.7% of the other lawyers (see Table 4.5.). These responses are more significant in terms of oil-related litigation than the replies by all respondents because they are more likely to be based on experiences with the oil industry. The results appear to strengthen the earlier finding that the problems of access to courts are more severe in oil-related litigation.

The chi-square and p-values for cross-tabulations between the attribute of environmental lawyer and attributes of obstacles of access to courts are as follows:

- for views on lack of general education: $\chi^2 = 3.39$, which exceeds the critical $\chi^2_{0.10}(1) = 2.706$, p = 0.065;
- for views on intimidation by public bodies: $\chi^2 = 11.61$, which exceeds the critical $\chi^2_{0.10}(2) = 4.605$, p = 0.003;
- for views on intimidation by tort-feasors: $\chi^2 = 8.58$, which exceeds the critical $\chi^2_{0.10}(2) = 4.605$, p = 0.014;
- for views on ethnic origin: $\chi^2 = 16.86$, which exceeds the critical $\chi^2_{0.10}(2) = 4.605$, p = 0.0002;
- for views on geographical distance to courts: $\chi^2 = 12.10$, which exceeds the critical $\chi^2_{0.10}(2) = 4.605$, p = 0.002;
- for views on uncertainty about the potential success of a suit: $\chi^2 = 5.18$, which exceeds the critical $\chi^2_{0.10}(2) = 4.605$, p = 0.074.

[239] These results also appear to strengthen the argument that the Nigerian government and private corporations sometimes frustrate the enforcement of environmental legislation (compare chapter 3).

[240] In other words, only one cross-tabulation produces a significant chi-square value: $\chi^2 = 5.30$, which clearly exceeds the critical $\chi^2_{0.10}(2) = 4.605$, p = 0.071.

Table 4.4. Answers to Questions 5 and 11b: Responses of environmental lawyers on reasons which may prevent potential litigants from seeking legal recourse (per cent)

	Very important reason	Important reason	Less important reason
Environmental lawyers on lack of general education	73.3	24.4	2.2
Other lawyers	54.7	30.7	14.7
Environmental lawyers on intimidation by public bodies	60.5	25.6	14.0
Other lawyers	28.2	46.5	25.4
Environmental lawyers on intimidation by tort-feasors	44.2	41.9	14.0
Other lawyers	20.0	50.0	30.0
Environmental lawyers on ethnic origin	25.0	45.5	29.5
Other lawyers	11.8	19.1	69.1
Environmental lawyers on geographical distance to courts	16.3	58.1	25.6
Other lawyers	11.8	29.4	58.8
Environmental lawyers on uncertainty about the potential success of a suit	15.9	75.0	9.1
Other lawyers	24.0	54.7	21.3

Table 4.5. Answers to Questions 6a and 11a: Responses of lawyers with previous contact with the oil industry on whether they met potential litigants who have been discouraged from seeking legal recourse (per cent)

	Very often	Often	Sometimes	Rarely	Never
Lawyers with previous contact in the oil industry	10.9	21.8	40.6	7.9	18.8
Cumulative percentage	10.9	32.7	73.3	81.2	100.0
Other lawyers	0	35.7	0	21.4	42.9
Cumulative percentage	0	35.7	35.7	57.1	100.0

Table 4.6. Answers to Questions 6b and 11b: Responses of oil industry lawyers on intimidation by tort-feasors (per cent)

	Very important reason	Important reason	Less important reason
Lawyers who acted as counsel for oil industry	24.7	45.5	29.9
Cumulative percentage	24.7	70.2	100.1
Other lawyers	31.6	56.1	12.3
Cumulative percentage	31.6	87.7	100.0

Somewhat surprisingly, the views of lawyers who previously worked for an oil company diverge from the views of the other lawyers on only one question, namely on the question of intimidation by tort-feasors.[241] The oil company lawyers attach less

---

[241] $\chi^2 = 5.84$, which clearly exceeds the critical $\chi^2_{0.10}(2) = 4.605$, p = 0.054.

importance to intimidation by tort-feasors than the other lawyers. Of the oil company lawyers, 24.7% and 45.5% consider this problem very important and important respectively, compared with 31.6% and 56.1% of the other lawyers respectively (see Table 4.6.). Clearly, significantly fewer oil company lawyers consider this a problem.

The responses of oil company lawyers do not necessarily suggest that intimidation by tort-feasors is a less severe problem in oil-related litigation. On the contrary, several respondents emphasise that intimidation by public bodies and oil companies is a more prevalent problem in oil-related litigation. Several lawyers have strong views on the question of intimidation. While commenting on oil-related litigation, one respondent from Port Harcourt states that problems are *'more severe because in oil-related matters the interest groups involved are powerful and highly connected, oil being the major revenue earner of the central government".*[242] Another lawyer from Port Harcourt comments that in cases involving oil companies the government may *"use security agents against litigants and their solicitors".*[243] An environmental lawyer from Lagos comments on the structural links between the government and oil companies: *'Most litigants are afraid of taking oil companies to court because of their connection with the government'.*[244] Judging by these responses, political influence of oil companies may, therefore, deter potential litigants, although in practice it may be difficult to document specific cases involving intimidation.[245] It is entirely consistent for oil company lawyers to minimise the importance of intimidation. No explanation can be entirely satisfactory, but one may expect that oil companies as tort-feasors are less likely to be accused of intimidation by the lawyers working for them. While our speculations on the question of intimidation cannot be adequately verified or falsified by the data, it is conceivable that oil company lawyers would want to minimise the extent of intimidation by their clients or would simply note fewer problems.

Our speculations on intimidation appear to be strengthened by the views of commercial lawyers.[246] Commercial lawyers consider intimidation by public bodies

---

[242] Lawyer no.144, 1998 survey of Nigerian lawyers.

[243] Lawyer no.146, 1998 survey of Nigerian lawyers.

[244] Lawyer no.8, 1998 survey of Nigerian lawyers.

[245] Non-governmental organisations have provided few examples. For instance, Human Rights Watch described one case in which a plaintiff, who lived near Elf's Obite gas installation, was reportedly threatened by a manager of an oil company sub-contractor when he refused to settle a compensation claim (HRW 1999, 177).

[246] In 3 out of 4 cross-tabulations, of which the results are not independent, commercial lawyers consider problems of access to courts more severe than the other lawyers. The p-value varies from p = 0.093 to p = 0.003, that means, all results are significant at $\alpha = 0.10$. The chi-square and p-values for cross-tabulations between the attribute of commercial lawyer and attributes of obstacles of access to courts are as follows:
- for views on intimidation by public bodies: $\chi^2 = 11.34$, which exceeds the critical $\chi^2_{0.10}(2) = 4.605$, p = 0.003;
- for views on intimidation by tort-feasors: $\chi^2 = 6.07$, which exceeds the critical $\chi^2_{0.10}(2) = 4.605$, p = 0.048;
- for views on ethnic origin: $\chi^2 = 2.83$, which exceeds the critical $\chi^2_{0.10}(1) = 2.706$, p = 0.093;
- for views on organisational structure of villages: $\chi^2 = 4.54$, which exceeds the critical $\chi^2_{0.10}(1) = 2.706$, p = 0.033.

and by tort-feasors more severe than the other lawyers. Of all commercial lawyers, 85.5% and 80.9% regard intimidation by public bodies and by tort-feasors respectively as a very important or an important problem, while the figures for the other lawyers are 54.2% and 58.4% (see Table 4.7.). These results would suggest that intimidation can be a crucial problem of access to Nigerian courts within a commercial environment. This appears to strengthen our earlier speculations that intimidation can be a very important factor in preventing oil-related litigation.

Table 4.7. Answers to Questions 5 and 11b: Responses of commercial lawyers on reasons which may prevent potential litigants from seeking legal recourse (per cent)

	Very important reason	Important reason	Less important reason
Commercial lawyers on intimidation by public bodies	44.4	41.1	14.4
Other lawyers	25.0	29.2	45.8
Commercial lawyers on intimidation by tort-feasors	29.2	51.7	19.1
Other lawyers	29.2	29.2	41.6
Commercial lawyers on ethnic origin	17.0	34.1	48.9
Other lawyers	16.7	12.5	70.8
Commercial lawyers on organisational structure of villages	8.0	21.6	70.5
Other lawyers	9.5	47.6	42.9

On the whole, the data in the last two sections has revealed that potential litigants in Nigeria face severe barriers to justice and that these problems are particularly severe in oil-related cases. As Degni-Segui argued, the obstacles of access to courts are further compounded by African political systems such as through authoritarian rule and its impact on the judiciary. The functioning of the judiciary and extra-judicial pressures in Nigeria are assessed in the next two sections.

4.5. Functioning of the Judiciary and the Court System

That access to courts is only one of the problems in the functioning of Nigeria's legal system is self-evident. Litigants also face problems once they have filed a lawsuit. These problems result from the deficiencies in the day-to-day operations of the judiciary and the legal system. Such impediments include interference from the executive branch of the government and underfunding. In 1994, the Eso Panel, under the retired judge of the Supreme Court Kayode Eso, submitted a report on the situation of the judiciary to the government. The Eso Panel reportedly described the judiciary as a 'disaster institution'. The report was said to have concluded that *'after 34 years of*

The results of the cross-tabulation between the attribute of commercial lawyer and problems of ethnic origin were only marginally significant at $\alpha = 0.10$ as they become significant at $p = 0.093$. All other results were highly significant. We are, of course, mainly interested in the commercial lawyers' views on intimidation.

[Nigeria's] *independence, there are not the necessary physical structures - that is, court halls, judges residence, libraries, vehicles, stationary, and indeed, toilets'* (CLO 1995, 165-168). The detailed findings of the report have never been disclosed in public but leaks to the press suggested that the Eso Panel produced four main findings. First, the judiciary was considered too dependent on the executive arm of the government. Second, the appointment of judges was regarded as too arbitrary. Third, the funding of the legal system was said to be too little. Fourth, congestion in the courts was seen as too high. Survey respondents confirm all the findings of the Eso Panel. Of all respondents, 89.6% agree that the judiciary is too dependent on the executive arm of the government, 74.7% agree that the appointment of judges is too arbitrary and 89.6% agree that the funding of the legal system is too little. Some 90.2% consider congestion in the courts too high (see Table 4.8.). If 'no responses' were subtracted, the results would become even more impressive. What emerges is that the Nigerian judiciary faces severe impediments to its functioning.

Table 4.8. Answers to Question 14 'Do you agree/disagree with the following statements?'

	Strongly disagree	Disagree	Neither agree/ disagree	Agree	Strongly agree	No response
The judiciary is too dependent on the executive arm of the government	1.3	0.6	4.5	5.2	84.4	3.9
Cumulative percentage	1.3	1.9	6.4	11.6	96.0	99.9
The appointment of judges is too arbitrary	9.1	3.2	9.1	20.8	53.9	3.9
Cumulative percentage	9.1	12.3	21.4	42.2	96.1	100.0
The funding of the legal system is too little	3.2	0.6	2.6	2.6	87.0	3.9
Cumulative percentage	3.2	3.8	6.4	9.0	96.0	99.9
Congestion in the courts is too high	3.9	1.3	0.6	0.6	89.6	3.9
Cumulative percentage	3.9	5.2	5.8	6.4	96.0	99.9

While there is generally little variation in the respondents' views on the Nigerian judiciary, the views of commercial lawyers differ on 3 out of 4 questions. Commercial lawyers regard the problems of the judiciary as more severe than the other lawyers. The most significant results concern the question on the funding of the legal system. Of all commercial lawyers, 94.9% strongly agree that the legal system is underfunded, compared with 69.2% of the other lawyers (see Table 4.9.).[247] It could be argued that commercial lawyers are predictably more concerned with monetary issues than the other lawyers. But this speculation cannot explain why commercial lawyers are more concerned about the situation of the judiciary in general. Of the commercial lawyers, 88.9% strongly agree that the judiciary is too dependent on the executive arm

---

[247] $\chi^2 = 11.99$, which clearly exceeds the critical $\chi^2_{0.10}(1) = 2.706$, p = 0.0005.

of the government, compared with 73.1% of the other lawyers.[248] A total of 96.0% of the commercial lawyers strongly agree that the congestion in the courts is too high, compared with 80.8% of the other lawyers (see Table 4.9.).[249] An explanation for these differences may simply be that the government is more likely to intervene in commercial cases than in other cases, which could explain why commercial lawyers experience more impediments to the functioning of the judiciary.

Lawyers in our survey appear to regard the non-democratic nature of military rule (1966-1979 and 1983-1999) as a key cause of the impediments faced by the judiciary. The military, which governed Nigeria for most of the country's history since 1966, ruled by decree and courts were forbidden from questioning the validity of a decree. The military, moreover, set up tribunals made up predominantly of members of the armed forces to try criminals and government critics.[250] With regards to military rule, Kayode Eso wrote in a newspaper article: 'There can never be independence of the judiciary in a non-democratic setting'.[251] According to Nigerian lawyers, the nature of military rule leads to interference from the executive and the arbitrary appointment of judges and, more generally, to a less favourable treatment of the Nigerian judiciary by the government. By implication, it has to be assumed that the transfer to civilian rule in May 1999 will lead to greater independence of the judiciary.

Table 4.9. Answers to Questions 5 and 14: Responses of commercial lawyers on whether they agree/disagree with the following statements (per cent)

	Strongly disagree	Disagree	Neither agree/ disagree	Agree	Strongly agree
The funding of the legal system is too little					
Commercial lawyers	2.0	0	1.0	2.0	94.9
Other lawyers	11.5	3.8	11.5	3.8	69.2
The judiciary is too dependent on the executive arm of the government					
Commercial lawyers	2.0	0	4.0	5.1	88.9
Other lawyers	0	3.8	11.5	11.5	73.1
Congestion in the courts is too high					
Commercial lawyers	3.0	0	1.0	0	96.0
Other lawyers	11.5	7.7	0	0	80.8

Two of the problems revealed by the Eso Panel and the survey further compound the obstacles of access to courts in Nigeria: congestion in the courts and the

---

[248] $\chi^2 = 2.99$, which exceeds the critical $\chi^2_{0.10}(1) = 2.706$, p = 0.084.

[249] $\chi^2 = 5.02$, which clearly exceeds the critical $\chi^2_{0.10}(1) = 2.706$, p = 0.025.

[250] On military rule and its effect on the Nigerian legal system, see Nwabueze (1992).

[251] Kayode Eso, 'Judicial Independence in the Post-Colonial Era' (*Guardian*, Lagos, 27 January 1997).

arbitrary appointment of judges. Congestion in the courts leads to the delay in the disposal of cases, while the appointment of government-backed judges increases the uncertainty about the potential success of a suit.

The congestion in the courts manifests itself through the high number of pending cases. Cases in Nigerian courts including appeals may take over 10 years before reaching a final verdict. Sometimes the original litigants will have died by the time the judgment is made. No published figures could be obtained for the whole of Nigeria on the number of pending cases, but a report commissioned for the Shell-initiated Niger Delta Environmental Survey (NDES) provides detailed figures for Rivers State, one of the key oil producing areas. The number of cases in Rivers State carried from the previous year has been steadily growing, for instance, 17,304 cases were carried over from 1995 to 1996, while only 2,847 cases were disposed of in 1995 (see Table 4.10.).

Table 4.10. Cases in Rivers State Disposed Of and Carried Over for 1993-1996 Legal Year

	1994	1995	1996
Cases filed	6,552	5,045	-
Cases pending	-	19,187	18,671
Cases disposed of	4,905	2,847	2,929
Cases carried from previous year	15,215	16,939	17,304

Source: Ogbnigwe (1996).

The delay in the disposal of cases together with uncertainty about the potential success of a suit may discourage a potential litigant. In addition, while the court case is pending, a litigant may be left without any means to support himself. In *Eze v. Agip*[252], the plaintiff sued Agip for the destruction of his house and his property at the Akri flowstation in Imo State. He reportedly lost his house as a result of oil operations but had received no compensation from the oil company. He testified that he had been squatting with a friend, while his family had to stay permanently away from him. So when the case was adjourned, he felt that he could not wait until the scheduled day of proceedings and asked for an accelerated hearing. The judge refused the application on the grounds that the plaintiff failed to '*show special and exceptional circumstances justifying such application*'.[253] The above case exemplifies that the delay in the disposal of cases may discourage potential plaintiffs from instituting a lawsuit.

While the delay in the disposal of cases may discourage potential plaintiffs, the arbitrary appointment of judges by the government may alter the outcome of court cases in favour of the government, its agencies and business partners in the private sector. A commercial lawyer from Lagos commented on the appointment of judges: '*The way our judges are being appointed can be said to be responsible for them being*

---

[252] (1979) IMSLR 540.

[253] Per Chianakwalam, J. at page 542.

subservient to the executive arm of government thus allowing it to manipulate the judges anyhow to serve their selfish ends as a result of which there is no justice in Nigeria'.[254] Before Obasanjo came to power in May 1999, judges of the federal courts and the State High Courts were appointed by the Provisional Ruling Council (PRC). Appointments were made on the advice of the Advisory Judicial Committee, whose membership included the Chief Justice of Nigeria, the Attorney-General and various other judges from the federal states. Judges of inferior state courts were appointed by the military governors of the federal states. Judges theoretically had a guaranteed tenure of office until retirement, but they could be dismissed by the PRC on the advice of the Advisory Judicial Committee (Nwankwo et al. 1993, 20-26; Guardian, Lagos, 30 June 1999).[255] In a few instances, the military removed judges without advice. For instance, the government removed sixty High Court judges in 1985 as part of a country-wide purge of the public service (Nwabueze 1992, 24). Following the transfer to civilian rule in May 1999, the appointment of judges is likely to be reformed.

Before May 1999, the problems of the arbitrary appointment of judges were probably most severe with regards to military tribunals, in which government-appointed judges decided upon a case jointly with military officers. In terms of oil-related litigation, the most prominent court case of a military tribunal was that against Ken Saro-Wiwa, leader of the Movement for the Survival of the Ogoni People (MOSOP), who was best known for his protests against Shell. Ken Saro-Wiwa and 14 other defendants were accused of murdering four traditional rulers in May 1994. Rather than allowing the case to be judged by a civilian court, General Abacha convened a so-called Civil Disturbances Special Tribunal in November 1994, which included two judges and a military officer. The tribunal's decisions were only considered effective upon confirmation by the ruling military council and they carried no right of appeal. A report by Michael Birnbaum QC (1995), a British barrister, suggested that the trial was not fair and that there were serious doubts as to its legality. Birnbaum (1995, 8) concluded that there was no reason for the appointment of the military tribunal in the Saro-Wiwa case 'other than the desire of the Federal Military government that any trial.. should take place before a tribunal which it hopes will favour the prosecution and a desire to avoid the scrutiny of its case by the ordinary courts'. Birnbaum further averred that, overall, the tribunal 'has behaved in a way which strongly suggests that it is biased in favour of' the government.[256] Despite concerns over the legality of the trial and the evidence presented, Ken Saro-Wiwa and eight others were sentenced to death in November 1995. The Saro-Wiwa case may have discouraged potential litigants from seeking legal redress in oil-related matters. A female lawyer from Lagos comments that 'after Ken Saro-Wiwa a lot of people might

---

[254] Lawyer no.84, 1998 survey of Nigerian lawyers.

[255] As Eze (1996, 143-144) pointed out, the 1979 Constitution provided for the appointment of judges through democratic processes. The Constitution provided, for example, that Supreme Court judges were to be appointed by the Nigerian president subject to confirmation by a majority in the Senate, on the advice of the Federal Judicial Service Commission. However, the re-introduction of military rule in 1983 shifted the responsibility for the appointment of judicial officers from democratic institutions to the military.

[256] On the proceedings of the Saro-Wiwa case, see Birnbaum (1995).

not sue any oil company again.[257] In any case, the above lawsuit exemplifies how the appointment of judges may influence the outcome of a court case in favour of the government, which in turn reduces the certainty of the potential success of a case based on the strength of a legal argument.

The delay in the disposal of cases and the uncertainty about the potential success of a case compound the problems of access to courts. Combined with ignorance, financial problems and intimidation, the problems of the judiciary thus reduce the frequency of oil-related litigation. Due to barriers to justice, compensation claims in the Nigerian oil industry are more likely to be settled before they come to court, even if the potential plaintiffs are dissatisfied with the payment offered by a company. Beyond the question of access to courts, the above discussion suggests that the judiciary faces substantial extra-judicial pressures from the government. It is not yet clear in what way the attitude of the government towards the judiciary will change under the civilian regime of Obasanjo, albeit an improvement in the functioning of the judiciary can be expected.

4.6. Extra-Judicial Pressures and Enforcement of Court Orders

The respondents confirm the view that the Nigerian judiciary is often under serious extra-judicial pressures from public and private bodies. Of all respondents, 50.0% state that judges, lawyers and other judicial officers encounter pressures from public or private institutions very often or often. According to 44.8% and 4.5%, pressures exist sometimes or rarely respectively. Not a single lawyer believes that there are never pressures (see Table 4.11.).

Table 4.11. Answers to Question 8a 'Would you say that lawyers, judges or other judicial officers encounter outside pressures from private or public institutions in their work?'

	Percentage of Respondents	Cumulative Percentage
Very often	20.1	20.1
Often	29.9	50.0
Sometimes	44.8	94.8
Rarely	4.5	99.3
Never	0	99.3
No response	0.6	99.9
Total	99.9	99.9

A significant proportion of the respondents suggest that the extra-judicial pressures are greater in oil-related litigation. Excluding 'no responses' and 'don't knows', a clear majority - 54.1% - note that the difficulties are greater or much more severe in oil-related litigation, while 35.0% state that the difficulties are the same. Only 10.8% state that the difficulties are less severe or much less severe (see columns 3 and

---

[257] Lawyer no.88, 1998 survey of Nigerian lawyers.

4, Table 4.12.). A Lagos lawyer comments that *'oil cases usually attract political considerations'.*[258] Another lawyer with 35 years of professional experience comments: *'oil cases often have political implications'.*[259] The relatively high percentage of respondents who note that the problems are the same or less severe in oil-related litigation may suggest that extra-judicial pressures are not necessarily a particularly serious problem in some oil-related cases, if compared with other types of litigation.

Table 4.12. Answers to question 8b 'Are the pressures more or less severe in oil company related litigation?'

	1	*2*	*3*	*4*
	Percentage of Respondents	*Cumulative Percentage*	*Percentage of Respondents (excl. 'no responses' and 'don't knows')*	*Cumulative Percentage (excl. 'no responses' and 'don't knows')*
Much more severe	14.3	14.3	18.3	18.3
Greater	27.9	42.2	35.8	54.1
The same	27.3	69.5	35.0	89.1
Less severe	7.8	77.3	10.0	99.1
Much less severe	0.6	77.9	0.8	99.9
Don't know	16.2	94.1	-	-
No response	5.8	99.9	-	-
Total	99.9	99.9	99.9	99.9

The extra-judicial pressures in oil-related cases appear to depend primarily on the subject matter of a case. A commercial lawyer from Lagos differentiates between cases involving environmental damage and employment-related cases. He argues that in court cases involving environmental damage, as opposed to employment-related cases, extra-judicial pressures from the government may be applied.[260] It is likely that the government does not intervene in every oil-related case as there is a substantial quantity of those cases and many cases do not directly infringe on the interests of the government. Nonetheless, the majority of respondents suggests that problems in oil-related litigation are, by and large, greater.

The views on extra-judicial pressures differ according to professional background.[261] The views of commercial lawyers differ significantly from the rest.[262]

---

[258] Lawyer no.58, 1998 survey of Nigerian lawyers.

[259] Lawyer no.74, 1998 survey of Nigerian lawyers.

[260] Lawyer no.108, 1998 survey of Nigerian lawyers.

[261] Lawyers who claim that they specialise in civil law or environmental law state that the extra-judicial pressures are more severe in oil-related litigation. Lawyers who claim to be specialists in criminal law are, overall, more likely to believe that the extra-judicial pressures are less severe in oil-related litigation. A cross-tabulation between the attribute of size of a law firm and views on extra-judicial pressures also produces a significant chi-square value. But there is no discernible pattern as to how the size of a law firm determines views on these pressures.

[262] $\chi^2 = 6.04$, which clearly exceeds the critical $\chi^2_{0.10}(2) = 4.605$, p = 0.049.

Of all commercial lawyers, 21.1% believe that extra-judicial pressures are much more severe in oil-related litigation, compared with 8.3% of the other lawyers. Some 57.9% of the commercial lawyers state that these pressures are much more or more severe in oil-related litigation, compared with 29.1% of the other lawyers (see Table 4.13.). These results appear to suggest that extra-judicial pressures are greater in litigation involving commercial enterprises.

Table 4.13. Answers to Questions 5 and 8b: Responses of commercial lawyers on whether the extra-judicial pressures are more or less severe in oil-related litigation (per cent)

	Much more severe	Greater	The same	Less severe	Much less severe
Commercial lawyers	21.1	36.8	31.6	9.2	1.3
Cumulative percentage	21.1	57.9	89.5	98.7	100.0
Other lawyers	8.3	20.8	54.2	16.7	0
Cumulative percentage	8.3	29.1	83.3	100.0	100.0

Interestingly, lawyers who had previous contact with oil companies regard extra-judicial pressures as more severe than the other lawyers.[263] Of the respondents with previous oil industry contact, 55.2% state that extra-judicial pressures exist very often or often, compared with 29.2% of the other lawyers (see Table 4.14.). These results appear to confirm the earlier finding that there are more extra-judicial pressures in oil-related cases than in other types of litigation.

Table 4.14. Answers to Questions 6a and 8a: Responses of lawyers with previous contact with the oil industry on whether the legal system experiences extra-judicial pressures (per cent)

	Very often	Often	Sometimes	Rarely	Never
Lawyers with previous contact in the oil industry	21.3	33.9	40.2	4.7	0
Cumulative percentage	21.3	55.2	95.4	100.1	100.1
Other lawyers	16.7	12.5	66.7	4.2	0
Cumulative percentage	16.7	29.2	95.9	100.1	100.1

Even if the outcome of a court case has not been influenced by extra-judicial pressures, the government may still attempt to prevent the enforcement of court orders, rulings and judgments. Of all respondents, 55.2% state that there are severe or very severe problems in the enforcement of court orders in Nigeria. A further 40.9% state that there are some difficulties and only 2.6% state that there are minor difficulties (see Table 4.15.). What emerges from these results is that the non-enforcement of court orders can be a major problem in litigation.

---

[263] $\chi^2 = 6.004$, which clearly exceeds the critical $\chi^2_{0.10}(2) = 4.605$, p = 0.05.

Table 4.15. Answers to Question 7a 'Would you say that there are difficulties in the enforcement of court orders, rulings or judgments?'

	Percentage of Respondents	*Cumulative Percentage*
Very severe problems	26.0	26.0
Severe problems	29.2	55.2
Some difficulties	40.9	96.1
Minor difficulties	2.6	98.7
No difficulties	0.6	99.3
No response	0.6	99.9
Total	99.9	99.9

Several lawyers stress that the enforcement of court orders depends primarily on the interest of the government in a specific court case. The only respondent, who states that there are no difficulties in the enforcement of court orders in Nigeria, adds that there are indeed difficulties in cases, in which *'the government has an interest to protect'*.[264] In order to enforce rulings against the government, a fiat of the Attorney-General is needed.[265] By implication, the Attorney-General decides in the last instance whether a ruling should be enforced or not. One lawyer from Lagos comments that *'It is pretty hard to enforce court orders in Nigeria, especially where the government has an interest and in any case one needs the blessing of the Attorney-General to enforce orders'*.[266] The Attorney-General has the power to stifle court judgments against the government.

Government interventions in the operations of the legal system do not only occur on behalf of federal agencies but also on behalf of local authorities and other public bodies. A lawyer from Lagos narrates a well-known court case in 1995, in which the Akwa Ibom State High Court pronounced a judgment against the state government. The government of the Akwa Ibom State refused to carry out the court order. The state government, moreover, put pressure on the high court judges to withdraw the court order by instructing the seizure of the official vehicles of all high court judges in the state and by evicting the judges from their residential quarters. At a later stage, the federal government reportedly mediated between the judges and the state government and the matter was settled.[267] Instances such as this may serve to intimidate judicial officers and may discourage judges from pronouncing judgments against government institutions.

It is not entirely clear in what way the difficulties in the enforcement of court judgments in oil-related litigation are different from other types of litigation. Excluding

---

[264] Lawyer no.152, 1998 survey of Nigerian lawyers.

[265] Constitution (Suspension and Modification) Decree No.107 of 1993.

[266] Lawyer no.77, 1998 survey of Nigerian lawyers.

[267] Lawyer no.1, 1998 survey of Nigerian lawyers. This incident in Akwa Ibom State was also reported in Olugboji (1996, 87). As another example of non-enforcement of court orders, Olugboji (1996, 89-90) reported a case involving unjust dismissal from the police force. In 1994, the Abeokuta High Court ruled that two police officers, who were dismissed from the police force, be re-instated in their previous jobs and be paid their outstanding salaries and allowances as their dismissal was *'irregular and unconstitutional'*. Police authorities reportedly ignored the ruling.

'don't knows' and 'no responses', some 44.4% of the surveyed lawyers state that the problems are the same in oil-related litigation and other types of litigation. 39.8% note that the problems are more severe or much more severe in oil-related litigation. Only 15.8% state that the problems are less or much less severe in oil-related litigation (see columns 3 and 4, Table 4.16.). The high percentage of respondents who note that the problems are greater in oil-related cases suggests that there may be somewhat greater problems in oil-related litigation, if compared with other types of litigation. Nonetheless, the data appears to indicate that the problems in oil-related litigation are, by and large, comparable with other types of litigation.

Table 4.16. Answers to Question 7b 'Are the difficulties more or less severe in oil company related litigation?'

	1	*2*	*3*	*4*
	Percentage of Respondents	*Cumulative Percentage*	*Percentage of Respondents (excl. 'no responses' and 'don't knows')*	*Cumulative Percentage (excl. 'no responses' and 'don't knows')*
Much more severe	13.0	13.0	15.0	15.0
More severe	21.4	34.4	24.8	39.8
The same	38.3	72.7	44.4	84.2
Less severe	9.7	82.4	11.3	95.5
Much less severe	3.9	86.3	4.5	100.0
Don't know	11.0	97.3	-	-
No response	2.6	99.9	-	-
Total	99.9	99.9	100.0	100.0

As previously mentioned, our results suggest that it may be somewhat more difficult to enforce court orders in oil-related cases but the data is not unequivocal on this point. What appears from some respondents' comments is that the difficulties in the enforcement of court orders in different types of litigation depend very much on the subject matter. As with general difficulties in the enforcement of court orders, lawyers state that the enforcement of court orders depends primarily on the interest of the government. A female lawyer from Lagos argues that the difficulties in oil-related litigation *'depend on the interest of the government in the matter'.*[268] For instance, Olugboji (1996, 90) reported a case, in which the Federal High Court in Benin City imposed a court order restraining the Oil Mineral Producing Areas Development Commission (OMPADEC) from swearing in Joseph Popo as the new commissioner for Delta State. The OMPADEC defied the court order and went ahead to swear in Popo as the new commissioner. The above discussion appears to suggest that a court order against the oil industry or the country's oil administration may not be enforced, if it is perceived as an infringement of the government's interests in the oil industry.

---

[268] Lawyer no.88, 1998 survey of Nigerian lawyers.

The views on the enforcement of court orders vary somewhat according to professional background.[269] Above all, the views of environmental lawyers differ from those of the other lawyers.[270] Of the environmental lawyers, 63.8% state that the difficulties in the enforcement of court orders are severe or very severe, compared with only 44.6% of the other lawyers (see Table 4.17.). A clear majority of the environmental lawyers - 53.3% - state that these difficulties are more severe in oil-related litigation, compared with only 23.5% of the other lawyers (see Table 4.18.). This suggests that the enforcement of court orders is more difficult in court cases involving environmental matters. By implication, it has to be assumed that the enforcement of court orders in oil-related cases involving environmental damage is likely to be more difficult than in other oil-related cases such as employment-related litigation.

The earlier speculation that the enforcement of court orders may be more difficult in oil-related litigation appears to be strengthened by the replies of lawyers who had prior contact with oil companies.[271] Of those lawyers, 55.2% state that the difficulties are more severe or much more severe in oil-related litigation, compared with 29.2% of the other lawyers (see Table 4.19.). These results appear to suggest that, overall, the enforcement of court orders in oil-related cases is more difficult than in other types of litigation.

Table 4.17. Answers to Questions 5 and 7a: Responses of environmental lawyers on whether there are problems in the enforcement of court orders (per cent)

	Very severe problems	Severe problems	Some difficulties	Minor difficulties	No difficulties
Environmental lawyers	40.4	23.4	31.9	4.3	0
Cumulative percentage	40.4	63.8	95.7	100.0	100.0
Other lawyers	15.7	28.9	54.2	1.2	0
Cumulative percentage	15.7	44.6	98.8	100.0	100.0

[269] Interesting findings concern the years of respondents' professional experience. In both cross-tabulations on attributes of years of professional experience and the enforcement of court orders, the chi-square tests for independence are significant. In general, the greater number of years of professional experience lawyers have, the more likely they are to state that there are serious difficulties in the enforcement of court orders. This may be explained by the assumption that lawyers with more years of professional experience are more likely to have experienced instances, in which court orders have not been enforced.

[270] In respect of question 7a on the general difficulties in the enforcement of court orders, the results of cross-tabulations are as follows: $\chi^2 = 10.11$, which clearly exceeds the critical $\chi^2_{0.10}(2) = 4.605$, p = 0.006. In respect of question 7b on the difficulties in oil-related litigation, the results of cross-tabulations are even more significant: $\chi^2 = 19.76$, which clearly exceeds the critical $\chi^2_{0.10}(3) = 6.251$, p = 0.0002.

[271] $\chi^2 = 6.00$, which clearly exceeds the critical $\chi^2_{0.10}(2) = 4.605$, p = 0.050.

Table 4.18. Answers to Questions 5 and 7b: Responses of environmental lawyers on whether these problems are more or less severe in oil-related litigation (per cent)

	Much more severe	More severe	The same	Less severe	Much less severe
Environmental lawyers	33.3	20.0	40.0	6.7	0
Cumulative percentage	33.3	53.3	93.3	100.0	100.0
Other lawyers	4.4	19.1	52.9	14.7	8.8
Cumulative percentage	4.4	23.5	76.4	91.1	99.9

Table 4.19. Answers to Questions 6a and 7b: Responses of lawyers with previous contact with oil companies on whether problems of enforcement are more or less severe in oil-related litigation (per cent)

	Much more severe	More severe	The same	Less severe	Much less severe
Lawyers with previous contact	21.3	33.9	40.2	4.7	0
Cumulative percentage	21.3	55.2	95.4	100.1	100.1
Other lawyers	16.7	12.5	66.7	4.2	0
Cumulative percentage	16.7	29.2	95.9	100.1	100.1

On the whole, the data in the last two sections has revealed that the Nigerian judiciary and the court system face severe impediments to their functioning. These problems further compound barriers to justice for potential litigants. The impediments to the functioning of the judiciary and the court system appear to be much greater in court cases involving the government and somewhat greater in oil-related litigation. Following the transfer to civilian rule in May 1999, these impediments are likely to become less severe. What must be remembered, nevertheless, is that the extent of these problems and the quality of legal services may continue to differ from court to court.

4.7. Types of Courts

That government pressure on judges or the quality of judicial services vary according to different types of courts is perhaps unsurprising. Of all respondents, 85.7% believe that there are major differences in the quality of judicial services in different Nigerian courts, only 8.4% believe the opposite, while 5.8% give no response. The Supreme Court, the highest Nigerian court, is regarded as the most competent Nigerian court, followed closely by the Court of Appeal. Of all surveyed lawyers, 38.3% and 50.6% consider the Supreme Court to be very competent and competent respectively. Some 31.2% and 59.1% regard the Court of Appeal as very competent and competent respectively. The other Nigerian courts are considered markedly less competent (see Table 4.20.). This can possibly be best explained by the fact that the Supreme Court and the Court of Appeal attract some of the best judicial officers within the court system. Judges of these two courts receive higher material benefits, including free housing, and enjoy higher prestige than those of the lower courts, which is likely to attract the most capable lawyers.[272] In addition, a court case in the Supreme Court is usually presided over by five judges, sometimes seven, while a court case in the Court of Appeal is usually presided over by three judges.[273] It is thus more likely that these courts can arrive at a more balanced and competent decision than all the other courts, which have only one judge presiding over a court case.

Of the other courts, the Federal High Court and the State High Courts are regarded as competent. Of all lawyers, 7.8% and 70.1% consider the Federal High Court very competent and competent respectively, while 3.9% and 74.0% consider the State High Courts very competent and competent respectively. The lower courts, the magistrates' courts and the customary courts, are generally considered incompetent (see Table 4.20.). These differences can possibly be best explained by the fact that the Federal High Court and the State High Courts attract some of the best judicial officers from the lower courts. The best judges from the magistrates' courts are often recruited by the State High Courts. The inadequacies of the magistrates' and the customary courts may be explained as a result of the appointments of unqualified judicial officers and inadequate remuneration.[274] A commercial lawyer from Lagos comments: *'The level of experience required to be a magistrate (mostly 3 years plus at the Nigerian Bar), low salary scale, large volume of criminal cases, lack of adequate technological support, inexperience and venality have conspired to make the magistrate court the acme of gross abuse of judicial process in Nigeria* [sic]*'*.[275]

Several respondents emphasise that there are regional differences between courts in different federal states and personal differences between different judicial officers.[276] Moreover, the quality of judicial services is not the same as the quality of

---

[272] While judges of the Supreme Court and the Court of Appeal earn more than those of other types of courts, their remuneration is not excessively high. According to Nwankwo et al. (1993, 28), the Chief Justice of Nigeria, the highest paid judicial officer in the country, received 77,400 Naira per annum in 1993 (excluding housing and other additional benefits). At the 1993 official rate of exchange, this translated to about US$ 3,500 per annum. In comparison, Ibidapo-Obe (1995, 186) revealed that some Nigerian legal practitioners charge a fee of between 250,000 and 1,000,000 Naira for a single brief. Nwankwo et al. (1993, 28) commented: *'The low wages attributed to judicial officers have discouraged independent-minded lawyers in private legal practice from taking up positions in the bench, as such lawyers are reluctant to give up relatively lucrative private practices for poor judicial positions'.*

[273] Section 214 of the 1979 Constitution provided that the Supreme Court must consist of not less than 5 justices for the purpose of an appeal from the Court of Appeal. If an appeal deals with constitutional issues, the court must be constituted by 7 justices. Section 226 of the 1979 Constitution provided that the Court of Appeal must consist of not less than 3 justices.

[274] A comprehensive report on the administration of justice in the magistrates' and customary courts in Southern Nigeria was undertaken by the Civil Liberties Organisation (Onyekpere 1996).

[275] Lawyer no.108, 1998 survey of Nigerian lawyers.

[276] Our survey results appear to support this view. In particular, lawyers from Lagos and Port Harcourt have different views on the competence of different courts. The most significant difference concerns the general question on the quality of judicial services in Nigeria. Three cross-tabulations between the attribute of location of law firm and questions on the court system produce significant chi-square tests: on the general view on differences, on the competence of the Federal High Court and the magistrates' courts. The chi-square test results for them are as follows:
- on views on the general differences between judicial services in different types of courts: $\chi^2 = 9.86$, which clearly exceeds the critical χ^2 0.10 (1) = 2.706, p = 0.007.
- on views on the Federal High Court: $\chi^2 = 4.11$, which clearly exceeds the critical χ^2 0.10 (1) = 2.706, p = 0.043.

justice. While a court may be competent in terms of substantive and procedural law, it is not necessarily independent from public or private bodies.

The views on the court system vary somewhat according to professional background.[277] Commercial lawyers are more likely than others to observe differences between different types of courts.[278] Of the commercial lawyers, 94.7% believe that there are major differences between the quality of judicial services in different types of courts, while the figure for the other lawyers is 78.6% (see Table 4.21.).

Table 4.20. Answers to Question 16b 'Which type of court would you judge as particularly competent or incompetent?' (per cent)

	Very competent	Competent	Incompetent	Don't know	No response
Supreme Court	38.3	50.6	3.9	1.9	5.2
Court of Appeal	31.2	59.1	4.5	0.6	4.5
Federal High Court	7.8	70.1	8.4	7.1	6.5
State High Courts	3.9	74.0	10.4	2.6	9.1
Magistrates' Courts	3.9	16.9	55.8	17.5	5.8
Customary Courts	5.2	7.1	52.6	29.2	5.8

Table 4.21. Answers to Questions 5 and 16a: Responses of commercial lawyers on whether there are major differences between the quality of judicial services in different types of courts (per cent)

	There are major differences	There are no major differences
Commercial lawyers	94.7	5.3
Cumulative percentage	94.7	100.0
Other lawyers	78.6	21.4
Cumulative percentage	78.6	100.0

- on views on the magistrates' courts: $\chi^2 = 6.33$, which clearly exceeds the critical χ^2 0.10 (1) = 2.706, p = 0.012.

Of the Port Harcourt lawyers, 70.6% believe that there are major differences between the quality of judicial services in different types of courts, compared with the figure of 93.8% for the Lagos lawyers. These results appear to support the earlier speculation that there are regional differences between the judicial services of different types of courts.

[277] Some of these differences cannot be easily explained. Environmental lawyers view the Supreme Court and the State High Courts as more competent than the other lawyers. Criminal lawyers view the Supreme Court and the magistrates' courts as more competent than other lawyers. The size of law firms also influences views on the competence of different types of courts. But the author is unable to adequately explain these diverging views.

[278] $\chi^2 = 6.94$, which clearly exceeds the critical $\chi^2_{0.10}(1) = 2.706$, p = 0.024.

Commercial lawyers hold different views on the competence of the Federal High Court to the other lawyers.[279] Of those lawyers, 93.5% believe that the Federal High Court is either competent or very competent, compared with the figure of 78.3% for the other lawyers (see Table 4.22.). These differences may be explained by the fact that the Federal High Court, which was formerly the Federal Revenue Court, is a court specialised in commercial litigation. It could be thus expected that the Federal High Court is more competent in commercial cases than other courts.

Table 4.22. Answers to Questions 5 and 16b: Responses of commercial lawyers on whether the judicial services in the Federal High Court are competent (per cent)

	Very competent	Competent	Incompetent
Commercial lawyers	8.6	84.9	6.5
Cumulative percentage	8.6	93.5	100.0
Other lawyers	8.7	69.6	21.7
Cumulative percentage	8.7	78.3	100.0

A number of respondents emphasise that the Federal High Court, albeit generally competent in terms of law, is particularly vulnerable to government pressures.[280] One lawyer, who regards the court as very competent, writes that the *'Federal High Court often seems to see itself as an appendage of the federal government and this tends to affect its judgments especially where the government is a party'*.[281] Another lawyer compares the independence of different types of courts and concludes: *'From my professional experience, judges of the Federal High Court are much more timid as compared, for instance, with the judges of the State High Courts'*.[282]

The vulnerability of the Federal High Court to government pressures has wide repercussions on oil-related litigation. The Constitution (Suspension and Modification) Decree No.107 divested State High Courts of jurisdiction over oil matters in 1993 (see chapter 3). In Nigeria, there were only twelve Federal High Court divisions in 1993, compared with well over 500 State High Court divisions (Nwankwo *et al.* 1993, 11; Robinson 1996, 38). In the oil producing Rivers State, there were eight High Court divisions, compared with a single Federal High Court division (Fawehinmi 1992).[283]

---

[279] $\chi^2 = 3.40$, which clearly exceeds the critical $\chi^2_{0.10}(1) = 2.706$, p = 0.065.

[280] This view has also been expressed by a number of Nigerian scholars. Oyakhirome (1995, 177), for instance, commented: '...It may be argued that the existence of Federal High Courts exercising exclusive jurisdiction in matters or causes on the exclusive list will enable the federal government to protect itself and enforce its own laws through its own judicial agencies'. Oyakhirome (1995, 179) further averred that, in a military dictatorship, the Federal High Court 'could become a ready tool to suppress advocates of human rights and democracy'.

[281] Lawyer no.63, 1998 survey of Nigerian lawyers.

[282] Lawyer no.16, 1998 survey of Nigerian lawyers.

[283] The Rivers State High Court divisions were Port Harcourt, Ahoada, Omoku, Yenagoa, Degema, Nchia, Isiokpo and Bori.

Until 1993, a potential litigant in Rivers State could approach the nearest of the eight High Court divisions to sue a company. From 1993, potential litigants may find it more difficult to travel to the Federal High Court. It can be thus expected that the Act will effectively reduce the amount of litigation against oil companies. Moreover, as indicated by respondents, the Federal High Court appears to be more dependent on the executive arm of the government. This is likely to result in more favourable court judgments for oil companies who have joint ventures and common interests with the government. A number of respondents stress that judges of the Federal High Court are also less likely to sympathise with the plight of village communities affected by oil operations because they tend to come from outside the oil producing areas. For instance, the sole judge of the Federal High Court in Port Harcourt, the main oil city, was appointed from Lagos, while a number of the State High Court judges in Rivers State have originally come from some of the oil producing areas.

What the above discussion suggests is that the Federal High Court is likely to be biased in favour of oil companies. A ruling by the Federal High Court can, of course, be appealed against, in which case the Court of Appeal or the Supreme Court will ultimately decide upon the case. But any appeal to a higher court is likely to be limited to questions of law. The witness evidence admitted by the Federal High Court is likely to be taken for granted by the appellate court. That means, a less sympathetic judge in the Federal High Court may dismiss some of the plaintiff's vital evidence. This would in turn decrease the chances of success for the plaintiff's appeal in oil-related litigation. In other words, it is conceivable that the Federal High Court is more likely to dismiss the plaintiff's evidence against an oil company or the government than a State High Court judge. For all the above reasons, the 1993 Act and the current structure of the court system benefit the oil companies more than the opposing litigants because they limit the access to courts for potential litigants and their prospects of success.[284]

While the Federal High Court appears to be less independent from the government, other courts may face government pressures, too. One lawyer with 20 years of professional experience argued that the Supreme Court, the most competent of all Nigerian courts, has become less independent since its re-location from Lagos to the capital in Abuja. While important distinctions remain between different types of courts, lawyers stress that, notwithstanding the type of court, the integrity of a particular judge and the subject matter of a lawsuit may often be the most important factors in determining the quality of justice.

On the whole, this section has shown that there are wide differences in the quality of judicial services between different types of courts. The Supreme Court and the Court of Appeal appear to be the most competent Nigerian courts. The Federal High Court, which became the court of first instance for oil-related litigation in 1993, appears to be biased in favour of oil companies.

---

[284] It has to be remembered, however, that the interpretation of the 1993 Decree has not been entirely unambiguous. In *Shell v. Isaiah* (1997) 6 NWLR (Pt. 508) 236, the Court of Appeal pronounced that the 1993 Decree does not affect oil spillage matters (see chapter 3).

4.8. Oil Companies and Court Procedure

Previous analysis indicates that the court system tends to be biased in favour of oil companies rather than the opposing litigants. This section discusses in greater detail how oil companies and courts conduct themselves in oil-related litigation which provides a background for analysing conflict and litigation between oil companies and village communities.

The answers of all respondents do not suggest that litigants in oil-related cases are treated particularly unfairly by the courts. Of all respondents, 36.3% state that litigants are treated unfairly or very unfairly, compared with 32.4% who state that litigants are treated fairly or very fairly (see Table 4.23.).

Table 4.23. Answers to Question 9a 'Are litigants treated fairly in court decisions involving oil companies?'

	Percentage of Respondents	Cumulative Percentage
Very fairly	1.9	1.9
Fairly	30.5	32.4
Neither fairly nor unfairly	10.4	42.8
Unfairly	24.0	66.8
Very unfairly	12.3	79.1
Don't know	14.9	94.0
No response	5.8	99.8
Total	99.8	99.8

There are significant differences between the views of different groups of lawyers on fair treatment in court proceedings. Interestingly, the commercial lawyers are more likely to observe unfair treatment of litigants in oil-related litigation.[285] Of the commercial lawyers, 46.9% state that litigants are treated unfairly or very unfairly, compared with 22.7% for the other lawyers (see Table 4.24.). These results suggest that unfair treatment of litigants is a realistic possibility in a commercial environment.

Table 4.24. Answers to Questions 5 and 9a: Responses of commercial lawyers on whether litigants are treated fairly in court decisions involving oil companies

	Very fairly	Fairly	Neither fairly nor unfairly	Unfairly	Very unfairly
Commercial lawyers	2.5	34.2	16.5	30.4	16.5
Cumulative percentage	2.5	36.7	53.2	83.6	100.1
Other lawyers	4.5	63.6	9.1	22.7	0
Cumulative percentage	4.6	68.1	77.2	99.9	99.9

---

[285] $\chi^2 = 3.18$, which clearly exceeds the critical $\chi^2_{0.10}(1) = 2.706$, p = 0.074.

Environmental lawyers, like commercial lawyers, are more likely to note unfair treatment of litigants in oil-related litigation.[286] Of those lawyers, 57.5% note that litigants are treated unfairly or very unfairly, compared with 31.2% of the other lawyers (see Table 4.25.). These results suggest that unfair treatment of litigants is a realistic possibility in environmental cases involving oil companies. Unfortunately, respondents do not provide examples of instances in which litigants were treated unfairly. What the views of commercial and environmental lawyers may indicate is that, while unfair treatment is not the norm in oil-related litigation, litigants may be treated unfairly in specific cases. In particular, litigants may be more likely to be treated unfairly in litigation involving environmental damage from oil operations.

Table 4.25. Answers to Questions 5 and 9a: Responses of environmental lawyers on whether litigants are treated fairly in court decisions involving oil companies

	Very fairly	Fairly	Neither fairly nor unfairly	Unfairly	Very unfairly
Environmental lawyers	5.0	32.5	5.0	35.0	22.5
Cumulative percentage	5.0	37.5	42.5	77.5	100.0
Other lawyers	1.6	45.9	21.3	24.6	6.6
Cumulative percentage	1.6	47.5	68.8	93.4	100.0

While there may be instances in which litigants have been treated unfairly in court decisions, one may also ask whether litigants have been treated fairly by the representatives of the oil companies in court proceedings. Excluding 'don't knows' and 'no responses', a significant minority of all respondents - 43.4% - state that oil companies, their subsidiaries or contractors conduct themselves ethically in court proceedings often or very often. Nonetheless, a majority of the respondents - 56.6% - believe that oil companies conduct themselves ethically only sometimes, rarely or never (see columns 3 and 4, Table 4.26.). Unfortunately, respondents do not provide examples of such instances. Our results suggest that, while the understanding of professional ethics may differ between lawyers, there appear to exist numerous instances, in which oil companies do not conduct themselves ethically in court proceedings.

Respondents' views on ethical conduct in court proceedings vary according to professional background and location. Oil company lawyers are less likely to believe that oil companies conduct themselves unethically.[287] Of those lawyers, 52.3% note that oil companies conduct themselves ethically in court proceedings often or very often, while the figure for the other lawyers is 30.0% (see Table 4.27.). These results are perhaps not surprising since, by answering the question on ethical conduct, oil company lawyers had to effectively assess their own work and the work of their clients in court proceedings. It could be expected that fewer oil company lawyers would accuse themselves, their colleagues or their clients of unethical conduct.

---

[286] $\chi^2 = 8.55$, which clearly exceeds the critical $\chi^2_{0.10}(2) = 4.605$, p = 0.014.

[287] $\chi^2 = 6.35$, which marginally exceeds the critical $\chi^2_{0.10}(3) = 6.251$, p = 0.096.

Table 4.26. Answers to Question 9b 'Do you think oil companies, their subsidiaries and contractors conduct themselves ethically in court proceedings?'

	1	2	3	4
	Percentage of Respondents	Cumulative Percentage	Percentage of Respondents (excl. 'don't knows' and 'no responses')	Cumulative Percentage (excl. 'don't knows' and 'no responses')
Very often	6.5	6.5	9.4	9.4
Often	23.4	29.9	34.0	43.4
Sometimes	32.5	62.4	47.2	90.6
Rarely	5.8	68.2	8.5	99.1
Never	0.6	68.8	0.9	100.0
Don't know	26.0	94.8	-	-
No response	5.2	100.0	-	-
Total	100.0	100.0	100.0	100.0

Table 4.27. Answers to Questions 6b and 9b: Responses of oil industry lawyers on whether oil companies, their subsidiaries and contractors conduct themselves ethically in court proceedings

	Very often	Often	Sometimes	Rarely	Never
Oil company lawyers	9.2	43.1	41.5	6.2	0
Cumulative percentage	9.2	52.3	90.8	100.0	100.0
Other lawyers	10.0	20.0	57.5	12.5	0
Cumulative percentage	10.0	30.0	87.5	100.0	100.0

Table 4.28. Answers to Question 9b: Responses of Lagos and Port Harcourt lawyers on whether oil companies, their subsidiaries and contractors conduct themselves ethically in court proceedings

	Very often	Often	Sometimes	Rarely	Never
Lagos lawyers	8.9	37.8	48.9	4.4	0
Cumulative percentage	8.9	46.7	91.1	100.0	100.0
Port Harcourt lawyers	13.3	13.3	40.0	33.3	0
Cumulative percentage	13.3	26.6	66.6	99.9	99.9

Interestingly, the views on ethical conduct vary according to location. Lagos lawyers are more likely to say that oil companies conduct themselves ethically, if compared with Port Harcourt lawyers.[288] Of the Lagos lawyers, 46.7% state that oil companies conduct themselves ethically in court proceedings often or very often, while the figure for the Port Harcourt lawyers is only 26.6% (see Table 4.28.). These results indicate that there are regional differences in the way that oil companies conduct

---

[288] $\chi^2 = 13.91$, which clearly exceeds the critical $\chi^2_{0.10}(2) = 4.605$, p = 0.001.

themselves in court proceedings. They may suggest that oil companies conduct themselves less ethically in court proceedings in the oil producing areas such as Port Harcourt than in Lagos.

While there may be numerous instances, in which oil companies conduct themselves unethically in court proceedings, one cannot take for granted that judges are necessarily biased in favour of oil companies. Some judges, especially those from the oil producing areas may indeed be biased against oil companies. A Port Harcourt lawyer states: *'Some judges especially from an oil producing area dislike oil companies because of their dirty politics in Nigeria'.*[289] The view that judges from the oil producing areas are biased against oil companies was supported by M.B. Belgore, Chief Justice of the Federal High Court. Belgore stated in an interview with the author of this book that judges from Port Harcourt or Warri are more likely to rule in favour of village communities. Said Belgore: *'Judges, who are from the area in which they are involved themselves, use their discretion more freely to the party than a judge who is a little more detached'.*[290] Nonetheless, roughly half of the respondents state that courts are biased in favour of oil companies, while only 16.8% state that courts are biased in favour of opposing litigants (see Table 4.29.). These results suggest that the courts are, overall, biased more in favour of oil companies than the opposing litigant.

There are significant differences between oil company lawyers and others on the bias of courts.[291] Of the oil company lawyers, 44.7% state that courts are biased in favour of opposing litigants, compared with 15.6% of the other lawyers (see Table 4.30.). Lawyers who acted as counsel in a lawsuit against an oil company are of the opposite view to oil company lawyers. Some 17.3% of those lawyers note that the courts are biased in favour of the opposing litigants, compared with 63.0% of the other lawyers (see Table 4.31.). These results are perhaps not surprising since lawyers are less likely to regard courts as biased in favour of their own clients.

While the courts appear to generally favour oil companies, respondents have also been asked what specific reasons exist as to why courts may encounter difficulties in judging oil-related cases fairly. Excluding 'no responses', some 51.6% of the surveyed lawyers note that the lack of funds is a very important reason why courts might encounter difficulties in judging oil-related cases fairly, while outside pressures are viewed as a very important reason by 49.6% of the respondents. Some 40.5% consider incompetence of witnesses a very important reason (see Table 4.32.). The former two reasons - the lack of funds and outside pressures - are general problems of the Nigerian judiciary. Incompetence of witnesses is a problem lying outside the scope of the judiciary and may be partly ascribed to the lack of general education. One could expect that the incompetence of witnesses is a particularly important problem in environmental cases against oil companies, in which expert evidence and technical knowledge is particularly relevant, if compared, for instance, with employment-related cases.

---

[289] Lawyer no.152, 1998 survey of Nigerian lawyers.

[290] Personal interview with M.B. Belgore, Chief Justice of the Federal High Court (Lagos, March 1998).

[291] $\chi^2 = 6.02$, which clearly exceeds the critical $\chi^2_{0.10}(1) = 2.706$, p = 0.014.

Table 4.29. Answers to Question 9c 'Would you say that courts are biased in favour of the oil company or the opposing litigant?'

	Percentage of Respondents	Cumulative Percentage		Percentage of Respondents	Cumulative Percentage
Severe bias in favour of oil company	5.2	5.2	Severe bias in favour of opposing litigant	3.2	3.2
Some bias in favour of oil company	44.8	50.0	Some bias in favour of opposing litigant	13.6	16.8
No bias in favour of oil company	18.2	68.2	No bias in favour of opposing litigant	34.4	51.2
Don't know	19.5	87.7	Don't know	18.8	70
No response	12.3	100.0	No response	29.9	99.9
Total	100.0	100.0	Total	99.9	99.9

Table 4.30. Answers to Questions 6b and 9c: Responses of oil industry lawyers on whether courts are biased in favour of the opposing litigant

	Severe bias in favour of opposing litigant	Some bias in favour of opposing litigant	No bias in favour of opposing litigant
Oil company lawyers	8.5	36.2	55.3
Cumulative percentage	8.5	44.7	100.0
Other lawyers	3.1	12.5	84.4
Cumulative percentage	3.1	15.6	100.0

Table 4.31. Answers to Questions 6b and 9c: Responses of lawyers who acted as counsel in a lawsuit against an oil company on whether courts are biased in favour of the opposing litigant

	Severe bias in favour of opposing litigant	Some bias in favour of opposing litigant	No bias in favour of opposing litigant
Lawyers who acted as counsel in a lawsuit against an oil company	3.8	13.5	82.7
Cumulative percentage	3.8	17.3	100.0
Other lawyers	11.1	51.9	37.0
Cumulative percentage	11.1	63.0	100.0

Table 4.32. Answers to Question 9d 'Amongst the following rank reasons why courts might encounter difficulties in judging oil-related cases fairly' (per cent) (excluding 'no responses')

	Very important reason	Important reason	Less important reason
Lack of funds	51.6	23.8	24.6
Outside pressures	49.6	39.5	10.9
Incompetence of witnesses	40.5	30.6	28.9
Lack of knowledge of oil technology	29.1	47.2	23.6
Lack of time	14.5	54.8	30.6
Lack of witnesses	12.2	38.2	49.6
Resources and skill of oil company's counsel	9.6	51.2	39.2

The respondents' views differ significantly with regards to reasons of why courts may encounter difficulties in judging oil-related cases fairly. Of all cross-tabulations performed, the most significant results occur in respect of the lack of funds, which is seen as the key reason why courts might encounter difficulties in oil-related litigation. Views differ according to experience and age. The more professional experience respondents have, the more importance they attach to the courts' lack of funds.[292] Similarly, the older the lawyers are, the more importance they attach to the courts' lack of funds.[293] If it is assumed that older and more experienced lawyers are in a better position to comment on the legal profession, it has to be assumed that the lack of funds is the crucial problem facing courts in judging oil-related litigation fairly.

Environmental lawyers, like older and more experienced lawyers, regard the lack of funds as the most important problem which courts face in judging oil-related cases.[294] Of the environmental lawyers, 68.6% believe that the lack of funds is a very important problem, compared with 36.2% of the other lawyers (see Table 4.33.). This may suggest that lack of funds is more important in oil-related litigation involving environmental damage than in other types of oil-related litigation.

The lack of funds has been identified as the key problem courts face in judging oil-related cases. Resources and skill of oil company's counsel have been identified by all respondents as the least important problem. But there is a wide disparity of views on the problem of resources and skill of oil company's counsel across professional background and age. Of the lawyers aged between 25 and 30, 39.1% regard resources and skill of oil company's counsel as an important or a very important problem, compared with the figure of 100.0% for the lawyers aged 46 years and over (see Table

---

[292] $\chi^2 = 9.36$, which clearly exceeds the critical $\chi^2_{0.10}(3) = 6.251$, p = 0.025. Of the lawyers with 1 to 5 years of professional experience, 31.8% consider the lack of funds a very important problem, while 80.0% of the lawyers with 21 or more years of professional experience consider it a very important problem.

[293] $\chi^2 = 21.28$, which clearly exceeds the critical $\chi^2_{0.10}(4) = 7.779$, p = 0.0002. Of the lawyers aged between 25 and 30, 26.1% consider the lack of funds a very important problem, while 83.3% of the lawyers aged 46 years and over view it as a very important problem.

[294] $\chi^2 = 9.96$, which clearly exceeds the critical $\chi^2_{0.10}(2) = 4.605$, p = 0.007.

4.34.).[295] If it is assumed that older lawyers are in a better position to comment on the legal profession, it has to be assumed that resources and skill of oil company's counsel may be a very prominent problem in oil-related cases.

This speculation appears to be confirmed by the views of the environmental lawyers. Of the environmental lawyers, 76.9% consider resources and skill of oil company's counsel an important or a very important problem, compared with 51.4% of the other lawyers (see Table 4.35).[296] This may suggest that resources and skill of oil company lawyers may play a greater role in oil-related cases involving environmental damage than in other types of oil-related litigation.

Table 4.33. Answers to Questions 5 and 9d: Responses of environmental lawyers on whether lack of funds is an important reason why courts might encounter difficulties in judging oil-related cases fairly (per cent)

	Very important reason	*Important reason*	*Less important reason*
Environmental lawyers	68.6	17.1	14.3
Cumulative percentage	68.6	85.7	100.0
Other lawyers	36.2	29.0	34.8
Cumulative percentage	36.2	65.2	100.0

Table 4.34. Answers to Questions 1 and 9d: Responses according to age of lawyers on whether resources and skill of oil company's counsel is an important reason why courts might encounter difficulties in judging oil-related cases fairly (per cent)

	Very important reason	*Important reason*	*Less important reason*
Lawyers between 25 and 30 years old	4.3	34.8	60.9
Cumulative percentage	4.3	39.1	100.0
Lawyers between 31 and 35 years old	7.9	42.1	50.0
Cumulative percentage	7.9	50.0	100.0
Lawyers between 36 and 40 years old	14.8	44.4	40.7
Cumulative percentage	14.8	59.2	99.9
Lawyers between 41 and 45 years old	11.8	58.8	29.4
Cumulative percentage	11.8	70.6	100.0
Lawyers 46 years old and over	8.3	91.7	0
Cumulative percentage	8.3	100.0	100.0

---

[295] $\chi^2 = 11.68$, which clearly exceeds the critical $\chi^2_{0.10}(3) = 6.251$, p = 0.009. The cross-tabulation with the attribute of professional experience also produces a significant chi-square value: $\chi^2 = 12.30$, which clearly exceeds the critical $\chi^2_{0.10}(3) = 6.251$, p = 0.006. While the results are somewhat less clear-cut than for the attribute of age, broadly speaking, one can say that, the more professional experience respondents have, the more importance they attach to the resources and skill of oil company's counsel.

[296] $\chi^2 = 6.74$, which clearly exceeds the critical $\chi^2_{0.10}(2) = 4.605$, p = 0.034.

Table 4.35. Answers to Questions 5 and 9d: Responses of environmental lawyers on whether resources and skill of oil company's counsel is an important reason why courts might encounter difficulties in judging oil-related cases fairly (per cent)

	Very important reason	*Important reason*	*Less important reason*
Environmental lawyers	12.8	64.1	23.1
Cumulative percentage	12.8	76.9	100.0
Other lawyers	8.8	42.6	48.5
Cumulative percentage	8.8	51.4	99.9

The above discussion suggests that Nigerian courts are heavily impeded in deciding upon oil-related cases, particularly in environmental litigation, and may tend to be biased in favour of oil companies. That these impediments have an impact on the final court judgments is self-evident. One indicator of the quality of final court judgments is the level of compensation awarded by courts. Respondents have been asked whether compensation paid by oil companies for damages in tort is unfair to either oil companies or the opposing litigant (tort will be explained in chapter 6). Excluding 'don't knows' and 'no responses', some 79.1% of the surveyed lawyers believe that the compensation paid by oil companies for damages in tort is unfair to the opposing litigant, while only 8.2% believe the opposite (see columns 3 and 4, Table 4.36.). These results unequivocally suggest that court judgments tend to be biased in favour of oil companies. Several lawyers, mainly environmental lawyers, note that the compensation regime for oil operations in Nigeria is grossly inadequate. One lawyer from Lagos, who previously worked for the oil industry, comments that *'compensation for oil pollution is not adequate. An independent commission might make a difference'*.[297] The views of environmental lawyers do not differ from the views of the other lawyers, so one cannot clearly say that compensation is more or less unfair to opposing litigants in environmental litigation. Nonetheless, it can be reasonably assumed that the respondents' views on compensation paid in tort are mainly based on their experiences with oil-related cases involving environmental damage because tort law in Nigeria's oil-related cases is mainly utilised in respect of environmental litigation such as litigation resulting from oil spills. By implication, it has to be assumed that compensation paid by oil companies in environmental litigation tends to be unfair to the opposing litigant.

Perhaps surprisingly, the oil company lawyers admit themselves that compensation payments are unfair to the opposing litigants.[298] A clear majority of the oil company lawyers - 71.6% - regard compensation payments as unfair to the opposing litigants, although this figure is smaller than the figure of 88.4% for the other lawyers (see Table 4.37.). These results are very revealing as oil company lawyers openly agree that compensation payments paid by their clients are unfair to those affected by oil operations.

---

[297] Lawyer no.24, 1998 survey of Nigerian lawyers.

[298] The views of the oil company lawyers differ significantly from those of the other lawyers: $\chi^2 = 6.22$, which clearly exceeds the critical $\chi^2_{0.10}(2) = 4.605$, p = 0.045.

On the whole, this section has shown that the functioning of the legal system largely favours oil companies, which manifests itself in inadequate compensation payments to the opposing litigants in oil-related litigation. The courts are generally biased in favour of oil companies.

Table 4.36. Answers to Question 10 'Would you consider the compensation paid by oil companies for damages in tort as...'

	1	2	3	4
	Percentage of Respondents	Cumulative Percentage	Percentage of Respondents (excl. 'don't knows and 'no responses')	Cumulative Percentage (excl. 'don't knows and 'no responses')
Unfair to oil companies as much too high	1.3	1.3	1.5	1.5
Unfair to oil companies as somewhat too high	5.8	7.1	6.7	8.2
Fair and justified	11.0	18.1	12.7	20.9
Unfair to opposing litigant as somewhat too low	39.0	57.1	44.8	65.7
Unfair to opposing litigant as much too low	29.9	87.0	34.3	100.0
Don't know	7.8	94.8	-	-
No response	5.2	100.00	-	-
Total	100.00	100.00	100.0	100.0

Table 4.37. Answers to Questions 6b and 10: Responses of oil industry lawyers on whether compensation paid by oil companies for damages in tort is fair

	Unfair to oil companies as much too high	Unfair to oil companies as somewhat too high	Fair and justified	Unfair to opposing litigant as somewhat too low	Unfair to opposing litigant as much too low
Oil company lawyers	1.4	12.2	14.9	43.2	28.4
Cumulative percentage	1.4	13.6	28.5	71.7	100.1
Other lawyers	1.7	0	10.0	46.7	41.7
Cumulative percentage	1.7	1.7	11.7	58.4	100.1

4.9. Legal Change and Legislation

It is not entirely clear how the potential bias of the legal system may change over time. Our discussion so far has said little about changes in the legal system and legislation. This is the focus of this section.

That the legal system changes is self-evident. But legal change is by no means apparent to Nigerian lawyers. A lawyer from Lagos with 35 years of professional experience boldly pronounces: *'Our laws, especially criminal, are virtually the same since the colonialists left'.*[299] Such a view appears to be shared by many Nigerian lawyers, if judged by some of the respondents' comments and interviews with lawyers. From the respondents' comments and interviews, it emerges, moreover, that lawyers tend to associate legal change with changes in statute law rather than with the evolution of judicial precedents. For instance, lawyers who believe that there has been change in environmental law appear to base their views mainly on the pronouncement of the Federal Environmental Protection Agency (FEPA) Act. With this background in mind, the respondents' views on legal change appear to reflect changes in statute law.

A clear majority of all respondents - 63.2% (excluding 'no responses') - note that there has been no change in criminal law since they were called to the Bar. A majority of respondents state that civil law, environmental law and commercial law have undergone some change, albeit not major change. Only 6.3% state that there has been major change in civil law, while 19.3% and 23.7% note that there has been major change in commercial law and environmental law respectively. Some 66.1% believe that there has been some change in civil law, while 64.4% and 57.3% believe that there has been some change in commercial law and environmental law respectively (see Table 4.38.). As indicated earlier, changes in environmental law are usually ascribed to the FEPA Act. Changes in commercial law are usually ascribed to legislative changes in laws relating to foreign investment, banking laws, company law and petroleum law. Commercial lawyers emphasise, above all, legislative de-regulation and removal of restrictions on foreign ownership of Nigerian enterprises as the major source of legal change.

Table 4.38. Answers to Question 12 'Which areas of law have undergone changes since you were called to the Bar?' (excluding 'don't knows' and 'no responses')

	Major change	Some change	No change
Criminal law	8.8	28.0	63.2
Civil law	6.3	66.1	27.6
Environmental law	23.7	57.3	19.1
Commercial law	19.3	64.4	16.3

The respondents' views on legal change vary considerably according to professional background and location. Interestingly, oil company lawyers are more likely to observe major changes in environmental law as opposed to the other lawyers.[300] Of those lawyers, 31.1% believe that there have been major changes in environmental law, compared with the figure of 14.0% for the other lawyers (see Table 4.39.). These results could suggest that changes in Nigeria's environmental law have affected oil companies more than other types of organisations or individuals. But this

---

[299] Lawyer no.74, 1998 survey of Nigerian lawyers.

[300] $\chi^2 = 5.30$, which clearly exceeds the critical $\chi^2_{0.10}(2) = 4.605$, p = 0.071.

speculation is put into question by the views of those lawyers who acted as counsel in a lawsuit against an oil company with regards to changes in environmental law.[301] Of those lawyers, 17.1% believe that there have been major changes in environmental law, compared with the figure of 34.7% for the other lawyers (see Table 4.40.). In other words, the trends in the views of oil company lawyers and lawyers who acted as counsel in lawsuits against oil companies run counter to each other. One group is more likely to believe that there have been major changes, while the other believes the opposite. What these results suggest is that views on the degree of change in environmental law can be highly subjective depending on a lawyer's personal and professional background.[302]

Table 4.39. Answers to Questions 6b and 12: Responses of oil industry lawyers on whether environmental law has undergone changes

	Major change	Some change	No change
Oil company lawyers	31.1	52.7	16.2
Cumulative percentage	31.1	83.8	100.0
Other lawyers	14.0	63.2	22.8
Cumulative percentage	14.0	77.2	100.0

Table 4.40. Answers to Questions 6b and 12: Responses of lawyers who acted as counsel in a lawsuit against an oil company on whether environmental law has undergone changes

	Major change	Some change	No change
Lawyers who acted as counsel in a lawsuit against an oil company	17.1	59.8	23.2
Cumulative percentage	17.1	76.9	100.1
Other lawyers	34.7	53.1	12.2
Cumulative percentage	34.7	87.8	100.0

The above discussion suggests that parts of civil law, environmental law and commercial law have undergone some change. That changes in statute law are not always implemented in Nigeria is self-evident. Respondents were asked whether five pieces of legislation affecting oil companies have, in practice, been effectively enforced or not. As with the expression 'legal change', the meaning of effective enforcement may differ considerably between lawyers. A useful test case is the Gas

---

[301] $\chi^2 = 6.18$, which clearly exceeds the critical $\chi^2_{0.10}(2) = 4.605$, p = 0.045.

[302] In terms of views on change in commercial law, the results are more clear-cut and unsurprising, if compared with respondents' views on changes in environmental law. Commercial lawyers and oil company lawyers are predictably more likely to believe that commercial law has undergone major changes than other lawyers. 24.7% of the commercial lawyers believe that there have been major changes in commercial law, compared with the figure of 4.8% for the other lawyers ($\chi^2 = 7.69$, which clearly exceeds the critical $\chi^2_{0.10}(1) = 2.706$, p = 0.006). 26.6% of the oil company lawyers believe that there have been major changes in commercial law, compared with the figure of 8.9% for the other lawyers ($\chi^2 = 7.25$, which clearly exceeds the critical $\chi^2_{0.10}(2) = 4.605$, p = 0.027).

Re-injection Act 1979. The Act has not been effectively enforced in Nigeria in the sense that a number of its main provisions prohibiting gas flaring have not been observed (see chapter 3). Nonetheless, as many as 35.0% of the respondents (excluding 'no responses') consider the Act partially enforced (see Table 4.41.). This may suggest that a considerable minority of respondents regard a piece of legislation as 'partially enforced', even if its main provisions are not enforced. In other words, some responses, which suggest that a piece of legislation has been 'partially enforced', may not necessarily indicate that any of the main provisions of a piece of legislation have been enforced.

Our survey results indicate that the Land Use Act is the best enforced legislation out of the five pieces of legislation. Excluding 'no responses', some 34.0% of the surveyed lawyers believe that the Land Use Act has been effectively enforced, while 50.0% believe that the Land Use Act has been partially enforced. Some 18.8% state that the Petroleum Act has been effectively enforced, while 41.0% state that the Act has been partially enforced. Only an insignificant minority of respondents believe that the other pieces of legislation - the FEPA Act (1.5%), the OMPADEC Act (3.3%) and the Gas Re-injection Act (2.9%) - have been effectively enforced (see Table 4.41.). What emerges from these results is that statute law which is likely to benefit oil companies as opposed to the village communities in the oil producing areas - the Land Use Act and the Petroleum Act - is more effectively enforced than statute law which is likely to benefit communities - the FEPA Act, the OMPADEC Decree and the Gas Re-injection Act. But it is difficult to determine to what extent legislation has been implemented because of the ambiguity of the term 'partially enforced'.

Table 4.41. Answers to Question 13 'Do you think that the following piece of legislation has been effectively enforced?' (excluding 'don't knows' and 'no responses')

	Effectively enforced	Partially enforced	Not enforced
Petroleum Act 1969	18.8	41.0	40.2
FEPA Act 1988	1.5	56.5	42.0
OMPADEC Decree 1992	3.3	56.1	40.7
Land Use Act 1978	34.0	50.0	16.0
Gas Re-injection Act 1979	2.9	35.0	62.1

The respondents' views differ significantly according to age and professional experience. The most significant survey results concern the enforcement of the FEPA Act. The older the lawyers, the more likely they are to believe that the FEPA Act has not been enforced.[303] Similarly, the more experienced the lawyers, the more likely they are to believe that the FEPA Act has not been enforced.[304] While the trend is not

---

[303] $\chi^2 = 29.50$, which clearly exceeds the critical $\chi^2_{0.10}(4) = 7.779$, $p = 0.000006$. Of the lawyers aged 46 years and over, 75.0% state that the FEPA Act has not been enforced, while only 30.4% of the lawyers aged between 25 and 30 years old note that the FEPA Act has not been enforced.

[304] $\chi^2 = 14.37$, which clearly exceeds the critical $\chi^2_{0.10}(4) = 7.779$, $p = 0.006$. Of the lawyers with 1 to 5 years of professional experience, 47.6% believe that the FEPA Act has not been enforced,

entirely consistent, one can convincingly argue that older and more experienced lawyers are more likely to state that legislation has not been enforced in Nigeria. If it is assumed that older and more experienced lawyers are in a better position to comment on the enforcement of legislation, it can be argued with more conviction that Nigerian legislation is generally unenforced in practice.

An interpretation of the responses on the enforcement of legislation is made complicated by the fact that a particular piece of legislation may contain some provisions which are enforced and some which are not. The Petroleum Act, for instance, comprises commercial provisions as well as environmental provisions for oil operations. It was hoped that an analysis of the views of environmental lawyers and commercial lawyers would provide some indication as to which specific provisions have been enforced and which have not. In this context, the responses of environmental lawyers are most interesting because their views differ from those of the other lawyers on almost all questions regarding enforcement, except for the question on the enforcement of the Gas Re-injection Act.[305] The views of environmental lawyers are particularly interesting on the enforcement of the Petroleum Act and the FEPA Act, both of which include explicit legal provisions for environmental protection. Of the environmental lawyers, 47.4% and 47.6% state that the Petroleum Act and the FEPA Act have not been enforced respectively, compared with figures of 26.2% and 27.5% for the other lawyers respectively (see Table 4.42.). The views of environmental lawyers may suggest that Nigerian statutory provisions on the environment are less likely to be enforced than other types of legislative provisions.

The views of commercial lawyers differ from those of the other lawyers only on the enforcement of the FEPA Act.[306] Interestingly, commercial lawyers are more likely than the other lawyers to state that the FEPA Act has not been enforced at all. Of the commercial lawyers, 39.6% state that the FEPA Act has not been enforced, compared with the figure of 15.0% for the other lawyers (see Table 4.43.). It is difficult to speculate on the meaning of these results but the respondents' views may suggest that the FEPA Act had relatively little impact on the business operations of their clients.

---

compared with the figure of 61.5% for the lawyers with 21 and more years of professional experience.

[305] In cross-tabulations, in which the responses of environmental lawyers vary from the rest, the p-value varies from p = 0.052 to p = 0.005, that means, all results are highly significant at $\alpha = 0.10$. The chi-square and p-values for cross-tabulations between the attribute of environmental lawyer and attributes of obstacles of access to courts are as follows:

- for views on the Petroleum Act: $\chi^2 = 6.44$, which exceeds the critical $\chi^2_{0.10}(2) = 4.605$, p = 0.040;
- for views on the FEPA Act: $\chi^2 = 3.78$, which exceeds the critical $\chi^2_{0.10}(1) = 2.706$, p = 0.052;
- for views on the OMPADEC Decree: $\chi^2 = 4.92$, which exceeds the critical $\chi^2_{0.10}(1) = 2.706$, p = 0.027;
- for views on the Land Use Act: $\chi^2 = 10.45$, which exceeds the critical $\chi^2_{0.10}(2) = 4.605$, p = 0.005.

[306] $\chi^2 = 3.33$, which exceeds the critical $\chi^2_{0.10}(1) = 2.706$, p = 0.068.

Table 4.42. Answers to Questions 5 and 13: Responses of environmental lawyers on the enforcement of different pieces of legislation (per cent)

	Effectively enforced	Partially enforced	Not enforced
Environmental lawyers on the enforcement of the Petroleum Act	10.5	42.1	47.4
Other lawyers	27.9	45.9	26.2
Environmental lawyers on the enforcement of the FEPA Act	2.4	50.0	47.6
Other lawyers	1.4	71.0	27.5
Environmental lawyers on the enforcement of OMPADEC Decree	2.5	47.5	50.0
Other lawyers	4.7	68.8	26.6
Environmental lawyers on the enforcement of the Land Use Act	18.2	61.4	20.5
Other lawyers	47.4	41.0	11.5

Table 4.43. Answers to Questions 5 and 13: Responses of commercial lawyers on whether the FEPA Act has been effectively enforced (per cent)

	Effectively enforced	Partially enforced	Not enforced
Commercial lawyers	2.2	58.2	39.6
Cumulative percentage	2.2	60.4	100.0
Other lawyers	0	85.0	15.0
Cumulative percentage	0	85.0	100.0

With regards to the enforcement of land legislation, oil company lawyers are more likely to believe that the Land Use Act has been effectively enforced than the other lawyers.[307] Of the oil company lawyers, 36.6% note that the Land Use Act has been effectively enforced, compared with the figure of 30.6% for the other lawyers. Only 9.8% of the oil company lawyers state that the Land Use Act has not been enforced, compared with the figure of 24.2% for the other lawyers (see Table 4.44.). Lawyers who acted as counsel in a lawsuit against an oil company are of the opposite view. They are less likely to believe that the Land Use Act has been effectively enforced than the other lawyers.[308] Of the lawyers who acted as counsel in a lawsuit against an oil company, 26.9% state that the Land Use Act has been effectively enforced, compared with the figure of 47.1% for the other lawyers. Of those lawyers, 18.3% note that the Land Use Act has not been enforced, compared with the figure of 11.8% for the other lawyers (see Table 4.45.). A simple explanation for these results may be that the Land Use Act had a different impact on oil companies, on the one hand, and on Nigerian landowners, on the other. On the one hand, the Land Use Act made it easier for oil companies to compulsorily obtain land in village communities for oil operations (see chapter 3). This may explain why oil company lawyers are more likely to believe that the Land Use Act has been effectively enforced. On the other

---

[307] $\chi^2 = 5.48$, which exceeds the critical $\chi^2_{0.10}$ (2) = 4.605, p = 0.064.

[308] $\chi^2 = 6.05$, which exceeds the critical $\chi^2_{0.10}$ (2) = 4.605, p = 0.049.

hand, the Land Use Act has not, overall, changed the communal and family ownership structures and the traditional way in which land is being allocated in the oil producing areas (see chapter 3). This may explain why lawyers who acted as counsel in a lawsuit against an oil company are less likely to believe that the Land Use Act has been effectively enforced.

Table 4.44. Answers to Questions 6b and 13: Responses of oil industry lawyers on whether the Land Use Act has been effectively enforced (per cent)

	Effectively enforced	Partially enforced	Not enforced
Oil company lawyers	36.6	53.7	9.8
Cumulative percentage	36.6	90.3	100.1
Other lawyers	30.6	45.2	24.2
Cumulative percentage	30.6	75.8	100.0

Table 4.45. Answers to Questions 6b and 13: Responses of lawyers who acted as counsel in a lawsuit against an oil company on whether the Land Use Act has been effectively enforced (per cent)

	Effectively enforced	Partially enforced	Not enforced
Lawyers who acted as counsel in a lawsuit against an oil company	26.9	54.8	18.3
Cumulative percentage	26.9	81.7	100.0
Other lawyers	47.1	41.2	11.8
Cumulative percentage	47.1	88.3	100.1

On the whole, this section has shown that there has been relatively little change in Nigerian statute law. There are severe problems of enforcement of legislation in Nigeria. Various questions remain largely unanswered on the question of enforcement and legal change, particularly with regards to the nature of legal change in case law.

4.10. Conclusion

This chapter discussed impediments to the functioning of the legal process and the judiciary with a focus on the problems of access to courts. Our discussion, of course, did not cover all of these impediments, most notably corruption on the bench. It could be expected that the prevalent corruption in Nigerian society has also had an effect on the judiciary. However, it is difficult to find evidence of such malpractices. Unfortunately, neither the Eso Panel nor our survey results indicate the extent of corruption amongst judges.[309] Yet it was not the goal of this study to cover all of the

---

[309] According to Justice Muhammed Mustapha Adebayo Akanbi, during the Eso Panel sitting, *'there was no evidence to back the allegations'* of corruption in the judiciary (*Guardian*, Lagos, 30 March 1999).

impediments in the functioning of the legal system. Rather we set out to analyse whether Nigeria's legal system is biased or not biased in favour of oil companies.

Our analysis was motivated by the perception of a paucity of studies on African legal systems in terms of the day-to-day operations of the legal system. Legal studies on Africa have hitherto often ignored the socio-legal context of law such as the problems of access to courts for potential litigants or the actual enforcement of legislation on the ground. They have largely confined their analyses to the formal legal process and/or the analysis of sources of law. This problem is particularly significant in the context of court cases between multinational companies and the local people in developing countries. In its modest way, our survey has sought to shed light on the legal processes associated with the interaction between village communities and oil companies. We believe that the survey has helped in the understanding of some of the key obstacles village communities encounter when seeking legal recourse for oil-related damage.

Previous scholars who have undertaken socio-legal studies on Africa have largely confined their analyses to qualitative, often speculative, evidence. Degni-Segui, who served as the starting point of our analysis of the barriers to justice, based his study mainly on secondary sources. At the outset of his study, he stated that there are five main barriers to justice: geographical distance to courts, delay in the disposal of cases, lack of funds, African political systems and ignorance of legal rights. Unfortunately, he has failed to provide evidence of why we should regard those specific factors as more important than other potential causes. Ultimately, his assessment of the hierarchy of the problems of access to courts hence appears speculative. We have attempted to quantify the hierarchy of access problems as perceived by Nigerian legal practitioners. In this context, we were able to show that the geographical distance to courts, which features among the key problems of access to courts cited by Degni-Segui, is not a particularly severe barrier to justice.[310] We believe that our quantitative analysis offers many advantages if compared with the existing qualitative studies.

As previously stated, the main theme of this chapter was access to courts for potential litigants. The results indicated that access to courts is a major obstacle in the functioning of Nigeria's legal system. The two main problems of access to courts were identified as the potential plaintiffs' lack of financial resources and their ignorance of general education and legal rights. The other main obstacles named by the respondents included delay in the disposal of cases, intimidation by public bodies, intimidation by tort-feasors and uncertainty about the potential success of a suit. The significance of the lack of funds as the key barrier to justice could be expected since the scope of Nigeria's legal aid scheme is largely limited to criminal cases. This prevents potential low income plaintiffs from instituting lawsuits in most civil cases. Access to contingency fees meanwhile may be limited due to the significant cost of expert witnesses and the financial risk faced by legal practitioners.

---

[310] Geographical distance should be regarded as part of financial problems which prevent litigants from travelling to courts. The other speculations of Degni-Segui on barriers to justice are largely confirmed by our survey. Three out of five problems cited by Degni-Segui - lack of funds, delay in the disposal of cases and ignorance - feature prominently among the problems of access to courts cited by Nigerian lawyers.

An analysis of the constraints in the functioning of the judiciary and the court system formed the second main theme in the discussion of the survey results. The data indicated that the Nigerian judiciary and the court system face severe problems in their day-to-day operations. The respondents were of the view that the Nigerian judiciary is frequently under serious extra-judicial pressures from public and private bodies. Extra-judicial pressures from the government can result in the non-enforcement of court orders in those cases, in which the government has an interest. A number of the problems noted in the context of the functioning of the judiciary, notably high congestion in the courts, further compound the obstacles of access to courts faced by potential litigants in Nigeria.

A discussion of the problems of access to courts and the functioning of the court system, which formed the initial part of the survey analysis, was followed by secondary survey results, which fell into three themes. First, we discussed the distinctions in the competency of judicial services in different courts in Nigeria. The data suggested that there are marked differences with the Supreme Court and the Court of Appeal being rated as the most competent Nigerian courts. Second, we explored in greater detail the lawyers' perceptions of the conduct of oil companies and courts in oil-related litigation. The data indicated that there exist numerous instances, in which oil companies do not conduct themselves ethically in court proceedings, and courts are regarded as biased in favour of oil companies. Third, legal change and legislation were discussed. It emerged that most lawyers perceive the legal changes that occurred in Nigeria as minor. There were strong indications that statute law which is likely to benefit oil companies as opposed to the village communities in the oil producing areas such as the Land Use Act is more effectively enforced than legislation which is likely to benefit communities such as the FEPA Act.

On the whole, our survey suggests that the inadequacies in the actual-practical operations of the legal system are not peculiar to oil-related court cases or cases involving the interests of the government and the ruling elite. The survey results have indicated that the Nigerian legal system has many deficiencies in terms of its day-to-day operations. Given the inadequacy of the legal system, any litigant, including litigants against the oil companies, may find it difficult to pursue a court case in a Nigerian court. It could be argued that Nigeria as a developing country still faces the problem of establishing efficient bureaucratic state structures (see chapters 2 and 3). One could then also argue that the legal system suffers problems of bureaucratic inefficiency. Nonetheless, our survey has indicated that the specific difficulties of village communities, who sue oil companies, are of a different scale than the difficulties faced by other potential plaintiffs.

Our survey results have revealed marked differences in the lawyers' views on the legal system across various sub-groups of respondents.[311] An analysis of the

---

[311] Of all chi-square tests for independence carried out between the personal characteristics of respondents and questions on the legal system, professional background plays the crucial role in shaping lawyers' views. The views of environmental lawyers and commercial lawyers deviate most from those of the other lawyers (in 21 cross-tabulations each). These results suggest that environmental and commercial lawyers may often encounter different sets of problems in dealing with the legal system than the other lawyers. As previously stated, the views of the oil company lawyers helped to denote specific differences between oil-related litigation and other types of litigation. The views of the environmental lawyers helped to indicate differences between general

differences between oil-related litigation and other types of litigation suggested that, in the view of the respondent lawyers, individual and community litigants are less likely to succeed in oil-related cases than in other types of litigation. A significant part of the data indicated that the problems of access to courts are greater in oil-related litigation. As in other types of litigation, the lack of funds and ignorance were rated as the main problems of access to courts in oil-related cases. If judged by the views of environmental lawyers, it could be assumed that the lack of general education and intimidation by the government as well as oil companies are more important barriers to justice for village communities suing oil companies than they are for other potential litigants.

The deficiencies in the day-to-day operations of the judiciary and the legal process also appear to be greater in oil-related litigation. Survey analysis indicated that the judiciary and the legal process are more biased in favour of oil companies rather than the opposing litigants and that judges encounter greater outside pressures in oil-related litigation. This bias manifests itself, for instance, in the award of compensation payments by Nigerian courts. A majority of legal practitioners regarded compensation payments in oil-related cases as more biased in favour of oil companies.

These findings support the initial hypothesis that the Nigerian legal system as a whole, not merely statute law and the structural character of the legal system, favours the interests of oil companies. While it is obvious that the Nigerian legal process is predisposed in favour of oil companies, it is less obvious which types of oil-related litigation are more affected. Nonetheless, the responses of environmental lawyers appear to suggest that the impediments to the exercise of justice are particularly severe in oil-related cases involving compensation claims for environmental damage. The greater part of environmental litigation in the oil industry involves compensation claims filed by members of village communities. By implication, it has to be assumed that the legal process is particularly predisposed in favour of oil interests in litigation between oil companies and village communities.

It is not yet clear in what way the judiciary will be affected by the civilian regime of Obasanjo. It could be expected that the quality of the legal system will be improved in a number of ways, for instance, by making the appointment of judges less arbitrary. However, impediments to justice are likely to continue. In particular, it could be expected that the problem of access to courts will remain since the socio-economic conditions in Nigeria are unlikely to change dramatically.

The analysis in this chapter has identified the constraints and opportunities faced by litigants in oil-related litigation. This sets the stage for the discussion of the dynamics of oil-related litigation in the consecutive chapters.

---

oil-related litigation (which could include e.g. employment cases) and litigation involving compensation claims for environmental damage. Somewhat surprisingly, the size of a law firm is also an important determinant of lawyers' views (significant chi-square results in 20 cross-tabulations), although in most cases it could not be discerned in what way the size of law firms determines lawyers' views. Somewhat surprisingly, contact with the oil industry does not appear to greatly influence the views of lawyers (significant chi-square results in only 3 cross-tabulations). It must be concluded that mere contact with oil companies does not change a lawyer's views on the legal system, whereas work for an oil company or specialisation in environmental law is far more likely to alter a lawyer's views.

Chapter 5: Environmental and Social Impact of Oil Operations on Village Communities

5.1. Introduction

Oil operations on the ground in Nigeria can have both a beneficial and an adverse impact on the well-being and property of village communities. The adverse effects can arguably be a source of conflict between oil companies and village communities. This chapter analyses the nature of these adverse effects as far as they relate to community conflict. Our goal is not to address comprehensively the correlates of the conflicts between village communities and oil companies such as economic inequality or the lack of political opportunities. Rather we use factual evidence to illustrate how the adverse effects of oil company field operations can be a source of conflict.

We illustrate the impact of oil operations by using exemplary court judgments from Nigerian courts. These court judgments provide examples of specific instances, in which village communities were adversely affected by oil operations. Rather than using court cases as legal material, we use them as factual evidence of the impact of oil operations on village communities. Since Nigerian courts produce a substantial quantity of written records on the conflicts between oil companies and village communities, court cases provide a significant number of references to particular events and disputes.[312]

The key problem in using court cases as a source of factual evidence is that courts rely on the interpretations presented by legal counsel and witnesses in court. In this context, one of the main obstacles faced by courts is to establish the processes which have resulted in oil-related environmental damage. Environmental damage in the oil producing areas originates from multiple activities. The oil industry is only one of a number of human activities in oil producing areas. In the Niger Delta, where the bulk of oil operations take place, other major human activities include farming, fishing and forestry. All these activities may cause adverse environmental and social effects on

---

[312] If compared with an analysis of court judgments, one of the alternative methodologies would be to conduct a sociological field study. Yet data gained from field studies can be very subjective as the number of objects of study may be severely limited, unless a standardised survey is used, a strategy which is difficult in a village setting in the Niger Delta. Data gained from court judgments is perhaps less subjective because judges are obliged to weigh the evidence of one party against that of the other party. A recent study by Omoweh (1998) exemplifies some of the methodological pitfalls involved in conducting field studies. Being influenced by the subjective perceptions of villagers, Omoweh concluded that oil companies, particularly Shell, have caused a land scarcity crisis in Nigeria's oil producing areas. This view is mistaken as studies with a scientific approach showed that there are more significant causes of the land crisis, particularly erosion and population growth (Ashton-Jones 1998, World Bank 1995 and 1990). A study by Onyige (1979) exemplified the same methodological problem. Being influenced by the subjective perceptions of villagers, Onyige (1979, 166 and 172-173) concluded that reduced crop yields of farmers and fishing losses were due to oil operations. Like Omoweh, he likewise failed to investigate other possible causes of these problems.

village communities (see Table 5.1.).[313] As the World Bank (1995, volume I, 102) showed, the Niger Delta faces many significant environmental problems including coastal and riverbank erosion, agricultural land degradation, forest degradation and biodiversity loss. A number of these environmental problems also have social consequences, for instance, agricultural land degradation leads to lower crop yields and, as a result, renders farming more difficult. Many of these social and environmental problems would be likely to prevail without the existence of the oil industry. Considering the multiple causes of environmental and social damage, it may be difficult to establish scientifically whether a specific adverse activity was caused by oil operations or not. For example, soil degradation may result from overfarming or from oil operations. By implication, a judge may find it difficult to decide on technical points arising out of oil-related litigation. While establishing causality may be an important problem, a judge is, nonetheless, obliged to admit the most credible factual evidence. On the balance of probabilities, factual information derived from litigation can hence yield potentially high returns. The key advantage in using evidence from court judgments is the reliability of Nigerian typed transcripts as a source of factual information.[314]

---

[313] Since the physical environment of the Niger Delta is dominated by the presence of water, it is instructive to indicate the sources of water pollution. Apart from oil pollution, water can also be polluted as a result of domestic sewage and other organic waste, infectious disease bacteria, fertiliser residues, pesticides and insecticides, industrial effluents, eroded sediments and other solid waste. Since there are no effective local pollution controls, sewage and other organic waste are probably the greatest sources of water pollution in the Niger Delta. The most significant consequence of water pollution is the lack of decent drinking water in many areas, which results in illness and death from water-borne illnesses and diseases such as diarrhoea, cholera and typhoid. Fishing, the main economic activity for many people in the Niger Delta, has been affected by environmental damage and over-fishing, with many fishermen suffering from declining catches (Ashton-Jones 1998, chapter 11). The above brief discussion indicates that oil operations are only a part of larger problems in the oil producing areas.

[314] In the 1998 survey of legal practitioners, respondents were asked whether typed transcripts of court judgments in Nigeria are usually written competently. Excluding 'no responses', a majority of the surveyed lawyers - 52.9% - noted that typed transcripts of court judgments are usually written competently, while 29.4% disagreed and 17.6% neither agreed nor disagreed (see columns 3 and 4, Table on the bottom of this footnote). Since a significant minority of lawyers has doubts about the reliability of typed transcripts, one needs to exercise some caution when interpreting typed court judgments. Nonetheless, our results would suggest that typed transcripts of court judgments can generally be utilised as reliable primary evidence of court proceedings. In Nigerian court procedure, while the judge does not type the transcripts himself, he must (at least in theory) proof-read each typed transcript to ensure that the transcript contains no mistakes before appending his signature. This ensures an adequate standard of the transcripts. On the whole, typed transcripts are likely to provide a more reliable source of information than alternative methodologies.

Table: Answer to Survey Question 15 'Do you agree/disagree with the following statement? "Typed transcripts of court judgments are usually written competently" '

	1 Percentage of Respondents	2 Cumulative Percentage	3 Percentage of Respondents (excl. 'no responses')	4 Cumulative Percentage (excl. 'no responses')
Strongly disagree	20.8	20.8	23.5	23.5
Disagree	5.2	26.0	5.9	29.4
Neither agree/disagree	15.6	41.6	17.6	47.0
Agree	18.8	60.4	21.3	68.3

Table 5.1. Human Activities in the Niger Delta

Ecozone	Approximate Area (in sq. km)	Major Human Activities
Lowland Equatorial Monsoon	7,400	• Oil operations and infrastructure • Arable agriculture • Oil palm and rubber exploitation • Urban and industrial activities
Freshwater	11,700	• Oil operations and infrastructure • Traditional forest exploitation • Modern forestry • Raffia and oil palm exploitation • Rice and arable agriculture • Fishing
Brackish Water	5,400	• Oil operations and infrastructure • Traditional mangrove exploitation • Port and associated activities
Sand Barrier Islands	1,140	• Oil operations and infrastructure • Fishing • Raffia and oil palm exploitation

Source: adapted from Ashton-Jones (1998, 116).

5.2. Mechanics of Oil Operations in Village Communities

Before we analyse evidence from court cases, it is instructive to explain the mechanics of oil operations in village communities. This serves as a background to the subsequent analysis of court cases.

Oil companies affect village communities through their exploration and production activities. In contrast, marketing and refining takes place mainly in urban areas, so it can be entirely disregarded here. Exploration operations in rural areas include seismic studies and drilling. Production operations include transportation of oil through pipelines and gas flaring. In addition, construction of pipelines and oil installations takes place.

On the most basic level, exploration for oil aims at locating sites with geological structures in which oil might be trapped. Exploration is mainly carried out by three methods: analysis of existing geological and other information, seismic surveys and exploration drilling. The first step for the survey team is to study geological as well as geochemical information and to prepare detailed maps, sometimes accompanied by aerial photographic surveys. Geologists study rock outcrops and analyse rock specimens and fossils in order to obtain clues about their origins and ages (Hyne 1995, 221-232). These activities involve little or no contact with village communities.

Strongly agree	27.9	88.3	31.6	99.9
No response	11.7	100.0	-	-
Total	100.0	100.0	99.9	99.9

Seismic surveys are intended to gather geophysical information for the oil companies. In a seismic survey, sound waves are sent into the earth's crust where they are reflected by the different rock layers. The sound energy from a source on the surface bounces off the different rock layers and returns to the surface where it is recorded by a detector (see Figure 5.1.). Surveys are carried out by seismic crews, which are usually sub-contractors of oil companies. The seismic crew measures the time taken for the wave to return to the surface, which reveals the depth of the layers. Such surveys also indicate what types of rock lie beneath the surface, since different rocks transmit sound at different rates (Hyne 1995, 233-254).

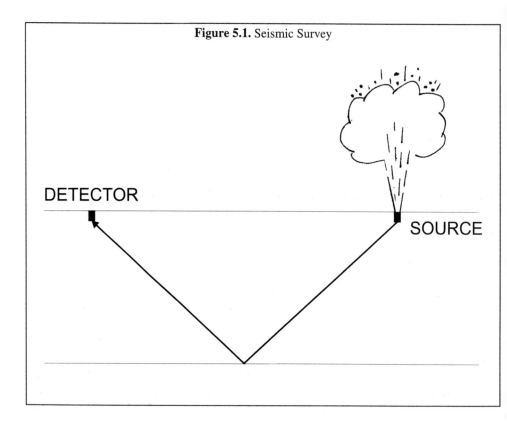

Figure 5.1. Seismic Survey

DETECTOR

SOURCE

A seismic survey starts by 'line cutting', that is, clearing the land or water surface from any plants in preparation for the survey. In Nigeria, a line is usually at least one meter in width. The cutting of plants is almost exclusively done by hand, using machetes. After completion of the lines, the seismic survey can start. Most surveys on land in Nigeria use explosives as the energy source. Explosives are detonated a few metres below the ground surface. In riverine areas, small boats or barges are used for seismic surveys, equipped with airguns which release compressed air into the water surface. This equipment is towed in the water behind the boat (see

Figure 5.2.). From the 1980s, oil companies have increasingly used the so-called 3-D seismic survey as opposed to the 2-D survey used in the past.

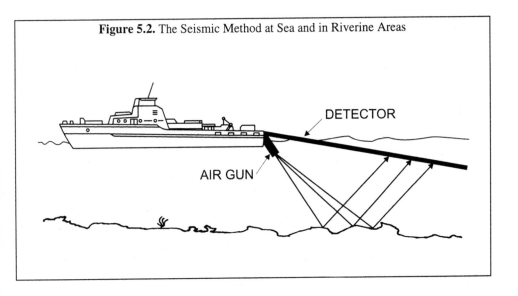

Figure 5.2. The Seismic Method at Sea and in Riverine Areas

DETECTOR

AIR GUN

A 3-D survey provides the oil company with a three-dimensional seismic image of the subsurface. On land, many seismic cables are laid close to each other to form a grid pattern, so that maximum information can be obtained from the surveyed area. In riverine areas, a single boat has two arrays of air guns being towed behind. The information is later processed in a high-speed computer. The subsurface can be viewed on a computer from different directions which allows a more accurate geophysical assessment than in a 2-D survey (Hyne 1995, 251-252).

3-D surveys were first employed by Shell in 1986 and have almost entirely replaced 2-D surveys in Shell's operations since (van Dessel 1995, 14-15). By the late 1990s, 3-D surveys played a much bigger role than 2-D surveys. Shell was the most active oil company conducting seismic surveys in 1997, while Western Geophysical was the most important seismic contractor in Nigeria (Petroconsultants 1998, 30).

Seismic surveys bring oil companies into close contact with village communities. 'Line cutting' requires a large number of workers to intrude on communal lands. 3-D surveys are particularly labour-intensive. In Nigeria, seismic crews usually carry all equipment by hand so a single 3-D crew can include over 1,000 people (van Dessel 1995, 14-15). The introduction of 3-D surveys has thus increased the physical presence of oil companies in village communities. Furthermore, oil companies sometimes use 3-D surveys in areas previously surveyed with the assistance of 2-D techniques since 3-D surveys provide more reliable data. The same area could hence be exposed to a seismic survey on several occasions.

Following seismic surveys, drilling of exploration wells begins by clearing the vegetation and building access roads and canals. Clearing of land is usually done by hand just as for seismic surveys. In riverine areas, canals are dredged to enable the company access to the well site. On land, an access road to the well site is constructed. Wells are drilled with rotary cutting tools with tough metal or diamond teeth that can bore through the hardest rock. These tools are suspended on a drilling string. During drilling operations, information about the oil field at various depths is collected by examining drill cuttings which are returned to the surface. The information about the rocks at various depths is recorded as a so-called 'sample' or 'lithographic log'. Drilling is the only way to exactly determine whether there is oil under the surface. If there is no oil in commercial quantity, this so-called 'dry hole' is plugged and abandoned. If oil is discovered in the exploration well, so-called appraisal wells are drilled in the area in order to establish the size of the field. If the field is to be commercially exploited, some of these appraisal wells may later be used as so-called development wells for oil production (Hyne 1995, 255-389).

Drilling information is much more precise than that taken from a seismic survey, but drilling costs are substantial which limits the quantity of drilling. For instance, in 1997, only 49 wells were drilled in Nigeria, of which 32 were situated in Nigeria's continental shelf areas (Petroconsultants 1998, 38-39). In 1997, Mobil was the most active oil company in drilling, with 14 exploration and appraisal wells drilled. The second most active company in drilling was Shell, with 7 wells drilled in the same year. Private indigenous oil companies such as Consolidated Oil are also becoming increasingly active in drilling (Petroconsultants 1998, 38-39). In general, thousands of wells have been drilled in Nigeria to-date. For instance, 1,300 wells were drilled by 1995 in Shell's Eastern Division alone, of which about half were still producing (van Dessel 1995, 16). Drilling activities involve a substantial number of oil workers using specialised drilling equipment, boats, road vehicles and helicopters. During these activities, company staff mainly meet with village communities. Dredging and road construction tend to infringe on communal lands.

Once the production stage starts, an oil/gas/water mixture flows to the surface. Oil companies cannot merely pump oil because gas and water are located in a petroleum trap together with the oil (see Figure 5.3.). Gas flows to the surface by itself because it is very light. Oil can also flow to the surface by itself if there is enough pressure in the reservoir, which is common in Nigeria. If there is not enough reservoir pressure, oil can be brought to the surface artificially by pumps or other methods. Once the natural reservoir drive has finished, water is injected into the earth's crust to force some of the remaining oil to flow to the surface (Hyne 1995, 8-10). Out of 2,251 producing oil wells in Nigeria in 1997, oil was flowing to the surface in 1,864 wells, while only 387 oil wells required an artificial lift (*OPEC Annual Statistical Bulletin* 1998).

From the well head on the surface, the oil/gas/water mixture is transported through a pipeline called a flowline to a gathering station called a flowstation. A flowstation usually gathers oil from a number of different wells. There, gas and liquids are separated. In Nigeria, most of the gas is flared, mainly in a horizontal flare laid on the ground close to the flowstation (van Dessel 1995, 17). The remaining oil/water mixture is transported from a flowstation through a pipeline to an export terminal on the coast where crude oil and water are separated. At the terminal, the crude oil is loaded onto tankers and shipped abroad (see Figure 5.4.).[315] Terminals have a strategic importance for oil companies. For instance, Shell alone operated 86 flowstations in Nigeria in 1995 (SPDC 1995a), but there were less than 20 oil loading terminals in the whole of Nigeria. All terminals are situated in the south-east of Nigeria, with the closest being 220 km from Lagos and the furthest being 650 km from Lagos (to the south-east). The largest storage capacities were available to Shell (approx. 13 million barrels) and Mobil (over 6.5 million barrels) (see Table 5.2.).

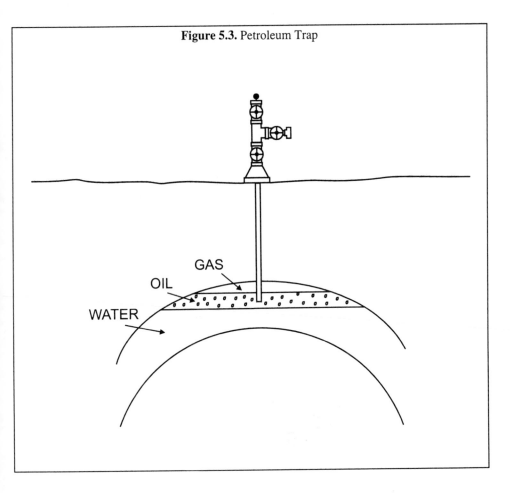

Figure 5.3. Petroleum Trap

The operation of a terminal is more important than that of a single flowstation. If the functioning of a flowstation is disturbed, only the production from the connected wells will be stopped. If a terminal is disturbed, oil export from all flowstations in the area may be stopped. When Biafra pulled out of the Nigerian Federation in 1967 at the beginning of the Civil War, Shell's flowstations were located on both sides of the new

---

[315] A small percentage of crude oil is transported to Nigerian refineries and utilised within the country.

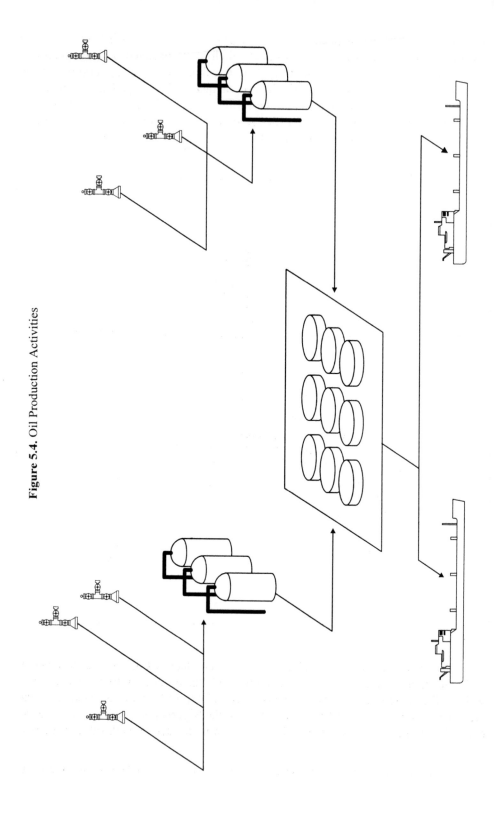

Figure 5.4. Oil Production Activities

border. However, Shell could not export any oil because the Bonny terminal was blockaded by the Biafran government (Forsyth 1969, 169). Unlike today, Shell had only one export terminal in 1967 and all Shell flowstations were connected through pipelines to Bonny. Even though there are many more export terminals today than thirty years ago, they are still the weakest point of the oil infrastructure and can suffer the most from political instability such as village community protests and from technical faults. When the main loading pipeline of the Qua Iboe terminal was damaged in June 1995, all exports from the terminal were halted and Mobil's oil production was cut to half of the normal production rate of 330,000 barrels/day (*Platt's Oilgram News*, 15 June 1995). This exemplified the strategic importance of terminals for oil production.

Table 5.2. Crude Oil Loading Terminals in Nigeria in 1998

Terminal	Operator	Location	Distance from Lagos (km)	Max. Tanker Size (000s dwt)	Loading Capacity (tons/hour)	Storage Capacity (million barrels)
Anten	Ashland/ Anten	offshore	n/a	270	n/a	1.75
Bonny	Shell	onshore	560	135	5,000	n/a
Bonny	Shell	offshore	560	320	6,000	n/a
Brass	Agip	offshore	470	300	5,000	3.5
Escravos	Chevron	offshore	220	300	4,100	3.6
Forcados	Shell	offshore/ onshore	260	254	9,000	13 (Bonny and Forcados combined)
Ima	LTS*	n/a	n/a	270	8,200	n/a
Odudu	Elf	n/a	n/a	280	n/a	n/a
Oso Field	Mobil	n/a	n/a	140	n/a	n/a
Pennigton	Texaco	offshore	370	250	3,000	2
Port Harcourt	NNPC	onshore	n/a	n/a	n/a	1.1
Qua Iboe	Mobil	offshore	650	300	7,200	6.5
Ukpokiti	Conoco	n/a	n/a	150	4,350	n/a

* Liberty Technical Services.
Sources: OECD (1998, II.39); Nigeria's Oil and Gas Publications (1996, 32).

The construction of permanent production facilities such as terminals and flowstations infringes on village communities because it involves large-scale construction work. The construction of flowstations infringes on village communities to a larger extent than the construction of terminals because their number is significantly greater. In any case, the above discussion suggests that the social interactions between oil companies and village communities are likely to be high. Whether those interactions translate into adverse environmental or social effects on village communities is the topic of the following two sections.

5.3. Impact of Oil Exploration on Village Communities

That oil operations such as the construction of flowstations have had an adverse impact on the environment and village communities is perhaps self-evident. The adverse effects of oil operations have been documented in great detail by van Dessel, Shell's former head of environmental studies in Nigeria. According to van Dessel, the most serious environmental damage of oil exploration and production activities is caused by: oil spills, gas flares, oily and other waste, land take and production/drainage of water.[316] The most serious damage occurs during oil production, but much environmental damage is also done by exploration, particularly if seismic surveys are carried out. Exploration activities are usually temporary but can still be highly damaging. A seismic crew may only stay in an area for a few days but the resulting damage may have long-lasting effects.

As explained earlier, significant areas of land are cleared in the process of laying seismic lines. In some areas such as farmland and uncultivated bush areas, the effect of line cutting is rather insignificant and little evidence of seismic lines is left after one year. In other areas, however, line cutting leaves long-term damage. The environmental impact of line cutting is particularly significant in mangrove swamps. It takes two to three years for mangrove bushes to recover after their roots are cut into, and it may take 30 years or more for mangrove trees to fully recover from line cutting. According to Shell's figures, 56.4 sq. km out of 91.4 sq. km of land cleared in the company's Eastern Division by 1995 was in mangrove areas (van Dessel 1995, 15). Detonation of explosives can affect the soil structure. If the holes for explosives are improperly drilled, a detonation can cause a crater. The environmental impact of seismic surveys in riverine areas is mostly restricted to sea mammals. The release of chemicals during a seismic survey is thought to be rather insignificant. The long-term ecological effects of surveys are largely unexplored. Some of the social effects of surveys, particularly losses to property, are meanwhile visible.

In order to illustrate the impact of oil exploration on village communities, we have selected a number of Nigerian court judgments. The issues discussed include the impact of seismic surveys, damage from an oil waste pit and the construction of access roads to oil installations.

There have been a number of court cases pleading damage from seismic surveys in Nigeria from the early days of oil operations.[317] In general, it is difficult to prove a

---

[316] J.P. van Dessel had resigned from Shell in protest at the company's environmental record in Nigeria. His insights on Shell's environmental record were described in van Dessel (1995).

[317] A significant number of early cases arising from seismic surveys were directed against Seismograph Service, an oil company sub-contractor. These included: *Seismograph Service v. Onokpasa* (1972) 1 All NLR (Pt. 1) 347, *Seismograph Service v. Akporuovo* (1974) All NLR 95,

direct link between a seismic survey and the particular damage. For instance, in *Shell-BP v. Usoro*[318] in 1960, Akpan Usoro sued Shell-BP for damage resulting from detonating explosives. Shell-BP came to Usoro's village to carry out a seismic survey and detonated explosives twenty yards from Usoro's unfinished building. The plaintiff claimed that the company did not warn him beforehand and that the explosion resulted in cracks in the building. The company did not dispute the fact that the explosion was carried out only twenty yards away from the building. But it denied that the seismic survey damaged the building. The company claimed that Usoro permitted the company staff to detonate explosives twenty yards away from his building. In addition, it claimed that the cement blocks of the house were of rather poor quality and that the cracks in the building existed before the explosion. The issue at the trial was for the plaintiff to prove that damage originated from oil company operations rather than from other activities. The plaintiff seemed to have a good case. Even witnesses called by Shell-BP appeared to support his case. The company called a civil engineer in the Public Works Department as a witness who testified that there were two types of cracks in the building. Some cracks could be ascribed to the poor quality of the cement blocks, but other cracks could have been caused by an explosion. He concluded: *'If I were building I would not permit an explosion as near as that'*. Another witness for the company, a so-called 'shooter' employed by Shell-BP, testified that he found *'two new cracks'* after the *'shooting'*. Judging by the evidence, the High Court of the Eastern Region in Calabar awarded the plaintiffs £644 and 5 shillings in damages. However, dissatisfied with the judgment, Shell-BP appealed against the decision to the Nigerian Supreme Court. The higher court concluded that the evidence was not conclusive enough and ordered a re-trial of the case. The case indicates the difficulties that villagers encounter in trying to prove damage caused by seismic surveys.

The damage from seismic operations is not restricted to buildings. In *Seismograph Service v. Mark*[319], the plaintiff claimed compensation for the destruction of his fishing nets by a seismic boat. Seismograph Service was carrying out a seismic survey as Shell's sub-contractor in the area. The plaintiff, a fisherman, claimed that he set his fishing nets in a fishing port with net floaters and buoys attached to warn approaching boats. A vessel called M.V.Verina, belonging to the seismic party, tore through the nets and damaged them, some parts were lost and others were dragged away by the vessel. The plaintiff won in the High Court of Ikot/Abasi, but Seismograph Service appealed against the decision to the Court of Appeal. Among other defences employed, the company claimed that seismic operations were not carried out on 20 February 1988 as the plaintiff alleged but on 21 February 1988. It was impossible for the plaintiff to prove the contrary. It was also impossible for the plaintiff to show that the company acted negligently by, for example, the vessel moving too fast.[320] As a result, the Court of Appeal allowed the company's appeal and dismissed the case.

Seismograph Service v. Ogbeni (1976) 4 S.C. 85, *Okorie v. Seismograph Service* (1975) ECSLR 286 and *Owabo v. Seismograph Service* (1974) ECSLR 455.

[318] (1960) SCNLR 121.

[319] (1993) 7 NWLR (Pt. 304) 203.

[320] The legal basis of negligence claims is discussed in the subsequent chapter.

Even where a judge visited the site of a seismic survey, evidence of damage could not always be established. In *Seismograph Service v. Onokpasa*[321], the plaintiff claimed compensation for damage from the destruction of buildings as a result of seismic operations. The plaintiff Benedict Etedjere Onokpasa claimed that detonations during a seismic survey heavily damaged eight college buildings, including a block of twelve class rooms and a dormitory block. According to the plaintiff, the oil company sent a representative, Paul Ossai, to inspect the building both before and after the 'shooting operations'. Ossai reportedly promised to *'make good all the damages to the college buildings* [sic]*'*, having admitted that the vibrations caused the damage. Seismograph Service initially denied that Paul Ossai was sent to the premises. Following the plaintiff's statement, the company altered its defence. The revised statement claimed that Ossai was only sent to the premises to check the distance to the place of 'shooting operations', not to inspect the premises. Since there was conflicting evidence in court, the trial judge decided to visit the premises. The judge saw a number of cracks in the wall going to the foundation, concluded that they were caused by the detonation and awarded damages to the plaintiff. Seismograph Service appealed against the decision. The Supreme Court allowed the appeal of the company, reversing the previous judgment. The court held that the trial judge's own observations could not be used as evidence and that it was erroneous for him to treat them as established facts.

The above cases have shown that it is difficult to establish both that seismic operations took place or that they caused any damage. In either case, the court encountered difficulty in attributing causality.

The drilling for exploration and appraisal wells is less common than seismic studies, albeit its impact has also been noted by secondary sources. Clearance of vegetation can lead to a long lasting or permanent loss of vegetation. Dredging destroys vegetation and life, especially if the dredged material is washed back into the water leading to a reduction of living organisms. The most damaging effect of drilling is probably the release of waste. Drilling activities require a significant quantity of 'mud' or drilling fluid. This is a special mixture of clay, various chemicals and water, which is constantly pumped down through the drill pipe and comes out through the nozzles in the cutting tool. The stream of mud returns upwards to the surface, carrying with it rock fragments cut away bit by bit. The waste which is generated is not particularly toxic or harmful but its impact is significant because of the substantial quantities. Discharge of this waste into water leads to the degradation of living organisms in the water (van Dessel 1995, 16 and 20-21).

While court judgments provide little factual evidence on drilling *per se*, there have been court cases pleading damages for activities related to drilling such as collection of oil waste or construction of access roads to drilling sites. In *Umudje v. Shell-BP*[322], the plaintiffs on behalf of the Enenurhie-Evwreni community in the East-Central State sued Shell-BP for damage resulting from an oil waste pit and the construction of a road. Shell-BP dug an oil waste pit during its exploration activities. In 1969-70, the pit was full and the waste spread over the plaintiffs' farms, ponds and

---

[321] (1972) 1 All NLR (Pt. 1) 347.

[322] (1975) 9-11 S.C. 155.

lakes, damaging the land and killing fish. The plaintiffs claimed that Shell-BP refused to pay any compensation. The trial judge of the lower court believed the evidence of the plaintiffs. His judgment in favour of the plaintiffs was later confirmed in the Supreme Court. Idigbe, J.S.C., delivering the judgment, said:

> The evidence which the trial judge accepted was that oil-waste collected in the location occupied by, or at least in the control of, the appellants, escaped... into Unenurhie land where it damaged the respondents' ponds. The trial judge on the evidence before him accepted the above facts as proved.[323]

In addition to the issue of oil waste, the case *Umudje v. Shell-BP*[324] also dealt with the construction of a road, which is another harmful aspect of oil operations. The oil company constructed a road across a waterway and failed to insert enough culverts under the road. At the location of the road, fish previously moved across the land into the plaintiffs' artificial ponds and lakes during the rainy season. After the road construction, fish could no longer move across. The local people were deprived of earnings from fishing. Said the trial judge of the lower court:

> I have no doubt in my mind that the access road blocked the passage of water during the flood season, and made it impossible for water and fish to go into the ponds on the right side of the access road during the flood season. It has definitely starved the ponds and lakes of water and fish, notwithstanding the fact that five culverts were erected under the access road.[325]

The lower court awarded 7,200 Naira to the plaintiffs in respect of the damaged ponds, lakes and farm land. The oil company appealed against the judgment. It claimed, among other things, that *'the facts alleged by the said plaintiffs in their evidence cannot support any of the reliefs claimed'*. The Supreme Court rejected this ground of appeal. Subsequently, the appeal by Shell-BP was dismissed and the judgment of the lower court was confirmed. However, the Supreme Court reduced the award of damages from 7,200 to 6,000 Naira as there was no sufficient evidence of damage to the plaintiffs' lakes and farm land.[326] The above case indicates that it may be difficult to prove the consequential damages arising from oil operations.

There have been a number of other lawsuits dealing with the construction of access roads. For instance, in *Nwadiaro v. Shell*[327], the plaintiffs on behalf of the Umusaziokwushi family of Obutu Village sued Shell for blocking the *'Utu Iyi Efi Creeks and Ponds'*. In 1966, Shell constructed an access road to an oil well location which blocked the village creeks, pond and lakes. Shell had never paid compensation to the family, although some payments were made to other persons disturbed by Shell's road construction. Meanwhile, the blockage continued and the plaintiffs were prevented from using their creeks, pond and lakes for almost three decades. In court,

---

[323] Per Idigbe, J.S.C. at page 168.

[324] (1975) 9-11 S.C. 155.

[325] Per Idigbe, J.S.C. at page 160.

[326] There were also legal grounds for this reduction.

[327] (1990) 5 NWLR (Pt. 150) 322.

Shell did not file a mandatory statement of defence for five years claiming that the plaintiffs had no right to sue the company over two decades after the road was constructed. The Court of Appeal ordered Shell to file a statement of defence in 1990, yet the case remained unresolved.

In contrast to the Umudje case, in the Nwadiaro case, the court did not encounter a difficulty in assessing the consequential damages because Shell had earlier admitted liability. But the case suggests that, even if damage has convincingly been proven in court, oil companies may continue to adversely affect village communities without paying compensation. As a whole, the cases discussed above would suggest that courts may encounter specific difficulties in attributing causality and assessing the consequential damages in oil-related litigation.

The above cases point to differences between temporary effects of oil operations and the effects of permanent oil company infrastructure on village communities. When permanent structures such as roads or canals are constructed, as in *Nwadiaro v. Shell*[328], the social effects of oil operations may remain for decades, while the local people receive no compensation. Indeed, the effects of road construction or canal dredging may be more damaging than the effects of any temporary exploration activity. For instance, in *Seismograph Service v. Mark*[329], the destruction of fishing nets constituted an adverse impact but this impact was temporary. In contrast, a road or a canal will remain in place for decades or longer. The effects of oil exploration on village communities are thus likely to be less severe in the long-term than the effects of oil production because they tend to involve temporary work rather than the establishment of permanent production facilities.

5.4. Impact of Oil Production on Village Communities

Secondary sources (e.g. van Dessel 1995) noted that oil production, like oil exploration, has a significant adverse impact on the environment (see Table 5.3.). Oil production and oil exploration activities have a number of adverse effects in common including waste management and disturbance during construction of the facilities and infrastructure. For instance, burial of oily or chemical waste in the process of exploration and production bears enormous ecological and health hazards as it can affect ground water, resurface during the rainy season or directly pollute the surrounding environment (van Dessel 1995). The issue of waste and the oil industry infrastructure have already been noted in the previous section. In this section, we deal with the adverse effects specific to oil production.

In order to illustrate the impact of oil production on village communities, we have selected a number of Nigerian court judgments. The issues discussed include gas flaring, oil spills and operational accidents such as well blow-outs.

---

[328] (1990) 5 NWLR (Pt. 150) 322.

[329] (1993) 7 NWLR (Pt. 304) 203.

Table 5.3. Potential Environmental Impact of Oil Production Activities

Production Activity	Potential Environmental Impact
All activities	• Loss of vegetation/ arable land • Hydrological changes • Disturbance of communities/ flora/ fauna • Waste pits in the field • Oily waste burned in the flare pit
Well operations	• Soil, water pollution • Disturbance of communities/ flora/ fauna
Flowlines, pipelines	• Soil, water pollution • Disturbance of communities/ flora/ fauna
Flowstations	• Ambient air quality • Acid rain • Soot/ heavy metal deposition • Greenhouse effect • Pollution/ fire affecting flora • Soil/ surface water pollution • Disturbance of communities/ flora/ fauna
Terminals	• Soil/ surface water pollution • Disturbance of communities/ flora/ fauna • Poor ambient air quality • Ozone depletion (fire fighting agents) • Soil, water, air pollution • Waste problems • Soil pollution

Source: van Dessel (1995).

The impact of gas flaring is difficult to evaluate as little is known about actual flame temperatures, which can range from 300 to 1400°C, and their effect. According to the World Bank, the total emission of coaldioxides from gas flaring in Nigeria in 1995 was estimated at 35 million tons per year, the total emission of nitricoxides and sulphurdioxides was 210,000 and 40,000 tons/year respectively (World Bank 1995, volume II, annex I). According to official figures, Shell was the greatest producer of gas emissions in Nigeria in absolute terms, followed by Chevron, Agip, Mobil and other companies. In 1994, Shell produced 37.9% of the total amount of gas flared in Nigeria. By 1997, Shell's share had declined to 27.7% but the company remained the largest source of gas flaring in Nigeria (see Table 5.4.). This is not surprising since Shell is the largest oil producer in Nigeria. Yet Shell flared a smaller proportion of associated gas than several other oil companies. Texaco flared a larger proportion of gas than any other oil company in Nigeria, followed by Agip Energy (a joint-venture between Agip and the NNPC). In 1997, Texaco flared 99.7% of the associated gas which the company produced, followed by Agip Energy with 99.1%. Agip's subsidiary NAOC flared the lowest percentage of associated gas - 53.5% of the company's associated gas production. Shell and Mobil reportedly flared 64.7% and 64.3% respectively of their total associated gas production (see Table 5.4.). What these figures appear to suggest is that there are some differences in terms of the environmental impact of different oil companies in Nigeria.

Table 5.4. Gas Flared in Nigeria in 1994 and 1997 by the Largest Oil Companies (in thousand cubic feet)

	Shell	Chevron	Agip	Mobil	Elf	Texaco	AENR*	Total Gas Flared
Gas Flared (cubic feet) in 1994	294,908	186,407	97,260	92,645	29,249	25,573	8,500	778,726**
Gas Flared (cubic feet) in 1997	222,013	176,966	150,690	116,465	33,894	44,770	7,914	801,847**
Gas Flared as % of Nigeria's Total in 1994	37.9	23.9	12.5	11.9	3.8	3.3	1.1	-
Gas Flared as % of Nigeria's Total in 1997	27.7	22.1	18.8	14.5	4.2	5.6	1.0	-
Gas Flared as % of Company's Total in 1997	64.7	91.3	53.5	64.3	95.1	99.7	99.1	-

* Agip Energy & Natural Resources; ** excluding the smaller oil producing companies such as Addax, Pan Ocean and Amni International.
Sources: 1994 figures from Nigeria's Oil and Gas Publications (1996, 51); 1997 figures from *Vanguard* (1 October 1998).

From a scientific point of view, gas flaring contributes significantly more to the greenhouse effect and air pollution which affects society at large rather than to specific damage in communities, which tends to be limited (van Dessel 1995, 23).[330] The low local significance of the adverse effect of gas flaring on specific communities in Nigeria can help to explain why little litigation has arisen from gas flaring and why court cases involving damage from gas flaring had little chance of success. However, some village communities feel disturbed by gas flares, as evidenced with the example of the case *Chinda v. Shell-BP*[331] below.

In *Chinda v. Shell-BP*[332], the Rumuokani community in Rivers State sued Shell-BP for damage from the *'heat, noise and vibration resulting from a flare'*. The plaintiffs claimed that gas flaring destroyed trees in the vicinity and damaged nearby houses. Holden, C.J., personally visited the site of the gas flare near the village. He

---

[330] A number of harmful effects of gas flaring on village communities have been noted by several non-governmental organisations in Nigeria (e.g. ERA 1995). The effects on village communities include the possible destruction of house roofs. Nigerian houses are often covered with steel roofs which may corrode as a result of acidification. But these effects of gas flaring are rather insignificant, if compared with the greenhouse effect or aggregate air pollution.

[331] (1974) 2 RSLR 1.

[332] (1974) 2 RSLR 1.

could not identify any tangible effects of the gas flare on the surrounding environment. Trees and crops near the gas flare seemed *'perfectly healthy'* to him.[333] From the evidence before him, the judge concluded that *'even if such damages are considered to be claimable in this action, I hold that there is no evidence of them so the claims must fail.'*.[334] In other words, the judge encountered a difficulty in establishing causality and hence dismissed the plaintiffs' claim.

While court cases highlight individual instances of the adverse effects of oil production with some precision, secondary sources have attempted to give broad estimates of the environmental impact of oil production. The following reproduces some of the findings of this research. According to the World Bank's figures, there were almost 300 oil spills per year in the Delta and the Rivers States alone between 1991 and 1993, which were the main oil-producing Nigerian federal states at the time (see Table 5.5). The key oil polluter was Shell, accounting for over 75% of the spills. According to Shell's own figures, the company had 190 spills per year in Nigeria from 1989 until around 1995, involving on average 319,200 US gallons of oil per year, damaging land and polluting water (Rowell 1996, 293). Depending on the location, oil spills can poison water, destroy vegetation and kill living organisms, which was shown by various 'post impact' studies (van Dessel 1995, 23; Amajor 1985). The adverse ecological impact of oil spills in the Niger Delta is increased by floods. During the rainy season, over 80% of the Niger Delta is flooded (Moffat and Linden 1995, 527). Water carries the oil to villages and onto farm lands. The floods also render the clean-up of oil spills more difficult.

Table 5.5. Oil Spills in the Delta and Rivers States of Nigeria, 1991-1993

	Delta State			Rivers State		
	Number of spills	Quantity spilled (barrels)	Number of spills at Shell	Number of spills	Quantity spilled (barrels)	Number of spills at Shell
1991	78	950	50	98	5103	86
1992	129	12,232	55	223	21,480	143
1993	116	909	58	232	8,101	248
Average per year	107	4,697	56	184	9,893	159

Source: World Bank (1995, volume II, annex M).

Oil spills in Nigeria are an undisputed fact yet their causes are disputed. Oil companies often claim that spills are caused by sabotage, while environmentalists claim that spills are due to deteriorating equipment. According to the World Bank (1995, volume II, annex M), oil spills are generally caused by companies themselves, with corrosion being the most frequent cause. Oil companies appear to have used

---

[333] Per Holden, C.J. at page 10.

[334] Per Holden, C.J. at page 10.

fictitious claims of sabotage to escape liability for compensation payments (this will be explained in chapter 6). Even according to Shell's own figures for the period 1991-1994, corrosion was the most frequent cause (see Table 5.6.).

While corrosion of equipment and equipment failure are important causes of oil spills, the age of installations appears to play a crucial role. Shell's own figures suggested that the age of pipelines and flowlines largely determined the frequency of leaks. The older the flowlines were, the more susceptible they were to leaks. Roughly 95% of all leaks occurred in flowlines 11 years or older (see Table 5.7.).

Table 5.6. Causes and Volume (in thousand barrels) of Shell's Oil Spills in Delta State, 1991-1994

	1991		*1992*		*1993*		*1994*	
	No. of spills	*Volume*	*No. of spills*	*Volume*	*No. of spills*	*Volume*	*No. of spills*	*Volume*
Corrosion	17	266	24	183	26	131	25	124
Equipment Failure	22	178	20	126	17	275	15	89
Sabotage	7	26	9	642	13	161	13	235
Other	23	233	19	269	16	50	20	65
Total	69	705	72	1220	72	617	73	515

Source: World Bank (1995, volume II, annex M).

Table 5.7. Age of Flowlines and Number of Flowlines in SPDC's Western Division in Nigeria

Age (years)	*No. of Flowlines*	*% of Total Flowlines*	*% of Leaks*
0-5	115	12.79	2.5
6-10	49	5.45	2.5
11-15	102	11.35	12
16-20	168	18.69	29
21 and over	465	51.72	54

Source: adopted from Ashton-Jones (1998, 187).

Evidence from court cases suggests that the impact of oil spills is more visible than, for instance, the impact of seismic surveys or gas flaring. The impact of oil spills is direct, immediate and can be easily detected by villagers. Damaged crops and polluted water can be easily identified as a result of oil spills. This can partly explain why a significant number of court cases against oil companies in Nigeria originate from oil spills.

In a recent case *Shell v. Isaiah*[335], three plaintiffs sued Shell for damage from an oil spill. In July 1988, an old tree fell on an oil pipeline which ran across the plaintiffs' land. A Shell sub-contractor was hired to repair the pipeline. In the process of repairing

---

[335] (1997) 6 NWLR (Pt. 508) 236.

the pipeline, the oil spill continued for several hours polluting the nearby swampland and farmland. The plaintiffs claimed that the sub-contractor failed to construct an 'oil trap' to contain the oil spill, which was denied by Shell. Having considered the evidence before him, the trial judge concluded that there was no oil trap to contain the oil spill.

Shell denied responsibility for the oil spill by claiming that the oil pipeline was 'cut by hacksaw' hence the spill amounted to sabotage. But Shell's defence witnesses contradicted themselves. Three of them admitted in court that the oil leak was caused by a fallen tree. A judge of the Court of Appeal commented in the court ruling:

> The issue of sabotage raised by the defendant [Shell] is neither here nor there. Sabotage was discovered after the second investigation. I am, having regard to the facts and circumstances of this case, convinced that the defence of sabotage was an afterthought.[336]

The Isaiah case indicates that oil pipelines in Nigeria are not adequately protected against external influences. It also suggests that the oil companies' efforts to clean up oil spills may be unsatisfactory in the sense that they negligently fail to contain an oil spill (sabotage claims will be discussed in greater detail in chapter 6).

As previously stated, the impact of oil spills is more visible than, for instance, the impact of seismic surveys. Nevertheless, even if a company admits an oil spill, the plaintiff's evidence may be rejected by a judge. In *Ogiale v. Shell*[337], Shell was sued by the Olomoro Isoko community in Delta State. The plaintiffs claimed compensation for damage to the land suffered as a result of oil production and gas flaring. The defence of the oil company rested on the contention that the *'company's activities were carried out on the area of land which the company legally acquired'*. Donald Otoakhia, Shell's Senior Lands Supervisor, admitted that the company had five oil spills in the area in the period 1973-80, yet he said that: *'We did not damage anything owned by Olomoro community. Individual families and quarters who own lands affected by our operations were duly paid. My company is not liable to the plaintiffs' claim'*.

The plaintiffs lost in the lower court, based on the judge's conclusion that they failed to prove their claim. The appeal of the plaintiffs was also dismissed by the Court of Appeal. The court proceedings centred around the question of admissibility of expert opinion which indicates how difficult it is to prove environmental damage. The long-term environmental effects of oil spills were not considered during the trial. T.E. Williams, Shell's lawyer at the appeal trial, claimed that *'the soil of the appellants' land would take a period of between 6 months and 5 years "to get normal" '* again. Such long-term effects of oil spills may not be competently considered by a court, as it has been difficult enough to prove short-term effects of visible oil spills.

Apart from gas flaring and oil spills, production activities bear a certain risk of operational accidents which can lead to major environmental disasters. An important adverse effect of oil operations appears to be well blow-outs. Since no statistical data could be obtained from the oil companies, it is instructive to analyse a specific case. In *Shell v. Farah*[338], several families sued Shell for compensation from a well blow-out.

---

[336] Per Katsina-Alu, J.C.A. at page 252.

[337] (1997) 1 NWLR (Pt. 480) 148.

[338] (1995) 3 NWLR (Pt. 382) 148.

In 1970, Shell-BP had a well blow-out at the Bomu II oil well. It took the oil company several weeks to bring the situation under control. Meanwhile, oil and other substances had polluted the adjoining land. Crops and trees were destroyed, while the farming land was rendered infertile. Shell had promised to rehabilitate a land area of 13.2 h and to hand the land back to the community afterwards. To facilitate land rehabilitation, the land was vacated by the community. Some 18 years after the blow-out, in March 1988, Shell wrote a letter to the plaintiffs' solicitor claiming that the land had already been rehabilitated and *'handed back'* to the plaintiffs. Moreover, Shell claimed that it had paid £22,000 in compensation for damaged crops, trees and other objects and another £1,000 for damage to the land. However, the company broke the promise and rehabilitation was not carried out. In the meantime, the local people could neither farm nor use the land in any other way. The plaintiffs claimed that they had never received any compensation for damage to the land. The families involved finally engaged in litigation in 1989, nineteen years after the blow-out.

Shell admitted that the blow-out had occurred. But the extent of the damage was disputed. A key witness in the trial was Professor C.T.I. Odu of the Department of Agronomy, University of Ibadan. Odu, the project co-ordinator of the land rehabilitation exercise, claimed that *'the area had returned back to normal'* by 1975. In 1989, Shell allegedly sent him to re-assess the ecology of the Bomu area. He claimed that only the area of about 1 out of 13 hectares indicated poor soil, the rest of the area was allegedly rehabilitated. He blamed the poor crop performance on erosion due to poor soil management by the community. The witness finished by saying:

> We concluded that the poor performance of the crops in this area was not due to the pressure (presence) of crude oil which several scientists both within and outside Nigeria have shown to be beneficial for crop production at level of about 1 per cent or below. [sic]

In effect, Odu's statement suggested that oil spills can be beneficial for village communities, but he failed to quote any environmental study to prove his claim. The trial judge doubted the genuineness of Prof. Odu's evidence. In his view, there was a conflict of interest between Odu's work for Shell and his court testimony. Said he:

> What did the defendant [Shell] do? They engaged the same man to go back to the area to re-assess the soil and the nature of the vegetation in the area.
> This is in effect asking the same expert to go back to the land and confirm that he actually did the job that he was commissioned to do some years ago. If I may ask, what kind of report do the defendant [sic] expect from Defence Witness 2 [Prof. Odu]? The defendant has been sued because the land has not been rehabilitated, obviously the Professor would not have come back with a report that the land has not been rehabilitated and that crops are not growing in the area that is said to be rehabilitated.[339]

Therefore, the court regarded Shell's main expert as an unreliable witness. The main expert of the plaintiffs was Dr. Edward Obiozo, lecturer in Biochemistry at the University of Port Harcourt. In his 1988 report he concluded that the soil around the

---

[339] Per Edozie, J.C.A. at page 184.

Bomu oil well continued to be heavily polluted with patches of crude oil tar and other chemicals, eighteen years after the accident. Among other things, the report concluded:

> 7. *On the average, 49-53 per cent of the land area affected are completely bare i.e. still do not support plant growth, and where there are plants at all, these are stunted, pollution-resistant siam weeds and guinea grass.*
>
> 8. *Agricultural crop productivity in the area was as patchy as the other plants and very low. The land in its present condition cannot support any good crop growth.*
>
> 9. *The area cannot be deemed to have been rehabilitated to its pre-impact conditions and cannot be so unless certain further actions are taken.*

The trial judge was initially uncertain about the evidence presented by the plaintiffs and by the defendants which contradicted each other. He subsequently appointed two referees to re-assess the evidence. One referee was nominated by Shell, the other by the plaintiffs. The joint report supported the evidence of the plaintiffs. The court established that Shell's evidence was not reliable. As a result, in the lower court, the plaintiffs were awarded 4,621,307 Naira in compensation. Dissatisfied with the judgment, Shell appealed against the decision. The Court of Appeal confirmed the award.

The case *Shell v. Farah*[340] illustrates the long-term damage arising from accidents in the oil industry. Two decades after an oil-related accident, the area was still considered unsuitable for effective farming. The Farah case, as well as the other cases, has demonstrated that oil operations may have highly damaging effects on the environment and thus on village communities. The case *Shell v. Farah*[341] also indicates that oil companies are unwilling to accept responsibility for damage from oil operations. Shell's expert witness even claimed that crude oil is beneficial to crop fertility. The same expert, Clifford Temple Idigi Odu[342] of the University of Ibadan, had claimed 20 years earlier in *Chinda v. Shell*[343] that damaged leaves near a gas flare were due to poor soil fertility, not due to the oil operations. Of course, those repeated claims are absurd, yet they have helped Shell to escape liability for environmental damage as in the Chinda case.

Evidence from the above cases on oil production confirms the earlier speculation that Nigerian courts may encounter difficulties in attributing causality and assessing consequential damage. Cases such as the Farah and the Chinda cases exemplify that the direct proof of damage from oil operations may frequently be disputed. In any case, the above discussion of oil production activities points to the significance of the adverse impact of oil operations. This adverse impact can directly result in litigation against oil companies.

---

[340] (1995) 3 NWLR (Pt. 382) 148.

[341] (1995) 3 NWLR (Pt. 382) 148.

[342] It appears from the court cases that C.T.I. Odu had been retained as an expert by Shell for well over 20 years.

[343] (1974) 2 RSLR 1.

5.5. Land Disputes and Oil Operations

The adverse impact of oil operations cannot be adequately explained without reference to land issues. Oil companies are dependent on access to land because they derive their wealth primarily and directly from below the earth's surface. Village communities are dependent on land as a natural resource for farming, fishing and hunting. Land disputes between companies and communities may, therefore, arise. This section discusses land disputes in the oil producing areas, by using evidence from Nigerian court judgments.

Oil operations affect the use of land in village communities in a number of ways. The use of land is, for instance, affected by the existence of pipelines and flowlines. As Ashton-Jones (1998, 187) pointed out, pipelines cut across the footpaths of the local people, thus severely disrupting foot communication, a primary method of movement in the oil producing areas.[344] Pipelines also forced some changes to traditional land use patterns. In particular, farmers cannot burn bushes in the vicinity of pipelines because pipelines could easily be set on fire (Ashton-Jones 1998). Court judgments on oil-related land issues do not provide factual evidence on topics such as pipelines and are largely limited to land disputes between villagers in the oil producing areas.

The social significance of land disputes in Nigeria's oil producing areas cannot be underestimated. According to a survey among over 300 local people in Rivers State by Onyige (1979, 148), 56% of the respondents had been involved in at least one land-related court case in their lives. Most of the respondents in Onyige's survey largely attributed their involvement in land disputes to oil operations.[345] It is likely that the significance of land disputes has further increased in the last two decades due to the expansion of oil operations.

From the preliminary analysis of the available court judgments, it would appear that there are two main sources of land disputes in oil-related litigation: disagreement over land titles between families and communities, and disagreement over the quantum of compensation to be paid by an oil company. Land disputes involving an oil company often arise when the company is prepared to pay compensation to a community in respect of land acquisition or damage. If two different communities dispute a piece of land and one community receives a payment, the other community may be aggrieved. Also, even if there is merely the prospect of receiving a payment, the local people may rush to receive a share. Different claimants might dispute the entitlement to compensation in respect of the same piece of land.

Oil companies are not the only source of land disputes associated with oil operations. Land disputes may have other causes such as ethnic conflicts. On the most

---

[344] The problem is particularly severe if a pipeline is fenced on both sides.

[345] Of all respondents in Onyige's survey, as many as 12% claimed that they had been involved in a land dispute roughly four times during their lifetime (Onyige 1979, 148). Unfortunately, Onyige did not compare his figures with the quantity of land disputes in areas unaffected by oil operations. Such a comparison could help to establish whether the quantity of land disputes in the oil producing areas is higher than average in Nigeria or not. Nonetheless, Onyige's results appear to suggest that land disputes are a very common type of conflict in the oil producing areas and that oil operations can trigger off land disputes.

basic level, oil operations may have no impact on land disputes, they may aggravate existing disputes or they may cause new ones.

Oil companies have often found themselves caught in long-standing disputes in oil producing areas. Those long-standing disputes with regards to land usually centre around issues such as boundaries between plots of land (as in *Adomba v. Odiesi*[346] below), ethnic conflict (as in *Otuedon v. Olughor*[347] below), the nature of land ownership or laws of inheritance (as in *Ogulu v. Shell*[348] below) or a combination of those factors. Some of these disputes started long before an oil company arrived in a particular area.

In this context, oil companies have often intensified existing disputes, as can be seen in *Adomba v. Odiesi*[349]. In that case, Agip entered communal land near Oloibiri in Rivers State in 1977. The plaintiffs, representing the Ekoni family of Opomatoba, sued the defendants, representing the Ake family, for having received rent and compensation arising from Agip's oil operations. Although land ownership was the disputed matter, compensation payments from oil companies appear to have been the motive behind the lawsuit. The plaintiffs asked the court for a declaration that they were entitled to all compensation payments, including those already paid and 143,234 Naira deposited in court by Agip, and they also asked the court to impose an injunction against Agip to prevent them from paying any compensation to any persons other than themselves. The plaintiffs won the case and were then entitled to Agip's compensation payments.

Even though the court case was over compensation from oil operations, there had been a long-standing land dispute already lasting for at least 20 years before Agip came to the area. The two families had been engaged in litigation since the 1950s over the said land. There had been two lawsuits Nos. 17/58 and 18/58 in the Oloibiri Native Court before the case was later transferred as Suit P/57/58 to the Port Harcourt High Court. From the court judgment, it appears that the defendants had continued to use the land in question despite an injunction by the Native Court *'to restrain the defendants from using the land in dispute until defendants establish their right of ownership over the land in dispute'*.[350] Oil operations only revived an old dispute.

The case *Adomba v. Odiesi*[351] also shows the problems of determining boundaries between different tracts of land. The Ake family did not deny that the Ekoni family won the lawsuit in the customary court. However, they denied the land rights of the plaintiffs, claiming that the customary court case involved a different plot of land from that in the later case. They disputed the boundaries of the land named by the plaintiffs. Similar disputes over boundaries are common in Nigeria's rural areas because the local people employ imperfect ways of describing land areas. Under English Law, land is usually described by reference to an attached plan unless verbal

---

[346] (1980) 1 RSLR 139.

[347] (1997) 9 NWLR (Pt. 521) 355.

[348] (1975/76) RSLR 68.

[349] (1980) 1 RSLR 139.

[350] Per Wai-Ogusu, J. at page 150.

[351] (1980) 1 RSLR 139.

description can accurately identify the land. In customary practice in Nigeria, land areas are given specific local names and the description of the area is often merely by reference to the name. In land contracts under customary law, boundaries are often inaccurately defined, being indicated by *'cairs, mounds, or ridges of earth, trees or grass, or by streams or other natural features'* (Onwuamaegbu 1966, 105-108).

In *Adomba v. Odiesi*[352], both parties presented plans showing the plot of land, but these did not provide adequate evidence to decide the case. The plaintiffs referred to the disputed land as *'Edumanyo'* or *'Edumato/Emeni'*, the defendants referred to *'Edum Ebela'* or *'Ebela'*, while Agip referred to *'Nembe A Location'*. In addition, the plaintiffs claimed that the land called *'Ebela Piri'* of the customary law case of 1958 was the same as *'Edumanyo'* of the lawsuit in 1980, which added to the confusion. In the lawsuit of 1958 no plan was attached because the case was decided under customary law, so no comparison could be made with a plan prepared by a land surveyor for the later case. According to the judge, *'the lands involved in those Oloibiri Native Court Suits cannot with certainty be said to be the same land as was involved in P/57/58'*.[353] Both the plaintiffs and the defendants claimed that Agip's Nembe A Location was within their communal land area, but none of them had a formal proof of land ownership.

The Adomba case is an example of a long-standing dispute between different communities in the same area. Many land disputes have an ethnic background, too. In *Otuedon v. Olughor*[354], the Gbolokposo people sued the Ugbomoro Village, Shell-BP and two other families over compensation owed to them in respect of Shell's operations. The plaintiffs from the Itsekiri ethnic group and the defendants from the Urhobo ethnic group had been engaged in litigation from 1925 at the very least. That means, the land dispute lasted over 70 years. Shell-BP only came to the area in 1963 when the land dispute had already lasted 40 years. The dispute was exacerbated when Shell-BP paid compensation in respect of land acquisition to the defendants rather than to the plaintiffs. The case shows, however, that oil companies may find themselves drawn into a long-standing ethnic dispute.

Sometimes an oil company may be drawn into a land dispute because land ownership or the laws of inheritance are disputed within a community. An interesting case is *Ogulu v. Shell-BP*[355], in which the plaintiff - Oyi Ogulu of Egbeama village - sued Shell-BP. The case is different from the Adomba and the Otuedon cases in that the land conflict involved members of the same village community.

The case *Ogulu v. Shell-BP*[356] was preceded by two earlier court judgments on the same subject matter involving community members in Egbeama. In the first court case which started in 1970 in the same High Court of Rivers State, members of the Egbeama community sued the elder brother of Oyi Ogulu, Chief Ibe Ogulu and Shell-

---

[352] (1980) 1 RSLR 139.

[353] Per Wai-Ogusu, J. at page 145.

[354] (1997) 9 NWLR (Pt. 521) 355.

[355] (1975/76) RSLR 68.

[356] (1975/76) RSLR 68.

BP.[357] The community representative sought an injunction against Chief Ogulu to restrain him from receiving any further rent payment from Shell-BP. Oyi Ogulu's elder brother had received payments from Shell-BP in respect of the *'Edum Ogboko Land'* claiming that the land was family-owned, while other community members claimed it was communal land. Said the trial judge: *'I am satisfied that the land on which these two locations are situated is not communal land but land belonging to first defendant's* [i.e. the elder brother of Oyi Ogulu] *family'*.[358] Oyi Ogulu's elder brother hence won the suit.

After the death of his elder brother, Oyi Ogulu claimed that he had succeeded him in the exercise of land rights on behalf of the family. Another lawsuit followed in 1971, in which the community representatives sued the Otu-Wariboko family including Oyi Ogulu.[359] They sought a declaratory judgment that the disputed land is the *'communal property of the entire Egbe Ogbogolo family including Otu-Wariboko family'*, not family land. The trial judge concluded that the disputed land was indeed the *'communal property of the entire Ogbogolo people and not the property of any unit of the Ogbogolo people'*.[360] Oyi Ogulu's family hence lost the case.

This court judgment was reaffirmed in the case *Ogulu v. Shell-BP*[361], in which Oyi Ogulu sued Shell-BP in order to receive rent payments due from the *'Edum Ogboko Land'*. In this third case on the subject matter, the judge concluded that the disputed land became communal, as opposed to family owned, after the death of Oyi Ogulu's elder brother. He thus dismissed the suit.

The court case examples above indicate that oil companies may find themselves involuntarily drawn into land disputes. Sometimes the company is sued directly as in *Ogulu v. Shell-BP*[362]. Sometimes the company is sued as the second or third defendant alongside the local community or family as in *Adomba v. Odiesi*[363]. But it appears that the oil companies do not wish to be drawn into land disputes. In the Adomba case, Agip's lawyers did not wish to appear in court. But the judge ordered that *'as stakeholders in the whole dispute it was necessary for them to have been joined'*.[364] The Agip lawyers still attempted to distance themselves from the dispute. Finally, Agip managed to stay away from the court proceedings by promising that they would, nevertheless, abide by the final decision of the court. Therefore, the oil companies often manage to keep aloof from local land disputes. Most frequently, when communities go to court over land issues, they tend to sue the neighbouring family or community, not the oil company, as in the case *Eze v. Okwosha*[365] below.

---

[357] PHC/11/1970, quoted in *Ogulu v. Shell-BP* (1975/76) RSLR 68.

[358] Per Manuel, J. at page 69.

[359] PHC/84/71, quoted in *Ogulu v. Shell-BP* (1975/76) RSLR 68.

[360] Per Manuel, J. at page 70.

[361] (1975/76) RSLR 68.

[362] (1975/76) RSLR 68.

[363] (1980) 1 RSLR 139.

[364] Per Wai-Ogusu, J. at page 144.

[365] (1977) 1 IMSLR 296.

While oil companies may be involuntarily drawn into land disputes, they can themselves trigger off fresh disputes - particularly litigation in courts - because of the careless manner in which they investigate land claims. In the case *Eze v. Okwosha*[366], the Ossai Oriaku Ezeoduwa family of the Umdei village in Imo State sued the Umuogini family of Obutu village over title to a plot of land and a stream. The lawsuit arose out of oil operations by Ashland. The plaintiffs claimed that Ashland had from 1973 entered and damaged their land. The land conflict was a direct result of oil operations. At the time of Ashland's arrival, the land ownership was not disputed and the Ossai Oriaku Ezeoduwa family was not bothered that the Umuogini family occupied the land. After the arrival of the oil company, both families scrambled to receive compensation payments from Ashland. Anthony Alphonso Nwakuche, a representative of Ashland, explained how the oil company went about settling the land question:

> When he received instructions to acquire the location called Urashi I, he placed public notices in the town and the Divisional Office and used the town Cryer to inform the people that the Company was to acquire the area. Before then the Company demarcated the area by cutting traces on the land. 1st defendant applied for compensation because he was there with members of the family on the day of the notice and the assessment. The Company paid them compensation.[367]

Nwakuche did not try to identify the rightful land owners but simply paid money to the first claimants who approached him. Under cross-examination in court, he admitted that compensation had already been paid by the time the plaintiffs filed a lawsuit to restrain the company from paying money. By the time the lawsuit was initiated in court, part of the land was already damaged by oil operations.

The different parties provided completely different accounts of traditional evidence for their respective claims. The plaintiffs claimed that the land belonged to them, while the defendants were merely their customary tenants. They claimed that their family obtained the land *'by conquest'* a long time ago. Their ancestor Ossai Oriaku allegedly farmed the land, which was originally owned by the Ogwu people. When the Ogwus started to steal his crops, he killed or expelled all of them and took possession of the land. Subsequently, the land remained in the possession of the Ossai Oriaku Ezeoduwa family. The defendants were merely allowed by the family to occupy the land as customary *'caretakers'*. As caretakers, the defendants had tenants who paid them rent in respect of the land. They allegedly performed a customary ceremony called Igo-Ife during every farming season. The ceremony, using items such as goats, fowls, kola nuts and palm wine, was aimed to certify that the plaintiffs as land owners allocated land to tenants. The defendants allegedly shared the rent payments with the plaintiffs.

However, the defendants gave an entirely different evidence in court. They claimed that the Umuogini family owned the land *'from time immemorial'* and denied that they were customary caretakers. The plaintiffs were allegedly not the owners of

---

[366] (1977) 1 IMSLR 296.

[367] Per Chianakwalam, J. at page 313.

the land in question. The defendants performed the Igo-ife ceremony to bless the land for the tenants. Each tenant paid the defendants 21 yarms as rent for a farming season. But they did not perform the Igo-ife ceremony to the plaintiffs. The land conflict only arose with the arrival of Ashland when the plaintiffs hoped to receive money from the oil company. For three years, the defendants could not fish in the Ugbo Nwaezike stream because the plaintiffs threatened them with a gun. The 1st defendant admitted that he had received money from Ashland but added that *'the plaintiffs did not claim the land when all these compensations were paid to him in respect of the land'*. The judge accepted the evidence of the defendants and their witnesses and rejected that of the plaintiffs. Chianakwalam, J. held that the plaintiffs' evidence of ownership rights was inconclusive and the defendants were the owners of the land.

If Nwakuche of Ashland had investigated the customary land rights more properly before negotiations over compensation with the villagers took place, many problems could probably have been avoided. Nwakuche negotiated with both parties in respect of the disputed ownership of the Ugbo Nwaezike stream without knowing the customary land rights properly. He agreed *'with plaintiffs to pay them 1000 Naira for the stream and agreed with the defendants to pay them 1100 Naira for the stream'*. He did not pay either the plaintiffs or the defendants in respect of the stream. The money was paid into court instead to remain there until the final settlement of the land dispute. By leaving the final decision to the judge, the company was able to largely keep out of the land conflict. However, by that time, Ashland had already triggered off the land dispute.

Even in cases when an oil company did not trigger off a land dispute, the ignorance of oil companies may have exacerbated an existing dispute. In *Adomba v. Odiesi*[368] mentioned earlier, Agip was drawn into a long-standing dispute. The ignorance of the company, however, exacerbated the conflict as Agip's representatives knew little about customary land rights in the area. According to Gabriel Chioloji, a land supervisor of Agip, the company assumed that the Akipelai community owned the Nimbe A Location partly because of *'the nearness of Akipelai village to the location'*. The Akipelai village was closer to the location than the Opomatoba village. However, he admitted that in Nigeria a plot of land can be some distance from the land owning community. It is unlikely that the company would have paid compensation to the wrong claimants, if the Agip staff had been adequately informed about the local customary rights. The above case thus exemplifies some of the problems that may result from the oil companies' ignorance of local land rights.

In another case *Shell-BP v. Abedi*[369], the plaintiffs on behalf of the Abadiama people sued Shell-BP for having damaged land previously cultivated by them. Jacob Abedi claimed that Shell-BP had removed soil from the land and that the excavated area of approximately 60 yards by 60 yards was later submerged in water. In addition, he claimed that Shell-BP destroyed property in the process, including 534 palm trees, 36 fishing ponds, 35 fishing canals and 3 religious juju shrines. Abedi claimed compensation from Shell-BP, but the oil company refused to pay to the Abadiama

---

[368] (1980) 1 RSLR 139.

[369] (1974) 1 All NLR 1.

people. Instead, they paid 6 Nigerian pounds and 12 shillings to the people of Gbekebor for the use of the land. Subsequently, the Abadiama people sued Shell-BP but lost the court case on legal technicalities.

The land conflict was probably unnecessary in this case and reflected Shell-BP's ignorance of the customary land rights in the area. When the oil company entered the area in December 1965, the company representatives approached the Gbekebor people but failed to approach the Abadiama people. Shell-BP used a surveyor and a so-called 'contact man' to identify the owners of the land. In those days, oil companies sometimes used indigenous contact men from their area of operations who provided local information to the oil companies. In the present case, it appears that Shell-BP's contact man was a native of Gbekebor, while the Abadiama people had no contact man. Since Shell-BP received information from an indigene of Gbekebor, the company may have been misinformed about the Abadiamas' true land claim.

If the Land Section of Shell-BP had in this case done its work properly, the company would have paid compensation to the Abadiamas as customary tenants for the destroyed ponds and other improvements, while money should have been paid to the Gbekebor people as land owners for the use of land only.

In general, the oil companies' ignorance of local customary rights causes problems for communities and companies alike. According to a confidential Shell report from 1993, the three main problems in land acquisition are: communication and wrong interpretations, identifying rightful owners, and resolving disputes and counter claims (SPDC 1993). It could be argued, however, that the key underlying problem was the lack of an economic incentive for oil companies to conduct land acquisition in a careful manner. If there is a land dispute, an oil company is able to compulsorily acquire a piece of land notwithstanding an existing conflict between land owners. The regulations introduced under the Petroleum Act 1969 provided that, in the event of a dispute, an amount was to be deposited by an oil company with the Accountant-General of a federal state in full or partial settlement, which was eventually due to the landowners.[370] The amount of compensation deposited was decided by the company. Even though the dispute might not have been resolved and families might have been left landless, a company was allowed to enter a piece of land.[371] Since 1978, oil companies have no longer been required to pay compensation for land but only for any crops, buildings and other objects destroyed on the land (see chapter 3). As a result, hostility may arise towards oil companies because the compensation payments are either insignificant or non-existent.

Oil companies have not always generated hostility when they entered a plot of land, particularly before 1978. Indeed, the relationship between oil companies and communities could have been one of co-operation as long as the oil company paid compensation. However, compulsory land acquisition and subsequent low compensation payments could be responsible for destroying the peaceful relationship

---

[370] Regulations 17(1)(c) and (2).

[371] The predicament of land owners under petroleum law was even worse under the Oil Pipelines Act, which did not require an oil company to pay a deposit. That means, a company was able to take possession of a piece of land for the construction of an oil pipeline notwithstanding a dispute and was not required to pay any compensation.

between companies and communities, as can be seen in *Nzekwu v. Attorney-General East-Central State*[372]. In that case, the Ogbo family sued the government for the compulsory acquisition of 397 acres of their land near Onitsha in the then Eastern Region of Nigeria. Initially, the family co-operated with the oil companies. In 1957, they leased 3.2 acres of land to Total Oil for ninety-nine years at the rate of £945 per annum. In the same year, they let out land to Shell-BP for a ferry ramp at the rate of £200 per annum.

However, in January 1960, the government published a notice of its intention to acquire almost 800 acres of land in the area, including the 397 acres owned by the plaintiffs, who demanded significantly higher compensation than they were offered. The government offered a rate of £10 per annum for 20 years, which was significantly lower than the rates previously offered by the oil companies. The Ogbo family rejected the offer and subsequently sued the government. The Supreme Court awarded the family a sum of £252,600 for the land and the houses thereon which was to be paid by the government. In this way, a land conflict had rendered the family rich. The above case is an example of how the courts could help a community or a family to capitalise on land acquisition for oil operations. Such a situation could no longer arise following the promulgation of the Land Use Act 1978, since the legal basis for compensation for land acquisition has been severely restricted since 1978 (see above and chapter 3).

Following the anti-oil protests of the 1990s, oil companies made substantial rent payments for land on a number of occasions. For instance, the T.S.K.J. consortium[373], a sub-contractor for the NLNG project, ear-marked US$ 1 million as the 8-year rent for a piece of land on Bonny Island.[374] However, it is not clear whether this new policy only applies to strategically important plots of land such as those required for the NLNG project. More importantly, oil companies are still not legally required to pay rent to local owners for land acquired for oil operations, so any rent payments are at the discretion of corporations.

On the whole, the cases discussed in this section illustrate that oil companies often find themselves caught in long-standing land disputes in the oil producing areas. But there is evidence that they may cause fresh conflicts or aggravate existing ones, particularly as a result of their ignorance of local land ownership structures. In this context, land acquisition may present a source of conflict between companies and communities.

5.6. Conclusion

This chapter assessed the impact of oil exploration, oil production and land acquisition on village communities in terms of the resulting environmental and social damage. This damage was analysed through the window of litigation. This window excludes

---

[372] (1972) All NLR 543.

[373] The consortium comprises Technip, Snamprogetti, Kelloggs and Japan Gasoline Corporation.

[374] The US$ 1 million rent payment was subject to a land dispute in *Hart v. T.S.K.J.* (1998) 12 NWLR (Pt. 578) 372.

those disputes which have not gone to court due to financial, technical or other factors. By looking at this type of litigation, we inevitably ignore evidence of the direct benefits of oil operations to village communities.[375] Court cases also fail to provide evidence of the adverse secondary effects of oil operations such as migration of oil workers into oil producing areas as well as the psychological and cultural effects of oil operations.[376] With regards to some secondary effects, it is difficult to say whether oil operations led to adverse or beneficial changes.[377] Court judgments, moreover, do not allow for a comparison between the scope of environmental damage in Nigeria and in other countries.[378] In this sense, our view is biased. Yet it was not the goal of this study to weigh the costs and benefits of oil operations. Rather we set out to analyse sources of conflict and civil strife. Evidence from 'real world' cases illustrated a number of those sources.

While the Niger Delta faces more significant ecological problems than oil pollution such as coastal erosion, oil operations adversely affect specific areas and people. Oil pollution has a limited impact on the ecology of the oil producing areas as a whole (World Bank 1995, volume I, 102; Ashton-Jones 1998, 150). But court cases have revealed that the destruction of crops or fishing sites by oil companies can have a disastrous effect on specific families and communities by depriving them of any means of subsistence. This inevitably leads to conflict.

That ecological and social damage is incidental to oil operations and that it can never be fully eliminated is perhaps self-evident. Commenting on the impact of seismic surveys, J.P. van Dessel, formerly Shell's head of environmental studies in Nigeria, remarked that *'further reduction of the impact of seismic operations in the mangrove (further reduction of the line width) is not possible without jeopardising the safety of*

---

[375] Onyige (1979, 189-191) mentioned a number of beneficial effects of oil operations such as the construction of access roads and scholarships.

[376] Onyige (1979, 151-152, 155-156 and 176) mentioned a number of adverse effects, which cannot be derived from court cases. These included the impact of migration of oil workers and the rise in food prices. Court cases, moreover, provide little evidence of the psychological and cultural effects of oil operations. Onyige (1979, 188), for example, pointed to the effect of temporary employment of young people by oil companies. Those young people who are employed by oil companies are highly paid for a short period of time. By increasing their spending habits and imitating a culture alien to them, their lifestyles may quickly become distinctive from the rest of the community. Both the young men and the village community as a whole may find it difficult to adjust to those sudden changes. In any case, more in-depth field research is needed into those issues.

[377] Writing on the Ogba/Egbeba district of Rivers State, Onyige (1979, 164-165) found that many farmers had shifted from yam to cassava production as a result of the influx of oil company workers. Oil company workers consumed a substantial amount of gari, which is made from cassava. It is not entirely clear whether this shift can be classified as either beneficial or adverse to the village communities.

[378] Secondary sources suggest that, from an international perspective, oil operations in Nigeria appear to cause greater environmental and social damage than in many other oil producing countries. For instance, gas flaring in Nigeria is more significant as a percentage of total gas production than elsewhere in the world. According to the World Bank (1995, volume I, 59), up to 76% of the associated gas from oil wells was flared in Nigeria in 1995, as compared with 0.6% in the US and 4.3% in the UK. By 1997, the percentage of flared gas had fallen to roughly 71% (*Vanguard*, 1 October 1998). This percentage was likely to fall further as a result of new investments in gas-related projects in Nigeria but a continuation of gas flaring was likely to continue in the short-term and the medium-term. If judged by the example of gas flaring, it would appear that oil companies have taken environmental concerns in Nigeria less seriously than in other countries.

the crews or the quality of the data' (van Dessel 1995, 19). Similarly, the oil industry cannot function without infrastructure such as access roads, which requires interactions between oil companies and village communities. Nonetheless, most forms of damage such as oil spills cannot be blamed on technical and geographical difficulties alone, but must be attributed to a lack of corporate effort and the failure of Nigeria's legal provisions to protect the environment and the village communities (see chapter 3).

The adverse impact of oil operations often appears as the result of careless operating practises and the lack of funding. By implication, it has to be assumed that this impact could be significantly minimised. As shown earlier, oil spills are often caused by operational faults and inadequate maintenance of oil installations. Oil companies in Nigeria could reduce the impact of oil operations in various ways.[379] For instance, many oil spills could be either avoided or better contained. In *Shell v. Isaiah*[380] mentioned earlier, Shell negligently failed to contain an oil spill. In *Umudje v. Shell-BP*[381] mentioned earlier, Shell-BP constructed a road across a waterway but failed to insert enough culverts under the road. In both cases, damage from oil operations could have been avoided or minimised.

Legal provisions in Nigeria do not appear to have been particularly effective in minimising the adverse impact of oil operations (see chapter 3). Indeed, Shell's Health, Safety and Environment Adviser in Nigeria stated in 1998: *'Law is the least important factor in terms of environmental protection'.*[382] According to him, the three main factors were: control over decision-making, culture and the age of installations, although the third factor appears to result from the first two. In terms of decision-making, funding is the key obstacle to the protection of the rural environment and the village communities. Environmental improvements are often costly, while oil companies are likely to be reluctant to spend money on environmental protection. The economic activity of oil companies is dictated by the profit motive. The federal government and the oil companies have a natural incentive to retain revenue and minimise costs in a competitive bidding system. Contractors are under pressure from Shell and the other oil companies to perform services at the lowest possible price, which further forces them to minimise costs. Therefore, contractors have little incentive to spend money on the maintenance of oil installations and, generally, on any projects related to village communities and environmental protection. Meanwhile, the purely environmental costs as part of the total oil company expenditure are potentially substantial. According to a 1996 survey on the Nigerian oil industry by the consultancy firms Arthur Andersen and Andersen Consulting, 54% of the oil company executives expect environmental issues in Nigeria such as oil spills and gas flaring to have the greatest effect on abandonment and restoration costs (Arthur Andersen 1997).

---

[379] Secondary sources on oil operations, for instance, suggested that abandoned wells can be plugged (Hyne 1995, 293). Yet, according to J.P. van Dessel, a small fraction of Shell's non-producing wells in Nigeria have been adequately abandoned, *'most of them were simply left behind'* (van Dessel 1995, 16).

[380] (1997) 6 NWLR (Pt. 508) 236.

[381] (1975) 9-11 S.C. 155.

[382] Personal interview with Chris Geerling, SPDC's Corporate Health, Safety and Environment Adviser (Lagos, February 1998).

While the financial costs of environmental protection can be assumed to play an important role in decision-making, cultural influences also appear to be very important, that means, social values which guide decisions made by company staff. Subsidiaries of multinational companies could be assumed to develop specific corporate cultures influenced by both the national culture of the country in which they operate and by the cultural values of the corporate headquarters. Unfortunately, there appears to have been no prior academic research on the dynamics of cultural change in Nigeria's oil companies. Within the cultural context, the most striking feature of the industry's environmental performance is probably the ignorance of oil company staff with regards to environmental and community issues. Referring to the Nigeria Liquefied Natural Gas (NLNG) project, Chris Geerling, Shell's Health, Safety and Environment Adviser, could not understand why anyone would be willing to oppose NLNG as the project would eliminate gas flaring in the long run. In Geerling's view, the NLNG project presents only beneficial effects to the environment and the village communities. Geerling obviously failed to recognise, however, that a project of that nature may also have a significant social and environmental impact on village communities such as compulsory acquisition of land, construction work, laying of gas pipelines or migration of oil workers into the area.[383] The views of Shell's environmental head in Nigeria may exemplify the oil companies' cultural ignorance of the problems faced by village communities as a result of oil operations. This ignorance has been reflected, for instance, in the failure of oil companies to properly investigate the local ownership structures before awarding compensation for land acquisition. In *Adomba v. Odiesi*[384] mentioned earlier, Agip's representatives knew little about customary land rights in the area. In general, factual evidence from court judgments, particularly in relation to land disputes, suggests that oil company staff are either ignorant of the problems faced by village communities as a result of oil operations or they attach little importance to those problems.

There are indications that cultural attitudes rather than funding problems are at the root of careless oil company operating practices in Nigeria. This speculation appears to be supported by evidence from court cases. In *Seismograph Service v. Mark*[385] mentioned earlier, the destruction of fishing nets by seismic boats, for example, could have been easily avoided through an adequate warning system and closer co-operation with village communities, which would have entailed only insignificant financial costs. In *Umudje v. Shell-BP*[386] mentioned earlier, the impact of the blockage could have been minimised through inserting enough culverts under the road at an insignificant financial cost. In general, evidence from court judgments indicated that many forms of damage from oil operations stem directly from the

---

[383] Personal interview with Chris Geerling, SPDC's Corporate Health, Safety and Environment Adviser (Lagos, February 1998). As Ashton-Jones (1998, 173) noted, Shell's 1995 Environmental Impact Assessment (EIA) study of the LNG plant in Bonny, which has been on the drawing board for over 30 years, did not, for instance, consider the impact of activities carried out in the process of preliminary works such as clearing of vegetation in 1979 and the re-location of the Finima village after 1979.

[384] (1980) 1 RSLR 139.

[385] (1993) 7 NWLR (Pt. 304) 203.

[386] (1975) 9-11 S.C. 155.

careless management by oil companies rather than from the lack of funding. From the perspective of oil companies, it would make good business sense to minimise the adverse impact of oil operations when the financial costs involved are low. By minimising the damage from oil operations, oil companies could help to reduce the frequency of community conflicts arising from oil activities on the ground. But cultural attitudes are likely to prevent many initiatives to minimise the adverse impact of oil operations.

On the whole, factual evidence from oil-related court judgments provided various indications that the adverse impact of oil operations has led to fresh disputes between village communities and oil companies or aggravated existing disputes. Some of these disputes have, in turn, resulted in litigation.

With regards to the legal side of disputes in the oil industry, our analysis provided indications that Nigerian courts may find it difficult to adequately adjudicate claims for damage from oil operations which are inevitably of a technical nature. Evidence from court judgments indicated that courts encounter specific difficulties in attributing causality and assessing the consequential damages in oil-related litigation. This is likely to have reduced the chances of success of those affected by oil operations in litigation against oil companies in Nigeria. In turn, this could partially explain why the adverse environmental and social impact of oil operations may result in extra legal forms of protest rather than in litigation.

The analysis in this chapter was confined to the use of court judgments as factual evidence. It cannot explain why more court cases filed by village communities against oil companies have succeeded and higher compensation payments were awarded to communities in the 1990s. The legal dynamics of oil-related litigation are explored in some detail in the following chapter.

Chapter 6: Compensation Claims in Oil-Related Litigation

6.1. Introduction

The evolution of litigation is inevitably related to the success of individual litigants. This chapter investigates how the Nigerian legal system has addressed the litigants' claims against oil companies over time. We observe that a number of legal innovations have been introduced in oil-related litigation and that these innovations may have benefited village communities. Our analysis indicates that there is an increased possibility of higher compensation awards to village communities. This seems to have had an impact on the quantity of litigation.

In the period 1981-86, 24 compensation claims against Shell went to court in Nigeria (Adewale 1989, 93). In early 1998, Shell was reportedly involved in over 500 pending court cases in Nigeria, out of which 70% or roughly 350 cases dealt with oil spills, the other 30% or 150 cases dealt mostly with other types of damage from oil operations, contracts, employment and taxation (Frynas 1999, chapter 6). In the whole of the 1980s, Chevron reportedly had only up to 50 court cases in Nigeria. In early 1998, Chevron was involved in over 200 cases, of which 80-90% or roughly 160-180 cases dealt with oil spills, other types of damage from oil operations or land acquisition for oil operations (Frynas 1999, chapter 6). This substantial increase cannot be solely ascribed to expanding oil operations. In the 1990s, a number of high profile cases have been won by village communities, notably *Shell v. Farah*[387], in which ca. 4.6 million Naira (ca. US$ 210,000) was awarded as damages to a community.

We have analysed 68 court cases, which involved disputes arising from oil company field operations. Reported cases were gathered from publicly available law reports, while a number of unreported cases were obtained from practising lawyers in Nigeria. The collection of cases was aided by Nigerian legal professionals, a Nigerian judge and the author's judgment. The sample of court cases is biased in favour of reported as opposed to unreported judgments because they are more readily available. But the sample probably represents the best possible judgment an outsider can gain on oil-related litigation in Nigeria. In this chapter, we utilise 31 of the most representative and relevant court cases.

6.2. Compensation Payments through Negotiation and Mediation

Before discussing legal rules, we investigate why many disputes in the Nigerian oil industry cannot be resolved through informal negotiations and mediation and may thus result in litigation and violence. This discussion can serve as a window to an

---

[387] (1995) 3 NWLR (Pt. 382) 148.

understanding of non-legal forms of disputes which in turn can help us to understand the dynamics underlying litigation. We analyse evidence from a number of court cases to illustrate specific instances, in which village communities tried to resolve a conflict before they actually went to court. In other words, in this section, we use court cases as factual evidence of non-legal forms of disputing.

Anthropological literature (e.g. Nader and Todd 1978) suggests that disputes can take a number of forms. Disputes may go through stages involving informal negotiation, mediation or violence without involving any litigation.[388] Even if a plaintiff initiates litigation, a case may be settled out of court before reaching a court judgment.[389] In disputes between village communities and oil companies in Nigeria, litigation is an important element but it may occur in only a fraction of disputes. For instance, in one of Shell's two divisions in Nigeria alone, 1081 compensation claims were made between 1981 and 1986, of which 124 claims were settled and only 24 claims went to court (Adewale 1989, 93). In 1979, Agip had roughly 600 unsettled compensation claims in Rivers State alone, but only 6 court cases were pending in Rivers State courts (Onyige 1979, 105 and 148-149). Before a compensation claim comes to court, it may be settled by informal agreement between those affected by oil operations and the oil company or by mediation.

A dispute may start with an attempt at informal negotiation. Once villagers decide to negotiate and to seek compensation for damage from oil operations, they contact the oil company. The company can decide whether to agree to negotiations or not. Negotiations are usually carried out between the oil company and the community leaders. If the company accepts liability, a subsequent assessment of the damage and a compensation payment may be made. The oil company tends to determine the amount of the compensation payment, which may then be rejected or accepted by the claimants. A confidential report commissioned for the Shell-initiated Niger Delta Environmental Survey (NDES) in 1996 criticised the way in which oil companies assess compensation payments in informal negotiations:

---

[388] As Nader and Todd (1978, 15) pointed out, 'these stages are not neat nor are they necessarily sequential'. The aggrieved party may, for instance, file a court suit without having earlier confronted an offender.

[389] An example of an out-of-court settlement in oil-related litigation in Nigeria is provided by the case *Gardline Shipping v. Joshua* Unreported Suit No. FHC/L/CS/1273/96. In that case, Gardline Shipping Limited sued 28 fishermen in order to limit the company's liability for damage towards the 28 fishermen, who claimed compensation for damage from oil operations. A boat owned by Gardline Shipping, while conducting a seismic survey, tore and dragged away fishing nets of fishermen in the Bonny area of the then Rivers State. 28 fishermen sought compensation from the company for the destroyed fishing nets. The company initiated a lawsuit against those fishermen in the Federal High Court in order to limit the aggregate compensation amount to 47,398 Naira for each ton of the tonnage of the ship in line with the Merchant Shipping Act. Subsequently, the matter was settled out-of-court at the initial request of the fishermen. In general terms, out-of-court settlements appear to be relatively infrequent in oil-related litigation in Nigeria. For instance, at Shell in Nigeria, out-of-court settlements reportedly involve between 5% and 15% of all court cases (Frynas 1999, chapter 6).

Our investigations revealed that the oil industry operators have their yardstick for assessing what they pay. The victim may reject the offer; if he makes a further appeal [to the company], *he may get another paltry upward review after a further delay of about 6 months to a year* (Ogbnigwe 1996).

Evidence from court cases suggests that an unsatisfactory outcome of informal negotiations for those affected by oil operations can lead to litigation. In *Odim v. Shell-BP*[390], the plaintiffs were paid compensation by Shell-BP in respect of destroyed crops, after negotiations took place. Subsequently, the plaintiffs went to court claiming a higher amount of compensation. They claimed that the negotiations with the oil company were not carried out in good faith and that the company fixed the compensation amounts without the consent of the recipients. A witness admitted that the plaintiffs were notified by the company about the assessment of crops for compensation and that they had received a payment. But the plaintiffs averred that they regarded the compensation payment as merely a temporary payment. When they heard about the promulgation of the Rivers State Minimum Crop Compensation Rates Edict of 1973, they instituted a lawsuit. Under the Edict of 1973, those adversely affected by oil operations were entitled to significantly higher compensation rates for crops than those actually paid by oil companies.

In the Odim case, Shell-BP lawyers relied on the provisions of the Oil Pipelines Act 1956, under which compensation payments were to be determined in negotiations with the claimants. There are indications that the 1973 Edict was biased against oil company interests because it involved higher compensation rates than those paid hitherto by the companies. Not surprisingly, Shell-BP lawyers argued against the Edict's provisions. The court judgment reported on the testimony of Shell-BP's Senior Lands Supervisor as follows:

The 1st defendants [Shell-BP] *do not accept for basis of calculation of compensation rates any other law than the Oil Pipeline Law; to accept the rates as fixed by the Rivers State Edict No.7 of 1973 was unrealistic and against the trend of open market prices.*[391]

The Odim case was dismissed because the court regarded the 1973 Edict as unconstitutional. The court further concluded that the plaintiffs had voluntarily accepted a compensation payment, so that they were not entitled to claim an additional compensation payment in respect of the same injury. If the villagers had been aware of the Edict during negotiations, it is likely that they probably would have used it as the basis of their compensation claim.

In another case *Nvogoro v. Shell-BP*[392], the oil company constructed a road through the middle of a farm occupied by Sunday Nvogoro in the Nweel community in the Ogoni area. While Mr. Nvogoro was away, his brother Bomu led negotiations with Shell-BP. During negotiations with Mr. Iworima of Shell-BP, Bomu claimed compensation for three banana trees and some bamboo trees. He demanded 5 shillings

---

[390] (1974) 2 RSLR 93.

[391] Per Wai-Ogosu, J. at page 98.

[392] (1973) 2 RSLR 75.

for each banana tree and 20 shillings for each bamboo tree, but settled for a sum of only 17 shillings for all the trees combined. In addition, he claimed £30 for an empty yam barn, but was only paid £3 by Shell-BP. When Sunday Nvogoro returned home, he was surprised that his illiterate brother had been paid compensation. Dissatisfied with the amount of compensation, he initiated a lawsuit against the oil company. Shell-BP used a receipt, thumb-printed by Bomu, as evidence in court. The plaintiff lost the case because Shell-BP had previously paid compensation in respect of the same damage.

The above cases appear to indicate that negotiations with oil companies are often unsatisfactory from the perspective of village communities. When negotiations break down, mediation may take place, though this appears to be less common in Nigeria than negotiation. Mediation involves a third party, usually officials from the Department of Petroleum Resources or the Nigerian National Petroleum Corporation (NNPC), who intervene in a dispute to help the two parties to reach an agreement.[393] In *Nwadiaro v. Shell*[394], the Umusaziokwushi family of Obutu village in Imo State sued Shell after having tried both negotiation and mediation in dealing with the company. In 1966, Shell constructed an access road to an oil well location which blocked the flow of water in the village creeks, pond and lakes. Shell had never paid compensation to the family, although some payments were made to other persons in 1972. At first, Shell denied any liability for damage from its oil operations, but later engaged in negotiations with those affected. When negotiations broke down, mediation was convened with the NNPC acting as intermediary. In late 1984, an investigation was carried out, which included two Shell employees, two NNPC employees and a representative of the Ikesco compensation claims agency, to investigate and assess the compensation claim of the Umusaziokwushi family. A report on the investigation found that Shell was responsible for the blockage. It recommended that the culverts under the road should be reconstructed to allow for a proper flow of water. It further recommended that compensation should be paid to the Umusaziokwushi family. In communication with the NNPC, Shell agreed to pay compensation. In reality, Shell still failed to pay the compensation so the plaintiffs filed a court case demanding 100,000 Naira in compensation. The case *Nwadiaro v. Shell*[395] illustrates the inadequacy of mediation. Although an investigation was carried out by the NNPC, Shell admitted liability for the damage in the process of mediation and agreed to pay, in reality, the oil company failed to pay compensation to the claimants.

In general, the main problem with mediation is that it is not legally binding and there is no agency in Nigeria to enforce the compensation payments. A further problem is that mediation is usually carried out by the NNPC or the oil ministry, which are

---

[393] In land disputes between the local people arising from an oil company's compensation payment, traditional rulers may act as mediators. For instance, in *Nteogwuija v. Ikuru* (1998) 10 NWLR (Pt. 569) 267, two communities - Okorobo and Ikuru Town - were involved in a dispute over compensation for a piece of land acquired by Shell-BP in the Bonny local government area in Rivers State. The Andoni Council of Chiefs appointed a five-man-peace panel to mediate between the two communities. The panel decided unanimously in favour of the Okorobo community. However, the representatives of Ikuru Town were dissatisfied with the ruling and subsequently went to court. This underlines the fact that the effectiveness of mediation is limited by the willingness of the participants to accept the ruling of mediators.

[394] (1990) 5 NWLR (Pt. 150) 322.

[395] (1990) 5 NWLR (Pt. 150) 322.

primarily concerned with the level of oil production and oil revenues rather than with the protection of those affected by oil operations. Compensation payments increase costs for companies, so companies are usually reluctant to pay. The NNPC operates as an oil exploration and production company and has itself refused to pay compensation for damage to communities in some cases.[396] Clearly, the NNPC and the oil ministry have an economic incentive to keep compensation claims to a minimum, so they are unsuitable to act as mediators in disputes between companies and communities. In contrast, as Adewale (1989, 98-99) pointed out, when the State Ministry of Lands acted as a mediator in those disputes on a number of occasions, both parties reportedly expressed greater satisfaction.

In addition to the above problems related to mediation and negotiation, secondary sources suggest that there have been many irregularities in respect of compensation payments made by oil companies. For instance, Onyige (1979, 144-146) investigated the payment of compensation to the Umuodogu family of Omoku in Rivers State by Agip. Agip acquired 20 acres of land in 1975. According to the directives of the Rivers State government at the time, the company should have paid 1,000 Naira per acre, so the Umuodogu family claimed 20,000 Naira. But Agip only paid 3,200 Naira to the family. Of the final sum, 800 Naira were reportedly retained by the company's acquisition officer, 800 Naira were paid to the lawyer who negotiated the settlement, 300 Naira were paid to the surveyor, 500 Naira were retained by the company's 'contact man' who provided information on the local property rights and another 300 Naira were reportedly paid as the lawyer's expenses. Of the 3,200 Naira paid, the family received merely 500 Naira or roughly 15% of the compensation sum in return for 20 acres of land acquired by the company for a period of five years. The above example indicates that neither the compensation payment nor the manner in which the money was paid to the family were adequate.

Irregularities in the payment of compensation appear to have persisted. A confidential report commissioned for the Shell-initiated Niger Delta Environmental Survey (NDES) in 1996 describes some of the problems:

> Oil industry operators approve compensation to be paid to victims whose crops, economic trees and shrines have been destroyed in course of operations [sic]. Such compensation (often tagged 'Ex gratia' payment) is made through various operators who are contractors to the oil industry operators. In such a situation the paltry sums which normally ranges [sic] from 500 to 5,000 Naira in extreme cases are forced down the throat of often dissatisfied victims who are in most cases too poor to undertake the expenses of initiating a suit (Ogbnigwe 1996).

The World Bank confirms the view that there are major irregularities regarding the payment of compensation to those affected by oil operations. Said a World Bank report in 1995: 'Compensation may not be paid to the affected community or individuals. Instead, other communities, disbursement agents, or powerful individuals may keep the compensation funds' (World Bank 1995, volume II, annex M, 75). Even if an oil company pays compensation to those adversely affected by oil operations, the inadequate OPTS rates or the official government rates are used (see chapter 3). In

---

[396] For instance, in *Eboigbe v. NNPC* (1994) 10 KLR (Pt 22) 68.

addition, damage assessments are often incomplete, according to the World Bank (1995, volume II, annex M, 76).

The above discussion suggests that, from the perspective of village communities, negotiation and mediation are currently unsatisfactory methods of settling compensation claims by communities against oil companies in Nigeria. Because of inadequate compensation payments and irregularities, communities may often be dissatisfied with the compensation procedures. Since mediation and negotiation may not satisfy the claimants and since there is no independent agency to monitor compensation payments, those affected by oil operations may feel that the only means of redress for them may be to either use violence or to initiate a lawsuit in court against an oil company.

The use of violence and community unrest against oil companies is by no means inevitable. But violence is more likely to escalate over time if those affected by oil operations continue to be aggrieved by those operations. Some evidence from court cases suggests that social unrest may directly result from the unresponsiveness of companies to demands for social amenities rather than the careless manner in which they operate. An interesting example involving violence is the case *Adizua v. Agip*[397], in which the Agorua Ajukwu family sued Agip for 800,000 Naira in compensation for damage. Agip used the plaintiffs' farmlands for its Akri and Akri West oil fields from 1967 and 1974 respectively. Initially, the relationship with the Agorua Ajukwu family was entirely peaceful as the company entered into an agreement to pay land rents and compensation, to award scholarships and to offer employment opportunities.

In the course of its operations, Agip operations reportedly caused severe damage to the family land, including the contamination of drinking water by oil spills. In 1982, a pipeline exploded, causing the death of six of the plaintiffs' tenants. Agip and the affected families engaged in negotiations. The company accepted liability for the accident, but the families of the deceased were dissatisfied with the insignificant compensation payments offered. Oil operations continued to have an adverse impact on the plaintiffs' land, so some members of the community decided to coerce the company into the payment of compensation.

It appears that the local people eventually engaged in violent conduct primarily because Agip went back on its earlier promises with regards to compensation payments, scholarships and jobs, rather than because of the actual environmental and social damage that the company was causing. In 1983, Agip stopped paying land rents, which the company had continuously paid from 1967 to 1982. The Agorua Ajukwu family claimed that, by 1997, only 15 scholarships had been awarded to secondary school pupils in the area in thirty years. They further averred that Agip had ceased awarding bush clearing contracts to the local people. The conflict between the family and the company escalated when Agip failed to respond to letters and representations from the local people.

It is not clear how violence erupted, but it appears that Agip had contributed to an atmosphere of fear and intimidation. Rather than engaging in negotiations with the local people, Agip decided to call on the security forces. In a letter dated 19 March 1984, Agip's district manager, A. Pirocchi wrote a letter to the Commissioner of Police

---

[397] Unreported Suit No. HOG/22/97, Imo State HC.

in Imo State, complaining about the Agorua Ajukwu family's unreasonable demands and asking for armed assistance. Wrote A. Pirocchi:

> *We therefore solicit your urgent action to step into this matter so that our production could start immediately and in fact we request that you provide a unit of your men to guard our installations in this area and to ensure that our current programmed activities are uninterrupted.*[398]

Following the company's requests for armed assistance in the 1980s and the 1990s, members of the Agorua Ajukwu family claimed that they were repeatedly harassed and intimidated by the police. In November 1996, the company's Akri flowstation was allegedly attacked by around 40 local people. Without investigating the incident, Agip's General Manager of the Port Harcourt District, Umberto Vergine, wrote to the Commissioner in Imo State blaming Chief Ugboma Adizua for the attack of *'some thugs carrying dangerous weapons'*. Once again Agip stressed that they would not bow to local demands. Wrote Umberto Vergine:

> *Sir, we believe that as good corporate citizens, we should be able to carry out our legitimate business without being subjected to blackmail and harassment of thugs and attacks on our staff when a landlord wants a contract. We would highly appreciate your intervention to bring book all those responsible for this attack [sic].*[399]

Agip has so far failed to resolve the conflict, relying on security protection rather than peaceful negotiations, which has led to a further escalation of the conflict. The entire truth about Agip's conflict with the Agorua Ajukwu family may never be known, but the case indicates that community disturbances are likely to result from a combination of unfulfilled social demands, broken oil company promises and the companies' traditional reliance on the security forces. Since both negotiations as well as the use of violence failed, the Agorua Ajukwu family decided to take Agip to court.

The Adizua case is indicative of a process in which communities come to use violence because they are inadequately compensated for damage from oil operations and faced with irregularities in the assessment and payment of compensation. The case also suggests that a dispute between a community and a company can evolve in stages from negotiation through violence to litigation.

In general, the above discussion illustrates that litigation is only a part of a dynamic process involving extra-legal and legal forms of conflict. The use of litigation as opposed to extra-legal forms of disputing depends on the company's legal liability for damage from oil operations.

---

[398] Letter from A.Pirocchi, Agip's district manager, to the Commissioner of Police, Imo State Police Command, Owerri, Agip Ref.No. JPO/WTC/PH/365/84 (19 March 1984).

[399] Letter from Umberto Vergine, Agip's General Manager, Port Harcourt District, to the Commissioner of Police, Imo State Police Command, Owerri (2 December 1996).

6.3. Basic Principles of Tort Law

Legal disputes between village communities and oil companies are governed by the
Nigerian law of torts. A Nigerian textbook on tort law by Kodilinye (1982, 1) defined a
tort as follows:

> *A tort may be defined broadly as a civil wrong involving a breach of duty
> fixed by the law, such duty being owed to persons generally and its
> breach being redressible primarily by an action for damages.*

> *The essential aim of the law of torts is to compensate persons harmed by
> the wrongful conduct of others, and the substantive law of torts consists
> of the rules and principles which have been developed to determine when
> the law will and when it will not grant redress for damage suffered. Such
> damage takes several different forms - such as physical injury to
> persons; physical damage to property; injury to reputation; and damage
> to economic interests. The law of torts requires every person not to cause
> harm to others in certain situations, and if harm is caused, the victim is
> entitled to sue the wrongdoer for damages by way of compensation.*

Therefore, the usual remedy for a tort is monetary compensation for damage.
This fact distinguishes tort law from criminal law. If the defendant loses a case, he may
have to pay compensation to the plaintiff, but will not be sentenced to imprisonment.
In addition to monetary compensation under tort law, a plaintiff can seek an injunction.
An injunction is a judicial order to the defendant to abstain from or to take a certain
action. Whether an injunction is granted or not depends on the subject matter. In
respect of oil operations in Nigeria, injunctions have sometimes been sought by
plaintiffs but were virtually never granted. In *Irou v. Shell-BP*[400], the judge refused to
grant an injunction in favour of the plaintiff whose land, fish pond and creek had been
polluted by Shell-BP. The judge explained his reasoning for not granting an injunction
as follows: '*To grant the order... would amount to asking the defendant* [Shell-BP] *to
stop operating in the area... The interest of third persons must be in some cases
considered e.g. where the injunction would cause stoppage of trade or throwing out a
large number of work people*'. The judge ruled that nothing should be done to disturb
the operations of the oil industry which '*is the main source of this country's revenue*'.
In other words, the economic interests of the oil industry appeared to be more
important to the judge than the course of justice. In *Chinda v. Shell-BP*[401], the plaintiffs
asked for an injunction against gas flaring. The judge rejected the request by saying:
'*The Statement of Claim demands an order that Defendants* [Shell-BP] *refrain from
operating a similar flare stack within five miles of Plaintiffs' village, an absurdly and
needlessly wide demand*'.[402] The above judgments indicate that Nigerian courts are
very reluctant to grant an injunction in oil-related cases. For oil companies, this
interpretation of the law by Nigerian judges is favourable because the law allows them
to continue with their exploration and production activities, notwithstanding the

---

[400] Unreported Suit No. W/89/71, Warri HC.

[401] (1974) 2 RSLR 1.

[402] Per Holden, C.J. at page 14.

adverse impact of oil operations on village communities. For instance, in early 1998, not a single injunction was in place against Shell in Nigeria (Frynas 1999, chapter 6).[403] The judges' reluctance to impose injunctions favours Shell and the other oil companies because, in the case of a dispute, they do not have to stop oil operations.

Seeking compensation for damage offers village communities greater prospects of success than injunctions. Oil-related compensation claims in Nigeria are usually based on specific torts, notably the 'tort of negligence', 'tort of nuisance' and on the rule of strict liability. These torts can sometimes overlap in a single case. For instance, a plaintiff could plead negligence in combination with nuisance.

6.4. Negligence

One of the main torts applied in oil-related litigation is negligence. In *Seismograph Service v. Mark*[404], the plaintiff claimed compensation for damage from the destruction of his fishing nets by a seismic boat. It was impossible for the plaintiff to show that the company acted negligently. In a negligence claim, the burden of proof is on the plaintiff, not the defendant. That means, it is not enough to show that an oil company destroyed property or lives, the plaintiff must actually prove that the oil company acted negligently. In a negligence claim, a plaintiff affected by oil operations must prove that the defendant owes him a duty of care, that the duty was breached and that damage resulted from the breach of duty.[405] In the present case, the Court of Appeal found that the plaintiff did not establish that the oil company breached the duty of care towards him. The fact that the seismic boat tore through the fishing nets was regarded as insufficient proof of negligence in itself. The judge said that *'the allegation that the vessel 'tore' through and carried the floaters etc. away is not by itself suggestive of excessive speed or any amount of negligence'*.[406] He found that, since the plaintiff had failed to provide details of a breach of duty of care towards him, the case had to be dismissed. Said Uwaifo, J.C.A.:

> In the present case, what did the defendants [Seismograph Service] do or fail to do which was the cause of the accident? Did the captain of the vessel engage in excessive speed in navigating her? Did he fail to sound the alarm or did he do so too late to signal her approach? Did the captain fail to keep a proper look out? Did he fail to slow down? Did he navigate at the time of the day he was not expected to? There is nothing to indicate as no particulars of negligence were given by the plaintiff.[407]

---

[403] While the imposition of injunctions against oil companies is not a realistic option in Nigeria, the substantial quantity of litigation continues to constitute a problem for the oil industry and entails financial costs for the companies. As a way of avoiding litigation, oil companies could introduce less harmful practices. This would ultimately reduce the quantity of litigation because village communities would have fewer legal grounds on which to sue. But oil companies have failed to change their harmful practices despite environmental legislation (see chapters 3 and 5).

[404] (1993) 7 NWLR (Pt. 304) 203.

[405] On negligence and duty of care, see e.g. Percy (1983, 10-15).

[406] Per Uwaifo, J.C.A. at page 212.

[407] Per Uwaifo, J.C.A. at page 214.

Seismograph Service v. Mark[408] illustrates that proving negligence can be difficult in oil-related litigation because of the technical nature of oil operations. The plaintiff must prove that the oil company violated against an accepted standard of behaviour. Environmental or technical standards are based on sophisticated scientific knowledge and data. For instance, the Petroleum Act 1969 provides that an oil company must adopt *'good oilfield practice'*. The oil industry normally has a superior technical knowledge as compared to individual litigants. Consequently, it may often be difficult for the plaintiff to argue that the oil company was unreasonably negligent or did not adopt accepted standards during its operations.[409]

In certain cases, a lawsuit based on the claim of negligence can succeed, even if the plaintiff cannot prove that the defendants breached a duty of care. The principle is called *'res ipsa loquitur'*, which literally means *'the facts speak for themselves'*. In the case *Mon v. Shell-BP*[410], the plaintiffs claimed compensation for damage from an oil spill. They won the case with the court justifying its decision as follows: *'Negligence on the part of defendants has been pleaded, and there is no evidence of it. None in fact is needed, for they must naturally be held responsible for the results arising from an escape of oil which they should have kept under control'*.[411] The plaintiffs were hence awarded compensation.

The case *Mon v. Shell-BP*[412] illustrates that shifting the burden of proof from the plaintiff to the defendant can significantly improve the chances of success for village communities in oil-related litigation. If the principle *res ipsa loquitur* is invoked, an oil company must prove that the oil operations constituted no harm to the plaintiffs.[413]

The discussion of the above cases suggests that plaintiffs in oil-related cases can sue more easily for some types of damage as opposed to others. As indicated in

---

[408] (1993) 7 NWLR (Pt. 304) 203.

[409] In a number of oil-related cases in Nigeria, the plaintiff won by inferring negligence without proving it. *Adhemove v. Shell-BP* Unreported Suit No. UHC 12/70, Ughelli HC is an example of such an instance. In that case, waste from an oil waste pit escaped and spread over the plaintiff's property destroying a fish pond and killing a substantial number of fish. It is not clear if the principle *res ipsa loquitur* was applied in this case (see the subsequent discussion of the rule). Unless *res ipsa loquitur* is evoked in a negligence case, the plaintiff must prove negligence. In those cases, in which a plaintiff won by inferring negligence without proving it and *res ipsa loquitur* could not be evoked, the judge did not appear to follow the correct legal procedure under the Common Law and, technically, the cases should have been dismissed. According to Percy (1983, 15), *'any failure to prove any one of these component elements* [duty of care, breach of duty and resulting damage] *must result in the plaintiff's action for damages being dismissed'*.

[410] (1970-1972) I RSLR 71.

[411] Per Holden, C.J. at page 73.

[412] (1970-1972) I RSLR 71.

[413] In order to rely on the principle, three conditions must be fulfilled. First, the plaintiff must prove that the accident occurred. Second, he must prove that the occurrence would not have happened *'in the ordinary course of things without negligence on the part of somebody other than the plaintiff'*. Third, the facts suggest that the defendant rather than the plaintiff was negligent. In line with the last condition, the plaintiff must usually show that the thing causing the damage was *'in the management and control of the defendant'* (Percy 1983, 350). An oil spill fulfils all three conditions of the principle *res ipsa loquitur*, as long as the plaintiff can show that the spill actually happened. An oil spill does not happen in the ordinary course of things and the oil installation is in the management of the oil company.

Seismograph Service v. Mark[414], it may be difficult to prove negligence when a seismic boat destroys property.[415] As denoted in *Mon v. Shell-BP*[416], a plaintiff may find it easier to succeed in an oil spill claim because *res ipsa loquitur* can be invoked.[417] If an accident such as an oil spill occurs, a court is likely to conclude that the oil company was negligent, unless the defendant company can show that the accident may have occurred without negligence on its part or on account of uncontrollable influences such as sabotage.

6.5. Nuisance

Another type of tort, albeit less common in oil-related litigation in Nigeria, is the 'tort of nuisance'. The tort of nuisance allows the plaintiff to sue for interference with the enjoyment of his land.[418]

There are two types of nuisance: private nuisance and public nuisance. A case of private nuisance was *Seismograph Service v. Akporuovo*[419]. In that case, the plaintiff claimed that vibrations destroyed his three buildings, two outhouses and household goods in the course of seismic operations in the 1960s. The trial judge awarded damages to the plaintiff. Dissatisfied with the judgment, the oil company appealed to the Supreme Court. The higher court allowed the appeal and set aside the judgment of the lower court. The court found that *'the evidence of plaintiff did not establish the liability, if any, of the appellant company'.*[420] The judges argued that there was a conflict of evidence as to whether the building was actually damaged. Since damage should have been proven, the trial judge should have visited the scene. Accordingly, the plaintiff lost the case.

Public nuisance is different from private nuisance in that public, not private, property is damaged. The plaintiff must prove that the nuisance caused damage which is particular to him or her. In addition, the damage must be much greater to the plaintiff than to the rest of the public. A case of public nuisance was *Amos v. Shell-BP*[421], in which the Ogbia community sued Shell-BP and its sub-contractor, the Niger

---

[414] (1993) 7 NWLR (Pt. 304) 203.

[415] It is also difficult to prove negligence as a result of gas flaring, see *Chinda v. Shell-BP* (1974) 2 RSLR 1.

[416] (1970-1972) I RSLR 71.

[417] *Res ipsa loquitur* was successfully applied in a number of more recent cases involving oil spills, for instance, in *Shell v. Enoch* (1992) 8 NWLR (Pt. 259) 335.

[418] The defendant can cause an interference through vibrations, flooding, fire, noise or other forms of invasion. Nuisance is slightly different from negligence, although it can also result from negligence. The plaintiff does not generally have to prove a duty of care, but he must show that the defendant's interference was unreasonable and that the interference was serious. On the most basic level, the court may ask the question *'Is it reasonable that the plaintiff should have to put up with this interference?'*. This is different from negligence where the question is asked about the duty of care. On nuisance, see e.g. Baker (1991, chapter 15).

[419] (1974) All NLR 95.

[420] Per Sowemimo, J.S.C. at page 106.

[421] 4 ECSLR 486.

Construction Company. The sub-contractor constructed a large earth dam across a creek, which was public property. Originally, the two companies had planned to build a bridge across Kolo Creek. Instead of going ahead with the original plan, they constructed a dam to enable heavy machinery to be moved across the creek. Witnesses testified that, as a result of the construction of the dam, flooding was caused upstream and the creek dried up downstream. Farms were flooded and damaged, canoes could not bring goods to the market and the life of the community was disrupted. The defendants denied that there was flooding, claiming that water continued to flow across the dam in two pipes. They also claimed that labourers helped villagers to carry canoes across the dam night and day. The court dismissed the plaintiffs' claim, holding that:

> *Kolo Creek is agreed by both sides to be a public waterway. Blocking it up is a public nuisance. No individual can normally recover damages for a public nuisance. For an individual claim to succeed there must be proof of the plaintiff having suffered special damage peculiar to himself from interference with a public right'.*[422]

In addition, the court ruled that the plaintiffs should have filed separate lawsuits since they had suffered separate losses. The plaintiffs had no right to sue as a community, since the losses were considered individual, not communal.

The two above cases suggest that a plaintiff's success in a lawsuit based on nuisance is uncertain. It appears, however, that those affected by oil operations are more likely to succeed on the basis of private nuisance claims. The plaintiffs in *Seismograph Service v. Akporuovo*[423] lost the case because of conflicting evidence. Otherwise, their claim would have been held valid. The plaintiffs in *Amos v. Shell*[424] lost because the nature of the claim itself was considered invalid. The main problem with public nuisance is that it has often relied on the goodwill of the executive branch of the government. In theory, the 1979 Constitution provided that judicial power extends to every type of legal action except those specifically excluded by the Constitution itself.[425] In practice, in a public nuisance case, the Attorney-General as the representative of the public is expected to sue the defendants rather than an unlimited number of private individuals, which has an understandable rationale behind it. In the case *Amos v. Shell*[426], the attorney-general (as a representative of the government and the public) rather than the plaintiffs should have pressed charges against Shell. The main problem in Nigeria is that the government was reluctant to act on behalf of those affected by oil operations.

---

[422] Per Holden, C.J. at page 488.

[423] (1974) All NLR 95.

[424] 4 ECSLR 486.

[425] Constitution of the Federal Republic of Nigeria 1979, section 6(6)(b).

[426] 4 ECSLR 486.

6.6. Strict Liability

Apart from the torts of negligence and nuisance, a plaintiff can rely on the rule of strict liability in *Rylands v. Fletcher*.[427] Until the introduction of strict liability in the 19th century, tort law limited liability to those cases where the defendant was at fault. Under the rule of strict liability, the defendant is liable for damage from his activities, even if he was not at fault and if there was no negligence on his part.

In *Umudje v. Shell-BP*[428], the plaintiffs were awarded compensation based on the rule of strict liability. In that case, the plaintiffs sued Shell-BP for damage resulting from an oil waste pit and the construction of a road. The oil company constructed a road across a waterway and failed to insert enough culverts under it. At the location of the road, fish previously moved across the land into the plaintiffs' artificial ponds and lakes during the rainy season. After the road construction, fish could no longer move across. The Supreme Court accepted those facts. But it found that Shell-BP was not liable under the rule of strict liability. The judge explained his reasoning as follows:

> There is no doubt that the appellants would be liable under the rule in
> *Rylands v. Fletcher* for damage arising from their interference with the
> natural flow of the Utefe stream and water from Ewu river into
> Unenurhie land had the judge found that the blockade [sic] caused by the
> access road resulted in the flooding of the Unenurhie land, together with
> the ponds and lakes therein; for liability under the rule does not arise
> unless there was an 'escape' of the dangerous substance from a place in
> the occupation, or control, of the defendant to another place which is
> outside his occupation or control... The position here... is that the access
> road blocked the flow of water through the waterway or channel and in
> consequence definitely starved the Unenurhie land... The award of
> damages, so far as they relate to the appellants' act in constructing the
> access road cannot, therefore, be sustained under the rule in *Rylands v.
> Fletcher.*[429]

---

[427] The legal rule was expressed by the British House of Lords in *Rylands v. Fletcher* (1868) L.R. 3 H.L. 330 as follows:

> We think that the true rule of law is, that the person who for his own purposes brings
> on his lands and collects and keeps there anything likely to do mischief if it escapes,
> must keep it in at his peril, and if he does not do so is prima facie answerable for all
> the damage which is the natural consequence of its escape.

The judgment in *Rylands v. Fletcher* laid down the rule for strict liability. Four conditions must be fulfilled for the rule to apply. First, the defendant must have brought the thing on his land for his own use. Second, the thing must be likely to cause harm if it escapes. Third, the defendant's use of the land must be non-natural, for instance, sewage or gas come under the rule, while weeds or flood water are natural things and do not come under the rule. Fourth, the thing must actually escape. On the principles of strict liability, see Baker (1991, chapter 16). An escape of crude oil or oily waste fulfils all the above four conditions. Accordingly, any dangerous incident involving crude oil can be potentially prosecuted. The defendant is strictly liable for damage, which removes the plaintiff's burden of proof. It is not necessary for the plaintiff to prove any negligence or breach of duty of care.

[428] (1975) 9-11 S.C. 155.

[429] Per Idigbe, J.S.C. at pages 170-171.

In other words, the rule in *Rylands v. Fletcher*[430] did not apply in this case because the court found that the blockage of the stream did not cause flooding but merely starvation of water and fish. If there had been an escape of water from the company's land rather than starvation of water, the rule of strict liability would have applied. For the courts, an escape of a substance is hence a necessary condition for the rule in *Rylands v. Fletcher*[431] to apply. But Shell-BP was found guilty of negligence for the blockage of the stream because it failed to insert enough culverts under the road, which caused damage. The Supreme Court ruled that *'the five culverts under the access road'* were *'inadequate'* and this *'inadequacy caused the blockade* [sic]*'* and therefore amounted to negligence.[432]

While the rule in *Rylands v. Fletcher*[433] did not apply to the road construction, it applied in respect of Shell-BP's oil waste pit. When the pit was full, the waste spread over the plaintiffs' farms, ponds and lakes, damaging the land and killing a substantial quantity of fish. Said Idigbe, J.S.C.:

> *Liability on the part of an owner or the person in control of an oil-waste pit, such as the one located at Location 'E' in the case in hand, exists under the rule in Rylands v. Fletcher although the 'escape' has not occurred as a result of negligence on his part.*[434]

The Umudje case exemplifies the differences in the application of the rule of strict liability and the rule of negligence.[435] In respect of the oil waste pit, the rule of strict liability applied but the rule of negligence did not. In contrast, in respect of the road construction, strict liability did not apply but the rule of negligence did. The Supreme Court consequently dismissed the appeal by Shell-BP.

The Umudje case illustrates that the legal rule of strict liability in *Rylands v. Fletcher*[436] can increase a plaintiff's chances of success in an oil-related case because it requires merely the proof of the escape of oil or waste rather than the proof of negligence by the tortfeasor.[437] However, the case also exemplifies some of the limitations of the rule of strict liability in oil-related cases. While an escape of waste from an oil waste pit would come under the strict liability rule, incidents such as the destruction of fishing nets by a seismic boat would not come under the rule.

The most important limitations of strict liability are posed by the various exceptions to the rule. Strict liability does not apply if the damage was due to: an 'act of God'; a default of the plaintiff; the consent of the plaintiff; statutory authority; or an

---

[430] (1868) L.R. 3 H.L. 330.

[431] (1868) L.R. 3 H.L. 330.

[432] Per Idigbe, J.S.C. at pages 171-172.

[433] (1868) L.R. 3 H.L. 330.

[434] Per Idigbe, J.S.C. at page 172.

[435] This insight was assisted by a discussion of the Umudje case in Kodilinye (1982, 116-117).

[436] (1868) L.R. 3 H.L. 330.

[437] Strict liability was successfully applied in a number of more recent cases involving oil spills, for instance, in *Shell v. Tiebo VII* (1996) 4 NWLR (Pt. 445) 657 and *Shell v. Isaiah* (1997) 6 NWLR (Pt. 508) 236.

act of a stranger (Kodilinye 1982, 117-121).[438] In Nigeria, oil companies have often alleged that damage from oil operations is due to sabotage, which is considered an act of a stranger. If the oil company can convince the court that sabotage was the cause of damage, it is not liable to pay compensation to the plaintiffs.

Oil companies have won a number of lawsuits by pleading sabotage. In *Shell v. Otoko*[439], a number of communities in Rivers State sued Shell for damage from an oil spill in October 1981, which polluted the Andoni River and creeks. Shell claimed that the spill was due to sabotage. The company's evidence of sabotage was dismissed by the lower court, but was allowed by the Court of Appeal. The appeal judge felt that the evidence of the plaintiffs supported the company's evidence. One of the plaintiff's witnesses testified that *'there was nothing else done again by the defendant company* [Shell] *to control the spillage apart from the corking of the manifold'.*[440] The judge concluded on the basis of this and other evidence that a screw or a bolt was removed by a 'third party', which caused the oil spill.

However, oil companies have not always succeeded in blaming oil spills on sabotage. In *Shell v. Enoch*[441], the Mumaija community in Rivers State sued Shell for damage as a result of an oil spill. Shell claimed that the spillage was caused *'by the malicious act of third persons'.* Said the trial judge:

> It is clear here that the plaintiffs had shown that there was an explosion
> at the defendant's manifold and that there was crude oil spillage which
> was extensive as a result of that explosion. There were extensive
> damages to economic crops, farm lands, yams, cocoyams, and so on.
> There was evidence that no third party caused the explosion, and that no
> one in the community did it.[442]

In another recent case *Shell v. Isaiah*[443], Shell also claimed that sabotage was involved. The Court of Appeal concluded that *'the defence of sabotage was an afterthought'* and dismissed Shell's appeal accordingly.[444]

Oil company allegations of sabotage often lack in merit or may be the result of exaggerations.[445] In general terms, a recent confidential report commissioned for the

---

[438] An act of a stranger may also be called an *'independent act of a third party'* (on limitations of strict liability, see also Percy 1983, 855-866).

[439] (1990) 6 NWLR (Pt. 159) 693.

[440] Per Omosun, J.C.A. at page 715.

[441] (1992) 8 NWLR (Pt. 259) 335.

[442] Per Jacks, J.C.A. at page 341.

[443] (1997) 6 NWLR (Pt. 508) 236.

[444] Per Katsina-Alu, J.C.A. at page 252. Another recent case was *Anare v. Shell* Unreported Suit No. HCB/35/89, in which four village communities sued Shell over oil spills in the 1980s. Shell claimed that the oil spills were caused by sabotage. The court, however, disbelieved Shell's witnesses and awarded over 30 million Naira in compensation to the plaintiffs. Shell appealed against the decision. By claiming sabotage, the company can save up to 30 million Naira in a single lawsuit.

[445] Secondary sources also provide strong indications that oil companies used claims of sabotage to avoid compensation payments to local communities in the past. S.K. Igbara of the Ahmadu Bello University in Zaria carried out an independent investigation into the causes of accidents at Shell's Afam 17 C and T wells in 1975 and at Bomu in 1973 (Ogbonna 1979, 254). With respect to the blow-out of the wellhead at Affam, Shell claimed sabotage. Evidence provided by some of the technicians at work revealed that negligence was the cause.

Shell-initiated Niger Delta Environmental Survey (NDES) concluded that *'Many operators have hidden under the cloak of sabotage to avoid remediation in cases of environmental spills, accidents and discharges'* (Ogbnigwe 1996). While vandalism of oil pipelines may occasionally occur in Nigeria, oil companies have an economic self-interest in claiming sabotage in court as they can escape the legal liability for damage.[446]

To sum up, the above discussion suggests that tort law has limitations as far as the claims of village communities against oil companies are concerned. The rules of negligence, nuisance and strict liability offer a legal remedy for plaintiffs suing oil companies but each legal rule imposes specific limitations on the plaintiffs' ability to sue. Even if a plaintiff can invoke a particular rule of tort law, oil companies can apply a number of standard legal defences in court.

6.7. Statutes of Limitation

The above discussion has only explained legal defences, which oil company lawyers can invoke in court, as far as they relate directly to a specific type of tort. The defendants can also employ various general legal defences. From a preliminary analysis of oil-related cases in Nigeria, one can distinguish at least three general legal defences: statutes of limitation, admissibility of scientific evidence, and misjoinder of parties, which are discussed below.

Statutes of limitation are laws which bar a lawsuit after a designated period of time. Many potential lawsuits against oil companies are barred by legislation. In this context, the most important Nigerian statute is the Nigerian National Petroleum Corporation (NNPC) Act 1977. The Act provides that no lawsuit against the NNPC, a member of its Board or any employee *'shall be instituted in any court unless it is commenced within twelve months next after the act, neglect or default complained of or, in the case of a continuance of damage or injury, within twelve months next after the ceasing thereof'.*[447] As a result, any lawsuits against the NNPC are statute barred after twelve months. That means, if a community, a family or an individual does not file a lawsuit against the NNPC within twelve months, it cannot claim any compensation for damage.

In the case *Eboigbe v. NNPC*[448], John Eboigbe sued the NNPC for damages on behalf of his family in Bendel State. He claimed that the NNPC destroyed trees and crops in the course of laying oil pipelines in February 1979. The NNPC allegedly bulldozed and destroyed a large part of his family's farm, which John Eboigbe was unaware of at the time. He claimed to have travelled to Northern Nigeria in 1979

---

[446] Interestingly, companies claim sabotage in court, but usually fail to take any action against suspected saboteurs. Adewale (1990), who argued that sabotage is an important problem in Nigeria, pointed out herself that, under Nigerian law, sabotage of oil installations can be punished by death. But there appear to have been very few instances in which saboteurs were tried for sabotage. Oil companies have usually not pressed charges for alleged sabotage.

[447] NNPC Act, section 12(1).

[448] (1994) 10 KLR (Pt. 22) 68.

where he stayed until July 1983. On his return, he learnt for the first time about the damage. He claimed that his family did not institute any court proceedings against the NNPC earlier because five out of six family members were illiterate and were hence ignorant of their legal rights. John Eboigbe took up the matter and wrote to the NNPC in July 1983 informing them of the damage. He exchanged letters with the NNPC until April 1984. The corporation did not admit liability. In a letter dated 1 February 1984, the NNPC told Eboigbe that they would not pay any compensation because the claim was *'not convincing'*. In a letter dated 9 March 1984, the corporation wrote that *'In the absence of any more facts we are regarding the matter as closed'*.[449]

In June 1985, John Eboigbe instituted a lawsuit against the NNPC demanding compensation. The NNPC won the court case by claiming that the action was statute barred. The Supreme Court held unanimously that *'time begins to run from the date that the cause of action accrues'*.[450] Accordingly, Eboigbe should have instituted a court case within twelve months of the damage to his family land in February 1979 by the NNPC. Notwithstanding any other legal rights or social problems involved, plaintiffs have no rights in respect of damage by the NNPC unless they act quickly. The twelve months provision of the NNPC Act can partly explain why little litigation has arisen against the NNPC for damage arising from oil operations.

Lawsuits against other oil companies must also be filed within a certain period of time. Apart from the NNPC Act, there are general statutes of limitation which tend to limit the period for instituting a lawsuit to six years from the date on which the cause of grievance accrues.[451] In most types of litigation, these statutes serve justice because they protect the individual defendant from old claims[452] and impose some finality on compensation claims. In oil-related litigation in Nigeria, they impede justice because of problems such as difficulties in obtaining access to courts and a latency period.[453]

As we have previously suggested, the villagers' access to courts is hampered by a number of factors (see chapter 4). If a plaintiff is illiterate or if there is no nearby court, a lawsuit may be delayed for a long time until he or she receives correct legal advice or collects the necessary funds to file a suit. In the meantime, the lawsuit may become statute barred. Courts do not accept excuses such as illiteracy. Said Edozie, J.C.A. in *Shell v. Farah*[454]:

> *The period of limitation begins to run from the date on which the cause of action accrued. It is immaterial that a party was absent from the jurisdiction or that there was no court within the jurisdiction to entertain the claim. Similarly, illiteracy will also not avail a plaintiff because ignorance of the law is no excuse.*[455]

---

[449] Quoted per Adio, J.S.C. at page 78.

[450] Per Adio, J.S.C. at page 75.

[451] On statutes of limitation in general, see e.g. Baker (1991, 436-437). The six year period of limitation was confirmed by Kolawole, J.C.A. in *Nwadiaro v. Shell* (1990) 5 NWLR (Pt. 150) 322.

[452] The lawyer commonly uses the term 'stale claim'.

[453] The problems of the latency period and scientific uncertainty in relation to court cases involving environmental damage are explained in general terms in Eggen (1995, 5-8).

[454] (1995) 3 NWLR (Pt. 382) 148.

[455] Per Edozie, J.C.A. at page 185.

Even if the plaintiffs have enough funds and are aware of their legal rights, a legal claim may become statute barred because of the latency period. The full effects of oil operations are not always immediately apparent. Damage such as long-term soil degradation requires a latency period for its development. The injury may not be immediately visible or may go undiscovered for a period of time. Conducting proper scientific studies may take many years to assess changes in vegetation or soil fertility, some of which can only be observed in the long-term. Because of the long latency period, potential litigants may not always have enough time to file a suit within the statutory period of limitation.

The statutes of limitation in Nigeria do not take account of the delay between economic activities and their long-term effects. Yet judges seem to be aware of the problem. In *Horsfall v. Shell-BP*[456], the judge stated that *'the cause of action accrues at the time of the negligence because it is then that the damage is caused, even though its consequences may not be apparent until later'.*[457] While judges may recognise some of the constraints posed by statutes of limitation, statutory limitations remain in place in Nigeria.

6.8. Admissibility of Scientific Evidence

In addition to problems posed by statutes of limitation, plaintiffs face the problem of the admissibility of scientific evidence. In any type of tort - negligence, nuisance and strict liability, the key problem is that of credible evidence. As a practical matter, since plaintiffs usually bear the burden of proof in oil-related litigation in Nigeria, providing scientific evidence in court is more difficult for village communities than for oil companies.

In *Shell v. Otoko*[458], the plaintiffs sued Shell for damage from an oil spill in 1981. Among other things, the judge doubted the plaintiffs' evidence of causation. The scientific report tendered in court by the plaintiffs was based on sediments and water samples taken in 1983. It was not clear to what extent the damage was caused by the oil spill of 1981. In the Court of Appeal, said the judge: *'There were spillages in 1980 and 1983. The question that invariably arises, is what spillage, that of 1980, 1981 and 1983 did Exhibit 'D' cover?'.*[459] In other words, it was not possible to establish to what extent the spill in 1981 caused the injury complained of or other factors, such as other spills. Ironically, the frequent occurrence of oil spills in the area could be exploited by oil company lawyers to frustrate the plaintiffs' evidence in respect of damage.

In *Ogiale v. Shell*[460], Shell was sued by the Olomoro Isoko community in Delta State. The plaintiff sued the defendants under the rule in *Rylands v. Fletcher*[461],

---

[456] (1974) 2 RSLR 126.

[457] Per Wai-Ogosu, J. at page 131.

[458] (1990) 6 NWLR (Pt. 159) 693.

[459] Per Omosun, J.C.A. at page 718.

[460] (1997) 1 NWLR (Pt. 480) 148.

[461] (1868) L.R. 3 H.L. 330.

nuisance as well as negligence. Nsofor, J.C.A. said that *'it was an issue of causation and consequential damage or liability. And the law, as I comprehend it, is that he who asserts ought to prove his assertion and this by credible evidence'*.[462] The plaintiffs could not prove the causation between oil operations and reduced soil fertility. The court dismissed the testimonies of the plaintiffs' witnesses as well as the experts. According to the judge, the testimonies of the witnesses amounted to a mere *'ocular inspection and comparism* [sic]*'*.[463] The testimonies of the experts were not admitted because the court doubted their skills and expertise. Dr. A.U. Salami, chief scientific expert for the plaintiffs, had specialist knowledge as a soil scientist and an agronomist. His testimony was not considered credible as he did not have additional knowledge of radiation and heat. According to Nigerian law, an expert must be specially skilled in the particular field in question.[464]

The court also doubted the evidence of Chief Birinengi Idoniboye-Obu, an environmental consultant. Said Akintan, J.C.A.:

> He said his team visited the place several times and wrote a report, admitted as Exhibit D. The witness said that he carried out scientific investigation of water in Olomoro. But he admitted under cross-examination that he did not do a quantitative analysis of water samples because of lack of funds for such investigation. He also admitted that such laboratory analysis could have shown the chemical contents of the water or other chemicals in the water. He also admitted that he did not carry out a scientific laboratory test of the air and heat radiation in Olomoro before arriving at the conclusions he set out in his report, Exhibit D.[465]

As indicated by the expert witness, scientific analysis requires substantial financial resources. In the present case, the plaintiffs did not have sufficient funds to afford a major scientific inquiry. Interestingly, Shell's defence witnesses did not conduct strict scientific analyses either. Shell hired Professor C.T.I. Odu, a professor of agronomy at the University of Ibadan, to study the Olomoro field area in 1983. Akintan, J.C.A. commented in the court judgment:

> The witness admitted under cross-examination that crops would not grow successfully where oil content is high. But he said he did not compare crop yield in Evwreni with crop yield in Olomoro. He said further that the opinion expressed on page 53 of their report, Exhibit G, about oil contents in soil was based on what he (the witness) was told by one Yomi Odewumi.[466]

---

[462] Per Nsofor, J.C.A. at page 180.

[463] Per Nsofor, J.C.A. at page 182.

[464] This principle was firmly established in *Seismograph Service v. Onokpasa* (1972) 1 All NLR (Pt. 1) 347 where the Supreme Court ruled that the correct test for the relevance of the witness's opinion as that of an expert is whether he or she is specially skilled in the particular scientific subject matter.

[465] Per Akintan, J.C.A. at pages 159-160.

[466] Per Akintan, J.C.A. at page 161.

Therefore, the quality of the scientific expert analysis did not appear to be much better for the defendant than for the plaintiffs. However, the weakness of the company's expert analysis did not assist the plaintiffs' case as the burden of proof was on the plaintiffs, not the defendants. According to Nsofor, J.C.A., *'the claimant ought to prove his case relying on the strength of his case and not on the weakness of the defendant's case'.*[467] Accordingly, the defendant had an advantage in terms of evidence. The plaintiffs lost in the lower court based on the judge's conclusion that they failed to prove their claim. The plaintiffs' appeal was dismissed by the Court of Appeal.

The Otoko and Ogiale cases exemplify some of the problems posed by the possibility that there are multiple causes of the same injury. In addition, they indicate that village communities may find it more difficult to provide scientific evidence than oil companies because the burden of proof is on them.

Even if a plaintiff can prove that oil operations caused an injury, he or she must also provide strict proof of 'special damages', that means, evidence of damage to specific crops, trees, buildings and other objects. The plaintiff cannot simply allege that oil operations resulted in destruction of trees or buildings. In *Shell v. Otoko*[468] mentioned earlier, the appeal judge dismissed the compensation award of the lower court. Among other things, the lower court awarded 30,000 Naira in respect of damaged juju shrines[469] and 30,000 Naira in respect of damaged fishing nets. On appeal, the judge ruled that the damages should have been strictly proven. The valuer, who prepared the valuation report for the plaintiffs, was not considered competent by the appeal court because he had no specialist knowledge of the different areas of expertise. In respect of the fishing nets, said Omosun, J.C.A.: *'Plaintiffs' Witness 5 [expert valuer] is not competent to offer his opinion as to the chemical composition of the oil and its effect on the nets'.*[470] In respect of the juju shrines, said he: *'He [expert valuer] is not an expert in juju shrines and the art of worship of juju, their discretion and purification or appeasement'.*[471] In order to prove all special damages in the Otoko case, the plaintiffs would have needed separate experts in juju worship, chemical engineering, land management and agriculture. If the plaintiffs decided to hire all those various experts, the financial cost of expert valuations would have been significantly more substantial indeed.

The Otoko and Ogiale cases indicated that a frequent problem village communities face is that of establishing a causal link between oil operations and the suffered injury. Even scientific studies may not always be entirely conclusive. For instance, it is often not entirely clear whether soil degradation is the result of oil operations or other factors such as intensive farming. As a consequence, it is often impossible to determine the extent to which the damage arose from oil operations and the extent to which it would have occurred in any case. Oil companies can thus use the

---

[467] Per Nsofor, J.C.A. at page 180.

[468] (1990) 6 NWLR (Pt. 159) 693.

[469] A juju shrine is a sacred religious place worshipped by Nigeria's Animist communities.

[470] Per Omosun, J.C.A. at page 721.

[471] Per Omosun, J.C.A. at page 720.

argument of scientific uncertainty and causation as a standard legal strategy to defend a case in court.

6.9. Misjoinder of Parties and Causes of Action

In addition to the defences based on statutory limitation and admissibility of evidence, oil companies can undermine the plaintiff's so-called *'locus standi'*. To initiate a lawsuit, the plaintiff must have a *locus standi*, which literally means 'standing to sue'.[472] The plaintiff must have either a special legal right to sue, or a personal interest in the lawsuit, or his interest must have been adversely affected, for instance, if personal property was damaged during oil operations. A judge usually decides on a case-by-case basis, if the plaintiff has a *locus standi*. A lawsuit may not be allowed, if the judge thinks that different plaintiffs in the same lawsuit suffered separate damage, which is called 'misjoinder of parties and causes of action'. That means, the plaintiffs cannot sue jointly because their grievances were separate and specific to each individual. In such a case, the different plaintiffs must sue separately in separate lawsuits.

In *Horsfall v. Shell-BP*[473], the community sued Shell-BP as the first defendant and Seismograph Service as the second defendant for damage to *'private buildings, communal buildings, churches inclusive'*.[474] The lawyers of Shell-BP claimed a misjoinder of parties and causes of action. The company argued that the plaintiffs should not sue jointly because the different buildings belonged to different individuals, not to the village as a whole. The trial judge concurred by stating that *'it was only the town hall that could be owned by the whole village'*.[475] In his view, even the claims for damage to churches should have been brought to court by registered trustees, not the community representatives. Interestingly, the judge seemed annoyed that the company filed a motion of misjoinder even before the plaintiffs had a chance to prove their allegations in court. Said the judge: *'The very pleading of the defendants [Shell-BP] here, in my opinion, envisaged this, and it was a mere gamble to bring up a separate motion for this'*.[476] The company lawyers used a standard legal strategy as a defence, without drafting a specific legal defence for the case. It would appear that oil companies have used the issue of misjoinder as a legal technicality to frustrate compensation claims by communities.

The company defences based on misjoinder succeeded in a number of recent cases such as in *Shell v. Enoch*[477], in which the Mumaija Community in Rivers State sued Shell for damage resulting from an oil spill. The plaintiffs testified that the explosion of an oil pipeline resulted in an oil spill. As a result, five children died from

---

[472] On some problems in the enforcement of *locus standi* in Nigeria, see Ogowewo (1995).

[473] (1974) 2 RSLR 126.

[474] Per Wai-Ogosu, J. at page 128.

[475] Per Wai-Ogosu, J. at page 129.

[476] Per Wai-Ogosu, J. at page 131.

[477] (1992) 8 NWLR (Pt. 259) 335.

drinking polluted water, farm lands were damaged and property was destroyed including crops and fishing nets. Shell claimed misjoinder of parties and causes of action. The trial judge in the Bori Division of the Rivers State High Court agreed with Shell that individual and communal claims were lumped together and, therefore, the community lawsuit could not succeed. He held that each member of the community should have started a lawsuit by himself for specific damages, while the community should also have started a lawsuit on behalf of communal issues. Said the trial judge: *'The estate or next friend of these children who died have their own personal action for the compensation and not the community'.*[478] He ordered a so-called 'non-suit' but did not strike out the case. Shell's lawyers were dissatisfied with the judgment and appealed to the Court of Appeal asking for the court to dismiss the case. The difference is that, under a non-suit, members of the community could again sue Shell in court for the same damage, this time as individual plaintiffs, not as the community. In contrast, a dismissal of the case would mean that members of the community were not allowed to go back to court again. The Court of Appeal confirmed the earlier judgment and ordered a non-suit.

A striking feature of the case is that the trial judge had no doubt that Shell had caused major damage to the community. The plaintiffs' scientific evidence was admitted by the court. Said Edozie, J.C.A.:

> *There was unchallenged and credible evidence that the appellant's oil pipeline exploded and the oil spillage therefore caused extensive damage to the respondent community. To that extent, the respondent's claim in negligence did not fail to warrant dismissal. They were however not entitled to judgment, for, as the appellants successfully pleaded and contended, the action was bad for misjoinder of parties and cause of action. In the circumstances, the proper order which meets the justice of the case is a non-suit.*[479]

The key problem with this and other similar cases is that English Law does not take full notice of communal issues in Nigeria's rural areas. Nigerian lawyers have tended to be reluctant to depart from the established English Law even though they recognise the problem. Said the judge in *Shell v. Enoch*[480]: *'In my view there would be a grave injustice if the respondents' case was dismissed with the resultant effect of denying the community and the various individuals* [sic] *of re-litigating their claims in separate and properly constituting actions'.*[481] But the problem with the above reasoning is that the individuals are less likely to be able to afford separate litigation. The community as a whole may afford a court action but not necessarily an individual villager. Therefore, the judgment of non-suit ultimately favours the oil companies, contrary to the intention of the court to do justice to both sides. By claiming misjoinder, oil companies have often escaped liability for compensation payments to those adversely affected by oil operations.

---

[478] BHC/2/83, quoted in *Shell v. Enoch* (1992) 8 NWLR (Pt. 259) 335.

[479] Per Edozie, J.C.A. at page 346.

[480] (1992) 8 NWLR (Pt. 259) 335.

[481] Per Jacks, J.C.A. at page 345.

Oil companies have not always succeeded in pleading misjoinder. In *Mon v. Shell-BP*[482], the plaintiffs claimed compensation for damage from an oil spill. The plaintiffs testified that oil destroyed their joint fishponds. Lawyers of Shell-BP claimed that the different plaintiffs should sue the company separately, not jointly. The court found that the plaintiffs were working together *'in a loose sort of partnership'*.[483] Having obtained advice from the Ministry of Agriculture, they jointly initiated a scheme to breed fish in fishponds for sale. Said the judge: *'On the evidence I am satisfied that each had contributed work or money or both to the jointly needed channel, and that they intended to share the profits in due time. Therefore it is proper that they should sue jointly'*.[484] However, the case *Mon v. Shell-BP*[485] is somewhat exceptional since it involved a new form of partnership. The judge made it clear that a community could not sue jointly in respect of damaged fish ponds. The rationale behind the decision was as follows: *'If plaintiffs had erected fishtraps in the creeks there and those traps had been damaged by oil, then they would have been entitled to compensation as individuals in just the same way as many others were, including some of the witnesses before me'*.[486] Although the land was communal, the fishtraps were individually owned.

The above cases suggest that, under normal circumstances, a community cannot sue jointly on behalf of individual property. It appears that a community can sue jointly on behalf of communal land or buildings. But it cannot sue jointly for damage to individual property such as trees, fishtraps or houses. This partly mirrors customary law, under which land does not include things growing or attached to the soil, including trees or buildings. Nevertheless, court judgments do not entirely take account of customary law. As Obi (1963, 94 and 98) pointed out, among the Ibo, fishing lakes and ponds, as well as trees growing wild on communal reserve land are usually communally, not individually, owned. On farmland, trees growing wild are treated as communal, as long as the land lies fallow. Where the farmland is under cultivation, the individuals who farm the area have exclusive rights over the trees. Under customary law, trees grown on individual landholdings generally belong to the individuals who farm the land. However, among the Ngwa, palm trees growing on 'private' land were open to communal use for certain periods of the year (Obi 1963, 94 and 98). From the analysis of oil-related litigation in Nigeria, it appears that courts may have often failed to take notice of those distinctions in customary rights.

On the whole, the above discussion has indicated that oil companies have at their disposal a wide range of general legal defences, which they can use in oil-related litigation. Companies can rely on statutes of limitation, plaintiff's problems in providing evidence and the rule of misjoinder of parties and causes of action. In addition, it has to be remembered that oil companies have generally superior financial and technical resources as compared to village communities. They are hence more

---

[482] (1970-1972) I RSLR 71.

[483] Per Holden, C.J. at page 72.

[484] Per Holden, C.J. at page 73.

[485] (1970-1972) I RSLR 71.

[486] Per Holden, C.J. at page 73.

likely to provide superior expertise in court. This places a limitation on justice for village communities in lawsuits against oil companies. Yet the fact that the quantity of litigation against oil companies and the quantum of compensation awards have increased would suggest that there has been legal transformation in oil-related cases which has lessened the limitation on justice for village communities.

6.10. Locus Standi

The principles of legal liability under tort law and the legal defences employed by oil companies have not changed fundamentally since Nigeria's independence in 1960. Nonetheless, our analysis of the court judgments indicates that, by the early 1990s, there had been a measure of legal transformation in the judicial interpretation of a number of legal rules in oil-related cases. This resulted in more favourable conditions for compensation claims by village communities. From a preliminary analysis of Nigerian litigation, one can distinguish at least three main legal changes: a broadening of the *locus standi*, a relaxation of evidence rules, and a broadening of compensation awards, which are analysed below.[487]

---

[487] These findings were, to a large extent, confirmed by a personal interview with M.B. Belgore, Chief Justice of the Federal High Court (Lagos, March 1998). Belgore was asked if he agreed with the author whether the three areas of law mentioned above have undergone any changes. On compensation awards, Belgore said:

> The law has changed because the law is more robust in awarding compensation now than it was before. This is very important where people bring evidence that their livelihood has been much affected. Some of them are farmers and the oil has poured on the area where they farm. Some of them are fishermen and they can't fish again. Of course, the law has to give them enough compensation, either to give them an alternative mode of livelihood or an alternative method of living a decent life. Therefore, on the issue of compensation, compensation is now more robust than it used to be. The damage is assessed more than before.

On evidence by experts, Belgore said:

> An expert is someone who knows the conditions, what it was before, what it is now. He need not to be a scientific person. For instance, a hand-writing expert may be somebody who is familiar with the hand-writing of Mr. X for a long time, when he looks at it, he is an expert, he doesn't need to go to any scientific school before becoming an expert. To that extent, the court now filled the issue of an expert with a broader sense than before in the definition of the word 'expert' because one has to do justice. Don't forget that most of these rural communities cannot afford a geologist, a soil expert etc. They may have someone who knows the conditions and who can explain things and we accept it.

This definition of an expert is quite different from the definition of the Supreme Court in *Seismograph Service v. Onokpasa* (1972) 1 All NLR (Pt. 1) 347 (see footnote 464). On *locus standi*, Belgore stated:

> We [Nigerian judges] are a little more liberal about locus standi. I had one or two cases, in which you have somebody from the community. He must be a member of that community but he may not necessarily be resident. If he is a member of that community, that gives him enough standing to issue a writ on behalf of the community.

These findings on legal change do not preclude that there have been other, equally significant, changes in the judicial interpretation of legal rules in Nigeria. But, based on our analysis of

A broadening of the *locus standi* has the potential of fundamentally changing the nature of oil-related litigation in Nigeria. In *Adediran v. Interland Transport*[488], the Nigerian Supreme Court broadened the scope of *locus standi* in terms of the so-called public right to sue. In that case, residents of a housing estate formed a housing association. The housing association filed a suit against Interland Transport, a transport firm with nearby offices. Interland Transport used its premises as a workshop and for parking trailers. The plaintiffs complained against the traffic of the trailers, which blocked the access roads to the estate, knocked down electric poles, damaged the roads and generated noise.

In the Adediran case, the court ruled that the nuisance caused by Interland Transport was private not public. But the Supreme Court considered the nature of *locus standi* in public nuisance in general terms. Until the Adediran case, in matters of public interest litigation the old rule was that only the Attorney-General could bring court action to protect a public right. The Adediran case has changed this state of affairs. Karibi-Whyte, J.S.C. pronounced: *'The restriction imposed at common law on the right of action in public nuisance is inconsistent with the provisions of section 6(6)(b) of the Constitution, 1979 and to that extent is void'.*[489] Karibi-Whyte, J.S.C. further stated: *'Having held that in the institution of actions, the distinction between public and private nuisance in this country has been abolished by the Constitution 1979, the exercise of the right of action for nuisance is no longer based on or determined by the distinction'.*[490] In other words, the Supreme Court found that the 1979 Constitution abolished the Common Law distinction between public and private nuisance as far as the right to institute actions in nuisance before Nigerian courts is concerned. Karibi-Whyte, J.S.C. explained the rationale behind the ruling in the following terms:

> *I think the high constitutional policy involved in section 6(6)(b) [of the 1979 Constitution] is the removal of the obstacles erected by common law requirements against individuals bringing actions before the court against the government and its institutions, and the preconditions of the requirement of the consent of the Attorney-General. This becomes the more important when the provisions are procedural encrustments designed to protect peculiar social or political institutions.*[491]

---

available litigation, the three main areas of change mentioned above appear most relevant to oil-related cases.

[488] (1991) 9 NWLR (Pt. 214) 155.

[489] Per Karibi-Whyte, J.S.C. at page 180. Section 6(6)(b) of the 1979 Constitution stated: *'The judicial powers vested in accordance with the foregoing provisions of this section shall extend to all matters between persons, or between government or authority and any person in Nigeria, and to all actions and proceedings relating thereto, for the determination of any question as to the civil rights and obligations of that person'.* Relying on this constitutional provision, Karibi-Whyte, J.S.C. stated: *'The Constitution has vested the Courts with the powers for the determination of any question as to the civil rights and obligations between government or authority and any person in Nigeria. See s.6(6)(b). Accordingly, where the determination of the civil rights and obligations of a person is in issue, any law which imposes conditions, is inconsistent with the free and unrestrained exercise of that right, is void to the extent of such inconsistency.'* Per Karibi-Whyte, J.S.C. at page 180. Based on this contention, the Supreme Court regarded the restriction on the right of action in public nuisance as inconsistent with the 1979 Constitution and to that extent void.

[490] Per Karibi-Whyte, J.S.C. at page 182.

[491] Per Karibi-Whyte, J.S.C. at page 180.

This suggests that the Supreme Court considered a limitation of *locus standi* in public interest litigation as an impediment to justice. The significance of the Adediran case lies in the recognition that private persons no longer require the Attorney-General's consent to press public right's litigation. They can bring an action themselves as long as they show sufficient interest in the matter.

The impact of the Adediran case on *locus standi* in Nigeria is as yet unclear. As Ogowewo (1995) argued, the law relating to *locus standi* in Nigeria is still unsettled. According to Ogowewo (1995), '*the position now seems to be that the courts proceed on a case-by-case basis, intuitively deciding who should have standing*'. Courts continue to rely on the so-called '*civil rights*' test laid down in the controversial ruling in *Adesanya v. President of the Federal Republic of Nigeria*[492]. The civil rights test was defined by Bello, J.S.C. as follows: '*standing will only be accorded to a plaintiff who shows that his civil rights and obligations have been or are in danger of being violated or adversely affected by the act complained of*'.[493] The Supreme Court judges disagreed on the issue of *locus standi* which left the law relating to *locus standi* in Nigeria unsettled. While subsequent court cases have, to a large extent, followed the civil rights test, a broader interpretation of *locus standi* was, for instance, applied in a criminal case. In *Fawehinmi v. Akilu*[494], the Supreme Court ruled that the Criminal Procedure Law of Lagos State gave every person a right to initiate private prosecution.[495]

In terms of oil-related litigation, the new rule in the Adediran case could mean that private persons or organisations, e.g. environmental pressure groups, could sue oil companies for damage from oil operations. Until now, only those directly affected by oil operations had a *locus standi*. The case *Douglas v. Shell*[496] could become a test case on the broadened interpretation of *locus standi* in oil-related litigation. In that case, Oronto Douglas - an environmental rights activist - sued Shell, the NNPC, the Nigerian Liquefied Natural Gas (NLNG) project, Mobil and the Attorney-General for non-compliance with the Environmental Impact Assessment (EIA) Decree No.86 of 1992 (see chapter 3). The Douglas case was dismissed in the Federal High Court, which ruled that the plaintiff had no right to sue. Belgore, C.J. held that Douglas's claim was baseless and that '*the plaintiff shows no prima facie evidence that his right was*

---

[492] (1981) 1 All NLR 1.

[493] Per Bello, J.S.C. at page 39.

[494] (1987) 4 NWLR (Pt. 61) 797.

[495] In that case, the court had to decide whether the applicant was entitled to apply for mandamus to compel private prosecution of certain persons. The Court of Appeal held that the applicant had no standing to sue as his legal rights had not been infringed. The Supreme Court set the rule of the Court of Appeal aside and held that the *locus standi* had been broadened since section 342 of the Criminal Procedure Law of Lagos State vests in every person a right to initiate a private prosecution. Nnamani, J.S.C. stated: '*It is my view that in these matters which are so interlined with the criminal law, our interpretation of Section 6(6)(b) of the Constitution must be approached with a true liberal spirit in the interest of the society at large. The Appellant has locus standi as any person to make the application he has brought to court, and if all other conditions are fulfilled, to initiate criminal proceedings*'. Per Nnamani, J.S.C. at page 855. The controversy on the issue of *locus standi* has continued. Ogowewo (1995) argued that the ruling in *Fawehinmi v. Akilu* does not broaden the *locus standi*. Owaboye (1995, 299), on the other hand, averred that the Akilu case broadens the *locus standi* and should be viewed as the locus classicus on the issue.

[496] Unreported Suit No. FHC/L/CS/573/96 in the Federal High Court, Lagos.

affected nor any direct injury caused to him'.[497] However, the court appeared to have failed to take into account all the facts related to the plaintiff's *locus standi*. The plaintiff's lawyers argued that Douglas had both a private interest in the suit as a native of a village affected by oil operations and a public interest as an environmentalist. In December 1998, the Court of Appeal ruled that the Federal High Court was in breach of a number of procedural rules when deciding the Douglas case. Accordingly, the earlier decision of the lower court was set aside and the case was remitted back to the Federal High Court to be retried before a different judge.[498] If the Douglas case or any subsequent oil-related cases are able to successfully apply the broadened rules of *locus standi* to oil-related litigation, this could open a floodgate for non-governmental organisations and other interested parties to sue oil companies in Nigeria. But the implementation of the rule laid down in the Adediran case may take some time to take effect since legal transformation is a slow process.

While the broadened rules of the public right to sue have so far failed to directly affect oil-related litigation, there are indications that oil-related litigation has undergone some transformation in terms of the private right to sue. Those affected by oil operations usually sue oil companies as a group rather than as individual plaintiffs. In the past, it was common for a judge to dismiss a suit or to limit its scope because he found that the plaintiffs had not proven their authority to sue as a group. For instance, in *Chinda v. Shell-BP*[499], the plaintiffs sued Shell-BP as representing the Rumuokani community in Rivers State for damage to houses and crops from gas flaring, and for general inconvenience and discomfort. Their claim was dismissed as the judge held that *'it is not proved that the six named plaintiffs sue as representatives of all the villagers'.*[500] Since they had no authority to sue in a representative capacity, they were deemed to be suing only in respect of themselves individually.

More recently, however, cases in which oil companies have successfully been sued by plaintiffs representing a village community or a family as a whole have become more widespread.[501] In *Shell v. Tiebo VII*[502], the plaintiffs sued Shell on behalf of the Peremabiri community for damage from an oil spill in 1987. The oil company lawyers pleaded misjoinder, among other legal defences. The Court of Appeal held in 1996 that there was no misjoinder and awarded the plaintiffs 6 million Naira in compensation. This case exemplifies the broader interpretation of communally owned property by Nigerian courts. In order to illustrate this broader interpretation, it is illuminating to compare the Tiebo case with two 1972 cases, *Chinda v. Shell-BP*[503] and

---

[497] Per Belgore, C.J. at page 2 of unreported judgment.

[498] Unreported Suit No. CA/L/143/97 in the Court of Appeal.

[499] (1974) 2 RSLR 1.

[500] Per Holden, C.J. at page 4.

[501] Several recent high-profile cases by communities against oil companies from the 1990s can be cited: *Geosource v. Biragbara* (1997) 5 NWLR (Pt. 506) 607, *Shell v. Tiebo VII* (1996) 4 NWLR (Pt. 445) 657, *Shell v. Farah* (1995) 3 NWLR (Pt. 382) 148. In all of these cases, plaintiffs sued an oil company in representative capacity, not as individuals.

[502] (1996) 4 NWLR (Pt. 445) 657.

[503] (1974) 2 RSLR 1.

Mon v. Shell-BP[504]. In the Chinda case, the court pronounced that the plaintiffs suing in representative capacity could not receive compensation for damage to trees. Said the trial judge: *'each separate tree owner has a separate personal claim for damage to his or her trees'*.[505] In the Tiebo case, the plaintiffs were awarded compensation for damage to raffia palms. In the Mon case, the judge indicated that a community could not sue jointly in respect of damage to communal fishponds. In the Tiebo case, the plaintiffs were awarded compensation for damage to communal fish ponds.

While the facts in the above cases are different, the Tiebo case illustrates that Nigerian courts have interpreted the right to compensation for damage to communally owned property in broader terms. This does not imply that the private standing to sue has been broadened *per se*. It is yet too early to say whether there has been a general shift in judicial attitudes towards claims instituted in representative capacity. But a broader interpretation of communal claims is likely to frustrate the oil companies' legal defence based on misjoinder of parties and causes of action. Communal claims of village communities are hence more likely to succeed. The changing interpretation of *locus standi* appears to allow a greater number of individuals to sue oil companies. This could partly explain the recent rise in oil-related litigation in Nigeria.

6.11. Evidence Rules

In respect of the rules on expert evidence in oil-related cases, there are also indications of legal changes which have benefited village communities. In *Elf v. Sillo*[506], in which the Sillo family sued Elf for damage arising from oil operations, the Supreme Court partially relaxed the rules on expert evidence in 1994. The court pronounced a novel interpretation of the standard of proof for damage where the evidence in support is unchallenged. Said Onu, J.S.C.:

> *The standard of proof required in establishing the amount of damages in a case such as the one in hand, namely a case where the evidence in support is unchallenged, the law is that the burden assumed by the plaintiff/respondents hereis, is discharge upon a minimum of proof.*[507]

The application of this minimal standard of proof is limited to cases in which evidence is not challenged by the opposing litigant. This rule, nonetheless, presents a marked contrast with the previous insistence of the Supreme Court on a high standard of proof and expert evidence in oil-related litigation.[508]

In addition to its ruling on the minimal standard of proof, the Supreme Court in the Sillo case held that a court would be correct in preferring the credible evidence of a non-expert witness on an issue to the evidence of an expert on the same issue where

---

[504] (1970-1972) I RSLR 71.

[505] Per Holden, C.J. at page 3.

[506] (1994) 6 NWLR (Pt. 350) 258.

[507] Per Onu, J.S.C. at pages 279-280.

[508] See, in particular, judgments of the Supreme Court in *Seismograph Service v. Onokpasa* (1972) 1 All NLR (Pt. 1) 347, *Seismograph Service v. Akporuovo* (1974) All NLR 95 and *Seismograph Service v. Ogbeni* (1976) 4 S.C. 85.

the former is an independent witness whilst the latter prepared his or her evidence specifically for the case on hand on the direction of the party calling him or her. In the particular case, Adio, J.S.C. said:

> The P.W.3 [third plaintiff's witness] *made an inspection of the area on the direction of the Hon. Attorney-General of the state at a time when the possibility of the matter being settled amicably out of court was being explored while the D.W.1 [first defendant's witness] prepared his own report specifically for this case on the basis of the direction of the appellant [Elf] to the firm of the witness. The learned trial Judge felt, rightly, that the P.W.3 was an independent witness and his report [more] acceptable than the report prepared, specifically for use in this case, at the instance of the appellant. In preferring the evidence of the P.W.3 to the evidence of the D.W.1, the learned trial Judge had regard, rightly in my view, to other evidence before the court.*[509]

This attitude of the court departs from the earlier insistence of the Supreme Court and the Court of Appeal on the use of specially skilled experts in providing evidence. In *Seismograph Service v. Onokpasa*[510], the Supreme Court declared in 1972:

> *If the learned trial judge had applied the correct test* [of the relevance of the witness's opinion as that of an expert] *he would have come to the conclusion that the only expert opinions before him were those of the defendant's experts, and so unless for good reasons otherwise should have accepted them.*[511]

In other words, the Supreme Court held that the evidence of an expert is absolutely necessary. In another important precedent *Seismograph Service v. Ogbeni*[512] in 1976, the Supreme Court reinforced the opinion that expert evidence is necessary to connect the damage with oil operations. A Supreme Court judge criticised the court ruling of the lower court: '*Surprisingly, the learned trial judge, while accepting that the evidence of an expert was necessary to establish that the damage to the house was traceable to seismic operations, held that it was not absolutely necessary*'.[513] In contrast to the above two cases, the significance of the case *Elf v. Sillo*[514] lies in its departure from the notion that an expert opinion is absolutely necessary to establish evidence in court, if only in relation to 'independent' non-expert evidence.

The application of the new interpretation of the rules of evidence laid down in the Sillo case has not been uniform as yet. Although a new precedent was set, the judiciary has resisted change to some extent, often preferring to rely on older

---

[509] Per Adio, J.S.C. at page 272.

[510] (1972) 1 All NLR (Pt. 1) 347.

[511] Per Sowemimo, J.S.C. at page 357.

[512] (1976) 4 S.C. 85.

[513] Per Obaseki, J.S.C. at page 171.

[514] (1994) 6 NWLR (Pt. 350) 258.

judgments.[515] Today there is some evidence that the rules on evidence have been relaxed in oil-related litigation. In *Shell v. Isaiah*[516], the Court of Appeal relied on the minimal standard of proof established in the Sillo case, although the court judgment also cited the cases *Seismograph Service v. Onokpasa*[517] and *Seismograph Service v. Ogbeni*[518]. In that case, the more relaxed rules of evidence assisted the plaintiffs in winning a compensation award for damage from an oil spill. In general, it is still too early to say how the courts have altered their attitude towards the rules of evidence. But the existence of a new trend towards relaxed rules of evidence in oil-related litigation cannot be denied.

6.12. Quantum of Compensation Awards

The changing judicial attitudes towards *locus standi* and evidence rules in Nigeria have the potential of significantly affecting the outcome in oil-related cases. But the most significant precedent in oil-related litigation was created in 1994 in relation to the quantum of compensation awards with the case *Shell v. Farah*[519]. In that case, several families sued Shell for compensation for a well blow-out in 1970. The court established that Shell's evidence was not reliable and the plaintiffs were awarded 4,621,307 Naira in compensation. Dissatisfied with the judgment, Shell appealed against the decision. The Court of Appeal confirmed the award.

The Farah case is an important judicial precedent regarding the quantum of compensation for damage. In order to understand the impact of the Farah case, it is necessary to understand the principles of compensation payments before 1994. In order to illustrate the different approaches taken by courts to compensation in the 1990s, it is illuminating to compare the 1975 case *Umudje v. Shell-BP*[520] mentioned earlier with the Farah case.

In the Umudje case, the plaintiffs demanded a sum of 100,000 Naira for the destruction of their ponds and lakes as a result of oil spills and the construction of a road. The lower court awarded 14,400 Naira to the plaintiffs for the damage to 300 ponds, lakes and the land. Dissatisfied with the judgment, Shell-BP appealed against the decision. The Supreme Court confirmed the judgment but lowered the compensation payment from 14,400 Naira to 12,000 Naira. The court found that there was no credible evidence for the damage to the lakes and the land.

On the surface, the basic principle of compensation in the Umudje case was identical to the Farah case. In the Umudje case, the judge said: '*The primary*

---

[515] See, for instance, *Ogiale v. Shell* (1997) 1 NWLR (Pt. 480) 148, in which the court relied on the evidence rules in *Seismograph Service v. Onokpasa* (1972) 1 All NLR (Pt. 1) 347 and *Seismograph Service v. Ogbeni* (1976) 4 S.C. 85.

[516] (1997) 6 NWLR (Pt. 508) 236.

[517] (1972) 1 All NLR (Pt. 1) 347.

[518] (1976) 4 S.C. 85.

[519] (1995) 3 NWLR (Pt. 382) 148.

[520] (1975) 9-11 S.C. 155.

theoretical notion is to place the plaintiff in a good a position [sic], *so far as money can do it, as if the matter complained of had not occurred'.*[521] In the Farah case, the principle of compensation was defined by the judge as to '*restore the person suffering the damnum* [damage] *as far as money can do that to the position he was* [sic] *before the damnum or would have been but for the damnum'.*[522] What distinguishes the Farah case from the Umudje case is the interpretation of the above principle by the court. In the Umudje case, this basic principle was interpreted very narrowly. Said the judge: '*We concede that a claim which asks for "a fair and reasonable compensation" ...is most inappropriate in an action for damages in tort'.*[523] In the Farah case, the judge accepted that the plaintiffs were entitled to '*fair and adequate compensation'*, as stipulated by the Petroleum Act. Onalaja, J.C.A. defined and broadened the basis of adequate compensation as '*market value of property when taken. It may include interest and may include the cost or value of the property in the owner for the purposes for which he designed it'.*[524] In other words, compensation must also be paid for the subsequent consequential and prospective future losses, not merely for the destroyed property. In addition, the court ruled that compensation should also be paid for the suffering of individuals as a result of the damage to land. The judge cited a textbook on damages as follows:

> Beyond physical damage to the land, however, a nuisance may cause annoyance, inconvenience, discomfort, or even illness to the plaintiff occupier. Recovery in respect of these principally non-pecuniary losses is allowable and may be regarded as part of the normal measure of damages.[525]

The above pronouncements in the Farah case changed the basis of the award of compensation payments to those adversely affected by oil operations. In the Umudje case, the social effect of oil operations was not even considered, while the Supreme Court set aside the lower court's award of 800 Naira for 'injurious affection' of the plaintiffs' farm land and 1,600 Naira for the damage to the plaintiffs' lakes. The plaintiffs merely received a single lump sum payment for the destruction of ponds. In contrast, in the Farah case, the plaintiffs were awarded compensation under multiple heads including the loss of income, the '*social effect/general inconvenience'* and the rehabilitation of the land. Before the Farah case arose, Shell had previously paid compensation to the community for the crops damaged as a result of oil operations. But the court found that the victims should also have been compensated for the loss of income. In the course of the two decades after the accident, the victims could not use the land for farming. On that basis, they were awarded 2,371,307 Naira for the loss of income for the period of 19 years. Since Shell failed to rehabilitate the land in that time, the community was also awarded 2,000,000 Naira for the rehabilitation of the

---

[521] Per Idigbe, J.S.C. at page 162.

[522] Per Edozie, J.C.A. at page 192. Lawyers call the principle '*restitutio in integrum'*. See Percy (1983, 251-252 and 588).

[523] Per Idigbe, J.S.C. at page 162.

[524] Per Onalaja, J.C.A. at page 199.

[525] Per Edozie, J.C.A. at page 194.

land. Furthermore, the community was awarded 250,000 Naira for the *'social effect/general inconvenience'*.

The compensation award in the Farah case is a marked departure from earlier court judgments in a number of respects. In earlier cases, oil companies often relied on federal legislation to limit the amount of compensation payments. On the question of the quantum of compensation, in the 1974 case *Odim v. Shell-BP*[526], the judge ruled that the 1963 Constitution and the Public Lands Acquisition Act *'are there to guide us on this point'*.[527] In contrast, in *Shell v. Farah*[528], the judge refused to accept the Public Lands Acquisition Act as the basis for the quantum of compensation. The oil company lawyer relied on federal legislation by referring to the Public Lands Acquisition (Miscellaneous Provisions) Act No.33 1976. The 1976 Act fixed the sum of 1,250 Naira per hectare as the maximum compensation for outright acquisition of arable land. If applied to 7 hectares, the plaintiffs in the Farah case would only receive 8,750 Naira (US$ 397 at 1994 exchange rate). Since the amount was rather insignificant, an application of the provisions of the Public Lands Acquisition Act in the Farah case would have favoured the interests of the oil industry. By relying on federal legislation and official compensation rates, Shell would not have to pay for loss of income and some other types of losses. The value of official rates also decreased over time because of currency depreciation and inflation. For instance, the maximum compensation rate of 1,250 Naira per hectare was worth US$ 1993.62 when the Act was promulgated in 1976 but declined to US$ 56.83 when the Farah case was decided in 1994. The consumer prices in Nigeria rose by over 1,100% between 1976 and 1994.[529] Because of inflation, it made economic sense for oil companies to delay compensation payments and to rely on official rates. In contrast to some earlier court judgments, in the Farah case, the court objected to the use of official compensation rates and to the application of statute law in determining the compensation sum. Said Edozie, J.C.A.:

> Where a tortuous act is committed, the injured party is entitled to damages in accordance with the measure of damages applicable to his injury. The measure of damages for injury affecting land bears no relevance to the amount of compensation for outright acquisition of the land under the Public Lands Acquisition Act.[530]

The new principles of compensation payments established in the Farah case worked against a number of the previous legal strategies employed by oil companies to avoid substantial compensation payments to village communities. A common strategy was to pay paltry sums for the destruction of crops in order to avoid other forms of compensation. In *Nvogoro v. Shell-BP*[531] mentioned earlier, the oil company paid a small sum of money to the plaintiff's illiterate brother, who thumb-printed a receipt for

---

[526] (1974) 2 RSLR 93.

[527] Per Wai-Ogosu J. in *Odim v. Shell-BP* (1974) 2 RSLR 93 at 109.

[528] (1995) 3 NWLR (Pt. 382) 148.

[529] Based on the IMF figures for Nigerian consumer prices, see IMF Financial Statistics Yearbook 1995.

[530] Per Edozie, J.C.A. at page 195.

[531] (1973) 2 RSLR 75.

the money. Shell-BP used the receipt in court, saying that any compensation due had been paid, and the plaintiff lost the case on those grounds. In the Farah case, Shell also tried to use the same strategy by arguing that the plaintiffs had already been paid compensation for damage to crops as a result of the well blow-out. The company argued that the plaintiffs should not receive more money as further compensation. The company lawyer argued that it was wrong for the court not to have held that Shell paid compensation for all the losses arising from the blow-out. As evidence of its payments, Shell tendered a receipt with the thumb prints of 84 illiterate villagers. The trial judge dismissed the company's evidence because the receipt did not include the names of the plaintiffs and referred to a different piece of land. He also pointed out that the plaintiffs claimed compensation for damage to land, not crops. In other words, in contrast to the Nvogoro case, the judge held that compensation for damage could be paid more than once in respect of the same cause of damage, if the claim was made in respect of different items of assessment.

The court further averred that a mere payment of compensation by an oil company in respect of a specific item did not necessarily discharge the company's obligation to make a fair and adequate payment to those affected by oil operations. Shell claimed that it had paid 2,000 Naira compensation for the damage to the land, but the trial judge rejected this objection by arguing: *'Even if the sum of N2,000 was paid to the plaintiffs, it cannot be a fair and adequate compensation for the damage to the land'*.[532] In other words, the court found that the mere fact of paying compensation is not an excuse, the payment must also be fair and adequate. The Court of Appeal did not disagree with this reasoning of the trial judge. The Farah case was thus a departure from previous court judgments in the sense that the court was prepared to compel an oil company to pay compensation more than once in respect of the same injury and the same item of assessment. This legal reasoning clearly frustrated previous oil company strategies, which relied on receipts signed or thumb printed by local people in respect of token compensation payments.

On the whole, the significance of the Farah case as a landmark ruling in terms of compensation payments lies in the court's departure from the previous narrow understanding of the basis of compensation awards. The precedent in the Farah case broadened this understanding to include items such as, for example, non-pecuniary losses. As a result of these innovations in the assessment of compensation, the understanding of what constitutes 'fair and adequate' compensation was broadened. If the precedent in the Farah case is followed in future case judgments, an oil company will no longer be able to discharge its legal obligation to pay 'fair and adequate' compensation for damage from oil operations by paying a paltry sum to those adversely affected by oil operations.

In the wake of the Farah case, substantial compensation payments were awarded to plaintiffs in a number of court cases between village communities and oil companies. It is difficult to compare different court cases because the facts in each case are unique and they involve different types of damage. But a comparison of compensation awards before and after the Farah case can tentatively illustrate the rise

---

[532] Per Edozie, J.C.A. at page 175.

in compensation payments. In *Mon v. Shell-BP*[533] in 1972, the plaintiffs did not prepare a valuation of their claims, so the judge assessed the compensation figure himself at 200 Naira (US$ 304 at the official exchange rate). The compensation payment was only 0.1% of the plaintiffs' original demand. One of the notable exceptions was *Fufeyin v. Shell-BP*[534] in 1978, in which the plaintiffs were awarded as much as 55,691 Naira (approx. US$ 88,189) for the destruction of houses, crops, fishing creeks, canals, fish ponds, traps and other property. The reason for this substantial payment was that Shell-BP had earlier agreed to the amount of compensation anyway. In contrast, in *Shell v. Tiebo VII*[535] in 1997, as much as 6,000,000 Naira (US$ 274,173) was awarded, while in *Shell v. Isaiah*[536] in 1996, 22,000,000 Naira (US$ 1,005,208) was awarded (see Table 6.1.).

Table 6.1. Compensation Awards in Selected Oil-Related Cases

Year of Judgment	Court Case	Plaintiff's Claim (000s Naira)	Defendant's Offer (000s Naira)	Payment Awarded (000s Naira)	Payment Awarded (US$)	Payment Awarded as Share of Claim
1972	Mon v. Shell-BP	200	0	0.2	304	0.1%
1975	Umudje v. Shell-BP	50	0	12	19,481	24%
1978	Fufeyin v. Shell-BP	56	56	56	88,189	100%
1978	Shell-BP v. Cole	n.a.	0	35	55,118	n.a.
1994	Shell v. Farah	26,490	0	4,621	210,084	17%
1996	Shell v. Tiebo VII	64,146	50	6,000	274,173	9%
1996	Shell v. Udi	50	0	39	1,782	78%
1997	Geosource v. Biragbara	2,000	0	197	9,001	10%
1997	Shell v. Isaiah	22,000	0	22,000	1,005,208	100%

Source: official currency exchange rates were derived from *IMF International Financial Statistics* (various years).

In *Shell v. Tiebo VII*[537], two years after the judgment in the Farah case, the plaintiffs sued Shell on behalf of the Peremabiri community in the then Rivers State for damage from an oil spill in 1987. The oil spill, estimated at 600 barrels of crude oil, polluted the River Nun, which had previously been used as a source of fresh water and for fishing. Members of the community who drank the water after the spill suffered from water-borne diseases. In addition, the oil spill damaged swampland, streams, ponds and the community's juju shrines. Shell did not deny the oil spill, but claimed that it had only affected an area of 2.3 hectares of seasonal swamp and fish flats. It

---

[533] (1970-1972) I RSLR 71.

[534] (1978) 2 ANSLR 210.

[535] (1996) 4 NWLR (Pt. 445) 657.

[536] (1997) 6 NWLR (Pt. 508) 236.

[537] (1996) 4 NWLR (Pt. 445) 657.

offered the community 5,500 Naira as 'fair and adequate compensation'.[538] The lower court awarded 6,000,000 Naira to the plaintiffs and the Court of Appeal affirmed the judgment. The substantial compensation sum awarded in the Tiebo VII case exemplified the trend towards higher compensation awards in the 1990s in respect of damage from oil operations. Interestingly, the Tiebo VII case did not cite the Farah case as a legal precedent. But Onalaja, J.C.A. who delivered the judgment, was one of the Court of Appeal judges in the Farah case. This would suggest that the Farah case, while important as a legal precedent, is in itself a reflection of a broader shift in judicial attitudes towards higher compensation payments.

As a whole, the previous three sections indicate that there have been a number of legal transformations in relation to *locus standi*, evidence rules and quantum of compensation. These transformations appear to have largely benefited village communities in oil-related litigation.

6.13. Changing Approach to Law

The previous section has highlighted a number of changes which occurred within Nigerian judicial decision making. It is less clear why legal change has occurred. In this section, we propose a framework for explaining this legal transformation.

Obviously, any analysis of the causes of legal change must remain speculative. Amongst the most likely explanations are, first, a different approach to law by judicial officers, second, the increased professional ability of legal counsel working for village communities, and third, the impact of changing social attitudes on judges. We have attempted to investigate these explanations in the context of an interview with a senior Nigerian judge M.B. Belgore, Chief Justice of the Federal High Court.[539]

First, contemporary Nigerian judges appear to approach law in a different manner from their predecessors. Said Belgore, C.J.: '*One possible explanation* [for legal change] *is that judges everywhere today are moving away from Common Law of the 17th and 18th centuries. We approach the 21st century. We are moving towards a new modern law tradition*'.[540] According to Belgore, one of the differences in the judges' approach is the greater importance attached to substantive rules as opposed to procedural ones.[541] One of the indicators of these changing attitudes is that judges have

---

[538] According to plaintiffs' witnesses, the sum was 50,000 Naira, not 5,500 Naira as Shell's witnesses maintained.

[539] Personal interview with M.B. Belgore, Chief Justice of the Federal High Court (Lagos, March 1998). Belgore largely confirmed our speculations that legal change was affected by the three factors: different approach to law by judicial officers, the increased professional ability of legal counsel working for village communities, and the influence of changing social attitudes on judges. He also maintained that legal change could also be attributed to the increased frequency of accidents in the oil industry and the resulting legal disputes. It is possible that the increased frequency of litigation has accelerated the process of social learning among judges. But the quantity of litigation cannot explain *per se* why courts have changed their interpretation of legal rules.

[540] Personal interview with M.B. Belgore, Chief Justice of the Federal High Court (Lagos, March 1998). On the shifting attitudes of Nigerian judges in general, see e.g. Nweze (1996).

[541] The case *Fawehinmi v. Aminu* Unreported Suit No. FHC/L/CS/54/92 in the Federal High Court, which was adjudicated by Belgore, illustrates that courts have come to interpret legal statutes and

increasingly cited court precedents, particularly Nigerian ones, rather than statute law. For instance, in *Seismograph Service v. Akporuovo*[542], only one Nigerian court case was referred to in the judgment. In the more recent case *Shell v. Farah*[543], 36 Nigerian and 12 foreign court cases were cited (see Table 6.2.). Evidence from court cases indicates that there is a dual development. Nigerian courts appear to move away from statute law towards a greater application of judicial precedents. Moreover, courts move towards a Nigerian case law.

Table 6.2. Number of Nigerian and Foreign Cases Cited in Selected Oil-Related Cases

Year of Judgment	Court Case	Court	Number of Foreign Cases	Number of Nigerian Cases
1972	Seismograph Service v. Onokpasa	Supreme Court	3	0
1974	Seismograph Service v. Akporuovo	Supreme Court	0	1
1975	Umudje v. Shell-BP	Supreme Court	8	0
1976	Seismograph Service v. Ogbeni	Supreme Court	0	2
1978	Shell-BP v. Cole	Supreme Court	1	6
1994	Shell v. Farah	Court of Appeal	12	36
1994	Eboigbe v. NNPC	Supreme Court	3	11
1994	Elf v. Sillo	Supreme Court	0	32
1996	Shell v. Tiebo VII	Court of Appeal	9	46
1996	Shell v. Udi	Court of Appeal	0	11
1996	Ogiale v. Shell	Court of Appeal	9	20
1997	NNPC v. Elumah	Court of Appeal	0	4
1997	Shell v. Isaiah	Court of Appeal	1	12

An analysis of Nigerian court cases provides examples of a changing approach to law. In the past, courts have seemed reluctant to adjudicate matters related to federal legislation and government affairs. In oil-related litigation, this could amount to the courts' reluctance to prosecute oil companies or to raise petroleum matters. In *Amos v. Shell-BP*[544], the trial judge commented in 1974:

---

legal rules in a less narrow fashion. In that case, a Nigerian legal practitioner sued the Minister of Petroleum Resources Jubril Aminu and other defendants, including the NNPC, over the use of Nigeria's oil revenues in 1990. The NNPC requested the court to discharge them on the grounds that the plaintiff did not give them 30 days statutory notice as required by section 12(2) of the NNPC Act 1977. The judge concluded:

> *The right to access to Court should not be impeded by a process giving special advantage to the defendant for no other reason than that it is an organ or semi-organ of the Government. Any law putting it in such a position is certainly against the Constitution, void and invalid.*

Belgore, therefore, dismissed the NNPC's application and declared the aforementioned section of the NNPC Act 1977 as unconstitutional.

[542] (1974) All NLR 95.

[543] (1995) 3 NWLR (Pt. 382) 148.

[544] 4 ECSLR 486.

I do not think the courts have any jurisdiction to hear any claims for compensation under the Minerals Law. Section 78 lays down clearly the method of assessment, which in the absence of agreement is purely administrative, first through the divisional or district officer with an appeal to the Governor, who may order arbitration. Such an order would in my view be the only way in which the courts could acquire jurisdiction.[545]

According to the above logic, courts could only decide matters related to compensation, if a specific piece of petroleum legislation mentioned the word 'court'. This narrow interpretation would imply that the government could dictate whether the courts could decide a particular type of lawsuit or not. In this context, the judge somewhat misinterpreted the role of courts under English Common Law.[546] In general, the Amos case exemplified the courts' reluctance to interfere with statute law and government affairs.

In more recent cases, the courts were more willing to interfere with statute law and government affairs. In *Shell v. Isaiah*[547], the court ruled on the meaning of the Constitution (Suspension and Modification) Decree No.107 of 1993, which extended the original jurisdiction of the Federal High Court to oil-related matters (see chapter 3). The Court of Appeal pronounced that the 1993 Decree does not affect oil spillage matters. Notwithstanding the impact of the Isaiah case on federal legislation, the court judgment illustrates that contemporary courts in Nigeria are more willing to re-interpret statute law.

A greater willingness to re-interpret statutes was accompanied by the courts' greater reluctance to apply procedural or substantive rules which impede or delay justice to the litigants. In *Nwadiaro v. Shell*[548], the oil company claimed that the compensation claim was statute barred according to the English Statute of Limitation 1623. The statute prescribes that a plaintiff must begin a lawsuit within six years of the cause of grievance. In the present case, the community started the lawsuit in 1985, nineteen years after Shell constructed a road which resulted in damage to communal ponds. The Court of Appeal found that the statute of limitation was not applicable because the oil company had admitted liability for damage during negotiations in 1985. Said the judge: *'If there has been admission of liability during negotiation and all that remains is fulfilment of the agreement it cannot be just and equitable that the action would be barred after the statutory period of limitation'*.[549] The judge dismissed, what he considered, a too narrow interpretation of the statute.

---

[545] Per Holden, C.J. at page 490.

[546] Under Common Law, statutes of limitation can limit the period of limitation, within which a lawsuit can be brought to court. But legislation cannot limit the jurisdiction of courts to hear a tort case. Under some circumstances, courts may also override statutory limitations. On limitation of action, see Percy (1983, 199-230).

[547] (1997) 6 NWLR (Pt. 508) 236.

[548] (1990) 5 NWLR (Pt. 150) 322.

[549] Per Kolawole, J.C.A. at page 339.

In *Shell v. Udi*[550], the Court of Appeal indicated that it was not prepared to tolerate undue delays to justice brought about by oil company lawyers. In that case, the plaintiff claimed compensation for the destruction of fish ponds and trees during oil operations. On the date of the hearing in the Ughelli High Court, neither a company representative nor a lawyer were in court. The lawyers working for Shell merely sent a letter requesting an adjournment. They also failed to file a statement of defence, even though the company had over four months to prepare it. The judge felt that Shell and its lawyers did not take the case seriously. In his words, the behaviour of company lawyers was an *'example of wilful refusal or neglect to comply with Rules of Court'*.[551] The judge hence refused to grant adjournment of the case and the plaintiffs were awarded compensation. On appeal, the Court of Appeal confirmed the judgment of the lower court. On the issue of adjournment, the appeal judge ruled that *'the grant of an adjournment in a case is a matter entirely within the discretionary jurisdiction of the court which the court should exercise in accordance with the particular facts and circumstances of the case'*.[552] The judge's uncompromising attitude towards the oil company was reflected in the following statement:

> The request for an adjournment was merely to further delay the court giving judgment in favour of the respondent since there was nothing done by the appellant [Shell] to show that it was going to oppose the application made to the court by the respondent. Similarly, no explanation was given for the absence of the representative of the appellant. This also could only be interpreted as showing lack of interest in the matter by the appellant.[553]

The above two cases suggest that Nigerian judges are no longer prepared to tolerate legal technicalities and delay tactics by legal practitioners as a reason for preventing plaintiffs from instituting claims. This appears to support the earlier speculation that there has been a change in the judges' approach to law in the sense that they have come to attach greater importance to the substance of law.

6.14. Increased Professional Ability of Legal Counsel

As another explanation for legal change, we suggest that increased professional ability of legal counsel working for village communities has influenced the outcome of oil-related court judgments. One of the indicators of this increased professional ability is the sophisticated use of evidence by plaintiffs. Belgore, C.J. confirmed: *The damage is assessed more than before. Plaintiffs increasingly bring scientific evidence of the effects of oil on the soil.*[554]

---

[550] (1996) 6 NWLR (Pt. 455) 483.

[551] Per Akintan, J.C.A. at page 495.

[552] Per Akintan, J.C.A. at page 496.

[553] Per Akintan, J.C.A. at page 497.

[554] Personal interview with M.B. Belgore, Chief Justice of the Federal High Court (Lagos, March 1998).

A number of recent Nigerian court cases provide examples of a more sophisticated use of evidence by legal counsel for village communities. In the past, the quality of witness evidence was frequently of an inadequate standard. In the 1974 case *Odim v. Shell-BP*[555], there was only one witness for the plaintiff - the second plaintiff and two witnesses for the defendant, two Shell-BP employees, but there were no expert witnesses. In contrast, in more recent cases, legal counsel for village communities has often used sophisticated expert evidence. In *Shell v. Tiebo VII*[556], nine witnesses testified for the plaintiffs. They included a licensed surveyor. The plaintiffs' success in *Shell v. Farah*[557] was to a large extent possible because the community provided credible and sophisticated evidence of damage. The plaintiffs were assisted by a joint team of scientists from the University of Port Harcourt. When the lower court was faced with conflicting evidence from the plaintiffs and the defendant, the plaintiffs' lawyer moved the court to appoint two referees to investigate the disputed facts. The lawyer's pro-active stance was rewarded as the referees' subsequent report largely supported the plaintiffs' evidence.

It is not entirely clear to what extent the legal innovations in the 1990s have been induced or aided by the sophisticated and innovative use of legal rules by legal counsel. But there are examples which indicate that the judge's views on the legal issues involved in a case and expressed in a court judgment reflect arguments in the lawyer's brief. In *Shell v. Farah*[558], the court judgment reflected the legal reasoning of the legal counsel for the plaintiffs, L.E. Nwosu, on a number of points. For instance, the court accepted Nwosu's reasoning that the Public Lands Acquisition (Miscellaneous Provisions) Act was irrelevant in the assessment of compensation in the Farah case.

Court judgments cannot fully reveal the extent to which courts follow arguments presented by legal counsel. But the increased professional ability of legal counsel may reflect a process of social learning among village communities and their legal counsel. This process could be partly explained by the increased reliance of village community lawyers on contingency fees (see chapter 4). A lawyer hired on a contingency fee does not receive any payment if he or she loses a case. It could be thus argued that contingency fees provide an economic incentive for a lawyer to be more innovative and pro-active in court proceedings in order to increase the chances of success in a case.

6.15. Impact of Changing Social Attitudes on Judges

While legal change has been affected by the attitudes of judges and the ability of legal counsel, it may also have been influenced by changing social attitudes. Said Belgore, C.J.:

---

[555] (1974) 2 RSLR 93.

[556] (1996) 4 NWLR (Pt. 445) 657.

[557] (1995) 3 NWLR (Pt. 382) 148.

[558] (1995) 3 NWLR (Pt. 382) 148.

Judges of today have seen a lot more development than twenty years ago. They are more aware now of oil industry problems than thirty years ago... As one American jurist said, the current affair doesn't pass by the judges. The judge cannot be isolated from what is currently going on in society in line with a particular subject.[559]

Court judgments cannot portray the mode by which changing social attitudes have influenced the judges. But evidence from court cases indicates that judges have become more critical of the behaviour of oil companies and their legal counsel which may reflect the increasingly critical attitudes towards oil operations in Nigeria in recent years.

In *Shell v. Uzoaru*[560], oil company lawyers argued that the plaintiffs' claim was statute barred. Relying on the previous precedent in *Nwadiaro v. Shell*[561] mentioned earlier, the Court of Appeal found that the statute of limitation was not applicable because the oil company had previously admitted liability. The judges hence considered Shell's claim unwarranted and criticised the behaviour of Shell's legal counsel. Said Onalaja, J.C.A.:

I put it succinctly, that abuse of judicial process is misuse of judicial procedure intentionally to feather one's interest to the detriment of one's adversary, no court shall support or permit the abuse of its process. With the decision in Nwadiaro v. Shell the further pursuit of this appeal is vexatious knowing fully well following the rule of judicial precedent that the Court of Appeal is bound by its previous decision as the issues decided therein are the same, the present appellant is estopped by record from pursuing this appeal which is frivolous and [sic] abuse of process of this court.[562]

In other words, the judge suggested that the oil company used a standard legal strategy to 'intentionally feather' its interest to the detriment of those affected by oil operations. Onalaja's statement may reflect the increasingly more critical attitudes of the judiciary towards the oil industry.

One of the indicators of the judges' changing attitude towards the oil companies and village communities is the amount of compensation awarded to those affected by oil operations. Said Belgore, C.J.:

While the law is there, the human element counts in the judge's discretion. If there is compensation and maybe the plaintiffs claim 5 million Naira, you cannot award 5 million but, at the same time, you cannot award 500 Naira. You go in-between and that's where the discretion and the sympathy of the judge comes in.[563]

---

[559] Personal interview with M.B. Belgore, Chief Justice of the Federal High Court (Lagos, March 1998).

[560] (1994) 9 NWLR (Pt. 366) 51.

[561] (1990) 5 NWLR (Pt. 150) 322.

[562] Per Onalaja, J.C.A. at page 73.

[563] Personal interview with M.B. Belgore, Chief Justice of the Federal High Court (Lagos, March 1998).

As previously shown, courts have recently come to award higher compensation payments to village communities. By implication, the increased compensation awards are likely to reflect the increased use of discretion by Nigerian courts to the benefit of village communities.

In conclusion, there appear to be multiple reasons why legal change has occurred. We have identified three parallel developments, which may explain more favourable judgments in favour of those affected by oil operations: a different approach to law by judicial officers, the increased professional ability of legal counsel working for village communities, and the influence of changing social attitudes on judges. Of these three developments, changing social attitudes is probably the key one. As Kermit Hall (1989, 245-246) noted, the business of the courts mirrors the economic and social changes brought by economic development, while judges play a part in allocating the costs, risks and benefits of this development. Even if the judges' approach to law changes and the skill of legal counsel improves, a judge will not use his or her discretion in favour of one party unless he or she is convinced of the merits of a particular allocation. In that sense, legal change in oil-related litigation has to be ultimately rooted in social attitudes towards the allocation of the social costs and benefits arising from oil operations in Nigerian society. No longer does the judiciary view itself as merely a part of the economic and political elite but it shows a greater concern with justice.[564] This concern could be attributed to a number of factors including public pressures and the existence of a new generation of judges.

6.16. Conclusion

This chapter has provided an in-depth analysis of the nature of the legal disputes between oil companies and village communities. To this end, we have utilised the evidence from a number of Nigerian court cases. We have focused on substantive rules applied in those disputes and on legal changes.

We set out by investigating why many disputes cannot be resolved through informal negotiations and mediation and may thus result in litigation and violence. This discussion has served as a window to an understanding of non-legal forms of disputes which in turn can help to understand the dynamics underlying legal disputes.

We have employed a number of court cases to illustrate how the legal remedies of tort law have been used by village communities in their suits against oil companies. We have focused on three types of remedies from tort law: negligence, nuisance and strict liability. Evidence from litigation indicated that the success of claimants was often limited because oil companies were able to use a number of substantive and procedural rules as effective legal defences in oil-related litigation. There were some indications that the principles of the Common Law worked in favour of oil

---

[564] In *Irou v. Shell-BP* Unreported Suit No. W/89/71, Warri HC mentioned earlier, the judge ruled that nothing should be done to disturb the operations of the oil industry which '*is the main source of this country's revenue*'. Such pronouncements in support of the oil industry cannot be found in more recent judgments.

companies.[565] For instance, in *Shell v. Enoch*[566] mentioned earlier, the plaintiffs had a valid legal claim to compensation for damage from oil operations but Shell's legal counsel was able to successfully invoke the defence of misjoinder of parties and causes of action. The Enoch case illustrated that legal defences provided by Common Law such as misjoinder may act to reduce the ability of Nigerian village communities to assert their legal rights in compensation claims arising from oil operations.

Our analysis was partly motivated by the perception of a paucity of studies on judicial law-making in Africa. This problem is particularly significant in the context of legal disputes between multinational companies and the local people in developing countries. These disputes have increased in quantity over the past few decades, in part as a result of legal changes in favour of the local people. Legal studies have too often overlooked this dynamic process. In respect of oil-related litigation in Nigeria, previous scholars who have discussed court cases have generally confined their analyses to a description of substantive law but have failed to discuss the dynamic aspects of litigation. For instance, Adewale (1987, 1989, 1995), who wrote a number of academic papers dealing with oil-related cases in Nigeria, has failed to investigate legal change. This failure has led scholars to believe that the principles of tort law cannot offer a remedy to those affected by oil operations. As recently as 1997, Okonmah (1997) wrote in the *Journal of African Law* that '*victims of oil pollution... are left to the vagaries of the common law regime based largely on the torts of trespass to land, nuisance, negligence and the rule in Rylands and Fletcher'*. Emphasising the problems of burden of proof with respect to causation, Okonmah (1997) concluded: '*Where he* [a claimant] *succeeds in discharging this burden, the amount of damages awarded by the courts is inadequate to assuage his losses'*. This analysis failed to take any account of important court judgments such as *Shell v. Farah*[567] or *Elf v. Sillo*[568] which were published in the *Nigerian Weekly Law Reports* several years before the publication of Okonmah's article. The studies by Adewale and Okonmah exemplify that the dynamic aspects of litigation have been ignored by Nigerian scholars which has left a gap in the literature on legal change in oil-related litigation. We have attempted to fill this gap by examining 68 Nigerian court cases. In this context, we were able to show that legal change plays an important role in oil-related litigation in Nigeria.

The evidence presented in this chapter suggested that there has been a trend towards the adoption of substantive and procedural rules which render it easier for village communities to successfully litigate against oil companies in Nigeria. The liberalisation of *locus standi* and evidence rules and a broader interpretation of the quantum of compensation have all helped village communities to win recent court cases against oil companies. Important precedents have been set in *Adediran v. Interland Transport*[569] and *Elf v. Sillo*[570]. Above all, the precedent in *Shell v. Farah*[571]

---

[565] A number of general, theoretical problems involved in introducing European legal concepts to Africa have been discussed in Nunn (1995).

[566] (1992) 8 NWLR (Pt. 259) 335.

[567] (1995) 3 NWLR (Pt. 382) 148.

[568] (1994) 6 NWLR (Pt. 350) 258.

[569] (1991) 9 NWLR (Pt. 214) 155.

has assisted with higher compensation awards for communities. It is perhaps too early to foresee the full impact of legal change on legal disputes between oil companies and village communities since legal transformation is a slow process. But legal change appears to have already resulted in tangible material benefits to community litigants. In a number of recent high profile cases, including *Shell v. Tiebo VII*[572] and *Shell v. Isaiah*[573], village communities won substantial amounts of compensation for damage from oil operations. The increased possibility of higher compensation awards may partly account for the increased quantity of litigation against oil companies.

We speculated that legal change could be explained by three parallel developments: a different approach to law by judicial officers, the increased professional ability of legal counsel working for village communities, and the impact of changing social attitudes on judges. We suggested that the key factor in legal change in oil-related litigation was probably the changing social attitudes towards the allocation of the social costs and benefits arising from oil operations in Nigerian society.

While there are indications that legal change may have benefited village communities, it has to be remembered that most plaintiffs face significant barriers in accessing courts and that legal practitioners tend to regard courts as biased in favour of oil companies (see chapter 4) and that there are indications of a bias in Nigeria's statute law in favour of oil companies (see chapter 3). The scope for law-making by Nigerian judges is also limited because they have to apply English Common Law, which ties judicial decisions to the pattern of development in the British Commonwealth. By relying on foreign legal precedents, Nigerian courts may sometimes be prevented from fully addressing specific local issues. English legal traditions, including strict standards of scientific evidence or statutes of limitation, decrease the chances of success for potential litigants in oil-related cases. Even if a plaintiff is able to win a lawsuit, litigation can only address the damage suffered by a specific individual, family or village community but not the impact of oil operations on the oil producing areas as a whole. Since courts are reluctant to make use of injunctions against oil companies, they are unlikely to be able to compel companies to reduce the damage from oil operations on the ground.

These basic limitations could help to explain why legal change in favour of village communities has so far failed to reduce the quantity of violent forms of protest against oil companies. Indeed, the ambiguous nature and the uncertainty of legal outcomes could partly help to explain why a significant number of frustrated litigants and potential litigants in oil-related disputes may resort to violence. In that sense, legal change could be said to have not gone far enough to discourage extra legal forms of protest such as the kidnapping of oil company staff. In its modest way, our analysis has contributed to an understanding of one of the elements of disputes between oil companies and village communities in Nigeria.

---

[570] (1994) 6 NWLR (Pt. 350) 258.

[571] (1995) 3 NWLR (Pt. 382) 148.

[572] (1996) 4 NWLR (Pt. 445) 657.

[573] (1997) 6 NWLR (Pt. 508) 236.

Chapter 7: Conclusion

7.1. Findings of the Book

This study has analysed conflict and litigation between village communities and oil companies in Nigeria by using legal materials. It is perhaps evident that an investigation of legal materials cannot address all correlates of disputes such as socio-economic and political factors including the marginalisation of ethnic minorities in the oil producing areas. We have thus looked at the political and legal context of oil operations with the aim of providing the background for the discussion of legal materials. This investigation has confirmed our initial expectation that an adequate investigation of litigation cannot be undertaken without reference to the social context.

In chapter 2 we have traced the making of Nigeria's oil industry. A discussion of secondary sources was not exhaustive but selective. It suggested that the rise in social unrest and litigation may be partly attributed to the unequal allocation of social costs and benefits arising from oil operations within Nigerian society which cannot be derived from an analysis of court cases. This discussion has indicated that the relationship between oil companies and village communities is an unequal one, in which oil companies can muster greater political support and economic muscle. By implication, it could be expected that the Nigerian state would be reluctant to support litigation against foreign oil companies since litigation could disrupt the flow of oil revenue to the government and private middlemen.

This speculative finding on the bias of the state in favour of oil companies found support in the analysis of the formal legal system. Chapter 3, which has discussed statute law and the structural character of the legal system, has provided a number of indications that the formal legal framework in Nigeria tends to be predisposed in favour of oil companies at the expense of village communities. The formal-institutional structure of the Nigerian legal system is well developed and sophisticated. But oil-related statute law appears to offer little protection for village communities in the oil producing areas. In this context, it could be argued that an alliance of the political elite and private interests in Nigeria obstructs the development of legal remedies for the adverse effects from oil operations. The inadequate legislative provisions and lack of legal enforcement may thus lead to social unrest and litigation against the oil industry.

The analysis of the survey of legal practitioners in chapter 4 examined the constraints and opportunities that are faced by litigants in oil-related cases. Our findings suggested that the Nigerian legal system as a whole, not merely statute law, government policy or superior resources of oil companies, favours the interests of oil companies. Being a developing country, Nigeria faces many inadequacies in the day-to-day operations of the legal system. But, in the views of legal practitioners, litigants who sue oil companies face greater constraints than other litigants. A significant part of the data indicated that the problems of access to courts are greater in oil-related litigation. In this context, the lack of funds and ignorance were rated as the main problems of access to courts in oil-related cases. There were indications that intimidation by the government as well as oil companies is a more important barrier to justice for village communities suing oil companies than it is for other potential litigants. This supports the view that the Nigerian regime is predisposed in favour of oil companies. Survey analysis also indicated that the judiciary and the legal process tended to be biased in favour of oil companies rather than the opposing litigants and that judges encounter greater outside pressures in oil-related litigation. This bias manifests itself, for instance, in the inadequate payment of compensation for damage from oil operations awarded by Nigerian courts.

The existence of these biases was not surprising given the speculative finding of the contextual chapters that the Nigerian state tended to favour oil companies. The constraints faced by individual and community litigants can help to explain why village communities may abandon litigation in favour of extra-legal, sometimes violent, forms of protest.

The persistence of conflicts between oil companies and village communities can be partly explained by the adverse effects caused by oil operations on the ground. Chapter 5 analysed the nature of those adverse effects by focusing on the impact of oil exploration and production on village communities and land disputes. We have found evidence that the traditional operating practices of the oil companies combined with their unwillingness to commit funds towards environmental protection have prompted disputes between oil companies and village communities. It is clear that only some of these disputes have resulted in litigation. From an economic perspective, it is somewhat surprising that oil companies have continued to cause damage which could have easily been avoided with small expenditure on their part. Our analysis in Nigeria suggests that many economic activities of the oil industry cannot be adequately understood without reference to cultural attitudes which may prevent otherwise rational economic choices.

Considering the importance of adverse effects from oil operations and the bias of the legal system, one could expect that the existing court cases between village communities and oil companies are only a small fraction of the potential litigation, which could arise as a result of valid legal claims to compensation for damage from oil operations. In other words, if the Nigerian legal system were less predisposed in favour of oil companies, then the quantity of litigation against oil companies would be greater. The suppression of litigation against oil companies has important consequences for conflicts in the oil producing areas. Difficulties in obtaining legal recourse may have contributed directly and indirectly to informal forms of conflict such as seizure of oil industry equipment or the kidnapping of oil company staff. These activities are undesirable from the point of view of oil companies. But it could be expected that they are also partly caused by the companies' use of their superior resources to frustrate the legal claims of village communities. The resulting paradox is that the companies' ability to stifle one form of protest may lead to different, perhaps more troublesome, forms of protest.

On the surface, it may seem surprising that, despite severe barriers to justice and despite the bias of the legal system in favour of oil companies, the frequency of litigation between oil companies and village communities has substantially increased in the 1990s. This seeming paradox could be attributed to a number of factors including state fragmentation on the micro-level, public pressures by interest groups and the dynamic character of Nigeria's legal system. For instance, several respondents indicated that a number of judges have become more sympathetic to the claims of village communities than judges of the past.

Nonetheless, the bias of the legal system and the rentier nature of the Nigerian state remain important obstacles in terms of access to courts for those affected by oil operations. We have, therefore, concluded that there may be other reasons why oil-related litigation has increased in the 1990s. It was expected that a shift in judicial pronouncements in favour of village communities played a role in encouraging a greater quantity of litigation against oil companies.

Chapter 6, which provided a detailed analysis of litigation between oil companies and village communities, largely confirmed the initial expectation that legal innovations in oil-related cases have benefited village communities. The success of litigants in oil-related cases was limited because oil companies were able to use a number of substantive and procedural rules as effective legal defences. But there has been a trend towards the adoption of rules which render it easier for village communities to litigate against oil companies. Above all, village communities have recently been awarded higher compensation payments for damage from oil operations following the ruling in *Shell v. Farah*[574]. We speculated that the key factor in legal change in oil-related litigation was probably the judges' changing social attitudes towards the allocation of the social costs and benefits arising from oil operations in Nigerian society. This would support our initial assumption that court judgments reflect the economic and social changes in society. Following the same logic, the higher compensation payments to village communities reflect society's greater preoccupation with the plight of the village communities in the oil producing areas. The increased possibility of higher compensation payments may partly explain the rise in oil-related litigation in the 1990s. In this context, this book not only portrays the legal disputes between village communities and oil companies but also the legal dynamics underlying those disputes.

7.2. Relevance of the Book

It may be held that a study of legal disputes in the Nigerian oil industry is an irrelevant and futile exercise, given the assumption that there is no rule of law in Nigeria and that the judiciary is little more than an extended arm of the executive branch of the federal government. The evidence presented in this book, however, demonstrated such a judgment to be superficial and a mistaken one which fails to take full account of the complex nature of the judicial process in Nigeria, dynamic processes of legal change and the possibility of using court cases as factual evidence. While our findings differ from some of the conventional analyses in the literature, they have not necessarily been unexpected. In this sense, the originality of this book does not stem so much from

---

[574] (1995) 3 NWLR (Pt. 382) 148.

unanticipated new insights on the nature of multinational business or legal systems in developing countries but rather from its socio-legal approach and from its treatment of a hitherto neglected subject.

Above all, our analysis has been guided by the perception of a lack of a socio-legal study on the legal disputes between oil companies and village communities in Nigeria and the role of the legal system as mediator and adjudicator. In chapter 5, we have been able to identify a number of the sources of those disputes, particularly in terms of the impact of oil operations on the ground. Chapters 4 and 6 have provided an analysis of the legal system in the light of oil-related litigation. The discussion of legal transformation in oil-related litigation has contributed to an understanding of a subject which has largely been ignored in academic publications. With regards to the academic writings on the Nigerian oil industry in general, our analysis has filled a gap in the literature. It may serve as a starting point for further future research on conflicts between oil companies and village communities in Nigeria.

Our socio-legal analysis, particularly in chapter 4, was also motivated by the perception of a paucity of studies on African legal systems in terms of the day-to-day operations of the legal system. This problem is particularly significant in the context of legal disputes between multinational companies and the local people in developing countries. Legal studies on Africa have hitherto largely ignored the socio-legal context of law such as the problems of access to courts for potential litigants or the actual enforcement of statutes on the ground. They have largely confined their analyses to the formal legal process and/or the analysis of sources of law. Our survey has sought to shed light on the legal processes associated with the interaction between village communities and oil multinationals. The methodology adopted in the survey has allowed us to quantify the hierarchy of access problems as perceived by Nigerian legal practitioners and to quantitatively assess the extent of the practical impediments in the day-to-day operations of the legal system. We believe that only an interdisciplinary framework such as the one devised for this study can fully account for the legal disputes between the companies and the local people, which is not offered by either a purely socio-economic or a purely legal study.

One of the goals of the book was to make a contribution to the research and the debate on the role of multinational companies in developing countries in the field of litigation. While numerous studies have addressed the role of multinational companies, there is still ample need to analyse the interactions between those affected by business operations and the companies, particularly in the field of litigation. In contrast to the field study method and macro-analytical studies, we have utilised court cases to portray conflicts between oil companies and village communities and the legal dynamic underlying those conflicts. We have used court cases as factual evidence and as legal material which has allowed a more in-depth analysis than conventional legal studies which limit their analysis of litigation to a discussion of substantive and procedural rules. In addition to the investigation of substantive and procedural rules, our socio-legal analysis of litigation has served as a window to an understanding of the sources of disputes and non-legal forms of disputes.

7.3. Directions for Future Research

As we have noted at the outset of this project, legal materials are not the only source of information on conflicts between oil companies and village communities. In this context, it may be instructive to consider the merits of potential alternative avenues for future research. Our discussion of legal materials could be complemented by alternative methodological approaches.

One of those alternative approaches would be a comprehensive sociological and social-anthropological field study of village communities in the oil producing areas. Such a study could investigate in greater detail the effects of oil operations on village communities on the ground such as the migration of oil workers and the resulting shifts in cultural attitudes. More importantly, a field study could examine the motivations of villagers when engaging in conflicts with oil companies. Issues discussed could include the villagers' perception of economic inequality in Nigerian society and their lack of political opportunities. In the context of oil-related litigation, a field study could highlight barriers to justice as perceived by community members. In general, it could analyse extra legal forms of dispute resolution including informal negotiations and settlements. A study of this nature would potentially allow for the development of a comprehensive model of social protest in village communities which would take into account all correlates of conflicts between companies and communities.

Another alternative approach would be to analyse the internal workings of business organisations with a view to an understanding of the motivations of company staff when choosing a specific strategy to deal with conflicts. In particular, such a study could investigate the cultural attitudes of oil company staff towards village communities in the oil producing areas. Subsidiaries of multinational companies could be assumed to develop specific corporate cultures influenced by both the local cultures of the country in which they operate and by the cultural values transmitted from the corporate headquarters. Unfortunately, there appears to have been no prior academic research on the dynamics of cultural change in Nigeria's oil companies.

In terms of legal change, an alternative approach would be to survey Nigerian judges. Such a survey could investigate the motivations of judges when adjudicating legal disputes. A study of this nature could potentially establish to what extent judicial decisions are influenced by the transformations in the wider society. Moreover, it could potentially explore the nature and scope of legal change as perceived by judicial officers.

In terms of public policy implications, there is a lack of prior academic research on institutional - state and company - responses to local conflicts. A cost-benefit analysis of different institutional responses could explore the alternative strategies pursued by oil companies in dealing with local conflicts and the financial costs attached to each of those strategies. Such a study, moreover, could investigate the implications of changes in the forms of protest adopted by village communities vis-à-vis oil companies. For instance, one could explore the implications for oil companies of a shift from one form of protest (e.g. litigation) towards another form of protest (e.g. vandalism).

While many benefits could be gained from the aforementioned methodological approaches, particularly from the anthropological and sociological perspective, there are problems with these methodologies. Interviews and written sources may be biased or ill-informed and, in any case, reflect personal perceptions of the issues. Data on the oil industry is generally thought to be particularly vulnerable to manipulation for a number of reasons (Stevens 1995). Data gained from field studies can be very subjective as the number of objects of study may be highly limited, unless a standardised survey is used, a strategy which is likely to be difficult in a village setting in Nigeria. For practical reasons, it may be difficult to find a sufficient number of respondents for conducting a survey amongst judges because there are fewer judicial officers than legal practitioners and access to them is likely to be limited for an outside researcher. In comparison with the above methodologies, the methodology adopted in this study hence has the advantage of providing a consistent framework of analysis and a wealth of relatively reliable legal materials.

Beyond our immediate concern with conflicts arising from oil operations in Nigeria, our analysis suggests a number of avenues for future research on conflicts between business organisations and the local people in developing countries.

Our research highlights the importance of further study of litigation and of legal change in relation to disputes between companies and the local people in developing countries. With the rise in litigation against multinational companies in those countries, scholars can no longer neglect the study of the dynamics of legal systems in relation to multinational investment. Recognising the capacity of the Nigerian judiciary to act autonomously from the executive arm of the government would weaken the temptation of scholars in the African Studies field to dismiss legal systems as unworthy of study. We hope that this book has served to undermine the mechanistic view that the judiciary in Africa, as an integral part of the state structures, lacks a dynamic of its own. Relinquishing this conceptualisation of the judiciary will not only allow scholars to make greater use of litigation in the analysis of social conflicts but also to re-discover the study of legal systems and their underlying dynamics.

Future research on the disputes between the local people affected by business operations and firms in developing countries could make greater use of litigation as an alternative to the study of open conflict. While this study has not attempted to explicitly formulate a methodological tool of analysis, we feel that a study of litigation should combine an investigation of the social context, a discussion of the day-to-day operations of the legal system and a detailed analysis of litigation, both in terms of factual evidence and legal principles. We believe that such a interdisciplinary mixture can provide explanations which are both causally and meaningfully adequate in the Weberian sense. With the rise in litigation between multinational companies and indigenous populations the need for a rigorous methodology to analyse these legal disputes is perhaps evident. Hence, the ultimate contribution of this book could be to lay the foundations for the study of a hitherto neglected subject.

7.4. Future of Niger Delta Conflicts

Any discussion of conflicts in the Niger Delta has a significance beyond academic interest. When the Obasanjo administration took office in May 1999, conflicts between oil companies and village communities looked set to continue unabated. As stated at the outset of this study, solving the 'Niger Delta question' is one of the key challenges facing General Obasanjo. The task is undoubtedly very complex and there is the threat that the cycle of violence in the Niger Delta cannot be broken. If judged by past experience, it is unlikely that a mere increase in the financial contributions to the oil producing areas will wipe out discontent. Given the demands of the anti-oil protesters, any policy measures will have to include greater financial control over oil resources for the local people, a significant reduction of the adverse impact of oil operations and a meaningful development programme for the oil producing areas. Furthermore, the new civilian administration of Olusegun Obasanjo will have to engage in a meaningful dialogue with all of the major ethnic and interest groups in the Niger Delta including the more radical IYC, MOSOP and ERA.

The willingness of the federal government to commit greater financial resources to the oil producing areas provides enormous development opportunities for the people in the Niger Delta. Roads and hospitals could be built, job opportunities could be created and environmental standards in the oil industry could be raised, as demanded by the local people. But important question marks remain. Above all, who should be responsible for distributing the oil revenue in the oil producing areas? The choice includes state governments, local government councils, oil companies, special government agencies such as the OMPADEC, councils of chiefs and elders, non-governmental organizations or ethnic groups such as the Ijaw Youth Council (IYC) and the Ijaw National Congress (INC). How can the effectiveness of the OMPADEC and the newly planned Niger Delta development agency be increased? Or, perhaps, should the OMPADEC be abolished all together?

Our study suggests that the government will have to address the question of bias in the Nigerian legal system in favour of the oil industry. By reducing the bias, the local people could perhaps in future be persuaded to opt for negotiations, mediation or litigation with oil companies rather than violence. This could be accomplished, amongst others, by abolishing the Land Use Act 1978 which deprives village communities of adequate compensation, by establishing an independent agency for mediating compensation claims and by raising the official rates of compensation for damage from oil operations.

While the prime responsibility for ending the Niger Delta conflicts lies with the federal government, any solutions must involve the oil companies in Nigeria. As previously shown, oil companies have contributed significantly towards discontent in the oil producing areas (see, especially, chapters 2 and 5). Oil companies could contribute towards resolving conflicts in several ways: by reducing the adverse impact of oil operations, by ending their over-reliance on security co-operation and by executing meaningful development projects in tandem with the local people.

Unless the government and the oil companies change their basic attitude towards the local people in the Niger Delta, conflict and litigation are there to stay.

Bibliography

Secondary Sources

Adaramola, Funso. 1992. *Basic Jurisprudence*. Lagos: Shabar International Enterprises.

Adepetun, Adesola. 1996. "Nigeria's Oil and Gas Potential," Paper presented at the Africa-Upstream '96 Conference, Cape Town, 18-20 September.

----------, and Kemi Segun. 1999. "Nigeria: Oil & Gas Sector - 1999 Budget," *Oil and Gas Law and Taxation Review* 3: N21-N24.

Adewale, Ombolaji. 1987. "Rylands v. Fletcher and the Nigerian Petroleum Industry," *Journal of Private and Property Law* (8/9): 37-56.

----------. 1989. "Oil Spill Compensation Claims in Nigeria: Principles, Guidelines and Criteria," *Journal of African Law*, 33 (1): 91-104.

----------. 1990. "Sabotage in the Nigerian Petroleum Industry: Some Socio-Legal Perspectives," Lagos: Nigerian Institute of Advanced Legal Studies.

----------. 1992. "The Federal Environmental Protection Agency Decree and the Petroleum Industry," *Journal of Private & Property Law* 16, 17 & 18: 51-64 (combined edition for 1992 and 1993).

----------. 1995. "Some Legal Aspects of Community Relations in the Petroleum Industry," in Kayode Soremekun (ed.), *Perspectives on the Nigerian Oil Industry*, Lagos: Amkra Books.

Adigun, Isaac O. and Geoffrey M. Stephenson. 1992. "Sources of Job Motivation and Satisfaction Among British and Nigerian employees," *Journal of Social Psychology* 132 (June): 369-377.

Ajai, Olawale. 1996. "Law, Judiciary and the Environment in Nigeria," in I. A. Umezulike and C. C. Nweze (eds.) *Perspectives in Law and Justice*, Enugu: Fourth Dimension.

Ajomo, M.A. 1976. "The 1969 Petroleum Decree: a Consolidating Legislation, Revolution in Nigeria's Oil Industry," *Nigerian Annual of International Law* 1: 57-78.

----------. 1982. "Ownership of Mineral Oils and the Land Use Act," *Nigerian Current Law Review*: 330-340.

Akande, Jadesola O. 1982. *The Constitution of the Federal Republic of Nigeria 1979*. London: Sweet and Maxwell.

Akpan, George S. 1997. "Nigeria's LNG Programme: Problems and Prospects," *Oil and Gas Law and Taxation Review* 7: 264-271.

Alli, Olayinka R. 1997. "Joint Venture Investments and MOU Incentives: An Appraisal," in Victor E. Eromosele (ed.) *Nigerian Petroleum Business - A Handbook*, Lagos: Advent Communications.

Allott, Antony N. 1960. *Essays in African Law*. London: Butterworths.

----------. 1965. "The Future of African Law," in Hilda Kuper and Leo Kuper (eds.) *African Law: Adaptation and Development*, Berkeley: University of California Press.

----------, A. L. Epstein and Max Gluckman. 1969. "Introduction," in Max Gluckman (ed.) *Ideas and Procedures in African Customary Law*, London: Oxford University Press.

Aluko, Olajide. 1990. "The Nationalisation of the Assets of British Petroleum," in Gabriel O. Olusanya (ed.), *The Structure and Processes of Foreign Policy Making and Implementation in Nigeria, 1960-1990*, Lagos: Nigerian Institute of International Affairs.

Aluko, Oluwole. 1998. *The Law of Real Property and Procedure*. Ibadan: Spectrum.

Amajor, I.C. 1985. "The Ejamah-Ebubu Oil Spill of 1970: a Case History of a 14 Years Old Spill," in *Petroleum Industry and the Nigerian Environment*, Lagos: NNPC/Federal Ministry of Works and Housing.

Areola, Olusegun. 1987. "The political reality of conservation in Nigeria," in David Anderson and Richard Grove (eds.) *Conservation in Africa: People, Policies and Practice*, Cambridge: Cambridge University Press.

Arthur Andersen. 1997. "1996 Nigeria Oil and Gas Industry Outlook Survey Results," (February). Lagos.

Ashton-Jones, Nick. 1998. *ERA Handbook to the Niger Delta*. London: Environmental Rights Action.

Atsegbua, Lawrence Asekome. 1993. *Nigerian Petroleum Law - The Acquisition of Oil Rights in Nigeria*, Benin City: Renstine.

----------. 1997. "The Assignment and Revocation of Oil Licences and Leases in Nigeria," *Oil and Gas Law and Taxation Review* 15(9): 346-348.

Avuru, Austin. 1997. "Indigenous Participation Upstream: The Challenges and Prospects," in Victor E. Eromosele (ed.) *Nigerian Petroleum Business - A Handbook*, Lagos: Advent Communications.

Baker, C.D. 1991. *Tort*. 5th ed. London: Sweet & Maxwell.

Barrows Company. 1995. *World Petroleum Arrangements, Volume II*. New York: Barrows Company.

Bell-Gam, Winston I. 1990. *Development of Coastal and Estuarine Settlements in the Niger Delta: the Case of the Bonny Local Government Area*. Berne: Peter Lang Publishing.

Biersteker, Thomas. 1987. *Multinationals, the State, and Control of the Nigerian Economy*. Princeton, New Jersey: Princeton University Press.

Birnbaum, Michael. 1995. "Nigeria: Fundamental Rights Denies - Report of the Trial of Ken Saro-Wiwa and Others," London: Article 19, the International Centre Against Censorship (June).

Chanock, Martin. 1985. *Law, Custom and Social Order: the Colonial Experience in Malawi and Zambia*. Cambridge: Cambridge University Press.

Chazan, Naomi, Robert Mortimer, John Ravenhill and Donald Rothchild. 1988. *Politics and Society in Contemporary Africa*. London: Macmillan.

CLO/Civil Liberties Organisation. 1995. *Annual Report 1994*. Lagos: CLO.

Collett, Adrian. 1980. "Legal Care in Nigeria: Beginnings," *Journal of African Law* 24 (8): 220-242.

Collins, Paul. 1983. "The State and Industrial Capitalism in West Africa," *Development and Change* 14 (3): 403-429.

Control Risks Group. 1997. *Outlook 97: the World in 1997*. London: Control Risks Group (January).

Daniels, W.C. Ekow. 1964. *The Common Law in West Africa*. London: Butterworths.

Danler, Doris, and Markus Brunner. 1996. "Shell in Nigeria," Köln: Brot für die Welt (August).

Danquah, J.B. 1928. *Akan Laws and Customs and the Akim Abuakwa Constitution*. London: Routledge.

Degni-Segui, Rene. 1995. "L'acces a la justice et ses obstacles," *Verfassung und Recht in Übersee* 28(4): 449-467.

van Dessel, J.P. 1995. "Internal Position Paper: The Environmental Situation in the Niger Delta," (February).

Dike, K.O. 1956. *Trade and Politics in the Niger Delta, 1830-1855*. Oxford: Oxford University Press.

Douglas, Oronto Natei. 1997. "Environmental Protection Law and Practice in the Niger Delta of Nigeria - An Overview," M.A. thesis at the School of Law, De Montfort University, Leicester.

Eggen, Jean Macchiaroli. 1995. *Toxic Torts in a Nutshell*. St Paul, Minn.: West Publishing.

Ekemike, Chief E. 1978. *Understanding the Nigerian Land Use Decree: Its Uses and Abuses*. Benin City: Kems.

Elias, T.O. 1962. *Ghana and Sierra Leone – the Development of their Laws and Constitutions*. London: Stevens.

----------. 1971. *Nigerian Land Law*. 4th ed. London: Sweet & Maxwell.

----------. 1989. "Fundamentals of Nigerian Law," in M.A. Ajomo (ed.) *Fundamentals of Nigerian Law*, Lagos: Nigerian Institute of Advanced Legal Studies.

Emembolu, G. 1975. "Petroleum and the Development of a Dual Economy: The Nigerian Example," Ph.D. thesis at the University of Colorado.

ERA (Environmental Rights Action). 1995. "Shell in Iko," Benin City: ERA.

----------. 1997. "Shell in Nigeria: Public Relations and Broken Promises," a report, St Andrews: ERA (March).

Eromosele, Victor E. 1997. "Accounting in the Oil and Gas Industry: The Challenges," in Victor E. Eromosele (ed.) *Nigerian Petroleum Business - A Handbook*, Lagos: Advent Communications.

Etikerentse, G. 1985. *Nigerian Petroleum Law*. London: Macmillan.

Eze, Osita C. 1996. "The Rule of Law and the Bench," in I. A. Umezulike and C. C. Nweze (eds.) *Perspectives in Law and Justice*, Enugu: Fourth Dimension.

Fabig, Heike. 1998. "Identity and Social Movements - The Ogoni Struggle for Environmental and Social Justice," Unpublished paper, University of Sussex, Brighton.

Fawehinmi, Gani. 1992. *Courts' System in Nigeria - A Guide*. Lagos: Nigerian Law Publications.

FEPA (Federal Environmental Protection Agency). 1991. *Guidelines and Standards for Environmental Pollution Control in Nigeria*, Abuja: Federal Government of Nigeria.

Forrest, Tom. 1977. "Notes on the Political Economy of State Intervention in Nigeria," *IDS Bulletin* 9 (1): 42-47.

----------. 1992. "The Advance of African Capital: The Growth of Nigerian Private Enterprises," in F. Stewart, S. Lall and S.M. Wangwe (eds.) *Alternative Development Strategies in Sub-Saharan Africa*, London: Macmillan.

----------. 1993. *Politics and Economic Development in Nigeria*. Oxford: Oxford University Press.

Forsyth, Frederick. 1969. *The Biafra Story*. Harmondsworth: Penguin.

Frynas, J.G. 1998. "Political Instability and Business: Focus on Shell in Nigeria," *Third World Quarterly* 19(3): 457-478.

----------. 1999. "Litigation in the Nigerian Oil Industry: a Socio-legal Analysis of the Legal Disputes between Oil Companies and Village Communities," Ph.D. Thesis at the Department of Economics, University of St Andrews.

----------, and Matthias P. Beck. 1998. "Corporate Hegemony and Colonial Heritage: the First Mover Advantage of Shell-BP in Nigeria," Paper presented at the Annual Conference of the African Studies Association (ASA), Chicago, Illinois, 29 October - 1 November.

Galeski, Boguslaw. 1972. *Basic Concepts of Rural Sociology*. Manchester: Manchester University Press.

Galtung, Johan. 1971. "Structural Theory of Imperialism," *Journal of Peace Research* 8(2): 81-117.

Ghai, Yash, Robin Luckham and Francis Snyder. 1987. *The Political Economy of Law*. Delhi: Oxford University Press.

Gibbs, David N. 1995. "Political Parties and International Relations: The United States and the Decolonization of Sub-Saharan Africa," *International History Review* 17(2): 306-327.

Giddens, Anthony. 1989. *Sociology*. Cambridge: Polity Press.

Gluckman, Max. 1965. *Custom and Conflict in Africa*. Oxford: Basil Blackwell.

Graf, William D. 1988. *The Nigerian State: Political Economy, State Class and Political System in the Post-Colonial Era*. London: James Currey.

Guobadia, Ameze. 1993. "The Nigerian Federal Environment Protection Agency Decree No.58 of 1988: An Appraisal," *Revue Africaine de Droit International et Compare*, 5 (5): 408-417.

Hall, Kermit L. 1989. *The Magic Mirror: Law in American History*. New York: Oxford University Press.

Hallmark, Terry. 1998. "Political Risks in West Africa: A Comparative Analysis," *Oil and Gas Law and Taxation Review* 11: 399-404.

HRW (Human Rights Watch). 1995. "Nigeria, The Ogoni Crisis: A Case-Study of Military Repression in Southeastern Nigeria," New York: Human Rights Watch.

----------. 1999a. *The Price of Oil - Corporate Responsibility and Human Rights Violations in Nigeria's Oil Producing Communities*, New York: Human Right Watch.

----------. 1999b. "Nigeria: Crackdown in the Niger Delta," New York: Human Right Watch.

Hunt, Alan. 1993. *Explorations in Law and Society*. New York: Routledge.

Hyne, Norman J. 1995. *Nontechnical Guide to Petroleum Geology, Exploration, Drilling and Production*. Tulsa, Oklahoma: PennWell.

Ibidapo-Obe, Akin. 1995. "The Jurisprudence of Social Justice in Nigeria," in Wole Owaboye (ed.), *Fundamental Legal Issues in Nigeria*, Lagos: Nigerian Law Research & Economic Development Projects.

Ibrahim, Jibrin. 1991. "Religion and Political Turbulence in Nigeria," *Journal of Modern African Studies* 29: 115-136.

Ihonvbere, Julius, and Timothy M. Shaw. 1988. *Towards a Political Economy of Nigeria: Petroleum and Politics at the (Semi-) Periphery*. Aldershot: Avebury.

Ikein, Augustine A. 1990. *The Impact of Oil on a Developing Country: The Case of Nigeria*. New York: Praeger.

Ilegbune, Theresa Oby. 1994. "Legal Regulation of Industrial Waste Management," in M.A.Ajomo and Ombolaji Adewale (eds.), *Environmental Law and Sustainable Development in Nigeria*, Lagos: Nigerian Institute of Advanced Legal Studies.

James, R.W. 1973. *Modern Land Law of Nigeria*. Ile-Ife: University of Ife Press.

Jones, Geoffrey Gareth. 1981. *The State and the Emergence of the British Oil Industry*. London: Macmillan.

Khan, Sarah Ahmad. 1994. *Nigeria: The Political Economy of Oil*. Oxford: Oxford University Press.

Kodilinye, Gilbert. 1982. *The Nigerian Law of Torts*. Ibadan: Spectrum.

Land Use Panel. 1977. *Report of the Land Use Panel*. Lagos: Federal Government of Nigeria.

Leis, Philip E. 1972. *Enculturation and Socialization in an Ijaw village*. New York: Holt, Rinehart and Winston.

Lugard, Lord. 1965. *The Dual Mandate in British Tropical Africa*. 5th ed. London: Frank Cass.

Madujibeya, S.A. 1975. "Nigerian Oil: A Review of Nigeria's Petroleum Industry," *Standard and Chartered Review* (May): 2-10.

----------. 1976. "Oil and Nigeria's Economic Development," *African Affairs* 75(300): 284-316.

Mbakwe, R.C. 1987. "Die Entwicklung des Landeigentums in Nigeria unter besonderer Berücksichtigung des Waldes," *Der Tropenlandwirt* 88 (April): 41-51.

Media Watch. 1997. "Shell, Nigeria und die Medien," Köln: Media Watch (July).

Meek, C.K. 1957. *Land Tenure and Land Administration in Nigeria and the Cameroons*. London: Her Majesty's Stationary Office.

Meier, Gerald M. 1975. "External Trade and Internal Development," in Peter Duignan and L.H.Gann (eds.), *Colonialism in Africa 1870-1960*, Cambridge: Cambridge University Press.

Mittler, Daniel. 1996. "The Ogoni Battle," Unpublished paper, University of Edinburgh.

Moffat, David, and Olof Linden. 1995. "Perception and Reality: Assessing Priorities for Sustainable Development in the Niger River Delta," *Ambio*, 24 (7-8): 527-538.

Nader, Laura and Harry F. Todd Jr. 1978. "Introduction," in Laura Nader and Harry F. Todd Jr. (eds.) *The Disputing Process - Law in Ten Societies*, New York: Columbia University Press.

Nanakumo, Ebipamone N. 1999. "Reflections on a New Nigeria," Paper presented at a symposium organised by the Association of the Bar of the City of New York, New York, 8 April.

Nigeria's Oil and Gas Publications. 1996. *Nigeria's Oil and Gas Annual Vol.2, 1995/96*. Lagos: Nigeria's Oil and Gas Publications.

Njeze, Cally C.O. 1978. "Oil Concessions and Land Acquisition in Nigeria," Ph.D. Thesis at the Department of Land Economy, University of Cambridge.

Nmoma, Veronica. 1995. "Ethnic Conflict, Constitutional Engineering and Democracy in Nigeria," in Harvey Glickman (ed.) *Ethnic Conflict and Democratization in Africa*. Atlanta, Georgia: African Studies Association Press.

NNPC (Nigerian National Petroleum Corporation). 1986a. "Annual Statistical Bulletin January-December 1985," Lagos: NNPC (January).

----------. 1986b. "Understanding the Nigerian Oil Industry," Lagos: NNPC.

Nunn, Kenneth B. 1995. "Law as a Eurocentric Enterprise," Paper presented at the Critical Legal Conference entitled 'Contested Communities: Critical Legal Perspectives', University of Edinburgh, 8-10 September.

Nwabueze, B.O. 1992. *Military Rule and Constitutionalism in Nigeria*. Ibadan: Spectrum.

Nwankwo, Clement, Basil Ugochukwu and Dulue Mbachu. 1993. *Nigeria: The Limits of Justice*. Lagos: Constitutional Rights Project.

Nweze, C.C. 1996. "A Survey of the Shifting Trends in Judicial Attitudes to Fundamental Rights in Nigeria," in I.A. Umezulike & C.C. Nweze (eds.), *Perspectives in Law and Justice*, Enugu: Fourth Dimension.

Obi, Cyril and Kayode Soremekun. 1995. "Oil and the Nigerian State: an Overview," in Kayode Soremekun (ed.), *Perspectives on the Nigerian Oil Industry*, Lagos: Amkra Books.

Obi, S.N. Chinwuba. 1963. *The Ibo Law of Property*. London: Butterworths.

Obilade, Akintunde Olusegun. 1979. *The Nigerian Legal System*. Ibadan: Spectrum.

Odofin, D.C. 1979. "The Impact of Multinational Oil Corporations on Nigeria's Economic Growth: Theoretical and Empirical Explorations," Ph.D. thesis at the American University, Washington.

Odogwu, E.C. 1991. "The Environment and Community Relations: The Shell Petroleum Development Co. of Nigeria Experience," Paper presented at the First International Conference on Health, Safety & Environment in Oil and Gas Exploration and Production, Volume 2, The Hague, November 11-14.

OECD (Organisation for Economic Co-operation and Development). 1998. *Oil Information 1997*. Paris: IEA (International Energy Agency), OECD.

Ogbnigwe, Akpezi. 1996. *Legal Sector, NDES Phase 1*. Port Harcourt: Anpez Environmental Law Centre.

Ogbonna, Okoro David. 1979. "The Geographic Consequences of Petroleum in Nigeria with Special Reference to the Rivers State," Ph.D. thesis at the University of California, Berkeley.

Ogowewo, Tunde I. 1995. "The Problem with Standing to Sue in Nigeria," *Journal of African Law* 39 (1): 1-18.

Ohiorhenuan, John F.E. 1984. "The Political Economy of Military Rule in Nigeria," *Review of Radical Political Economics* 16 (2/3): 1-27.

Oko, Okechukwu. 1994. "Legal Education and Training in Nigeria," *Revue Africaine de Droit International et Compare* 6 (6): 271-292.

Okonmah, Patrick D. 1997. "Right to a Clean Environment: The Case for the People of Oil-Producing Communities in the Nigerian Delta," *Journal of African Law* 41 (1): 43-67.

Okonkwo, C.O. 1980. *Introduction to Nigerian Law*. London: Sweet and Maxwell.

Okonta, Ike and Oronto Douglas. 1998. *Where Vultures Feast: Forty Years of Shell in the Niger Delta*. Draft of a forthcoming book.

Okoosi, Antonia T. and Banji Oyelaran-Oyeyinka. 1995. "Conflict and Environmental Change: Responses of Indigenous People to Oil Exploration in Nigeria's Delta Basin," Paper presented at the Conference on Environment & Development in Africa, Leeds, 14-16 September.

Okoro, Nwakamma. 1966. *The Customary Laws of Succession in Eastern Nigeria*. London: Sweet & Maxwell.

Olawoye, C.O. 1982. "Statutory Shaping of Land Law and Land Administration up to the Land Use Act," in J.A.Omotola (ed.), *The Land Use Act*, Report of a national workshop held at the University of Lagos, May 25-28, 1981, Lagos: Lagos University Press.

Olisa, Martin M. 1987. *Nigerian Petroleum Law and Practise*. Ibadan: Fountain Books.

Olowu, Dele. 1990. "Centralization, Self-Governance and Development in Nigeria," in James S. Wunsch and Dele Olowu (eds.) *The Failure of the Centralized State*, Boulder, Colorado: Westview Press.

Olugboji, Babatunde. 1996. *Human Rights Practices in Nigeria*. Lagos: Constitutional Rights Project.

Omalu, Mirian Kene. 1996. "Developments in Petroleum Exploration and Production Arrangements in Nigeria," *Oil and Gas Law and Taxation Review* 14: 70-76.

Omotola, J.A. 1980. *Essays on the Nigerian Land Use Act 1978*. Lagos: Lagos University Press.

----------. 1982. "The Land Use Act 1978 and Customary System of Tenure," in J.A.Omotola (ed.) *The Land Use Act,* Report of a national workshop held at the University of Lagos, May 25-28, 1981, Lagos: Lagos University Press.

----------. 1990. "The Quantum of Compensation for Oil Pollution: an Overview," in J.A.Omotola (ed.), *Environmental Laws in Nigeria including Compensation*, Lagos: University of Lagos, Department of Law.

Omoweh, Daniel A. 1994. "The Role of Shell Petroleum Development Company and the State in the Underdevelopment of the Niger Delta of Nigeria," Ph.D. thesis at the Obafemi Awolowo University, Ife-Ife.

----------. 1998. *Shell, the State and Underdevelopment of Nigeria's Niger Delta*. Draft of a forthcoming book.

Onoh, J.K. 1983. *The Nigerian Oil Economy: From Prosperity to Glut*. New York: St Martin's Press.

Onwuamaegbu, M. Obumneme. 1966. *Nigerian Law of Landlord and Tenant*. London: Sweet & Maxwell.

Onyekpere, Eze. 1996. *Justice for Sale: A Report on the Administration of Justice in the Magistrates and Customary Courts of Southern Nigeria*. Lagos: Civil Liberties Organisation.

Onyenkpa, Victor. 1998. "Nigeria: The 1998 Federal Budget and the Oil and Gas Industry," *Oil & Gas Law and Taxation Review* 5: 213-216.

Onyige, Peter Usutu. 1979. "The Impact of Mineral Oil Exploitation on Rural Communities in Nigeria: The Case of Ogba/Egbema District," Ph.D. thesis at the Centre of West African Studies, University of Birmingham.

OPEC. 1992. *OPEC: General Information and Chronology, 1960-1992*. Vienna: OPEC Secretariat.

Osaghae, Eghosa E. 1995. "The Ogoni Uprising: Oil Politics, Minority Agitation and the Future of the Nigerian State," *African Affairs* 94: 325-344.

----------. 1998. "Managing Multiple Minority Problems in a Divided Society: Nigerian Experience," *Journal of Modern African Studies* 36(1): 1-24.

Oshio, P.Ehi. 1990. "The Land Use Act and the Institution of Family Property in Nigeria," *Journal of African Law* 34 (2): 79-92.

Othman, Shehu. 1989. "Nigeria: Power for Profit - Class, Corporatism, and Factionalism in the Military," in Donald B. Cruise O'Brien, John Dunn and Richard Rathbone (eds.) *Contemporary West African States*, Cambridge: Cambridge University Press.

Owaboye, Wole. 1995. "Denial of Justice and Concept of Locus Standi in Nigeria," in Wole Owaboye (ed.), *Fundamental Legal Issues in Nigeria*, Lagos: Nigerian Law Research & Economic Development Projects.

Oyakhirome, J. Aigbuloko. 1995. "The 'New' Federal High Court," *University of Benin Law Journal* 2(1): 171-180.

Park, A.E.W. 1963. *The Sources of Nigerian Law*. London: Sweet & Maxwell.

Pearson, Scott R. 1970. *Petroleum and the Nigerian Economy*. Stanford, California: Stanford University Press.

Percy, R.A. 1983. *Charlesworth & Percy on Negligence*. 7th ed. London: Sweet & Maxwell.

Petroconsultants. 1996. "Annual Review of Petroleum Fiscal Regimes," Geneva: Petroconsultants.

----------. 1997. "Review and Comparison of Environmental Legislation in Nigeria: Report for Shell International Exploration and Production BV," Geneva: Petroconsultants.

----------. 1998. "Foreign Scouting Service: Nigeria, December 1997," Geneva: Petroconsultants (December).

Posner, Richard A. 1986. *Economic Analysis of Law*. 3rd ed. Boston: Little, Brown and Company.

Quinlan, Martin. 1992. "New Look comes with New Risks, Nigeria - a Special Report," *Petroleum Economist* 59 (3): 21-25.

----------. 1999. "Prospects for a New Beginning," *Petroleum Economist* 66 (May): 3-5.

Rivers State of Nigeria. 1991. "Judicial Commission of Inquiry into Umuechem Disturbances under the Chairmanship of Hon. Justice Opubo Inko-Tariah," a report (January), Port Harcourt: Rivers State of Nigeria.

Roberts, Simon A. 1972. *Botswana I, Tswana Family Law*. London: Sweet & Maxwell.

Robinson, Deborah. 1996. *Ogoni - The Struggle Continues*. Geneva: World Council of Churches.

Rowell, Andrew. 1996. *Green Backlash*. London: Routledge.

Sampson, Anthony. 1975. *The Seven Sisters*. London: Hodder and Stoughton.

Sarbah, J.M. 1968. *Fanti Customary Law*. 3rd ed. London: Frank Cass.

Schapera, I. 1935. *A Handbook of Tswana Law and Custom*. London: Oxford University Press.

Schätzl, L.H. 1969. *Petroleum in Nigeria*. Ibadan: Oxford University Press.

Seidman, Robert B. 1968. "Law and Economic Development in Independent, English-Speaking, Sub-Saharan Africa," in Thomas W. Hutchison (ed.) *Africa and Law*, Madison, Milwaukee: University of Wisconsin Press.

Shell-BP. 1960. *The Story of Oil in Nigeria*. Lagos: Shell-BP.

Snyder, Francis G. 1981. *Capitalism and Legal Change: An African Transformation*. New York: Academic Press.

Soremekun, Kayode. 1995a. *Perspectives on the Nigerian Oil Industry* (edited). Lagos: Amkra Books.

----------. 1995b. "Presidential System and Petroleum Policy (1979-1983)," in Kayode Soremekun (ed.), *Perspectives on the Nigerian Oil Industry*, Lagos: Amkra Books.

SPDC (Shell Petroleum Development Company of Nigeria). 1993. "Fact Book '93," Confidential report, Port Harcourt: Shell Petroleum Development Company, Eastern Division, Public and Government Affairs, Environment Department.

----------. 1995a. "Nigeria Brief: the Environment," Lagos (May).

----------. 1995b. "Nigeria Brief: the Ogoni Issue," Lagos (January).

----------. 1996. "Harnessing Gas," Lagos (August).

----------. 1997. "People and the Environment: Annual Report 1996," Lagos (May).

Stevens, Paul. 1995. "Understanding the Oil Industry: Economics as a Help or a Hindrance," *Energy Journal* 16 (January 1).

Suberu, Rotimi T. 1996. *Ethnic Minority Conflicts and Governance in Nigeria*. Ibadan: Spectrum.

Synge, Richard. 1986. *Energy in Nigeria*. London: Middle East Economic Digest.

Thomas, David. 1995. "Niger Delta Oil Production, Reserves, Field Sizes Assessed," *Oil & Gas Journal* (13 Nov.): 101-104.

Tobi, Niki. 1992. *Cases and Materials on Nigerian Land Law*. Lagos: Mabrochi.

Todd, Harry F. Jr. 1978. "Litigious Marginals: Character and Disputing in a Bavarian Village," in Laura Nader and Harry F. Todd Jr. (eds.) *The Disputing Process - Law in Ten Societies*, New York: Columbia University Press.

Turner, Terisa. 1976. "Multinational Corporations and the Instability of the Nigerian State," *Review of African Political Economy* 5: 63-79.

----------. 1977. "Government and Oil in Nigeria: A Study of the Making and Implementation of Petroleum Policy," Ph.D. thesis at the London School of Economics.

----------. 1978. "Commercial Capitalism and the 1975 Coup," in Keith Panter-Brick (ed.) *Soldiers and Oil: the Political Transformation of Nigeria*. London: Frank Cass.

----------. 1980. "The Working of the Nigerian National Oil Corporation," in Paul Collins (ed.) *Administration for Development in Nigeria*, Lagos: African Education Press.

---------- & Pade Badru. 1984. "Oil and Instability: Class Contradictions and the 1983 Coup in Nigeria," *Journal of African Marxists* 7(March): 4-21.

Udoma, Udo, and Myma Belo-Osagie. 1995. "The Nigerian Liquefied Natural Gas Project: Current Structure and Future Prospects," *Petroleum Economist* 62, Special Supplement (May): xvi-xviii.

Uduehi, Godfrey O. 1987. *Public Lands Acquisition and Compensation Practice in Nigeria*. Lagos: John West.

Umezulike, I.A. 1986. "Does the Land Use Act 1978 Expropriate? Another View," *Journal of Private and Property Law* 5: 61-69.

Uwazie, Ernest E. 1994. "Modes of Indigenous Disputing and Legal Interactions among the Ibos of Eastern Nigeria," *Journal of Legal Pluralism* 34: 87-103.

Vanderlinden, Jacques. 1983. *Les Systemes Juridiques Africains*. Paris: Presses Universitaires de France.

Whitaker, C.S. 1991. "A Coda on Afrocentricity," in Richard L. Sklar and C.S. Whitaker (eds.) *African Politics and Problems in Development*, Boulder, Colorado: Lynne Rienner.

Whiteman, Arthur. 1982. *Nigeria: Its Petroleum Geology, Resources and Potential, Volume 2*. London: Graham & Trotman.

Williams, Donald C. 1992. "Accommodation in the Midst of Crisis? Assessing Governance in Nigeria," in Goran Hyden and Michael Bratton (eds.) *Governance and Politics in Africa*. Boulder, Colorado: Lynne Rienner Publishers.

World Bank. 1990. *National Environmental Action Plan: Towards the Development of an Environmental Action Plan for Nigeria*. World Bank: Washington (December).

----------. 1995. *Defining an Environmental Development Strategy for the Niger Delta*. Industry and Energy Operations Division, West Central Africa Department of the World Bank (May 25).

----------. 1996. *Nigeria: Poverty in the Midst of Plenty: The Challenge of Growth with Inclusion*. Population and Human Resources Division, Western Africa Department, Africa Region, World Bank (31 May).

Annual Publications, Periodicals, Newspapers and News Agencies

Africa Confidential (London)

AFP (Agence France-Presse) (Paris)

AP (Associated Press) (New York)

BP Statistical Review of World Energy (London)

Central Bank of Nigeria, *Annual Reports* (Lagos)

Central Bank of Nigeria, *Economic and Financial Review* (Lagos)

Constitutional Rights Journal (Lagos)

Daily Times (Lagos)

Delta Magazine (Leicester)

Economist Intelligence Unit Country Report: Nigeria (London)

Energy Compass (London)

Guardian (Lagos)

Guardian (London)

Hart's Africa Oil and Gas (London)

IMF International Financial Statistics Yearbook (Washington)

Inter-Press Service (Washington/New York)

NewReport Journal (Lagos)

Newswatch (Lagos)

Observer (London)

Oil & Gas Journal (Tulsa)

Oil & Gas Update (Lagos)

OPEC Annual Statistical Bulletin (Geneva)

Petroleum Economist (London)

Petroleum Intelligence Weekly (New York)

Petroleum Review (London)

Phone News International (London)

Platt's Oilgram News (New York)

PostExpressWired (Lagos)

Reuters (London)

Tell (Lagos)

The News (Lagos),

ThisDay (Lagos)

Vanguard (Lagos)

Weekly Petroleum Argus (London)

World Oil (Houston)

APPENDIX A: 1998 Survey Questionnaire

Survey of Nigerian lawyers

Your views are very important for this survey. You can help to assess the condition of the legal profession in Nigeria. Please fill in the following 16 questions. It should only take approx. 10 minutes of your time. Your answers will be kept anonymous and confidential.

1. What is your Birth Year?

19____

2. Are you

☐ Male   ☐ Female

3. When were you called to the Bar?

19____

4a. What is the approx. size of your law firm and/or organization including support staff?

____

4b. How many persons would you categorize as support staff?

____

5. What are you specialised in?

☐ Criminal law

☐ Civil law

☐ Environmental law

☐ Commercial law

☐ Other

Please feel free to be more specific

....

....

....

....

....

6a. Has your work involved contacts with an oil company?

☐ yes

☐ no

6b. Have you acted as

☐ counsel for an oil company, its subsidiary or a contractor

☐ counsel in a lawsuit against an oil company

(tick both if applicable)

7a. In your professional experience, would you say that there are difficulties in the enforcement of court orders, rulings or judgments?

☐ very severe problems

☐ severe problems

☐ some difficulties

☐ minor difficulties

☐ no difficulties

7b. Are the difficulties more or less severe in oil company related litigation?

☐ much more severe

☐ greater

☐ the same

☐ less severe

☐ much less severe

☐ don't know

8a. In your professional experience, would you say that lawyers, judges or other judicial officers encounter outside pressures from private or public institutions in their work?

☐ very often

☐ often

☐ sometimes

☐ rarely

☐ never

8b. Are these pressures more or less severe in oil company related litigation?

☐ much more severe

☐ greater

☐ the same

☐ less severe

☐ much less severe

☐ don't know

9a. In your professional experience, are litigants treated fairly in court decisions involving oil companies?

☐ very fairly

☐ fairly

☐ neither fairly nor unfairly

☐ unfairly

☐ very unfairly

☐ don't know

9b. Do you think oil companies, their subsidiares and contractors conduct themselves ethically in court proceedings?

☐ very often

☐ often

☐ sometimes

☐ rarely

☐ never

☐ don't know

9c. Would you say that courts are biased in favour of the oil company or the opposing litigant?

☐ severe bias in favour of oil company   ☐ severe bias in favour of opposing litigant

☐ some bias in favour of oil company   ☐ some bias in favour of opposing litigant

☐ no bias in favour of oil company   ☐ no bias in favour of opposing litigant

☐ don't know   ☐ don't know

[please tick one field on each side]

9d. Amongst the following, rank reasons [1=very important reason, 2=important reason, 3=less important reason] why courts might encounter difficulties in judging oil related cases fairly?

____ lack of knowledge on oil technology

____ lack of funds

____ lack of time

____ outside pressures

____ resources and skill of oil company's counsel

____ lack of witnesses

____ incompetence of witnesses

[feel free to use the same number as often as you wish or simply ignore specific fields]

---

10. In your professional experience, would you consider the compensation paid by oil companies for damages in tort as

☐ unfair to oil companies as much too high

☐ unfair to oil companies as somewhat too high

☐ fair and justified

☐ unfair to opposing litigant as somewhat too low

☐ unfair to opposing litigant as much too low

☐ don't know

11a. Have you encountered instances in which potential litigants have been discouraged from legal action although they had a valid claim to compensation, an injunction or another form of legal recourse?

☐ very often

☐ often

☐ sometimes

☐ rarely

☐ never

☐ don't know

11b. Amongst the following, rank reasons [1=very important reason, 2=important reason, 3=less important reason] which you think would prevent a potential litigants from seeking legal recourse?

_____ ignorance of legal rights

_____ lack of funds

_____ lack of general education

_____ geographical distance to courts

_____ intimidation by tort-feasors

_____ intimidation by public bodies

_____ organisational structure of villages

_____ uncertainty about the potential success of a suit

_____ delay in the disposal of cases by courts

_____ ethnic origin

_____ living in a rural area

_____ being a woman

_____ young age

[feel free to use the same number as often as you wish or simply ignore specific fields]

11c. In your opinion are the problems particularly severe in oil related litigation?

☐ much less severe

☐ less severe

☐ the same

☐ more severe

☐ much more severe

☐ don't know

Please feel free to be more specific

....
....
....
....

12. In your professional experience, which areas of law have undergone changes since you were called to the Bar?

	no change	some change	major change	don't know
Criminal law	☐	☐	☐	☐
Civil law	☐	☐	☐	☐
Environmental law	☐	☐	☐	☐
Commercial law	☐	☐	☐	☐
Other	☐	☐	☐	☐

Please feel free to be more specific

....
....
....

13. Do you think that the following piece of legislation has been effectively enforced?

	not enforced	partially enforced	effectively enforced	don't know
Petroleum Act 1969	☐	☐	☐	☐
FEPA Decree 1988[1]	☐	☐	☐	☐
OMPADEC Decree 1992[2]	☐	☐	☐	☐
Land Use Act 1978	☐	☐	☐	☐
Gas Re-Injection Act 1979	☐	☐	☐	☐

[1] Federal Environmental Protection Agency (FEPA)
[2] Oil Mineral Producing Areas Developm. Commission

14. The Eso Panel in 1994 submitted a report on the situation of the judiciary. Do you agree/disagree with the following findings of the Panel? For each statement, give a rating between 1 and 5 [1 = strongly disagree, 5=strongly agree]

_____ the judiciary is too dependent on the executive arm of the Government

_____ the appointment of judges is too arbitrary

_____ the funding of the legal system is too little

_____ congestion in the courts is too high

15. Do you agree/disagree with the following statement? [1 = strongly disagree, 5=strongly agree]

_____ typed transcripts of court judgements are usually written competently

16a. Do you think that there are major differences in the quality of judicial services in different Nigerian courts?

☐ yes   ☐ no

16b. Which type of court would you judge as particularly competent or incompetent?

	very competent	competent	incompetent	don't know
Supreme Court	☐	☐	☐	☐
Court of Appeal	☐	☐	☐	☐
Federal High Court	☐	☐	☐	☐
State High Courts	☐	☐	☐	☐
Magistrates Courts	☐	☐	☐	☐
Customary Courts	☐	☐	☐	☐

Do you have additional comments you would like to make? Please write below or attach pages if you want.

APPENDIX B: Oil Companies with OMLs and OPLs in Nigeria in 1998

Operator (interest)	Other Partners (interest)	Oil Licences (in sq. km)
Addax (100%)		4,770
Afric Oil & Marketing (97.5%)	Camac (2.5%)	1,500
Agip (NAOC) (20%)	NNPC (60%), Phillips Oil (20%)	5,259
Agip (NAOC) (65%)	Amoco (35%)	4,700
Agip (AENR) (0%)	NNPC (100%)	360
Alfred James Petroleum (60%)	Abacan (40%)	1,900
Allied Energy Resources (60%)	BP (20%), Statoil (20%)	1,700
Amalgamated Oil (100%)		520
Amni International (60%)	Abacan (40%)	491
Arewa (100%)		2,560
Aries (100%)		1,280
Atlas Petroleum (60%)	Occidental (20%), Profco Resources (10%), Summit Partners Management (10%)	785
Brass Petroleum (100%)		1,880
Cavendish Petroleum (57.5%)	Tuskar Resources (40%), Camac (2.5%)	966
Chevron (100%)		15,000
Chevron (40%)	NNPC (60%)	8,726
Consolidated Oil (100%)		2,550
Crescent City (100%)		1,380
Crownwell (100%)		3,320
Dania (100%)		1,160
Devine (100%)		3,060
Du Pont (47.5%)	Esso (47.5%), Medal Oil (5%)	2,421
Dubri Oil (100%)		232
Elf (40%)	NNPC (60%)	10,927
Elf (40%)	Chevron (30%), Esso (30%)	10,615
Esso (80%)	Amoco (20%)	2,200
Express Petroleum & Gas (57.5%)	Du Pont (40%), Camac (2.5%)	500
Famfa Oil (60%)	Texaco (40%)	2,550
General Oil (100%)		1,580
International Petro-Energy (100%)		3,390
Jerez Energy (100%)		1,898
Lamont (100%)		1,700

APPENDIX B: Oil Companies with OMLs and OPLs in Nigeria in 1998 (continued)

Operator (interest)	Other Partners (interest)	Oil Licences (in sq. km)
Mareena Petroleum (100%)		237
Mobil (40%)	NNPC (60%)	3,332
Mobil (50%)	Amoco (50%)	2,287
Moncrief Oil International (100%)		1,375
Moni Pulo (60%)	Brass Exploration (40%)	290
NAPIMS (100%)		24,000
Nigerian Bitumen (100%)		5,800
Nima Minerals (100%)		2,440
NNPC (100%)		690
Noreast Petroleum (100%)		4,985
Noreast Petroleum (60%)	Mobil (40%)	2,428
NPDC (100%)		1,170
NPDC (80%)	Tenneco Oil (15%), Sun DX (5%)	1,455
Obekpa (100%)		1,300
Optimum Petroleum (60%)	Abacan (40%)	1,850
Oriental Energy Resources (97.5%)	Camac (2.5%)	305
Pan Ocean (40%)	NNPC (60%)	503
Peak Petroleum (60%)	NTI Resources (40%)	1,632
Petroleum Products (60%)	Abacan (40%)	127
Queens Petroleum (60%)	Geo International (40%)	2,780
Seawolf (100%)		2,280
Shell (SPDC) (30%)	NNPC (55%), Elf (10%), Agip (5%)	31,118
Shell (SNEPCO) (55%)	Esso (20%), Elf (12.5%), Agip (12.5%)	11,934
Solgas Petroleum (60%)	Niko Resources (40%)	1,500
Statoil (35%)	BP (35%), Texaco (30%)	6,059
Summit Oil (100%)		4,440
Sunlink Petroleum (100%)		2,176
Texaco (20%)	NNPC (60%), Chevron (20%)	2,570
Ultramar International Energy (100%)		900
Yinka Folawiyo Petroleum (60%)	Abacan (40%)	1,600
		225,443

Source: Petroconsultants (1998).

APPENDIX C: Nigerian Private Oil Companies in 1998

Issue Date of First Licence	Nigerian Firm (equity share)	Partner (equity share)	Oil Licence	Licence Area (sq. km)
Aug. 1987	Dubri Oil (100%)		OML96	232
Nov. 1990	Queens Petroleum (100%)	Geo International (40%)	OPL135+228	2,780
Nov. 1990	Cavendish Petroleum (57.5%)	Tuskar Resources (40%); Camac (2.5%)	OML110	966
Nov. 1990	Consolidated Oil (100%)		OML103+ OPL458	950 1,600
Nov. 1990	Express Petroleum & Gas (57.5%)	Du Pont (40%); Camac (2.5%)	OML108	500
Nov. 1990	Summit Oil (100%)		OPL205+206	4,440
Nov. 1990	IPEC* (100%)		OPL202+229	3,390
Nov. 1990	Paclantic Oil (n/a)	n/a	n/a	n/a
Nov. 1990	Inki Petroleum** (97.5%)	Camac (2.5%)	OPL224	305
Nov. 1990	Ultramar Energy (100%)		OPL227	900
Feb. 1991	Solgas (60%)	Niko Resources (40%)	OPL226	1,500
Feb. 1991	Atlas Petroleum	Canadian Occidental Petroleum (20%); Profco Resources (10%); Summit Partners Management (10%)	OML109	785
May 1991	Supra Investments*** (100%)		OPL452	520
July 1991	Union Square Petrogas (n/a)	n/a	n/a	n/a
July 1991	Seagull (n/a)	n/a	n/a	n/a
July 1991	Moncrief Oil (100%)		OPL471	1,375
July 1991	Yinka Folawiyo Petroleum (60%)	Abacan (40%)	OPL309	1,600
July 1991	Alfred James Petroleum (60%)	Abacan (40%)	OPL302	1,900
July 1991	General Oil (100%)		OPL304	1,580
June 1992	Allied Energy Resources (60%)	Statoil (20%); BP (20%)	OPL210	1,700
June 1992	Noreast Petroleum (100%)****		OPL840+902	4,985
1993	Amni Petroleum (60%)	Abacan (40%)	OPL237+469	491
1993	Peak Petroleum (60%)	NTI Resources (40%)	OPL460	1,632
1993	Intoil (n/a)	n/a	n/a	n/a
1993	Optimum Petroleum (60%)	Abacan (40%)	OPL310	1,850
1993	Famfa Oil (60%)	Texaco (40%)	OPL216	2,550
1993	Azenith (n/a)	n/a	n/a	n/a
1993	Crescent City (100%)		OPL234	1,380
1993	First Aries (100%)		OPL235	1,280
1993	Asaris	n/a	n/a	n/a
1993	Petroleum Products (60%)	Abacan (40%)	OPL233	127
1993	Nyemoni Petroleum (n/a)	n/a	n/a	n/a
1993	Sunlink Petroleum (n/a)	n/a	n/a	n/a
1993	MLM Petroleum (n/a)	n/a	n/a	n/a
1993	Mareena (100%)		OPL231	237
1993	Brass Petroleum (100%)		OPL208	1,880
1993	Dania Oil (100%)		OPL236	1,160
1993	Lamont Oil (100%)		OPL207	1,700

* International Petrol Energy Co.; ** renamed Oriental Energy; *** renamed Amalgamated; **** Noreast was also part of a joint-venture with Mobil (40% equity share in the Noreast venture) to exploit OPL215.
Sources: Avuru (1997, 294); Petroconsultants (1998).

APPENDIX D:

Chronology of Nigeria's Political Economy of Oil

1907		Nigerian Bitumen Corporation, a Nigerian subsidiary of a German company, starts oil exploration
1908		Nigerian Bitumen Corporation discovers crude oil near Lagos
1914		Nigerian Bitumen Corporation withdraws from Nigeria at the beginning of the First World War
1937		Shell D'Arcy (later re-named Shell-BP) formed as a joint-venture between Shell and Anglo-Iranian (British Petroleum from 1954) to operate in Nigeria
1938		Shell D'Arcy granted a licence to explore oil covering the entire territory of Nigeria
1941		Oil exploration suspended due to the Second World War
1946		Oil exploration resumes
1951		First deep exploration well drilled by Shell D'Arcy at Ihuo but no oil found, Shell D'Arcy's original oil exploration licence covering the entire Nigerian territory reduced to an area of 58,000 square miles in Southern Nigeria
1953		Shell D'Arcy's first non-commercial oil find at Akata-1
1955		Socony-Vacuum (later re-named Mobil) obtains its first oil exploration licence in Northern Nigeria
1956		Oil found in commercial quantity at Oloibiri
	April	Shell D'Arcy re-named Shell-BP
1957	Dec.	Oil production starts
1959		Petroleum Profits Tax Ordinance promulgated
1960	April	Tennessee (also known as Tenneco) obtains its first oil exploration licence
	Oct.	Nigerian independence
1961		Gulf (later Chevron) and American Overseas (also known as Amoseas) obtain their first exploration licences
	April	Shell-BP's Bonny Terminal commissioned
1962		Agip and Safrap (later re-named Elf) obtain their first exploration licences
1963		The number of Nigerian regions increased from three to four

	Oct.	Nigeria becomes a republic, Nigeria's president replaces the British Crown as head of state
1964	Jan.	First offshore discovery at Okan made by Gulf (later Chevron) (production began in March 1965)
1965	Oct.	Port Harcourt refinery commissioned
1966	Jan.	Coup d'état, end of the First Republic, Balewa replaced by Major-General Ironsi
	June	Second military coup, Ironsi replaced by Colonel Gowon
1967	May	Regions abolished and replaced by twelve federal states, Eastern region of Nigeria secedes as Biafra, led by Ojukwu, Petroleum Profits Tax Ordinance amended (retroactively valid from January 1966), Rivers State created
	July	Civil War starts, oil production disrupted
1969	Nov.	Petroleum Act promulgated
1970	Jan.	End of Civil War
	April	Nigeria's oil production exceeds 1 million barrels/day for the first time
1971	April	Creation of the Nigerian National Oil Corporation (NNOC), the NNOC acquires 35% in the Safrap (later Elf) venture - the first oil producing joint venture established with government participation
	July	Nigeria joins the Organisation of the Petroleum Exporting Countries (OPEC)
	Sept.	Nigerian government acquires 33.33% in the Agip and Agip/Phillips ventures
1972	Feb.	First Indigenization Decree
1973	April	Nigerian government acquires 35% in the joint-venture with Shell-BP
	June	First production-sharing contract with Ashland
1974		Safrap re-named Elf Nigeria
	April	Nigerian government acquires 55% in the joint-ventures with Shell-BP, Mobil, Gulf (later Chevron), Agip and Elf
1975	May	Nigerian government acquires 55% in the joint-venture with Texaco
	July	Third coup d'état, Gowon replaced by Murtala Mohammad
1976	Feb.	Mohammad assassinated, replaced by Obasanjo
	April	Twelve federal states replaced by nineteen, Bendel State created
	Sept.	First Nigerian tanker 'Oloibiri' launched
1977	Jan.	Second Indigenization Decree

April	Nigerian National Petroleum Corporation (NNPC) established to replace the Nigerian National Oil Corporation (NNOC) and the Ministry of Petroleum Resources
July	Fiscal incentives for oil companies introduced including exploration incentives, petroleum profit tax and royalty rate modification
1978 Jan.	Nigerian government acquires 55% in the joint-venture with Pan Ocean
Sept.	Warri refinery commissioned
1979 July	Nigerian government acquires 60% in the joint-ventures with Shell-BP, Mobil, Gulf (later Chevron), Agip, Elf, Texaco and Pan Ocean, elections to the Senate, House of Representatives, State Houses of Assembly and state governors
Aug.	BP's assets nationalised, Shell left with only 20% in the joint-venture with the government, presidential elections
Oct.	Shagari elected as civilian president
1980 Jan.	Installation of the Second Republic under Shagari
Oct.	Kaduna refinery commissioned
1982 July	New fiscal incentives for oil companies introduced
1983 Feb.	Further fiscal incentives for oil companies introduced
Aug.	Shagari re-elected as president
Dec.	Military coup, end of the Second Republic, Buhari takes over
1984	New Liquefied Natural Gas (LNG) project launched with Shell as main partner of the government
1985 Aug.	Coup d'état, Babangida replaces Buhari
1986	1986 Memorandum of Understanding between the government and oil companies, Ministry of Petroleum Resources re-established
June	Structural Adjustment Programme (SAP) announced
1987	New fiscal incentives for oil companies
Sept.	Creation of two additional federal states, which increases the number of states from 19 to 21
1989	Second refinery in Port Harcourt commissioned
June	Government share in the Shell joint-venture reduced from 80% to 60%
1991	Memorandum of Understanding revised, the number of federal states increases from 21 to 30, Delta State created
1992	Oil Mineral Producing Areas Development Commission (OMPADEC) established
Dec.	Mobil's Oso Condensate field begins production

1993	Jan.	Formation of transitional council under Shonekan, a former non-executive director of Shell, expected to manage the country for seven months until the installation of a civilian government
	June	Presidential elections, Abiola emerged as election victor but election results annulled by Babangida
	Aug.	Babangida resigns, Shonekan sworn in as head of Interim National Government, government share in the Shell joint-venture reduced from 60% to 55%
	Nov.	General Abacha installs himself as head of state
1994	May	Ken Saro-Wiwa, leader of the Movement for the Survival of the Ogoni People (MOSOP), detained and later charged
	June	Abiola declares himself president, Abacha declares him wanted, Abiola arrested and later charged
1995	Nov.	Ken Saro-Wiwa and eight other Ogoni leaders executed
1996	Oct.	Creation of six additional federal states, which increases the number of states from 30 to 36, Bayelsa State created
1997	April	Chevron's Escravos Gas Project begins production
	June	Nigerian government terminates its production-sharing contracts with Ashland
1998		Addax takes over Ashland's oil exploration and production operations, fiscal incentives for gas projects
	June	Abacha dies, General Abubakar becomes president
	July	Mobil's Oso Natural Gas Liquid (NGL) project begins production
	Aug.	Ministry of Petroleum Resources scrapped
1999		Nigeria Liquefied Natural Gas (NLNG) Project (Shell, NNPC, Elf, Agip venture) expected to start production
	Feb.	National Assembly and presidential elections, Obasanjo elected as president
	May	Transfer to civilian rule

Sources: Khan (1994); Whiteman (1982); Turner (1977, 1980); Frynas and Beck (1998); various newspapers and periodicals.

NAME INDEX

Ogowewo, Tunde I., 202, 207
Ohiorhenuan, John F.E., 25
Ojukwu, Colonel, 30
Oko, Okechukwu, 105
Okocha, O.C.J., 56
Okonkwo, C.O., 59
Okonmah, Patrick D., 223
Okonta, Ike and O. Douglas, 49, 50
Okoosi, Antonia T. and B. Oyelaran-
    Oyeyinka, 110
Okoro, Nwakamma, 73
Okuntimo, Paul, 54
Olawoye, C.O., 75, 78
Olisa, Martin M., 4, 59, 83, 88
Olowu, Dele, 42
Olugboji, Babatunde, 123, 124
Omatsola, Preston, 50
Omosun, J.C.A., 196, 199, 201
Omotola, J.A., 5, 77, 78, 95, 96
Omoweh, Daniel A., 4, 5, 149
Onalaja, J.C.A., 212, 216, 221
Onoh, J.K., 3
Onu, J.S.C., 209
Onwuamaegbu, M. Obumneme, 172
Onyekpere, Eze, 127
Onyenkpa, Victor, 20
Onyige, Peter Usutu, 4, 101, 149, 170, 178,
    183, 186
Opia, Eric, 50
Oroh, Abdul, 102
Osaghae, Eghosa E., 44, 45, 46, 47, 49, 50
Oshio, P.Ehi, 78
Othman, Shehu, 42, 43
Owaboye, Wole, 207
Owonaro, Sam, 46
Oyakhirome, J. Aigbuloko, 92, 129

P

Park, A.E.W., 60, 62, 63, 66
Pearce, E.J., 31
Pearson, Scott R., 3, 30
Percy, R.A., 190, 191, 196, 212, 218
Pirocchi, A., 187, 188
Popo, Joseph, 124
Popoola, Oladayo, 49
Posner, Richard A., 68, 70

Q

Quinlan, Martin, 15, 16, 20, 21, 24, 35, 48

R

Roberts, Simon A., 61
Robinson, Deborah, 4, 129

Rowell, Andrew, 165

S

Sadler, J.S., 30
Sampson, Anthony, 30
Sarbah, J.M., 61
Saro-Wiwa, Ken, 1, 46, 50, 54, 119
Schapera, I., 61
Schätzl, L.H., 3, 11, 15, 36
Schiller, A.A., 68
Seidman, Robert B., 68
Shagari, Shehu, 43, 84
Shonekan, Ernest, 42, 43, 56
Snyder, Francis G., 61
Soremekun, Kayode, 3, 39; *see also* Obi, Cyril
    and K. Soremekun
Sowemimo, J.S.C., 192, 210
Stevens, Paul, 230
Suberu, Rotimi T., 43, 46, 50

T

Thomas, David, 22, 23
Tobi, Niki, 72
Todd, Harry F. Jr., 1, 183
Turner, Terisa, 3, 8, 20, 27, 28, 31, 32, 33, 39,
    40, 81, 87, 88
Turner, Terisa, and P. Badru, 41

U

Udoma, Udo, and M. Belo-Osagie, 22
Uduehi, Godfrey O., 97
Umezulike, I.A., 78
Uwaifo, J.C.A., 190
Uwazie, Ernest E., 64, 65

V

van den Berg, Ron, 55
van Dessel, J.P., 88, 153, 154, 158, 160, 162,
    163, 164, 165, 178, 179
Vanderlinden, Jacques, 69
Vergine, Umberto, 188

W

Wai-Ogosu, J., 184, 199, 202, 213
Watts, Philip B., 55
Whitaker, C.S., 5
Whiteman, Arthur 11, 12, 32
Williams, Donald C., 44

Y

Ya'Ardua, Musa, 78

SUBJECT INDEX

A

Abacan, 37
Accountant-General, 176
Addax, 16, 40, 164
admissibility of evidence, *see* legal defences
Advisory Judicial Committee, 119
African Petroleum, 38
Agip, 4, 11, 15, 16, 20, 30, 32, 33, 36, 37, 76,
    80, 81, 89, 118, 157, 163, 164, 171,
    172, 173, 175, 180, 183, 186, 187, 188
agriculture, 9, 25, 151, 201, 204
air pollution, 163, 164; *see also* gas flaring
Alfred James Petroleum, 37
American Overseas (Amoseas), 11, 36
American Petroleum Institute, 23
Amnesty International, 47
Amni International, 37, 40, 164
Andoni, 42, 45, 185
Anglo-Iranian, *see* BP, Shell-BP and Statoil-
    BP
Anglo-Persian, *see* BP, Shell-BP and Statoil-
    BP
appellate courts, *see* Court of Appeal, Supreme
    Court, House of Lords and Privy
    Council
Arcadia, 40
area courts, 92, 93
arms imports, 55
Arthur Andersen, 21, 179
Ashland, 16, 31, 81, 88, 157, 174, 175
Attorney-General, 56, 75, 90, 119, 123, 177,
    193, 206, 207, 210
Azerbaijan, 20

B

Bar Association, 102, 105
barriers to justice, *see* courts, access to
Barrows Company, 34, 82
Bayelsa Indigenes Association, 45
Bayelsa State, 42, 44, 45, 54, 108, 111
Belgore Commission of Inquiry, 49
Bendel State, 44, 45, 197
Benin, 20
Biafran War, *see* Civil War
BP, 9, 11, 12, 20, 30, 32, 34, 51; *see also*
    Shell-BP and Statoil-BP
BP's nationalization, 32, 34
Britain, 18, 32, 48, 62, 66, 68
British Colonial Office, 13

British Commonwealth Relations Office, 30
British Commonwealth, 11, 224
British Foreign Office, 30
British government, 9, 11, 12, 13, 15, 32, 61
British Ministry of Overseas Development,
    48, 49, 51
British Ministry of Power, 30
British Petroleum, *see* BP, Shell-BP and
    Statoil-BP
Brunei, 10, 11, 55
burden of proof, *see* legal defences

C

California Asiatic, 12
Canada, 10, 11, 18
carelessness of oil companies, *see* oil
    companies in Nigeria
Caribbean, 18
centre-periphery relationship, 27
Chevron, 2, 11, 12, 15, 16, 20, 32, 33, 36, 37,
    38, 45, 47, 51, 53, 54, 88, 89, 157,
    163, 164, 182
Chief Justice of Nigeria, 68, 76, 92, 109, 119,
    127
Chikoko movement, 47, 90
Civil Disturbances Special Tribunal, 119
civil law, 105, 106, 121, 140, 141
Civil Liberties Organisation (CLO), 102, 103,
    104, 116
Civil War, 16, 29, 30, 31, 155
civilian rule, 1, 39, 43, 84, 117, 119, 126
clients, *see* litigants
Coal Corporation, 10
Colonial Office, *see* British Colonial Office
commercial law, 68, 105, 140, 141
commercial lawyers, 108, 111, 114, 115, 116,
    117, 118, 121, 122, 127, 128, 129,
    131, 132, 140, 141, 143, 144, 147
commercialization of state oil corporation, 38,
    41; *see also* privatization of oil assets
Common law,
  bias in favour of oil companies, 65, 68, 70,
    71
  differences England/Nigeria, 59, 60, 67, 71,
    72
  economic development, and, 68, 70
  efficiency theory of, 68, 70
  reception of, 66
Commonwealth, *see* British Commonwealth

Texaco, 11, 12, 15, 16, 32, 33, 36, 37, 82, 88, 89, 157, 163, 164
Togo, 20
tort,
  duty of care, 190, 191, 192, 194
  expression defined, 189
  negligence, 159, 190, 191, 192, 194, 195, 196, 197, 199, 200, 203, 222, 223
  nuisance, 66, 190, 192, 193, 194, 197, 199, 200, 206, 212, 222, 223
  res ipsa loquitur, 191, 192
  restitutio in integrum, 211, 212
  strict liability, 190, 194, 195, 196, 197, 199, 222, 223
  see also legal defences, legal remedies and *locus standi*
Total, 39, 177
Tradoil, 40
trees, damage to, 94, 111, 158, 164, 168, 175, 186, 197, 201, 204, 209, 219
Trinidad, 10, 11
Turkmenistan, 20

U

Umuechem incident, 55, 56
unfair treatment of litigants, *see* litigants
United Kingdom, *see* Britain
United States of America, 13, 15, 18, 22, 24, 84, 178
Urhobo Progressive Union, 47
Urhobo, 42, 46, 47, 172

V

vandalism, *see* sabotage of oil installations

Venezuela, 23
Vietnam, 22, 23
village community, expression defined, 1
violence, 45, 54, 55, 182, 183, 187, 188, 222, 224, 226, 231

W

water pollution, 150, 158, 160, 162, 163, 165, 166, 203; *see also* oil spills
West African Gas Pipeline Project (WAGP), 20
Westates Petroleum, 35
Western Europe, 18, 23
Western Geophysical, 153
Western Niger Delta Development Programme, 53
Whitehall Petroleum Corporation, 9
Willbros, 47
witnesses,
  expert, 108, 110, 146, 169, 200, 209, 210, 211, 220
  incompetence of, 134, 136
  lack of, 136
World Bank, 42, 86, 87, 89, 90, 96, 97, 110, 149, 150, 163, 165, 166, 178, 186

X

XM Federal, 54, 55

Y

Yinka Folawiyo Petroleum, 36, 37, 40

Bremer Afrika-Studien

herausgegeben vom Informationszentrum Afrika (IZA), Bremen

Werner Korte
Ethnische Tradition und militärische Intervention in Afrika
Essay über den Putsch in Liberia
Bd. 10, 1995, 100 S., 19,80 DM, br., ISBN 3-8258-2009-2

Joe Lugalla
Adjustment and Poverty in Tanzania
In his book Lugalla looks at the relationship between adjustment policies and poverty in Tanzania. He understands Tanzanian poverty in the context of dominant social relations of inequality and not in terms of poverty lines. The author's main argument is that adjustment policies are intensifying these relations in Tanzania rather than reducing or eliminating them. He concludes that adjustment policies are not able to solve but create and even intensify poverty in Tanzania.
Bd. 12, 1996, 136 S., 34,80 DM, br., ISBN 3-8258-2007-6

Hans H. Bass (Hrsg.)
Enterprise Promotion and Vocational Training in Nigeria's Informal Sector
A joint publication of the Frederick-Ebert-Foundation Lagos, Nigeria and the Small Enterprise Promotion and Training Programme (SEPT) of the University of Bremen, Germany
Small enterprises, most of them operating informally, are Nigeria's most important providers of employment. Nevertheless, they have to face many disadvantages in their business activities. A conducive policy environment would be necessary to overcome the difficulties of small enterprises and take advantage of their various positive features.
Structural Adjustment Programmes (SAP) promised to enhance the opportunities of the small enterprise sector. Why were these hopes not fulfilled? What are the actual effects of SAP's prominent instruments on the small enterprise sector? Which is the framework for small enterprise promotion after the implementation of SAP?
The book addresses these questions and deals with institutional arrangements and promotional projects, focusing on skills acquisition as a bottleneck for employment generation.
Of particular interest is the Nigerian Open Apprenticeship Scheme NOAS, which originated in the desire to alleviate the social and labour

market problems of SAP. One of the scheme's important features – and almost unique in the developing world – , is its combination of in-firm training with schooling. Can this project be further enhanced by learning from the German vocational training system, where a similar approach is considered to be responsible for its successful performance?
The book also offers information on other aspects of development co-operation between German agencies and Nigerian counterparts in the field of small-enterprise promotion: The Friedrich Ebert Foundation gives an overview of its various activities to promote SSE performance in Nigeria, and an evaluation of a German-Nigerian Vocational Training Project provides one of only a few published first-hand insights into the practical problems of co-operation on the project level.
Bd. 13, 1995, 250 S., 38,80 DM, br., ISBN 3-8258-2149-8

Tesfatsion Medhanie
Eritrea & Neighbors in the 'New World Order'
Geopolitics, Democracy and 'Islamic Fundamentalism'
Eritrea, which formally became independent in May 1993, is Africa's youngest state. Its relations with Ethiopia, whose government is now dominated by the EPRDF, are very close and cooperative; but those with the Sudan have been strained ever since January 1994, when the EPLF government accused Khartoum of supporting Islamic fundamentalist incursions into Eritrea. This book examines, among other topics, the state of democracy in Eritrea under the EPLF regime, the nature of Eritrea's burgeoning ties with Israel, the basis of the alliance between the present regimes in Eritrea and Ethiopia, the politics behind the outrage of the Eritrean government against "Islamic fundamentalist" movements, and the ideals and problematics of political Islam. Through the focus of this book is on Eritrea, the political problems of Ethiopia and the Sudan are also explored. Ethiopia has been going through a process of democratisation which is increasingly beset with difficulties and controversies. In the Sudan, where an Islamist regime is in power, there is a bitter struggle over issues of democracy and human rights. The war in the Southern region is the country's most grave problem.
These questions are considered in the context of the new world situation in which the US is the uni-super-power, at least in the military sense of the term. In this connection, the doctrine of the USSR attention has been concentrated on some "threats" in the developing world to justify policy

LIT Verlag Münster – Hamburg – London
Bestellungen über:
Grevener Str. 179 48159 Münster
Tel.: 0251 – 23 50 91 – Fax: 0251 – 23 19 72
e-Mail: lit@lit-verlag.de – http://www.lit-verlag.de
Preise: unverbindliche Preisempfehlung

of intervention, including military intervention. These "threats" are also briefly discussed in this book.

Bd. 15, 1995, 144 S., 29,80 DM, br., ISBN 3-8258-2193-5

Susanna Adam
Competence Utilization and Transfer in Informal Sector Production and Services in Ibadan/Nigeria
The general aim of this study is to identify and illuminate factors which have affected the survival and development of informal, small-scale businesses in Ibadan, Nigeria, during recent years. The primary focus is on professional competences, in particular as gained through apprenticeship. The way in which such competences are acquired and the extent to which they are utilized in the businesses concerned are investigated.
Competence of the entrepreneurs is regarded as one of the factors which are most important for survival and development in the informal sector. However, an educational perspective alone would not have been an appropriate approach to this sector. Therefore an interdisciplinary approach, combining educational with socio-economic research, was chosen for this study: The research included other important factors such as infrastructure, financing, marketing, technology and informal relations. Thus, the author goes beyond the narrow perspective of vocational training.
The finding on entrepreneurs' responses to the changing environment, especially the innovative competences and the formation of interest groups, are of special interest. They indicate self-regulating tendencies in the informal sector which clearly show that the "informal" sector is not a "non-structured" sector.

Bd. 16, 1995, 208 S., 34,80 DM, br., ISBN 3-8258-2375-X

Dereje Alemayehu
The Crisis of Capitalist Development in Africa
The Case of Côte d'Ivoire
In the first two decades after independence the Côte d'Ivoire enjoyed not only political stability, but also economic progress almost unparalleled in sub-Saharan Africa. Since the beginning of the 80s the country is going through a severe economic and social crisis. The purpose of this study is to discuss the contradicitions of the Ivorian development model and analyse the historial and structural roots of its crisis. The discussion in this study is placed within the context of the current development discourse. It is intended as a contribution to the critique of past development policies within the framework of the Ivorian development model, and as a critique of the current structural adjustment programmes (SAP) as a set of policy measures to remedy the unfolding Ivorian crisis.

Bd. 18, 1997, 256 S., 38,80 DM, br., ISBN 3-8258-3014-4

Werner Korte
Ethnic Tradition and Military Intervention in Africa
The Case of Liberia
Bd. 19, Frühjahr 2000, 120 S., 29,80 DM, br., ISBN 3-8258-3167-1

Social Research on Africa
edited by Werner Biermann
(Universität-Gesamthochschule Paderborn)

Werner Biermann
Tanganyika Railways – Carrier of Colonialism
An Account of Economic Indicators and Social Fragments
Bd. 1 (zugleich Afrikanische Studien Bd. 9), 1996, 150 S., 38,80 DM, br., ISBN 3-8258-2524-8

Werner Biermann;
Humphrey P. B. Moshi (eds.)
Contextualizing Poverty in Tanzania
Historical Origins, Policy Failures and Recent Trends
Co-published with Dar es Salaam University Press.
Bd. 2, 1997, 208 S., 38,80 DM, br., ISBN 3-8258-3027-6

Werner Biermann; Karl-Ludwig Hesse;
Arno Klönne
Zaire – A Political Economy of Predation
Zaire's march into post-colonial modernity accompanied geopolitics and dictatorship. At the height of the Cold War Africa appeared as one important asset in the United States' hegemonial planning. This thinking persistent inspite of structural changes in world politics. Precisely as US-hegemony antagonised the lesser Western powers Europe under French guidance set out to restore politico-military influence in the former colonies. For reasons of resource and geopolitics Zaire was turned into the new contesting ground of Western rivalry. This helps to understand the survival of a military regime that managed the regional balance of power. The preponderance of geopolitics seemingly tolerates the economics of plunder to the detriment of Western capital interests. Predation enabled the regime's policy

LIT Verlag Münster – Hamburg – London
Bestellungen über:
Grevener Str. 179 48159 Münster
Tel.: 0251 – 23 50 91 – Fax: 0251 – 23 19 72
e-Mail: lit@lit-verlag.de – http://www.lit-verlag.de
Preise: unverbindliche Preisempfehlung

of buying local clients. The rise of warlordism in the nineties points towards the crisis of this policy for shrinking economic resources. At the same time, Europe under the impact of globalization, lacks the potentials for wider engagements. These factors define the present political constellation in Zaire where the major players the military regime, the various warlords, and the European overlords are too weak to restore stability what makes an 'atomization' of Zaire as one national entity most likely.
Bd. 3, Frühjahr 2000, 256 S., 38,80 DM, br., ISBN 3-8258-3218-x

Werner Biermann
The Tanzanian Economy 1920–1985: Colonial Valorization, Reconstruction, and Crisis
Bd. 4, 1998, 232 S., 39,80 DM, br., ISBN 3-8258-2525-6

Carl Peez; Josef Raudnitz
Maria-Theresien-Thaler
Edited with an introduction by
Werner Biermann
The following account by Carl Peetz and Dr. Josef Raudnitz, two high-ranking Austrian officials, portrays the 'biography' of a money that accompanied the apogee of commerce particularly in East Africa. Both authors served in the Austrian-Habsburg civil service where they held seniors posts with the consular service and the fiscal administration, respectively. Writing in the '90s of the 19th century, they – understandably – deplored the empire's economic decay. The story of the Maria Theresa Taler, therefore, should also inform on former glory and missed opportunities. Whatever fascinating this account is, it seems appropriate to restict the presentation to eastern Africa in particular.
Bd. 5, 1998, 128 S., 34,80 DM, br., ISBN 3-8258-3765-3

Werner Biermann (ed.)
African Crisis Response Initiative – the new U. S. Africa Policy
A Documentation, edited and commented by
Werner Biermann
The publication looks at the most recent turn in the United States' policy in Africa. The so-called ACRI–African Crisis Response Initiative–defines the new policy outlook that restores the U.S. as the major player in Africa's political games. Backing from local client states combines with military elements and both seem to promise earliest possible intervention in emerging socio-political crises that–if unimpeded-might easily threatened international politics and American global leadership.
The author is reader in sociology and co-director of ikoplan, a research network of economics and social science at the University of Paderborn.
Bd. 6, 1999, 184 S., 39,80 DM, br., ISBN 3-8258-4155-3

African Studies Centre
(Leiden, The Netherlands)

Piet Konings
Unilever Estates in Crisis and the Power of Organizations in Cameroon
The current economic crisis and political liberalization process in Africa have led in many cases to a partial withdrawal of the state, creating more space for autonomous forms of organization and action. Most analyses of these developments focus only on the national level, overlooking forms of organization and action at regional and local levels. This monograph tries to fill this gap. It first examines the impact of the current economic crisis on one of the oldest private agro-industrial enterprises in Cameroon, the Plantations Pamol du Cameroun Ltd, or Pamol, as it is still popularly called. It is a subsidiary of the giant Unilever company located in the South West Province of Anglophone Cameroon. The Francophone-dominated Cameroonian state denied any assistance to the ailing company during the crisis, leading to Pamol's liquidation in 1987. Interestingly, the newly appointed liquidator then decided to run the company as an ongoing business until a prospective buyer was found. The book also assesses the roles played by Pamol's trade unions and contract farmers' cooperatives, as well as by newly created regional elite groups and associations, in defence of their members' interests. Their capacity to act appears to be strengthened by the current political liberalization process.
1998, 160 S., 38,80 DM, br., ISBN 3-8258-3530-8

E. Adriaan B. van Rouveroy van Nieuwaal; Rijk van Dijk (eds.)
African Chieftaincy in a New Socio-Political Landscape
Many contemporary studies of African chieftaincy are devoted to the unravelling of "chiefly tradition". They have tried to unmask chieftaincy as an artefact of modernist projects of colonial rule, missionary activity and postcolonial stateformation. "Tradition" and "customs" have been interpreted as products of codification, petrification and coercion, all applied in the furtherance of such projects.

LIT Verlag Münster – Hamburg – London
Bestellungen über:
Grevener Str. 179 48159 Münster
Tel.: 0251 – 23 50 91 – Fax: 0251 – 23 19 72
e-Mail: lit@lit-verlag.de – http://www.lit-verlag.de
Preise: unverbindliche Preisempfehlung

Beyond such processes of imposition, however, African chiefs and their authority have often been focal points in the *imagination* of social und political power, and in the creation and subjugation of ethnicities. Research on chieftaincy has revealed continuities and discontinuities that are highly pertinent to the understanding of African societies today. This research froms the core of the contribution of this volume. Chiefs are shown to be richly varied in their responses to state authority and to the wishes and contestations of their subjects. They are viewed and analysed here in the light of the many diverse forces that determine their positions, their symbolic functions, and the resources they can mobilise within African societies and polities.

New light is also shed on the precolonial history of chieftaincy and on its diasporic spread to places both insided and outside Africa. The book will give further breath and depth to the study of contemporary African chieftaincy.

Contents:
Chieftancy in Africa: Three Facets of a Hybrid Role, E.Adriaan B. van Rouveroy van Nieuwaal; *The Elusive Chief: Authority and Leadership in Surma Society (Ethiopia),* Jan Abbink; *Modern Local Administration and Traditional Authority in Zaire. Duality or unity? An inquiry in the Kuvu,* Dirk Beke; *Nkoya Royal Chiefs and the Kazanga Cultural Association in Western Central Zambia today – Resilience, Decline or Folklorisation?,* Wim van Binsbergen; *Traditional Chiefs and Modern Land Tenure Law in Niger,* Christian Lund/Gerti Hesseling; *"One Chief, One Vote": The Revival of Traditional Authorities in Post-Apartheid South Africa,* Ineke van Kessel/Barbara Oomen; *The "Anglophone Problem" and Chieftaincy in Anglophone Cameroon,* Piet Konings; *Primus Inter Pares: Ideology or Praxis? A historical analysis of chieftaincy in Jamaican Maroon societies,* Werner Zips.
1999, 256 S., 39,80 DM, br., ISBN 3-8258-3549-9

Dick W. J. Foeken; Jan Hoorweg; R. A. Obudho (eds.)
The Kenya Coast
Problems and Perspectives
This volume is a standard work on the Kenya Coast and its hinterland. By many, the region ist considered relatively undeveloped within Kenya, despite the presence of the country's second town and East Africa's major port, Mombasa, and the large number of foreign tourists visiting the area each year. The book explores the background of this situation by means of presenting the current state of knowledge regarding a broad range of

topics related to the development possibilities in the region. In 25 chapters, aspects ranging from physical resources and environment to ethnicity, politics, tourism, education and nutrition are discussed under five main headings: *general background, historical background, economic resources, human resources,* and *development effort.* The book also contains a large bibliography and statistical information. It is a 'must' for anyone with a professional interest in the East-African coastal region in general and the Kenya Coast in particular.
Frühjahr 2000, 504 S., 99,80 DM, gb., ISBN 3-8258-3937-0

Materialien zu Afrika

Thomas Bierschenk (éd.)
Les effets socio-politiques de la démocratisation en milieu rural au Bénin
Résultats des recherches
Bd. 1/2, Frühjahr 2000, 928 S., 78,80 DM, br., ISBN 3-8258-2975-8

African Development Perspectives Yearbook
Research Group on African Development Perspectives University of Bremen

Frank Messner; Karl Wohlmuth (eds.)
Active Labour and Employment Policies
This fourth volume of the African Development Perspectives Yearbook gives a comprehensive account of the employment and labour situation in Africa and presents a coherent strategy of employment creation and poverty alleviation. A broad concept of active labour and employment policies for countries in sub-Saharan Africa is followed throughout this volume, emphasising not only the importance of employment-friendly macroeconomic and sectoral policies, but also the necessity of appropriate labour policies with regard to labour institutions, labour relations and labor conditions. In this context the new regional and international demands to redesign structural adjustment policies and development co-operation in order to lay greater emphasis on the employment issue are considered as well. Finally, the potential conflict between employment generation and environmental protection is examined and options for sustainable development policies are discussed.
Bd. 4, 1997, 504 S., 78,80 DM, br., ISBN 3-8258-2150-1

LIT Verlag Münster – Hamburg – London
Bestellungen über:
Grevener Str. 179 48159 Münster
Tel.: 0251 – 23 50 91 – Fax: 0251 – 23 19 72
e-Mail: lit@lit-verlag.de – http://www.lit-verlag.de
Preise: unverbindliche Preisempfehlung

Hans H. Bass; Robert Kappel;
Frank Messner; Markus Wauschkuhn;
Karl Wohlmuth (eds..)
Regional Perspectives on Labour and Employment
The fifth volume is to be understood as a complement to this volume with a specific regional focus. While volume 4 gives an account of general employment trends and active labour and employment policies in the context of structural adjustment and sustainable development, volume 5 focuses on specific countries (South Africa, Nigeria), examines the employment impacts of development co-operation.
This two volumes Active Labour and Employment Policies and Regional Perspectives on Labour and Employment do not only present facts, trends and analyses, but also lay the foundation for a comprehensive strategy of employment creation and poverty alleviation in Africa. Therefore, the two books may be used for all those working for Africa's development – at the country, the sectoral and the project level. Development practitioners, government officials, business executives, and development researchers will experience the two volumes as indispensable works of reference. Up to now, there is no comparable work on Africa's labour and employment situation on the market.
Bd. 5, 1997, 500 S., 78,80 DM, br., ISBN 3-8258-3101-9

Karl Wohlmuth; Hans H. Bass;
Frank Messner (eds.)
Good Governance and Economic Development
This volume gives a comprehnsive account of the role of good governance for African development. Major concepts and strategies to enhance good governance in Africa are presented, evaluated and analysed. A new strategy to strengthen governance systems in Africa is outlined. Various national case studies document the wide diversity of country experiences with regard to governance systems. At the level of local government and local development, various case studies show how decentralisation policies and local development strategies can benefit from improved local governance systems. The human rights situation in African countries in relation to social and economic performance is also reviewed, and the implications for development cooperation are discussed. Most important in this Yearbook is also the dimension of strengthening the systems of good governance with regard to resource use and environmental protection. Major initiatives by development institutions and research institutions,

as well as important African declarations and statements on the role of good governance in Africa are documented.
Bd. 6, 1999, 696 S., 99,80 DM, br., ISBN 3-8258-4215-0

Karl Wohlmuth; Achim Gutowski;
Elke Grawert; Markus Wauschkuhn (Eds.)
Empowerment and Economic Development in Africa
This seventh volume of the *African Development Perspectives Yearbook* on *"Empowerment and Economic Development in Africa"* goes in content beyond Volume 6 in presenting strategies of empowerment and programmes of assistance towards those groups that are important at local and national levels to strengthen governance systems and to make them more responsive to the civil society. The empowerment of selected groups, associations and small industry sectors is therefore an important subject regarding the sustainab le development of African countries. It is important to notice that there is an increasing awareness about the topic at international levels and regional levels in Africa. The sustainable social and economic development and empowerment of groups and actors in society and economy is considered to be an increasingly important objective in the context of state reconstruction and peace-building efforts in Africa.
Bd. 7, 1999, 760 S., 89,90 DM, br., ISBN 3-8258-4330-0

Schriften der Vereinigung von Afrikanisten in Deutschland (VAD e. V.)

Peter Meyns (Hrsg.)
Staat und Gesellschaft in Afrika
Erosions- und Reformprozesse. Jahrestagung der VAD vom 28. – 30. April 1995 in Duisburg
Die Nachrichten, die aus Afrika kommen, sind heutzutage selten gut. Wir erleben einen Kontinent, der seit einem Jahrzehnt von tiefgreifenden Entwicklungsproblemen geprägt ist. Bei aller Vorsicht, Krisensituationen ganz unterschiedlicher Ausprägung auf einen Nenner zu bringen, dürfte die Feststellung unstrittig sein, daß sich in den Entwicklungen der 80er Jahre und bis heute das Scheitern des nachkolonialen Modernisierungsprojekts in Afrika manifestiert. Sowohl die Modernisierungstheorie selbst als auch die alternativ dazu konzipierten dependenztheoretischen Ansätze, die beiden dominierenden entwicklungstheoretischen

LIT Verlag Münster – Hamburg – London
Bestellungen über:
Grevener Str. 179 48159 Münster
Tel.: 0251 – 23 50 91 – Fax: 0251 – 23 19 72
e-Mail: lit@lit-verlag.de – http://www.lit-verlag.de
Preise: unverbindliche Preisempfehlung

Paradigmen der 60er und 70er Jahre, haben zu diesem Scheitern beigetragen.
Vor diesem Hintergrund kann es indessen nicht darum gehen, alle bisherigen Entwicklungserfahrungen als unbrauchbar abzuschreiben. "Modernisierung" ist nach wie vor ein vielfach angestrebtes Ziel in Afrika; das verdeutlicht allein schon die zentrale Stellung der Demokratisierungsprozesse zu Beginn der 90er Jahre. Nicht minder wichtig ist die Feststellung, daß die Menschen in Afrika in der Krise eine Fülle von Überlebensstrategien in verschiedensten Lebensbereichen entwickelt haben.
Dieser Überlebenswille und diese Überlebensfähigkeiten werden nur zu oft vor den Hiobsbotschaften von Bürgerkriegen, Flucht, Dürre, Hungersnöten und Krankheitsepidemien ausgeblendet. Das übergreifende Thema "Staat und Gesellschaft in Afrika – Erosions- und Reformprozesse" zielt daher ausdrücklich darauf ab, beide Seiten der Entwicklung in Afrika, Niedergang und Neuanfang, einzubeziehen. Zudem hebt es mit Bedacht auf die Vielfältigkeit der zu beobachtenden und zu untersuchenden Entwicklungsprozesse in Afrika ab.
Bd. 16, 1996, 552 S., 68,80 DM, br., ISBN 3-8258-2461-6

Heike Schmidt; Albert Wirz (Hrsg.)
Afrika und das Andere
Alterität und Innovation
Afrika und das Andere. Alterität und Innovation.
Mit diesem thematischen Schwerpunkt knüpfte die gemeinsame Fachtagung von Afrikanistentag und VAD 1996 an die Diskussion um die Möglichkeiten der kulturellen und sozialen Differenz an, welche im Zeichen von Postkolonialismus und Globalisierung neue Dringlichkeit erreicht haben. Jede Gesellschaft, jede Zeit imaginiert sich ihr Anderes und entwickelt eigene Formen des Umgangs mit diesem Anderen. Wie aber sind afrikanische Gesellschaften in Vergangenheit und Gegenwart mit dem Problem der Alterität umgegangen? Zusätzliche Sprengkraft erhält die Fragestellung, wenn man sich vergewissert, daß der rationale Umgang mit dem Anderen in der Form von Neuem ein Wesensmerkmal der Moderne ist. Sollten afrikanische Gesellschaften in wichtigen Bereichen des gesellschaftlichen Lebens vielleicht moderner sein als die europäischen? Der Sammelband legt Zeugnis ab vom Stand der aktuellen Diskussion, wie er in der 1996er Tagung zum Ausdruck kam. Es melden sich Literaturwissenschaftler und Ethnologen zu Wort, Soziologen, Agrarwissenschaftler, Religionswissenschaftler, Politologen und Historiker, Theoretiker und Praktiker.
Bd. 17, 1998, 408 S., 58,80 DM, br., ISBN 3-8258-3395-x

Hans Peter Hahn; Gerd Spittler (Hrsg.)
Afrika und die Globalisierung
Bd. 18, Frühjahr 2000, 528 S., 59,80 DM, br., ISBN 3-8258-4363-7

Afrikanische Studien

Gabriele Altheimer; Veit Dietrich Hopf; Bernhard Weimer (Hrsg.)
Botswana
Vom Land der Betschuanen zum Frontstaat. Wirtschaft, Gesellschaft, Kultur
Mit Botswana begegnet uns eine scheinbar friedliche und wohlhabende Insel inmitten der Krisenregion des südlichen Afrika. Afrikanische und europäische AutorInnen zeichnen in 28 Beiträgen dem deutschsprachigen Leser hier erstmalig ein ausführliches Bild von der Geschichte, Wirtschaft und Kultur dieses Landes, das viele Beobachter als Wirtschaftswunder und demokratisches „Musterland" in Afrika einschätzen. In Gesprächen, Fallstudien und literarischen Texten entfaltet sich lesebuchartig das vielgestaltige und widersprüchliche Leben in Botswana.
Bd. 1, 2. Aufl., 1997, 350 S., 38,80 DM, br., ISBN 3-88660-511-6

Ulrich van der Heyden;
Achim von Oppen (Hrsg.)
Tanzania: Koloniale Vergangenheit und neuer Aufbruch
Die Frage nach den Chancen und Grenzen eines neuen Aufbruchs stellt sich angesichts der "Wende" in Tanzania, wie auch in anderen Staaten Afrikas, heute ganz neu. Sie bildet den Ausgangspunkt des hier zusammengefaßten Rückblicks auf 100 Jahre kolonialer und nachkolonialer Vergangenheit dieses ostafrikanischen Landes. Die einzelnen, thematisch gegliederten Beiträge beschäftigen sich dabei auch mit der besonderen Rolle, die Deutsche in Tanzania immer wieder gespielt haben: als Entdeckungsreisende, Kaufleute, Missionare, Soldaten, Kolonialbeamte, Pflanzer, Wissenschaftler und Entwicklungsexperten. Andererseits kamen auch immer wieder Menschen aus Tanzania nach Deutschland, um hier zu arbeiten, zu lernen und zu leben. Die Geschichte dieser wechselseitigen, wenn auch meist ungleichen Verknüpfung wirft erneut die Frage nach der Verantwortung für die Zukunft auf.
Bd. 7, 1996, 160 S., 29,80 DM, br., ISBN 3-8258-2146-3

LIT Verlag Münster – Hamburg – London
Bestellungen über:
Grevener Str. 179 48159 Münster
Tel.: 0251 – 23 50 91 – Fax: 0251 – 23 19 72
e-Mail: lit@lit-verlag.de – http://www.lit-verlag.de
Preise: unverbindliche Preisempfehlung

Werner Biermann
Tanganyika Railways – Carrier of Colonialism
An Account of Economic Indicators and Social Fragments
Bd. 9, 1996, 150 S., 38,80 DM, br., ISBN 3-8258-2524-8

E. Adriaan B. van Rouveroy van Nieuwaal; Werner Zips (eds.)
Sovereignty, Legitimacy, and Power in West African Societies
Perspectives from Legal Anthropology
Africa has been persistently the negative image of the lost continent: political turmoil, economic failures, hunger, disease, irresponsible and irrational warlords and corrupt regimes. Such a bias calls for a critique. The authors seek to analyse power divisions and struggles over sovereignty and legitimacy in African societies from a historical point of view. Possibilities for peaceful social relations are taken as much into account as internal frictions between state and "traditional authorities". In a striking difference to the legitimacy claims of single-rooted states, political legitimacy in many African states derives from two sources: the imposed European colonial states and the pre-colonial African polities. State and traditional authorities (systems of chieftaincy) depend on each other's contributions in striving towards the goals they both desire to achieve in the fields of development, stable *democratic* governance and human rights.
"Indigenous" institutions are not necessarily inferior to state institutions. The opposite might be true in view of the capacity of the traditional institutions not just to decide internal disputes, but actually to solve them and thus contribute to social cohesion. Such a perspective is highly relevant for a variety of concrete social relations of which gender relations are one important aspect.
Bd. 10, 1998, 264 S., 38,80 DM, br., ISBN 3-8258-3036-5

Beat Sottas; Thomas Hammer; Lilo Roost Vischer; Anne Mayor (Hrsg./éd.)
Werkschau Afrikastudien – Le forum suisse des africanistes
Die Werkschau versucht eine Standortbestimmung des gegenwärtigen Schaffens einer jüngeren Generation schweizerischer Forscherinnen und Forscher, welche sich mit Afrika beschäftigen. Der innere Bezug zwischen den verschiedenen Aufsätzen wird in den Ausführungen zur Entstehung und zur Bedeutung des Forums dargelegt. Einige Überlegungen zur Wissenschaftspolitik zeigen Entwicklungsperspektiven auf. Die insgesamt

34 Beiträge aus Geschichte, Ethnologie und Archäologie, zu den Geschlechterbeziehungen, zu Gesundheitsfragen, zu Umwelt und Raumplanung, zur Afrikalinguistik sowie zum Themenkreis Literatur und aktuelles Theaterschaffen sind sieben thematischen Schwerpunkten zugeordnet. Während einige der AutorInnen mit ihren Beiträgen nur einen flüchtigen Blick auf Ideenskizzen oder work in progress gewähren, gelingt es anderen, innovative Impulse zu vermitteln, ja neue Themen aufzugreifen und mögliche Annäherungen zu skizzieren.
Bd. 11, 1997, 392 S., 48,80 DM, br., ISBN 3-8258-3506-5

Hans van den Breemer; Bernhard Venema (eds.)
Towards Negotiated Co-management of Natural Resources in Africa
Within the field of management of natural resources, this book focuses on the various approaches of policy formulation and implementation. The queston central to this book is how to co-operate with people, the various categories of residents as well as non-residents, in the rural areas: in a top-down, a participatory or a contractual (co-management) way. On the basis of a comparative analysis of 12 case studies in the book, these three approaches are thoroughly discussed and their internal and external constraints examined.
The book starts with an editorial chapter, discussing the recent administrative and political developments in Africa as well as the new opportunities, which they offer for policies in the field of environment, and development.
The question is brought up whether the recent processes of decentralization, democratization, and empowerment of local organizations have indeed created new opportunities or that they have only superficially changed the political culture of the countries concerned.
In the concluding chapter of the book, the approaches are contrasted to each other as logical models, each with its own potentiality and limitations. Conclusions are formulated why the top down approach must result in improvization to escape from failure, and why the participatory approach risks to end up into a mixed balance. Special attention is given to the conditions and the prospects for the contractual or co-management approach, which has been introduced into Africa only recently. Under certain conditions, this approach seems rather promising.
Bd. 12, 1999, 368 S., 49,80 DM, pb., ISBN 3-8258-3948-6

LIT Verlag Münster – Hamburg – London
Bestellungen über:
Grevener Str. 179 48159 Münster
Tel.: 0251 – 23 50 91 – Fax: 0251 – 23 19 72
e-Mail: lit@lit-verlag.de – http://www.lit-verlag.de
Preise: unverbindliche Preisempfehlung